The MCSE™ Windows® 2000 Security Design Cram Sheet

This Cram Sheet contains the key facts and strategies relevant to the Windows 2000 Security Design exam. Review this information last thing before entering the test room, paying special attention to those areas where you feel you need the most review. Identify the key items listed on the Security Punchlist as you read each case study. You can transfer any of the facts onto a blank piece of paper before beginning the exam.

SECURITY PUNCHLIST

Analyze Corporate Business Objectives

1. Identify any statements about company priorities, tolerance to risk, recent security breaches, relevant laws, regulations, or standards.
2. Understand the business model in terms of information, physical constraints, and whether services are distributed or networked.
3. Identify specific requirements for end users, special groups, and business partners.
4. Understand the management model/structure as centralized or decentralized, functional areas and scopes of responsibility, and geographical constraints in relation to LAN/WAN.

Analyze the Technical Requirements

5. Evaluate the technical structure:
   - Physical distribution of users and resources
   - Methods of system access: networked, remote, Internet
   - Inventory of services and methods of access to those services
   - Current and projected demands on available bandwidth
   - Roles and responsibilities in terms of security and resource permissions

Analyze Security Risk

6. IT security controls include availability of services or resources, optimized use of resources, compliance, reliability, integrity, and confidentiality.
7. Table 1 compares the three attack modalities.

Table 1 Attack modalities and IT security controls.

Dimension	Interference	Interception	Impersonation
Active	Access control	Integrity	Authenticity
Passive	Availability	Compliance, nonrepudiation	Confidentiality

8. Table 2 shows examples of security breaches.

Table 2 Examples of security breaches.

Dimension	Interference	Interception	Impersonation
Active	Denial of service	Web page redirection	Spoof, replay, crack
Passive	Active viruses, bacteria	Wire taps	Trap door, Trojan horse

9. Determine a security baseline that includes users, groups, and services.
10. Analyze the impact of security design on both current and projected environments.

11. Identify required levels of security for resources and services.

DESIGNING SECURITY SOLUTIONS

Distributed Services Security Design

12. In a security design, consider the strategic areas of authentication methods, security group membership and placement, delegation of authority, Group Policy inheritance, loopback support, and audit policy.

Physical Topology

13. A site is a set of computers in one or more IP subnets, described as well-connected, providing efficient exchange of information.
14. There is no correlation between physical structure and domain structure nor a connection between sites and domain namespaces.
15. Active Directory allows multiple domains in a single site, as well as multiple sites in a single domain.
16. Remember the order of GPO processing using the acronym SDOU, which stands for site, domain, Organizational Unit (OU), OU within OU.

Network Protocols

17. Table 3 shows which security protocols map to which layers of the Open Systems Interconnection (OSI) and Microsoft models.

TRUSTS

18. A trusting (resource) domain points to a trusted (master, account) domain; the direction of user access is in the reverse direction of the arrow.
    - *Two-way*—All domain trusts in a Windows 2000 forest
    - *One-way*—Windows 2000 domains in different forests, NT 4 domains, and Kerberos 5 realms
    - *Transitive*—Always two-way and unbounded, flows upward through domain tree
    - *Nontransitive*—One-way by default; in mixed mode, all trusts are nontransitive; bounded by the two domains, does not flow upstream; nontransitive trusts are the only form of trust possible between the following pairs of items: a Windows 2000 domain and an NT domain, a Windows 2000 domain in one forest and another Windows 2000 domain in another forest, and a Windows 2000 domain and a Kerberos 5 realm

Security Configurations

19. The security templates, designed to satisfy common security needs, are:
    - *Basic (basicwk.inf, basicsv.inf, basicdc.inf)*—Default workstation, server, or domain controller (DC) for Windows 2000, respectively. Templates reapply default settings to all security areas except user and group rights.
    - *Compatible (compatws.inf)*—Compatible workstation or server. Not a secure environment. Templates implement an ideal user configuration but a less secure power user configuration; the template lowers security levels on specific files, folders, and Registry keys accessed by software applications so

Table 3 How key security protocols relate to the OSI and Microsoft models.

Layer Number	Layer Name (OSI)	Layer Name (Microsoft)	Security Protocols
7 6 5	Application Presentation Session	API	Secure Multipurpose Internet Mail Extensions (S/MIME); Kerberos protocol and other AAA servers; Proxy services; Secure Electronic Transaction (SET) service; IPSec: Internet Key Exchange Protocol (formerly ISAKMP/Oakley)
4	Transport	TDI	SOCKS (Sockets for Unix compatibility); Secure Sockets Layer/Transport Layer Security (SSL3/TLS1)
3	Network	NDIS	IPSec: Authentication Header (AH), Encapsulated Security Payload (ESP); packet filtering; Point-To-Point Tunneling Protocol (PPTP); Challenge Handshake Authentication Protocol (CHAP); Password Authentication Protocol (PAP); Microsoft CHAP (MS-CHAP)
2 1	Data Link Physical	Physical	PPP, L2TP, Hardware CSP

EXAM CRAM™

MCSE™ Windows® 2000 Security Design

Phillip G. Schein

CORIOLIS™

MCSE™ Windows® 2000 Security Design Exam Cram

The Coriolis Group, LLC
14455 N. Hayden Road
Suite 220
Scottsdale, Arizona 85260

(480)483-0192
FAX (480)483-0193
www.coriolis.com

Library of Congress Cataloging-in-Publication Data
Schein, Phillip G.
MCSE Windows 2000 security design exam cram / by Phillip G. Schein.
p. cm.
Includes index.
ISBN 1-57610-715-9
1. Electronic data processing personnel--Certification. 2. Microsoft software--Examinations--Study guides. 3. Microsoft Windows (Computer file) 4. Computer security--Examinations--Study guides.
I. Title.
QA76.3.S35 2000
005.8--dc21 00-058992
CIP

President and CEO
Keith Weiskamp

Publisher
Steve Sayre

Acquisitions Editor
Lee Anderson

Marketing Specialist
Brett Woolley

Project Editor
Meredith Brittain

Technical Reviewer
Jason A. Appel

Production Coordinator
Carla J. Schuder

Cover Designer
Jesse Dunn

Layout Designer
April Nielsen

Printed in the United States of America
10 9 8 7 6 5 4 3 2 1

The Coriolis Group, LLC • 14455 North Hayden Road, Suite 220 • Scottsdale, Arizona 85260

ExamCram.com Connects You to the Ultimate Study Center!

Our goal has always been to provide you with the best study tools on the planet to help you achieve your certification in record time. Time is so valuable these days that none of us can afford to waste a second of it, especially when it comes to exam preparation.

Over the past few years, we've created an extensive line of *Exam Cram* and *Exam Prep* study guides, practice exams, and interactive training. To help you study even better, we have now created an e-learning and certification destination called **ExamCram.com**. (You can access the site at **www.examcram.com**.) Now, with every study product you purchase from us, you'll be connected to a large community of people like yourself who are actively studying for their certifications, developing their careers, seeking advice, and sharing their insights and stories.

I believe that the future is all about collaborative learning. Our **ExamCram.com** destination is our approach to creating a highly interactive, easily accessible collaborative environment, where you can take practice exams and discuss your experiences with others, sign up for features like "Questions of the Day," plan your certifications using our interactive planners, create your own personal study pages, and keep up with all of the latest study tips and techniques.

I hope that whatever study products you purchase from us—*Exam Cram* or *Exam Prep* study guides, *Personal Trainers*, *Personal Test Centers*, or one of our interactive Web courses—will make your studying fun and productive. Our commitment is to build the kind of learning tools that will allow you to study the way you want to, whenever you want to.

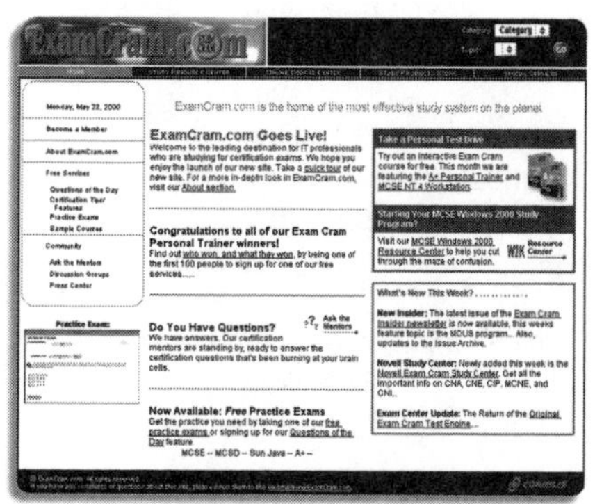

Visit ExamCram.com now to enhance your study program.

Help us continue to provide the very best certification study materials possible. Write us or email us at **learn@examcram.com** and let us know how our study products have helped you study. Tell us about new features that you'd like us to add. Send us a story about how we've helped you. We're listening!

Good luck with your certification exam and your career. Thank you for allowing us to help you achieve your goals.

Keith Weiskamp

Keith Weiskamp
President and CEO

To the grandmother I never met. You have visited me on many of these long, dark nights since our walks along the banks of the Genesee River. Promises have been kept.

❧

About the Author

Phillip G. Schein is a specialist in technical training whose expertise is in Web application development, courseware design and publishing, and in-house training programs. He has written articles about the computer industry for a regional publication (circ. 35,000) in Westchester/Rockland counties, New York. Phil has led corporate training seminars for Fortune 100 publishing companies, agricultural research firms, insurance reinvestment concerns, and business leaders in the insurance industry.

In addition to being a Microsoft Certified Systems Engineer/Trainer (MCSE/MCT) and Novell Certified Network Engineer (CNE), Phil is also recognized by The Chauncey Group International as a Certified Technical Trainer (CTT). He has CompTIA A+ certification in both Windows/DOS and Macintosh, as well as the latest CompTIA i-Net+ certification. In addition, he is a Certified Internet Webmaster (CIW-Site Designer). Phil is also a Microsoft Office User Specialist (MOUS) and Product Specialist (MCP+I) in several Microsoft products.

Phil's experience extends beyond the classroom; he hosts his own Web site, has developed in-house and commercial software, has served as a Unix administrator, and has done consulting work for more than 15 years. As for training, Phil has taught in both corporate and retail environments. His course list includes basic through advanced levels of all Microsoft operating systems, Novell OS, Macintosh OS, Web application development and Internet-related subjects, relational database management systems, leading mail systems, most of the popular accounting packages, and all Microsoft Office applications.

A native New Yorker, Phil completed undergraduate studies at the University of Rochester, NY, and graduate course requirements for a doctoral degree in physiological psychology at Indiana University in Bloomington. Formerly a staff instructor and interim network administrator at a local college, Phil is currently the Site Manager/Advanced Technology Trainer of a 78-seat training facility located in lower Manhattan in New York City. Prior to his career in the computer industry, Phil spent more than 10 years as an accounting manager in the transportation industry. He has served on the Board of Trustees for two not-for-profit organizations, owns a male chow named Marcus and a female keeshond named Cleo, and is an enthusiastic supporter of the dramatic arts.

You can reach the author for comment, correction, or criticism by email at **pschein@tchouse.com**, his personal home page at **www.tchouse.com/pgsbio.htm**, or through his Web site, The Clearing House Web Site, at **www.tchouse.com**.

Acknowledgments

Books are the original virtual machine. Like any Windows 2000 operating system, they have a user mode and a kernel mode. These brief paragraphs acknowledge the many service providers who run in that privileged area, the kernel mode. Without their invisible support, user mode activities would either run poorly or cease to function at all. The author is the keyboard, the monitor, the mouse. The services that drive the graphic device interface on which you read this text expend boundless energy, especially during development. A service provider (a.k.a. copyeditor) named Bonnie Trenga has incessantly, though correctly, returned a stream of error messages to the monitor: "Please specify... Please specify". Said the keyboard to the mouse, "She's made you a better writer ('rather than xx')!" Another service provider (a.k.a. technical reviewer), Jason A. Appel, is responsible for fault management. Said the keyboard to the mouse, "His insights turned background to foreground, his gentle nudges were in the right directions." Said the mouse to the keyboard, "Don't forget Lee Anderson (a.k.a. acquisitions editor) for giving me the opportunity to do the project, Carla Schuder (a.k.a. production coordinator) for making it flow; April Nielsen (a.k.a. interior designer) for turning words into pictures; and Jesse Dunn (a.k.a. cover designer) for guaranteeing the book will be favorably judged by its cover."

Other more peripheral, albeit no less significant, service providers never were aware they provided a service. To the instructors who arrived at my training center on time to work on mornings after my all-night vigils, thank you. I didn't want to have to cover a class at the last minute! Thank you, Arthur Epstein, for providing me with a black couch on which to sleep and a bird's-eye view of a 300-year-old cemetery on which to reflect. Though you didn't realize it, I couldn't have completed this project without either one providing much-needed background support. Thank you Evan Benjamin, Tharon Clausen, and David Safford for making yourselves available and waiting for a remote call. To friends who go unnamed, please forgive a driven individual—a Sisyphus who is, when writing, more often than not, less than communicative, unnaturally intense, and typically in need of a shave. Said the mouse to the keyboard, "And what of the ones you haven't mentioned?" Said the keyboard to the mouse, "There will be other server sessions."

A change in metaphor and a final thank you. It is written that the Buddha shows favor on the slowest horse even as the horse feels the stinging lash of the whip. That whip, in the hands of a wise equestrian, is a tool that shapes the performance of this strong, recalcitrant beast of burden—a performance that ranges from pulling plowshares through the fields in student's minds to clearing hurdles and finishing races. There is no horse without a rider and no rider without a horse. In the heat, sweat and pain of the race, the two are as one. Thank you, Meredith Brittain, project editor, for knowing when and when not to use the whip. We make a great team.

Contents at a Glance

Chapter 1 Microsoft Certification Exams 1

Chapter 2 Security Overview 25

Chapter 3 Public Key Infrastructure (PKI) 59

Chapter 4 Kerberos Security 87

Chapter 5 IP Security Architecture 125

Chapter 6 Remote Connectivity Issues 153

Chapter 7 Other Network Issues 183

Chapter 8 Constructing a Security Policy 213

Chapter 9 Identity Management Issues 251

Chapter 10 Group Policy 275

Chapter 11 Security and Configuration Tools 299

Chapter 12 Other Technical Issues 325

Chapter 13 Sample Test 361

Chapter 14 Answer Key 389

Table of Contents

Introduction xxi

Self-Assessment xxxiii

Chapter 1
Microsoft Certification Exams 1

Assessing Exam-Readiness 2
The Exam Situation 3
Exam Layout and Design: New Case Study Format 4
Multiple-Choice Question Format 5
Build-List-and-Reorder Question Format 7
Create-a-Tree Question Format 8
Drag-and-Connect Question Format 10
Select-and-Place Question Format 11
Microsoft's Testing Formats 13
Strategies for Different Testing Formats 15
The Case Study Exam Strategy 15
The Fixed-Length and Short-Form Exam Strategy 16
The Adaptive Exam Strategy 17
Question-Handling Strategies 18
Mastering the Inner Game 19
Additional Resources 20

Chapter 2
Security Overview 25

The Key Questions 26
Required Technical Background 27
IT Controls and Corporate Objectives 28
IT Security Controls 28
Corporate Objectives 30
Physical and Logical Access 30
System Security Audits 31

Risk Management 32
Security Requirements 33
Deployment of a Security System 34
Problems with Procedural Paradigms 34
A Microsoft Historical Perspective 35
Key Historical Trends 36
Active Directory 38
Integrating Security Account Management 41
Physical Organization 42
A Layered Security Paradigm 43
Evaluating Risks 45
Documenting Nontechnical Procedures 48
Using Security Protocols 49
Mapping Security Technologies 49
Competencies 50
Practice Questions 53
Need to Know More? 58

Chapter 3
Public Key Infrastructure (PKI) 59
Applying the Basic Security Scheme 61
Encrypted Exchanges 62
Symmetric Key Encryption 63
Cryptanalysis 65
Distribution Problems 66
Asymmetric Key Encryption 66
Active Interception 68
Authentication and Integrity Controls 68
One-Way Hash Functions 69
The Windows 2000 Implementation 70
Entity Authentication through Proof of Possession 70
Secret Key Agreements 71
Bulk Data Encryption 71
Digital Envelope 71
Certificates and Key Management Services 72
Digital Signatures 73
Extensibility 73
Certificates 74

The PKI Suite 76
Microsoft CryptoAPI 78
Global Encryption Policies 79
Practice Questions 80
Need to Know More? 85

Chapter 4
Kerberos Security 87
MIT Kerberos: The Basis for Microsoft's Implementation 88
Goals and Requirements 88
Assumptions 89
Components of the Protocol 89
Version 5 Enhancements 90
Microsoft's Implementation of Kerberos 5 91
Public Key Infrastructure (PKI) 92
Ticket Structure 92
Other Enhancements 92
KDC 94
Cross-Domain Authentication 98
Delegation of Authentication 100
Account Database 101
Kerberos Policy 101
Interoperability 102
Kerberos and Alternative Protocols 103
The Big Picture 103
SSPs 104
A Kerberos Case Study 110
ExamCram Ltd.: Sharing Resources with Other Companies 110
Commentary 112
Practice Questions 114
Need to Know More? 123

Chapter 5
IP Security Architecture 125
IP and Security 126
Examples of IPSec Deployment 128

Building upon IPSec 129
Industry Standards 131
Security Protocols 131
IPSec Architecture 132
Encryption Techniques 133
Key Management Protocols 134
TCO 135
Software Upgrades 135
Training 135
Cryptographic Key Management 136
Deployment Strategy 136
Analyze Information 136
Create Communications Scenarios 136
Determine Security Levels 137
Build Security Policies 137
An IP Security Architecture Case Study 141
ExamCram Ltd.: Considering Network Layer Security Solutions 141
Commentary 142
Practice Questions 144
Need to Know More? 150

Chapter 6
Remote Connectivity Issues 153
An Overview of VPN 154
Security Protocols 155
Basic Remote Access Models 156
Tunneling 158
NAT 159
VPN Security Protocols 159
Design Considerations 160
IPSec Tunnel and Transport Modes 162
Security Protocols Compared 162
VPN Management Policies 164
Remote Access Policy Management 164
Client Management 165
Firewall Technologies 165
Firewall Components 166

Firewall Architectures 167
Firewall Policies 171
Practice Questions 173
Need to Know More? 180

Chapter 7
Other Network Issues 183
IIS 5 185
Network Addressing and Domain Name Security 185
IIS Authentication Security 186
IIS Permissions 189
Combining NTFS and IIS Permissions 189
Other Security Methods 190
Secure Channel (SChannel) Protocols 191
SSL3/TLS1 192
Deployment of SSL 192
Certificate Services 193
Deploying Security for Distributed Services 194
SSL in Windows 2000 195
Application Standards and Policies 195
Authenticode 196
Secure Multipurpose Internet Mail Extensions (S/MIME) 197
Permission Management 197
Identity Management 198
Requirements for Identity Management 199
Deployment of Identity Management 200
Practice Questions 205
Need to Know More? 211

Chapter 8
Constructing a Security Policy 213
Steps in Planning Network Security 214
Identifying the User Population 216
Determining the Scope, Sizing, and Placement of IT Resources 217
Scoping Physical Assets 217
Scoping Logical Assets 218
Assessing Network Security Risks 220
Attack Modalities 220

Ring Model 221
Creating Secure Boundaries: Physical Scoping 224
Creating Secure Boundaries: Protocol Scoping 225
Creating Secure Boundaries: Application Scoping 225
Creating Secure Boundaries: Policy Scoping 225
Preparing a Support Team 226
Monitoring and Auditing 227
Help Desk Support 228
Developing a Security Deployment Plan 228
Creating and Publishing a Security Policy 228
Developing Strategies for Secure Network Connections 228
Deploying Network Strategies for the Everyone Group 229
Deploying Network Strategies for Staff Members 229
Deploying Network Strategies for Users and Applications 232
Deploying Network Strategies for Business Partners 233
A Security Policy Case Study 234
ExamCram Ltd. Reformulates Its Plans 234
Commentary 236
Practice Questions 243
Need to Know More? 248

Chapter 9
Identity Management Issues 251
Basic Directory Services 252
The X.500 Standard 253
LDAP v3 254
AD Directory Services 254
Objects and Attributes 255
Names/Name Resolution 256
Terms and Components 257
Access Control 262
Limiting Authenticated Access 262
Managing Access Control Lists 264
Managing Security Administration 264
Establishing Trust Relationships 266

Resources 267
EFS 267
Practice Questions 269
Need to Know More? 274

Chapter 10
Group Policy 275
The Concept of Group 276
Enhancements 277
Policies and Settings 278
Securing the Desktop Environment 281
Securing Access and Permissions 281
Policy Scoping: Secured Boundaries 282
Types of Policy Management 283
Group Policy Administration 284
Group Policy Processing 286
Permission Management Tools 290
Practice Questions 292
Need to Know More? 296

Chapter 11
Security and Configuration Tools 299
Centralized Administration Tools 301
WMI 301
WSH 302
TSA 302
RIS 303
AD 303
MMC 303
Desktop Management with IntelliMirror 304
The Security Configuration (SC) Tool Set 306
Security Areas 306
Security Settings 307
Tool Set Components 308
Security Templates 309
The secedit.exe Tool 310
Other System and Security Tools 312
IPSec Monitoring Tool 313
Certificate Services CLI Tools 313

Support Security Management Tools 314
Tools from the *Windows 2000 Server Resource Kit* CD 317
Practice Questions 319
Need to Know More? 323

Chapter 12
Other Technical Issues 325
Centralized Identity Management 326
Identity Administration 327
Community Management 328
Identity Integration 329
Standardizing Access for Users 330
Single Sign-On (SSO) 331
Securing Access for Users 333
Enhancement: Smart Cards 334
Terminal Services Uses 339
RIS 340
SNMP 341
SMB Signing 342
OS Migration vs. Coexistence 343
Interoperability/Migration: NetWare 343
Interoperability/Migration: Unix 345
Interoperability/Migration: Apple Macintosh 349
Extensibility: COM+ 350
Distributed Services 351
Security and RBAC 353
Practice Questions 354
Need to Know More? 358

Chapter 13
Sample Test 361

Chapter 14
Answer Key 389

Glossary 409

Index 421

Introduction

Welcome to *MCSE Windows 2000 Security Design Exam Cram*! Whether this is your first or your fifteenth *Exam Cram* book, you'll find information here and in Chapter 1 that will help ensure your success as you pursue knowledge, experience, and certification. This book aims to help you get ready to take—and pass—Microsoft certification Exam 70-220, titled "Designing Security for a Microsoft Windows 2000 Network." This Introduction explains Microsoft's certification programs in general and talks about how the *Exam Cram* series can help you prepare for Microsoft's Windows 2000 certification exams.

Exam Cram books help you understand and appreciate the subjects and materials you need to pass Microsoft certification exams. *Exam Cram* books are aimed strictly at test preparation and review. They do not teach you everything you need to know about a topic. Instead, I present and dissect the questions and problems I've found that you're likely to encounter on a test. I've worked to bring together as much information as possible about Microsoft certification exams.

Nevertheless, to completely prepare yourself for any Microsoft test, I recommend that you begin by taking the Self-Assessment included in this book immediately following this Introduction. This tool will help you evaluate your knowledge base against the requirements for an MCSE under both ideal and real circumstances.

Based on what you learn from that exercise, you might decide to begin your studies with some classroom training or some background reading. On the other hand, you might decide to pick up and read one of the many study guides available from Microsoft or third-party vendors on certain topics, including The Coriolis Group's *Exam Prep* series. I also recommend that you supplement your study program with visits to **ExamCram.com** to receive additional practice questions, get advice, and track the Windows 2000 MCSE program.

I also strongly recommend that you install, configure, and acquire significant "seat time" with the software that you'll be tested on, because nothing compares with hands-on experience and familiarity when it comes to understanding the questions you're likely to encounter on a certification test. Book learning is essential, but hands-on experience is the best teacher of all!

The Microsoft Certified Professional (MCP) Program

The MCP Program currently includes the following separate tracks, each of which boasts its own special acronym (as a certification candidate, you need to have a high tolerance for alphabet soup of all kinds):

- *MCP (Microsoft Certified Professional)*—This is the least prestigious of all the certification tracks from Microsoft. Passing one of the major Microsoft exams qualifies an individual for the MCP credential. Individuals can demonstrate proficiency with additional Microsoft products by passing additional certification exams.
- *MCP+SB (Microsoft Certified Professional + Site Building)*—This certification program is designed for individuals who are planning, building, managing, and maintaining Web sites. Individuals with the MCP+SB credential will have demonstrated the ability to develop Web sites that include multimedia and searchable content and Web sites that connect to and communicate with a back-end database. It requires one MCP exam, plus two of these three exams: "70-055: Designing and Implementing Web Sites with Microsoft FrontPage 98," "70-057: Designing and Implementing Commerce Solutions with Microsoft Site Server 3.0, Commerce Edition," and "70-152: Designing and Implementing Web Solutions with Microsoft Visual InterDev 6.0."
- *MCSE (Microsoft Certified Systems Engineer)*—Anyone who has a current MCSE is warranted to possess a high level of networking expertise with Microsoft operating systems and products. This credential is designed to prepare individuals to plan, implement, maintain, and support information systems, networks, and internetworks built around Microsoft Windows 2000 and its BackOffice Server 2000 family of products.

  To obtain an MCSE, an individual must pass four core operating system exams, one optional core exam, and two elective exams. The operating system exams require individuals to prove their competence with desktop and server operating systems and networking/internetworking components.

  For Windows NT 4 MCSEs, the Accelerated exam, "70-240: Microsoft Windows 2000 Accelerated Exam for MCPs Certified on Microsoft Windows NT 4.0," is an option. This free exam covers all of the material tested in the Core Four exams. The hitch in this plan is that you can take the test only once. If you fail, you must take all four core exams to recertify. The Core Four exams are: "70-210: Installing, Configuring and Administering Microsoft Windows 2000 Professional," "70-215: Installing, Configuring and Administering Microsoft

Windows 2000 Server," "70-216: Implementing and Administering a Microsoft Windows 2000 Network Infrastructure," and "70-217: Implementing and Administering a Microsoft Windows 2000 Directory Services Infrastructure."

To fulfill the fifth core exam requirement, you can choose from three design exams: "70-219: Designing a Microsoft Windows 2000 Directory Services Infrastructure," "70-220: Designing Security for a Microsoft Windows 2000 Network," or "70-221: Designing a Microsoft Windows 2000 Network Infrastructure." You are also required to take two elective exams. An elective exam can fall in any number of subject or product areas, primarily BackOffice Server 2000 components. The two design exams that you don't select as your fifth core exam also qualify as electives. If you are on your way to becoming an MCSE and have already taken some exams, visit **www.microsoft.com/trainingandservices/** for information about how to complete your MCSE certification.

In September 1999, Microsoft announced its Windows 2000 track for MCSE and also announced retirement of Windows NT 4.0 MCSE core exams on 12/31/2000. Individuals who wish to remain certified MCSEs after 12/31/2001 must "upgrade" their certifications on or before 12/31/2001. For more detailed information than is included here, visit **www.microsoft.com/trainingandservices/**.

New MCSE candidates must pass seven tests to meet the MCSE requirements. It's not uncommon for the entire process to take a year or so, and many individuals find that they must take a test more than once to pass. The primary goal of the *Exam Prep* series and the *Exam Cram* series test preparation books is to make it possible, given proper study and preparation, to pass all Microsoft certification tests on the first try. Table 1 shows the required and elective exams for the Windows 2000 MCSE certification.

- *MCSD (Microsoft Certified Solution Developer)*—The MCSD credential reflects the skills required to create multitier, distributed, and COM-based solutions, in addition to desktop and Internet applications, using new technologies. To obtain an MCSD, an individual must demonstrate the ability to analyze and interpret user requirements; select and integrate products, platforms, tools, and technologies; design and implement code, and customize applications; and perform necessary software tests and quality assurance operations.

  To become an MCSD, you must pass a total of four exams: three core exams and one elective exam. Each candidate must choose one of these three desktop application exams—"70-016: Designing and Implementing Desktop Applications with Microsoft Visual C++ 6.0," "70-156: Designing and Implementing

Table 1 MCSE Windows 2000 Requirements

Core

If you have not passed these 3 Windows NT 4 exams	
Exam 70-067	Implementing and Supporting Microsoft Windows NT Server 4.0
Exam 70-068	Implementing and Supporting Microsoft Windows NT Server 4.0 in the Enterprise
Exam 70-073	Microsoft Windows NT Workstation 4.0
then you must take these 4 exams	
Exam 70-210	Installing, Configuring and Administering Microsoft Windows 2000 Professional
Exam 70-215	Installing, Configuring and Administering Microsoft Windows 2000 Server
Exam 70-216	Implementing and Administering a Microsoft Windows 2000 Network Infrastructure
Exam 70-217	Implementing and Administering a Microsoft Windows 2000 Directory Services Infrastructure
If you have already passed exams 70-067, 70-068, and 70-073, you may take this exam	
Exam 70-240	Microsoft Windows 2000 Accelerated Exam for MCPs Certified on Microsoft Windows NT 4.0

5th Core Option

Choose 1 from this group	
Exam 70-219*	Designing a Microsoft Windows 2000 Directory Services Infrastructure
➤ **Exam 70-220***	Designing Security for a Microsoft Windows 2000 Network
Exam 70-221*	Designing a Microsoft Windows 2000 Network Infrastructure

Elective

Choose 2 from this group	
Exam 70-019	Designing and Implementing Data Warehouse with Microsoft SQL Server 7.0
Exam 70-219*	Designing a Microsoft Windows 2000 Directory Services Infrastructure
➤ **Exam 70-220***	Designing Security for a Microsoft Windows 2000 Network
Exam 70-221*	Designing a Microsoft Windows 2000 Network Infrastructure
Exam 70-222	Migrating from Microsoft Windows NT 4.0 to Microsoft Windows 2000
Exam 70-028	Administering Microsoft SQL Server 7.0
Exam 70-029	Designing and Implementing Databases on Microsoft SQL Server 7.0
Exam 70-080	Implementing and Supporting Microsoft Internet Explorer 5.0 by Using the Internet Explorer Administration Kit
Exam 70-081	Implementing and Supporting Microsoft Exchange Server 5.5
Exam 70-085	Implementing and Supporting Microsoft SNA Server 4.0
Exam 70-086	Implementing and Supporting Microsoft Systems Management Server 2.0
Exam 70-088	Implementing and Supporting Microsoft Proxy Server 2.0

This is not a complete listing—you can still be tested on some earlier versions of these products. However, we have included mainly the most recent versions so that you may test on these versions and thus be certified longer. We have not included any tests that are scheduled to be retired.

* The 5th Core Option exam does not double as an elective.

Desktop Applications with Microsoft Visual FoxPro 6.0," or "70-176: Designing and Implementing Desktop Applications with Microsoft Visual Basic 6.0"—*plus* one of these three distributed application exams—"70-015: Designing and Implementing Distributed Applications with Microsoft Visual C++ 6.0," "70-155: Designing and Implementing Distributed Applications with Microsoft Visual FoxPro 6.0," or "70-175: Designing and Implementing Distributed Applications with Microsoft Visual Basic 6.0." The third core exam is "70-100: Analyzing Requirements and Defining Solution Architectures." Elective exams cover specific Microsoft applications and languages, including Visual Basic, C++, the Microsoft Foundation Classes, Access, SQL Server, Excel, and more.

- *MCDBA (Microsoft Certified Database Administrator)*—The MCDBA credential reflects the skills required to implement and administer Microsoft SQL Server databases. To obtain an MCDBA, an individual must demonstrate the ability to derive physical database designs, develop logical data models, create physical databases, create data services by using Transact-SQL, manage and maintain databases, configure and manage security, monitor and optimize databases, and install and configure Microsoft SQL Server.

  To become an MCDBA, you must pass a total of three core exams and one elective exam. The required core exams are "70-028: Administering Microsoft SQL Server 7.0," "70-029: Designing and Implementing Databases with Microsoft SQL Server 7.0," and "70-215: Installing, Configuring and Administering Microsoft Windows 2000 Server."

  The elective exams that you can choose from cover specific uses of SQL Server and include "70-015: Designing and Implementing Distributed Applications with Microsoft Visual C++ 6.0," "70-019: Designing and Implementing Data Warehouses with Microsoft SQL Server 7.0," "70-155: Designing and Implementing Distributed Applications with Microsoft Visual FoxPro 6.0," "70-175: Designing and Implementing Distributed Applications with Microsoft Visual Basic 6.0," and two exams that relate to Windows 2000: "70-216: Implementing and Administering a Microsoft Windows 2000 Network Infrastructure," and "70-087: Implementing and Supporting Microsoft Internet Information Server 4.0."

  If you have taken the three core Windows NT 4 exams on your path to becoming an MCSE, you qualify for the Accelerated exam (it replaces the Network Infrastructure exam requirement). The Accelerated exam covers the objectives of all four of the Windows 2000 core exams. In addition to taking the Accelerated exam, you must take only the two SQL exams—Administering and Database Design.

- *MCT (Microsoft Certified Trainer)*—Microsoft Certified Trainers are deemed able to deliver elements of the official Microsoft curriculum, based on technical knowledge and instructional ability. Thus, it is necessary for an individual seeking MCT credentials (which are granted on a course-by-course basis) to pass the related certification exam for a course and complete the official Microsoft training in the subject area, and to demonstrate an ability to teach.

  This teaching skill criterion may be satisfied by proving that one has already attained training certification from Novell, Banyan, Lotus, the Santa Cruz Operation, or Cisco, or by taking a Microsoft-sanctioned workshop on instruction. Microsoft makes it clear that MCTs are important cogs in the Microsoft training channels. Instructors must be MCTs before Microsoft will allow them to teach in any of its official training channels, including Microsoft's affiliated Certified Technical Education Centers (CTECs) and its online training partner network. As of January 1, 2001, MCT candidates must also possess a current MCSE.

Microsoft has announced that the MCP+I and MCSE+I credentials will not be continued when the MCSE exams for Windows 2000 are in full swing because the skill set for the Internet portion of the program has been included in the new MCSE program. Therefore, details on these tracks are not provided here; go to **www.microsoft.com/trainingandservices/** if you need more information.

Once a Microsoft product becomes obsolete, MCPs typically have to recertify on current versions. (If individuals do not recertify, their certifications become invalid.) Because technology keeps changing and new products continually supplant old ones, this should come as no surprise. This explains why Microsoft has announced that MCSEs have 12 months past the scheduled retirement date for the Windows NT 4 exams to recertify on Windows 2000 topics. (Note that this means taking at least two exams, if not more.)

The best place to keep up with the MCP Program and its related certifications is on the Web. The URL for the MCP program is **www.microsoft.com/trainingandservices/**. But Microsoft's Web site changes often, so if this URL doesn't work, try using the Search tool on Microsoft's site with either "MCP" or the quoted phrase "Microsoft Certified Professional" as a search string. This will help you find the latest and most accurate information about Microsoft's certification programs.

Taking a Certification Exam

Once you've prepared for your exam, you need to register with a testing center. Each computer-based MCP exam costs $100, and if you don't pass, you may retest for an additional $100 for each additional try. In the United States and Canada, tests are administered by Prometric and by Virtual University Enterprises (VUE). Here's how you can contact them:

- *Prometric*—You can sign up for a test through the company's Web site at **www.prometric.com**. Or, you can register by phone at 800-755-3926 (within the United States or Canada) or at 410-843-8000 (outside the United States and Canada).
- *Virtual University Enterprises*—You can sign up for a test or get the phone numbers for local testing centers through the Web page at **www.vue.com/ms/**.

To sign up for a test, you must possess a valid credit card, or contact either company for mailing instructions to send them a check (in the U.S.). Only when payment is verified, or a check has cleared, can you actually register for a test.

To schedule an exam, call the number or visit either of the Web pages at least one day in advance. To cancel or reschedule an exam, you must call before 7 P.M. pacific standard time the day before the scheduled test time (or you may be charged, even if you don't appear to take the test). When you want to schedule a test, have the following information ready:

- Your name, organization, and mailing address.
- Your Microsoft Test ID. (Inside the United States, this means your Social Security number; citizens of other nations should call ahead to find out what type of identification number is required to register for a test.)
- The name and number of the exam you wish to take.
- A method of payment. (As I've already mentioned, a credit card is the most convenient method, but alternate means can be arranged in advance, if necessary.)

Once you sign up for a test, you'll be informed as to when and where the test is scheduled. Try to arrive at least 15 minutes early. You must supply two forms of identification—one of which must be a photo ID—to be admitted into the testing room.

All exams are completely closed-book. In fact, you will not be permitted to take anything with you into the testing area, but you will be furnished with a blank sheet of paper and a pen or, in some cases, an erasable plastic sheet and an erasable pen. I suggest that you immediately write down on that sheet of paper all the information you've memorized for the test. In *Exam Cram* books, this information appears on a tear-out sheet inside the front cover of each book. You will have some time to compose yourself, record this information, and take a sample orientation exam before you begin the real thing. I suggest you take the orientation test before taking your first exam, but because they're all more or less identical in layout, behavior, and controls, you probably won't need to do this more than once.

When you complete a Microsoft certification exam, the software will tell you whether you've passed or failed. If you need to retake an exam, you'll have to schedule a new test with Prometric or VUE and pay another $100.

The first time you fail a test, you can retake the test the next day. However, if you fail a second time, you must wait 14 days before retaking that test. The 14-day waiting period remains in effect for all retakes after the second failure.

Tracking MCP Status

As soon as you pass any Microsoft exam (except Networking Essentials), you'll attain Microsoft Certified Professional (MCP) status. Microsoft also generates transcripts that indicate which exams you have passed. You can view a copy of your transcript at any time by going to the MCP secured site and selecting Transcript Tool. This tool will allow you to print a copy of your current transcript and confirm your certification status.

Once you pass the necessary set of exams, you'll be certified. Official certification normally takes anywhere from six to eight weeks, so don't expect to get your credentials overnight. When the package for a qualified certification arrives, it includes a Welcome Kit that contains a number of elements (see Microsoft's Web site for other benefits of specific certifications):

- A certificate suitable for framing, along with a wallet card and lapel pin.
- A license to use the MCP logo, thereby allowing you to use the logo in advertisements, promotions, and documents, and on letterhead, business cards, and so on. Along with the license comes an MCP logo sheet, which includes camera-ready artwork. (Note: Before using any of the artwork, individuals must sign and return a licensing agreement that indicates they'll abide by its terms and conditions.)
- A subscription to *Microsoft Certified Professional Magazine*, which provides ongoing data about testing and certification activities, requirements, and changes to the program.

Many people believe that the benefits of MCP certification go well beyond the perks that Microsoft provides to newly anointed members of this elite group. I'm starting to see more job listings that request or require applicants to have an MCP, MCSE, and so on, and many individuals who complete the program can qualify for increases in pay and/or responsibility. As an official recognition of hard work and broad knowledge, one of the MCP credentials is a badge of honor in many IT organizations.

How to Prepare for an Exam

Preparing for any Windows 2000 Server-related test (including "Designing Security for a Microsoft Windows 2000 Network") requires that you obtain and study materials designed to provide comprehensive information about the product and its capabilities that will appear on the specific exam for which you are preparing. The following list of materials will help you study and prepare:

- The Windows 2000 Server product CD includes comprehensive online documentation and related materials; it should be a primary resource when you are preparing for the test.

- The exam preparation materials, practice tests, and self-assessment exams on the Microsoft Training & Services page at **www.microsoft.com/trainingandservices/default.asp?PageID=mcp**. The Testing Innovations link offers samples of the new question types found on the Windows 2000 MCSE exams. Find the materials, download them, and use them!

- The exam preparation advice, practice tests, questions of the day, and discussion groups on the **ExamCram.com** e-learning and certification destination Web site (**www.examcram.com**).

In addition, you'll probably find any or all of the following materials useful in your quest for Security Design expertise:

- *Microsoft training kits*—Microsoft Press offers training kits that target specific exams. For more information, visit: **http://mspress.microsoft.com/findabook/list/series_ak.htm**. This training kit contains information that you will find useful in preparing for the test.

- *Microsoft TechNet CD*—This monthly CD-based publication delivers numerous electronic titles that include coverage of Security Design and related topics on the Technical Information (TechNet) CD. Its offerings include product facts, technical notes, tools and utilities, and information on how to access the Seminars Online training materials for Security Design. A subscription to TechNet costs $299 per year, but it is well worth the price. Visit **www.microsoft.com/technet/** and check out the information under the "TechNet Subscription" menu entry for more details.

- *Study guides*—Several publishers—including The Coriolis Group—offer Windows 2000 titles. The Coriolis Group series includes the following:

  - *The Exam Cram series*—These books give you information about the material you need to know to pass the tests.

  - *The Exam Prep series*—These books provide a greater level of detail than the *Exam Cram* books and are designed to teach you everything you need to know from an exam perspective. Each book comes with a CD that contains interactive practice exams in a variety of testing formats.

  Together, the two series make a perfect pair.

- *Multimedia*—These Coriolis Group materials are designed to support learners of all types—whether you learn best by reading or doing:

  - *The Exam Cram Personal Trainer*—Offers a unique, personalized self-paced training course based on the exam.

  - *The Exam Cram Personal Test Center*—Features multiple test options that simulate the actual exam, including Fixed-Length, Random, Review, and Test All. Explanations of correct and incorrect answers reinforce concepts learned.

- *Classroom training*—CTECs, online partners, and third-party training companies (like Wave Technologies, Learning Tree, Data-Tech, and others) all offer classroom training on Windows 2000. These companies aim to help you prepare to pass Exam 70-220. Although such training runs upwards of $350 per day in class, most of the individuals lucky enough to partake find it to be quite worthwhile.

- *Other publications*—There's no shortage of materials available about Security Design. The resource sections at the end of each chapter should give you an idea of where I think you should look for further discussion.

By far, this set of required and recommended materials represents a nonpareil collection of sources and resources for Security Design and related topics. I anticipate that you'll find that this book belongs in this company

About this Book

Each topical *Exam Cram* chapter follows a regular structure, along with graphical cues about important or useful information. Here's the structure of a typical chapter:

- *Opening hotlists*—Each chapter begins with a list of the terms, tools, and techniques that you must learn and understand before you can be fully conversant with that chapter's subject matter. I follow the hotlists with one or two introductory paragraphs to set the stage for the rest of the chapter.

- *Topical coverage*—After the opening hotlists, each chapter covers a series of topics related to the chapter's subject title. Throughout this section, I highlight topics or concepts likely to appear on a test using a special Exam Alert layout, like this:

This is what an Exam Alert looks like. Normally, an Exam Alert stresses concepts, terms, software, or activities that are likely to relate to one or more certification test questions. For that reason, I think any information found offset in Exam Alert format is worthy of unusual attentiveness on your part. Indeed, most of the information that appears on The Cram Sheet appears as Exam Alerts within the text.

Pay close attention to material flagged as an Exam Alert; although all the information in this book pertains to what you need to know to pass the exam, I flag certain items that are really important. You'll find what appears in the meat of each chapter to be worth knowing, too, when preparing for the test. Because this book's material is very condensed, I recommend that you use this book along with other resources to achieve the maximum benefit.

In addition to the Exam Alerts, I have provided tips that will help you build a better foundation for Security Design knowledge. Although the information may not be on the exam, it is certainly related and will help you become a better test-taker.

This is how tips are formatted. Keep your eyes open for these, and you'll become a Security Design guru in no time!

- *Practice questions*—Although I talk about test questions and topics throughout the book, a section at the end of each chapter presents a series of mock test questions and explanations of both correct and incorrect answers.

- *Details and resources*—Every chapter ends with a section titled "Need to Know More?". This section provides direct pointers to Microsoft and third-party resources offering more details on the chapter's subject. In addition, this section tries to rank or at least rate the quality and thoroughness of the topic's coverage by each resource. If you find a resource you like in this collection, use it, but don't feel compelled to use all the resources. On the other hand, I recommend only resources I use on a regular basis, so none of my recommendations will be a waste of your time or money (but purchasing them all at once probably represents an expense that many network administrators and would-be MCPs and MCSEs might find hard to justify).

The bulk of the book follows this chapter structure slavishly, but there are a few other elements that I'd like to point out. Chapters 2 through 4 present key concepts used to analyze a case study, such as methodology, vocabulary, and tools. Practice questions at the end of Chapters 2 and 3 target topical discussions with both traditional multiple-choice questions and questions in some of Microsoft's new testing formats (see Chapter 1 for details). At the end of Chapter 4 and subsequent chapters, I use actual case studies to simulate an examination experience.

Chapter 13 includes a case-study–based sample test that provides a good review of the material presented throughout the book to ensure you're ready for the exam. Chapter 14 is an answer key to the sample test that appears in Chapter 13. In addition, you'll find a handy glossary and an index.

Finally, the tear-out Cram Sheet attached next to the inside front cover of this *Exam Cram* book represents a condensed and compiled collection of facts and tips that I think you should memorize before taking the test. Because you can dump this information out of your head onto a piece of paper before taking the exam, you can master this information by brute force—you need to remember it only long enough to write it down when you walk into the test room. You might even want to look at it in the car or in the lobby of the testing center just before you walk in to take the test.

How to Use this Book

I've structured the topics in this book to build on one another. Therefore, some topics in later chapters make more sense after you've read earlier chapters. That's why I suggest you read this book from front to back for your initial test preparation. If you need to brush up on a topic or you have to bone up for a second try, use the index or table of contents to go straight to the topics and questions that you need to study. Beyond helping you prepare for the test, I think you'll find this book useful as a tightly focused reference to some of the most important aspects of Security Design.

Given all the book's elements and its specialized focus, I've tried to create a tool that will help you prepare for—and pass—Microsoft Exam 70-220. Please share your feedback on the book, especially if you have ideas about how it can be improved for future test-takers.

Send your questions or comments to Coriolis at **learn@examcram.com**. Please remember to include the title of the book in your message. Also, be sure to check out the Web pages at **www.examcram.com**, where you'll find information updates, commentary, and certification information.

Thanks, and enjoy the book!

Self-Assessment

The reason I included a Self-Assessment in this *Exam Cram* book is to help you evaluate your readiness to tackle MCSE certification. It should also help you understand what you need to know to master the topic of this book—namely, Exam 70-220, "Designing Security for a Microsoft Windows 2000 Network." But before you tackle this Self-Assessment, let's talk about concerns you may face when pursuing an MCSE for Windows 2000, and what an ideal MCSE candidate might look like.

MCSEs in the Real World

In the next section, I describe an ideal MCSE candidate, knowing full well that only a few real candidates will meet this ideal. In fact, my description of that ideal candidate might seem downright scary, especially with the changes that have been made to the program to support Windows 2000. But take heart: Although the requirements to obtain an MCSE may seem formidable, they are by no means impossible to meet. However, be keenly aware that it does take "seat time," involves some expense, and requires real effort to get through the process.

Increasing numbers of people are attaining Microsoft certifications, so the goal is within reach. You can get all the real-world motivation you need from knowing that many others have gone before, so you will be able to follow in their footsteps. If you're willing to tackle the process seriously and do what it takes to obtain the necessary experience and knowledge, you can take—and pass—all the certification tests involved in obtaining an MCSE. In fact, *Exam Preps*, the companion *Exam Crams*, *Exam Cram Personal Trainers*, and *Exam Cram Personal Test Centers* are designed to make it as easy on you as possible to prepare for these exams. Coriolis has also greatly expanded its Web site, **www.examcram.com**, to provide a host of resources to help you prepare for the complexities of Windows 2000.

Besides MCSE, other Microsoft certifications include:

- MCSD, which is aimed at software developers and requires one specific exam, two more exams on client and distributed topics, plus a fourth elective exam drawn from a different, but limited, pool of options.

- Other Microsoft certifications, whose requirements range from one test (MCP) to several tests (MCP+SB, MCDBA).

The Ideal Windows 2000 MCSE Candidate

Just to give you some idea of what an ideal MCSE candidate is like, here are some relevant statistics about the background and experience such an individual might have. Don't worry if you don't meet these qualifications, or don't come that close—this is a far from ideal world, and where you fall short is simply where you'll have more work to do.

- Academic or professional training in network theory, concepts, and operations. This includes everything from networking media and transmission techniques through network operating systems, services, and applications.
- Three-plus years of professional networking experience, including experience with Ethernet, token ring, modems, and other networking media. This must include installation, configuration, upgrade, and troubleshooting experience.

Note: The Windows 2000 MCSE program is much more rigorous than the previous NT MCSE program; therefore, you'll really need some hands-on experience. Some of the exams require you to solve real-world case studies and network design issues, so the more hands-on experience you have, the better.

- Two-plus years in a networked environment that includes hands-on experience with Windows 2000 Server, Windows 2000 Professional, Windows NT Server, Windows NT Workstation, and Windows 95 or Windows 98. A solid understanding of each system's architecture, installation, configuration, maintenance, and troubleshooting is also essential.
- Knowledge of the various methods for installing Windows 2000, including manual and unattended installations.
- A thorough understanding of key networking protocols, addressing, and name resolution, including TCP/IP, IPX/SPX, and NetBEUI.
- A thorough understanding of NetBIOS naming, browsing, and file and print services.
- Familiarity with key Windows 2000-based TCP/IP-based services, including HTTP (Web servers), DHCP, WINS, DNS, plus familiarity with one or more of the following: Internet Information Server (IIS), Index Server, and Proxy Server.
- An understanding of how to implement security for key network data in a Windows 2000 environment.

- Working knowledge of NetWare 4.x and 5.x, including IPX/SPX frame formats, NetWare file, print, and directory services, and both Novell and Microsoft client software. Working knowledge of Microsoft's Client Service For NetWare (CSNW), Gateway Service For NetWare (GSNW), the NetWare Migration Tool (NWCONV), and the NetWare Client For Windows (NT, 95, and 98) is essential.
- A good working understanding of Active Directory. The more you work with Windows 2000, the more you'll realize that this new operating system is quite different than Windows NT. New technologies like Active Directory have really changed the way that Windows is configured and used. I recommend that you find out as much as you can about Active Directory and acquire as much experience using this technology as possible. The time you take learning about Active Directory will be time very well spent!

Fundamentally, this boils down to a bachelor's degree in computer science, plus three years' experience working in a position involving network design, installation, configuration, and maintenance. I believe that well under half of all certification candidates meet these requirements, and that, in fact, most meet less than half of these requirements—at least, when they begin the certification process. But because all the people who already have been certified have survived this ordeal, you can survive it too—especially if you heed what our Self-Assessment can tell you about what you already know and what you need to learn.

Put Yourself to the Test

The following series of questions and observations is designed to help you figure out how much work you must do to pursue Microsoft certification and what kinds of resources you may consult on your quest. Be absolutely honest in your answers, or you'll end up wasting money on exams you're not yet ready to take. There are no right or wrong answers, only steps along the path to certification. Only you can decide where you really belong in the broad spectrum of aspiring candidates.

Two things should be clear from the outset, however:

- Even a modest background in computer science will be helpful.
- Hands-on experience with Microsoft products and technologies is an essential ingredient to certification success.

Educational Background

1. Have you ever taken any computer-related classes? [Yes or No]

   If Yes, proceed to question 2; if No, proceed to question 4.

2. Have you taken any classes on computer operating systems? [Yes or No]

   If Yes, you will probably be able to handle Microsoft's architecture and system component discussions. If you're rusty, brush up on basic operating system concepts, especially virtual memory, multitasking regimes, user mode versus kernel mode operation, and general computer security topics.

   If No, consider some basic reading in this area. I strongly recommend a good general operating systems book, such as *Operating System Concepts, 5th Edition*, by Abraham Silberschatz and Peter Baer Galvin (John Wiley & Sons, 1998, ISBN 0-471-36414-2). If this title doesn't appeal to you, check out reviews for other, similar titles at your favorite online bookstore.

3. Have you taken any networking concepts or technologies classes or any classes that deal with security-related topics? [Yes or No]

   If Yes, you will probably be able to handle both Microsoft and generic networking terminology, concepts, and technologies (brace yourself for frequent departures from normal usage). If you're rusty, brush up on basic networking and Internet-related concepts and terminology, especially networking media, transmission types, the OSI Reference Model, and networking technologies such as Ethernet, token ring, FDDI, and WAN links.

   If No, you might want to read one or two books in this topic area. If you haven't purchased it already, the *MCSE Training Kit, Networking Essentials Plus, 3rd Edition*, by Microsoft Corporation (Microsoft Press, 1999, ISBN 1-57231-902-X) is the official documentation for the self-study course of the same name. Two other books that I know of are *Computer Networks, 3rd Edition*, by Andrew S. Tanenbaum (Prentice-Hall, 1996, ISBN 0-13-349945-6) and *Computer Networks and Internets, 2nd Edition*, by Douglas E. Comer (Prentice-Hall, 1998, ISBN 0-130-83617-6).

   For those of you specifically interested in security issues and Internet-related topics, consider *Practical Unix & Internet Security, 2nd Edition*, by Simson Garfinkel and Genee Spafford (O'Reilly, 1996, ISBN 1-56592-148-8) and *Network Security Essentials*, by William Stallings (Prentice-Hall, 1996, ISBN 0-13-016093-8). Although security is discussed in the context of the Unix environment, both books provide a comprehensive treatment of topics I encounter every day dealing with Microsoft operating systems. Differences in cultural viewpoint between the two network operating systems (Unix as opposed to Microsoft) when describing the same problems the IT professional faces daily is often insightful.

   Skip to the next section, "Hands-on Experience."

4. Have you done any reading on operating systems or networks? [Yes or No]

   If Yes, review the requirements stated in the first paragraphs after questions 2 and 3. If you meet those requirements, move on to the next section. If No, consult the recommended reading for both topics. A strong background will help you prepare for the Microsoft exams better than just about anything else.

Hands-on Experience

The most important key to success on all of the Microsoft tests is hands-on experience, especially with Windows 2000 Server and Professional, plus the many add-on services and BackOffice components around which so many of the Microsoft certification exams revolve. If I leave you with only one realization after taking this Self-Assessment, it should be that there's no substitute for time spent installing, configuring, and using the various Microsoft products upon which you'll be tested repeatedly and in depth.

5. Have you installed, configured, and worked with:

   - Windows 2000 Server? [Yes or No]

     If Yes, make sure you understand basic concepts as covered in Exam 70-215. You should also study the TCP/IP interfaces, utilities, and services for Exam 70-216, plus implementing security features for Exam 70-220.

You can download objectives, practice exams, and other data about Microsoft exams from the Training and Certification page at **www.microsoft.com/trainingandservices/default.asp?PageID= mcp/**. Use the "Exams" link to obtain specific exam information.

If you haven't worked with Windows 2000 Server, you must obtain one or two machines and a copy of Windows 2000 Server. Then, learn the operating system and whatever other software components on which you'll also be tested.

In fact, I recommend that you obtain at least three computers (two servers and one workstation), each with a network interface, and set up a three-node network on which to practice. With generic Windows 2000-capable computers selling for about $500 to $600 apiece these days, this personal investment is small compared to the potential financial rewards and career satisfaction Microsoft certification can bring you in future years. To reduce your total cost of ownership (TCO), also consider a KVM (keyboard, video, mouse) device to consolidate your machine connections to a reliable monitor and keyboard. You should also consider yet another inexpensive "spare" machine with the fastest possible Internet access speed. I personally consider 24/7 Internet connectivity to be an essential part of my work environment and my "computer lab" when I am preparing to take an exam or when I am teaching a class. No matter what the state of my "lab" machines, I can always use the "spare" machine to reference online technical material, download software, or email a friend for help.

You may have to scrounge to come up with the necessary software, but if you scour the Microsoft Web site and ftp site (**ftp://ftp.microsoft.com/bussys/winnt/winnt-public/reskit/**) you can usually find low-cost options to obtain evaluation copies of most of the software that you'll need. A more expensive but excellent investment is a professional subscription to the Microsoft Developer Network (**http://msdn.microsoft.com**), which provides software subscription programs, technical information, Web sites, and other material, including evaluation copies of the latest server products. You do not have to be a certified IT professional to subscribe to this subscription service.

- Windows 2000 Professional? [Yes or No]

  If Yes, make sure you understand the concepts covered in Exam 70-210.

  If No, you will want to obtain a copy of Windows 2000 Professional and learn how to install, configure, and maintain it. You can use *MCSE Windows 2000 Professional Exam Cram* to guide your activities and studies, or work straight from Microsoft's test objectives if you prefer.

For any and all of these Microsoft exams, the Resource Kits for the topics involved are a good study resource. You can purchase softcover Resource Kits from Microsoft Press (search for them at **http://mspress.microsoft.com/**), but they also appear on the TechNet CDs (**www.microsoft.com/technet**). Along with *Exam Crams* and *Exam Preps*, I believe that Resource Kits are among the best tools you can use to prepare for Microsoft exams.

6. For any specific Microsoft product that is not itself an operating system (for example, SQL Server), have you installed, configured, used, and upgraded this software? [Yes or No]

   If the answer is Yes, skip to the next section. If it's No, you must get some experience. Read on for suggestions on how to do this.

   Experience is a must with any Microsoft product exam, be it something as simple as FrontPage 2000 or as challenging as SQL Server 7.0. For trial copies of other software, search Microsoft's Web site using the name of the product as your search term. Also, search for bundles like "BackOffice" or "Small Business Server."

If you have the funds, or your employer will pay your way, consider taking a class at a Certified Training and Education Center (CTEC) or at an Authorized Academic Training Partner (AATP). Not all certified training facilities are the same; you should evaluate each candidate facility careful based on the kind of classroom equipment, the size of the classes, the frequency and reliability of class offerings, the experience of the certified instructors, and, most important, available lab time. In addition to classroom exposure to the topic of your choice, you get a copy of the software that is the focus of your course, along with a trial version of whatever operating system it needs, with the training materials for that class.

Before you even think about taking any Microsoft exam, make sure you've spent enough time with the related software to understand how it may be installed and configured, how to maintain such an installation, and how to troubleshoot that software when things go wrong. This will help you in the exam, and in real life!

Testing Your Exam-Readiness

Whether you attend a formal class on a specific topic to get ready for an exam or use written materials to study on your own, some preparation for the Microsoft certification exams is essential. At $100 a try, pass or fail, you want to do everything you can to pass on your first try. That's where studying comes in.

I have included a practice exam in this book, so if you don't score that well on the test, you can study more and then tackle the test again. There are also exams that you can take online through the **ExamCram.com** Web site at **www.examcram.com**. If you still don't hit a score of at least 70 percent after these tests, you'll want to investigate the other practice test resources I mention in this section.

For any given subject, consider taking a class if you've tackled self-study materials, taken the test, and failed anyway. The opportunity to interact with an instructor and fellow students can make all the difference in the world, if you can afford that privilege. For information about Microsoft classes, visit the Training and Certification page at **www.microsoft.com/education/partners/ctec.asp** for Microsoft Certified Education Centers or **www.microsoft.com/aatp/default.htm** for Microsoft Authorized Training Providers.

If you can't afford to take a class, visit the Training and Certification page anyway, because it also includes pointers to free practice exams and to Microsoft Certified Professional Approved Study Guides and other self-study tools. And even if you can't afford to spend much at all, you should still invest in some low-cost practice exams from commercial vendors.

7. Have you taken a practice exam on your chosen test subject? [Yes or No]

   If Yes, and you scored 70 percent or better, you're probably ready to tackle the real thing. If your score isn't above that threshold, keep at it until you break that barrier.

   If No, obtain all the free and low-budget practice tests you can find and get to work. Keep at it until you can break the passing threshold comfortably.

When it comes to assessing your test readiness, there is no better way than to take a good-quality practice exam and pass with a score of 70 percent or better. When I'm preparing myself, I shoot for 80-plus percent, just to leave room for the unexpected questions that sometimes show up on Microsoft exams. We all know about Murphy's Law: What can go wrong invariably will. Based on my real-world experiences, I suggest you also remember O'Brian's Law: Murphy was an optimist!

Assessing Readiness for Exam 70-220

In addition to the general exam-readiness information in the previous section, there are several things you can do to prepare for the Designing Security for a Microsoft Windows 2000 Network exam. As you're getting ready for Exam 70-220, visit the Exam Cram Windows 2000 Resource Center at **www.examcram.com/studyresource/w2kresource/**. Another valuable resource is the Exam Cram Insider newsletter. Sign up at **www.examcram.com** or send a blank email message to **subscribe-ec@mars.coriolis.com**. I also suggest that you join an active MCSE mailing list. One of the better ones is managed by Sunbelt Software. Sign up at **www.sunbelt-software.com** (look for the Subscribe button).

You can also cruise the Web looking for "braindumps" (recollections of test topics and experiences recorded by others) to help you anticipate topics you're likely to encounter on the test. The MCSE mailing list is a good place to ask where the useful braindumps are, or you can check Shawn Gamble's list at **www.commandcentral.com**.

You can't be sure that a braindump's author can provide correct answers. Thus, use the questions to guide your studies, but don't rely on the answers in a braindump to lead you to the truth. Double-check everything you find in any braindump.

Microsoft exam mavens also recommend checking the Microsoft Knowledge Base (available on its own CD as part of the TechNet collection, or on the Microsoft Web site at **http://support.microsoft.com/support/**) for "meaningful technical support issues" that relate to your exam's topics. Although I'm not sure exactly what the quoted phrase means, I have also noticed some overlap between technical support questions on particular products and troubleshooting questions on the exams for those products.

Onward, through the Fog!

Once you've assessed your readiness, undertaken the right background studies, obtained the hands-on experience that will help you understand the products and technologies at work, and reviewed the many sources of information to help you prepare for a test, you'll be ready to take a round of practice tests. When your scores come back positive enough to get you through the exam, you're ready to go after the real thing. If you follow our assessment regime, you'll not only know what you need to study, but when you're ready to make a test date at Prometric or VUE.

By the way, there is no shame in failing an exam; it is a rite of passage for all of us. But your diligence in following the recommendations set out here and in using the material in this book should all but eliminate that possibility. I wish you good luck and remind you to enjoy the excitement of living the adventure!

Microsoft Certification Exams

Terms you'll need to understand:

- ✓ Case study
- ✓ Multiple-choice question formats
- ✓ Build-list-and-reorder question format
- ✓ Create-a-tree question format
- ✓ Drag-and-connect question format
- ✓ Select-and-place question format
- ✓ Fixed-length tests
- ✓ Simulations
- ✓ Adaptive tests
- ✓ Short-form tests

Techniques you'll need to master:

- ✓ Assessing your exam-readiness
- ✓ Answering Microsoft's varying question types
- ✓ Altering your test strategy depending on the exam format
- ✓ Practicing (to make perfect)
- ✓ Making the best use of the testing software
- ✓ Budgeting your time
- ✓ Guessing (as a last resort)

Exam taking is not something that most people anticipate eagerly, no matter how well prepared they may be. In most cases, familiarity helps offset test anxiety. In plain English, this means you probably won't be as nervous when you take your fourth or fifth Microsoft certification exam as you'll be when you take your first one.

Whether it's your first exam or your tenth, understanding the details of taking the new exams (how much time to spend on questions, the environment you'll be in, and so on) and the new exam software will help you concentrate on the material rather than on the setting. Likewise, mastering a few basic exam-taking skills should help you recognize—and perhaps even outfox—some of the tricks and snares you're bound to find in some exam questions.

This chapter, besides explaining the exam environment and software, describes some proven exam-taking strategies that you should be able to use to your advantage.

Assessing Exam-Readiness

I strongly recommend that you read through and take the Self-Assessment included with this book (it appears just before this chapter, in fact). This will help you compare your knowledge base to the requirements for obtaining an MCSE, and it will also help you identify parts of your background or experience that may be in need of improvement, enhancement, or further learning. If you get the right set of basics under your belt, obtaining Microsoft certification will be that much easier.

Once you've gone through the Self-Assessment, you can remedy those topical areas where your background or experience may not measure up to an ideal certification candidate. But you can also tackle subject matter for individual tests at the same time, so you can continue making progress while you're catching up in some areas.

Once you have worked through an *Exam Cram*, read the supplementary materials, and taken the practice test, you'll have a pretty clear idea of when you should be ready to take the real exam. Although I strongly recommend that you keep practicing until your scores top the 75 percent mark, 80 percent would be a good goal to give yourself some margin for error in a real exam situation (where stress will play more of a role than when you practice). Once you hit that point, you should be ready to go. But if you get through the practice exam in this book without attaining that score, you should keep taking practice tests and studying the materials until you get there. You'll find more pointers on how to study and prepare in the Self-Assessment. But now, on to the exam itself!

The Exam Situation

When you arrive at the testing center where you scheduled your exam, you'll need to sign in with an exam coordinator. He or she will ask you to show two forms of identification, one of which must be a photo ID. After you've signed in and your time slot arrives, you'll be asked to deposit any books, bags, or other items you brought with you. Then, you'll be escorted into a closed room.

All exams are completely closed book. In fact, you will not be permitted to take anything with you into the testing area, but you will be furnished with a blank sheet of paper and a pen or, in some cases, an erasable plastic sheet and an erasable pen. Before the exam, you should memorize as much of the important material as you can, so you can write that information on the blank sheet as soon as you are seated in front of the computer. You can refer to this piece of paper anytime you like during the test, but you'll have to surrender the sheet when you leave the room.

You will have some time to compose yourself, to record this information, and to take a sample orientation exam before you begin the real thing. I suggest you take the orientation test before taking your first exam, but because they're all more or less identical in layout, behavior, and controls, you probably won't need to do this more than once.

Typically, the room will be furnished with anywhere from one to half a dozen computers, and each workstation will be separated from the others by dividers designed to keep you from seeing what's happening on someone else's computer. Most test rooms feature a wall with a large picture window. This permits the exam coordinator to monitor the room, to prevent exam-takers from talking to one another, and to observe anything out of the ordinary that might go on. The exam coordinator will have preloaded the appropriate Microsoft certification exam—for this book, that's Exam 70-220—and you'll be permitted to start as soon as you're seated in front of the computer.

All Microsoft certification exams allow a certain maximum amount of time in which to complete your work (this time is indicated on the exam by an on-screen counter/clock, so you can check the time remaining whenever you like). All Microsoft certification exams are computer generated. In addition to multiple choice, you'll encounter select and place (drag and drop), create a tree (categorization and prioritization), drag and connect, and build list and reorder (list prioritization) on most exams. Although this may sound quite simple, the questions are constructed not only to check your mastery of basic facts and figures about Security Design, but also to require you to evaluate one or more sets of circumstances or requirements. Often, you'll be asked to give more than one answer to a question. Likewise, you might be asked to select the best or most effective solution to a problem from a range of choices, all of which technically are correct. Taking the exam is quite an adventure, and it involves real thinking. This book shows you what to expect and how to deal with the potential problems, puzzles, and predicaments.

In the next section, you'll learn more about how Microsoft test questions look and how they must be answered.

Exam Layout and Design: New Case Study Format

The format of Microsoft's Windows 2000 exams is different from that of its previous exams. For the design exams (70-219, 70-220, 70-221), each exam consists entirely of a series of case studies, and the questions can be of six types. For the Core Four exams (70-210, 70-215, 70-216, 70-217), the same six types of questions can appear, but you are not likely to encounter complex multiquestion case studies.

For design exams, each case study or "testlet" presents a detailed problem that you must read and analyze. Figure 1.1 shows an example of what a case study looks like. For each case study, you will be presented with a dialog box with a series of tabs that contain geographical information, network topologies, current network composition and configuration, expansion plans, and specific interviews by key members of an organization. While you're taking the exam, click on the All tab to recast the set of separate items on one scrollable page.

Following each case study is a set of questions related to the case study; these questions can be one of six types (which are discussed next). Careful attention to details provided in the case study is the key to success. Be prepared to toggle frequently between the case study and the questions as you work. Some of the case studies also include diagrams, which are called *exhibits*, that you'll need to examine closely to understand how to answer the questions.

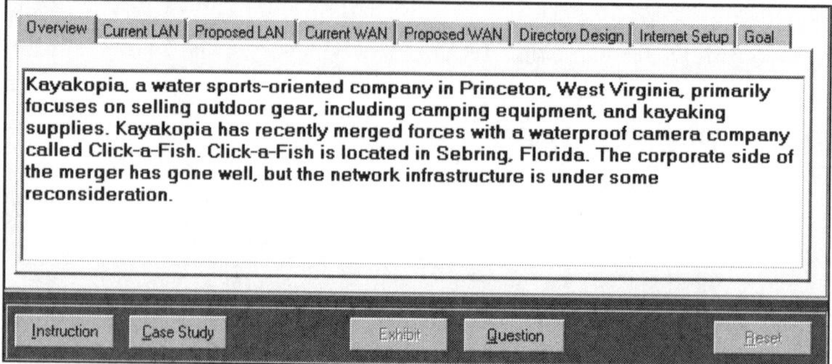

Figure 1.1 This is how case studies appear.

Once you complete a case study, you can review all the questions and your answers. However, once you move on to the next case study, you may not be able to return to the previous case study and make any changes.

It is possible that two or more case studies or scenarios on a Microsoft exam will use the same or similar names during the same test session. Therefore, this book will also use the same or similar names and details in different case studies. Always read the case study carefully and assume that whatever is stated takes precedence over any statements made in earlier case studies.

The case study format is probably the most natural way to present and analyze security issues because it mirrors a real-world situation. One would typically base a security plan on information gathered in interviews with several key members of an organization. This book approaches the analysis of such case studies in a manner appropriate to both the certification candidate and the IT practitioner. For example, the security analysis discussed in Chapter 8 could easily be delivered to a client in a real-world situation.

The six types of question formats are:

- Multiple choice, single answer
- Multiple choice, multiple answers
- Build list and reorder (list prioritization)
- Create a tree
- Drag and connect
- Select and place (drag and drop)

*Note: Exam formats may vary by test center location. Although most design exams consist entirely of a series of case studies or testlets, a test-taker may occasionally encounter a strictly multiple-choice test. You may want to call the test center or visit **ExamCram.com** to see if you can find out which type of test you'll encounter.*

Multiple-Choice Question Format

Some exam questions require you to select a single answer, whereas others ask you to select multiple correct answers. The following multiple-choice question requires you to select a single correct answer. Following the question is a brief summary of each potential answer and why it is either right or wrong.

Question 1

What factor guarantees message confidentiality?

❍ a. Proper social attitudes in the user community

❍ b. Length of the message

❍ c. Length of the key

❍ d. Authenticity of the sender

Answer c is correct. Length of the key guarantees message confidentiality. Proper social attitudes in the user community, length of the message, and authenticity of the sender do not guarantee confidentiality. Therefore, answers a, b, and d are incorrect.

This sample question format corresponds closely to the Microsoft certification exam format—the only difference on the exam is that questions are not followed by answer keys. To select an answer, you would position the cursor over the radio button next to the answer. Then, click the mouse button to select the answer.

Let's examine a question where one or more answers are possible. This type of question provides checkboxes rather than radio buttons for marking all appropriate selections.

Question 2

Which of the following are encryption technologies? [Check all correct answers]

❑ a. Asymmetric key encryption

❑ b. Symmetric key encryption

❑ c. Hash function

❑ d. All of the above

Answers a and b are correct. Asymmetric key encryption and symmetric key encryption are encryption technologies. Hash functions convert a message to some hash value for comparison, not for decryption or reading, so answers c and d are incorrect.

For this particular question, two answers are required. Microsoft sometimes gives partial credit for partially correct answers. For Question 2, you have to check the boxes next to items a and b to obtain credit for a correct answer. Notice that picking the right answers also means knowing why the other answers are wrong!

Build-List-and-Reorder Question Format

Questions in the build-list-and-reorder format present two lists of items—one on the left and one on the right. To answer the question, you must move items from the list on the right to the list on the left. The final list must then be reordered into a specific order.

These questions can best be characterized as "From the following list of choices, pick the choices that answer the question. Arrange the list in a certain order." To give you practice with this type of question, some questions of this type are included in this study guide. Here's an example of how they appear in this book; for a sample of how they appear on the test, see Figure 1.2.

Question 3

From the following list of famous people, pick those that have been elected President of the United States. Arrange the list in the order that they served.

Thomas Jefferson

Ben Franklin

Abe Lincoln

George Washington

Andrew Jackson

Paul Revere

The correct answer is:

George Washington

Thomas Jefferson

Andrew Jackson

Abe Lincoln

On an actual exam, the entire list of famous people would initially appear in the list on the right. You would move the four correct answers to the list on the left, and then reorder the list on the left. Notice that the answer to the question did not include all items from the initial list. However, this may not always be the case.

To move an item from the right list to the left list, first select the item by clicking on it, and then click on the Add button (left arrow). Once you move an item from one list to the other, you can move the item back by first selecting the item and

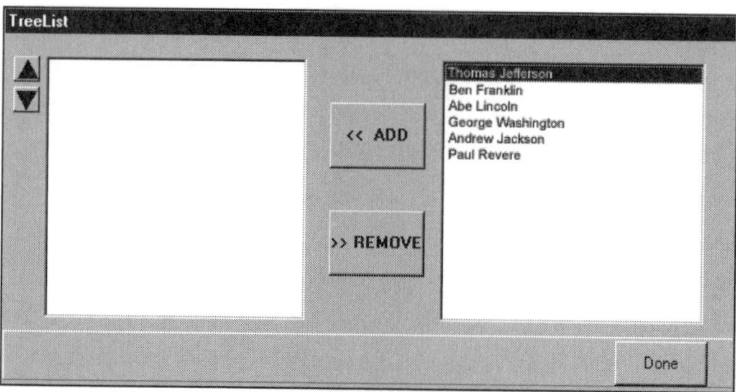

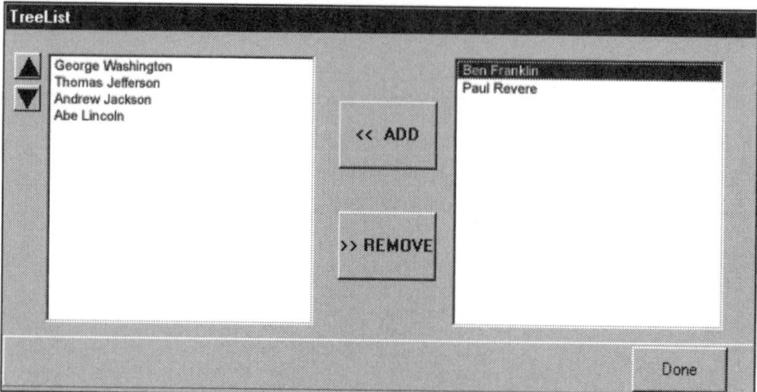

Figure 1.2 This is how build-list-and-reorder questions appear.

then clicking on the appropriate button (either the Add button or the Remove button). Once items have been moved to the left list, you can reorder an item by selecting the item and clicking on the up or down button.

Create-a-Tree Question Format

Questions in the create-a-tree format also present two lists—one on the left side of the screen and one on the right side of the screen. The list on the right consists of individual items, and the list on the left consists of nodes in a tree. To answer the question, you must move items from the list on the right to the appropriate node in the tree.

These questions can best be characterized as simply a matching exercise. Items from the list on the right are placed under the appropriate category in the list on the left. Here's an example of how they appear in this book; for a sample of how they appear on the test, see Figure 1.3.

Question 4

> The calendar year is divided into four seasons:
>
> Winter
>
> Spring
>
> Summer
>
> Fall
>
> Identify the season when each of the following holidays occurs:
>
> Christmas
>
> Fourth of July
>
> Labor Day
>
> Flag Day
>
> Memorial Day
>
> Washington's Birthday
>
> Thanksgiving
>
> Easter

The correct answer is:

- Winter
  - Christmas
  - Washington's Birthday
- Spring
  - Flag Day
  - Memorial Day
  - Easter
- Summer
  - Fourth of July
  - Labor Day
- Fall
  - Thanksgiving

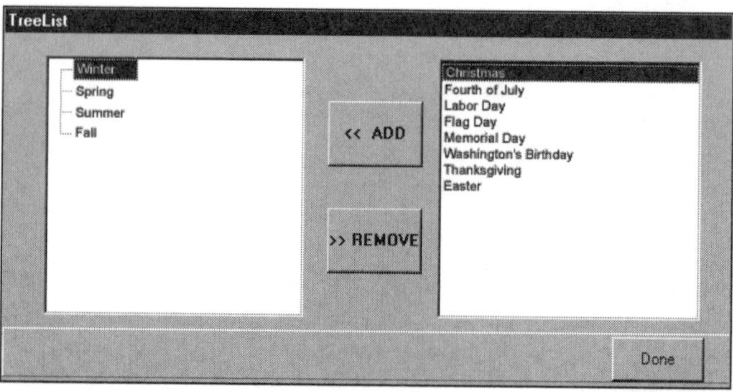

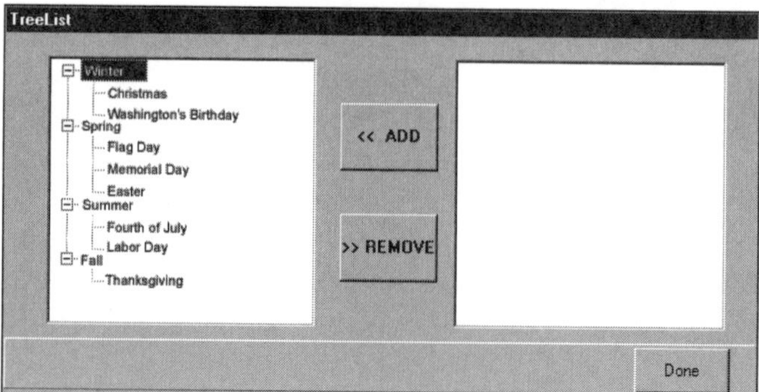

Figure 1.3 This is how create-a-tree questions appear.

In this case, all the items in the list were used. However, this may not always be the case.

To move an item from the right list to its appropriate location in the tree, you must first select the appropriate tree node by clicking on it. Then, you select the item to be moved and click on the Add button. If one or more items have been added to a tree node, the node will be displayed with a "+" icon to the left of the node name. You can click on this icon to expand the node and view the item(s) that have been added. If any item has been added to the wrong tree node, you can remove it by selecting it and clicking on the Remove button.

Drag-and-Connect Question Format

Questions in the drag-and-connect format present a group of objects and a list of "connections." To answer the question, you must move the appropriate connections between the objects.

This type of question is best described using graphics. Here's an example.

Question 5

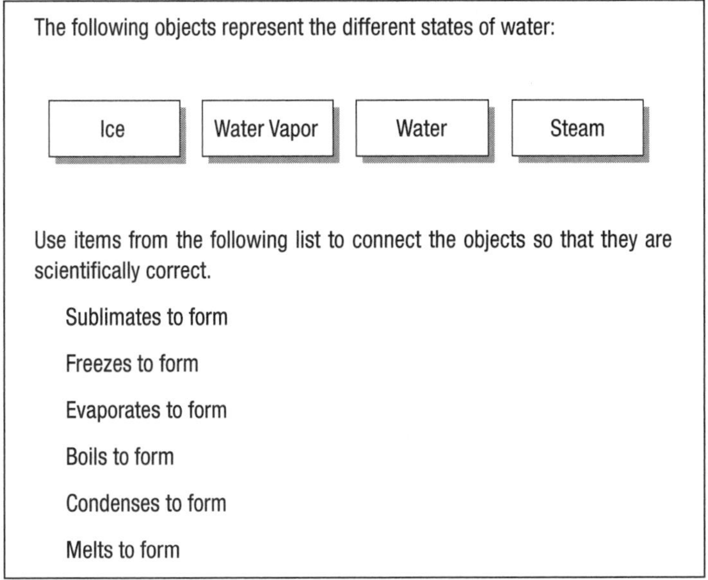

The following objects represent the different states of water:
Ice
Water Vapor
Water
Steam
Use items from the following list to connect the objects so that they are scientifically correct.
Sublimates to form
Freezes to form
Evaporates to form
Boils to form
Condenses to form
Melts to form

The correct answer is:

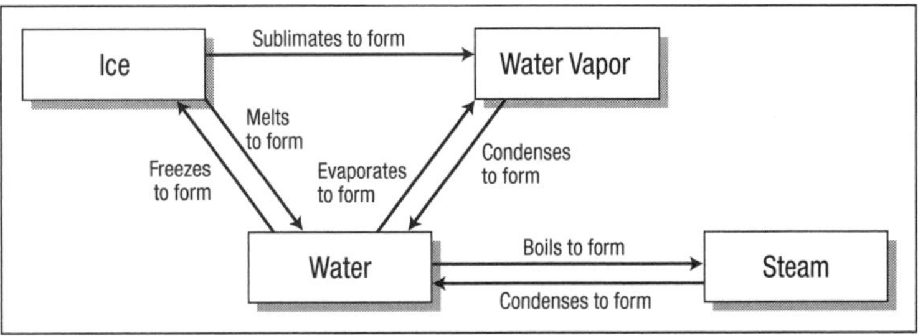

For this type of question, it's not necessary to use every object, and each connection can be used multiple times.

Select-and-Place Question Format

Questions in the select-and-place (drag-and-drop) format present a diagram with blank boxes, and a list of labels that need to be dragged to correctly fill in the blank boxes. To answer the question, you must move the labels to their appropriate positions on the diagram.

This type of question is best described using graphics. Here's an example.

Question 6

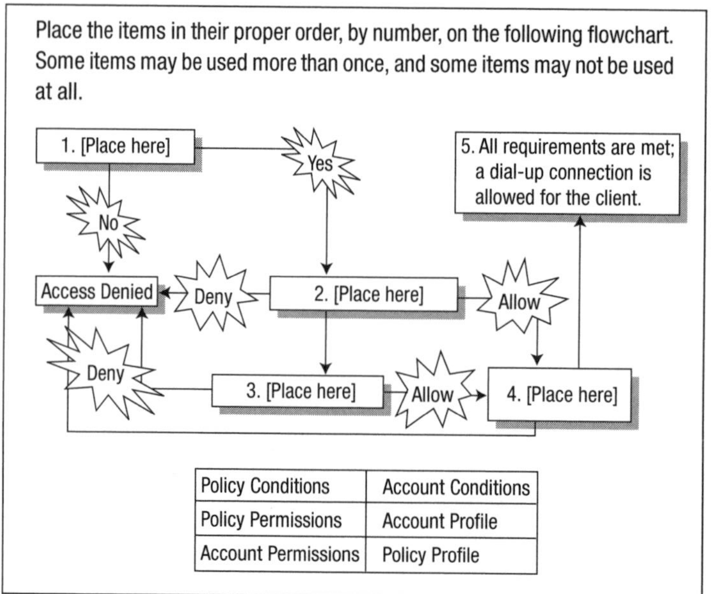

The correct answer is:

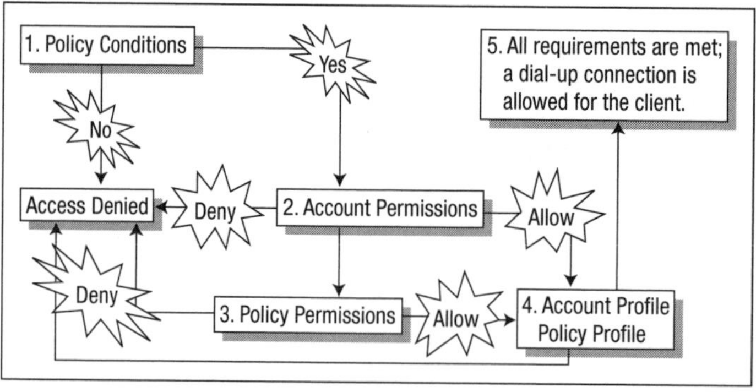

Microsoft's Testing Formats

Currently, Microsoft uses four different testing formats:

- Case study
- Fixed length
- Adaptive
- Short form

As I mentioned earlier, the case study approach is used with Microsoft's design exams, such as the one covered by this book. These exams consist of a set of case studies that you must analyze to enable you to answer questions related to the case studies. Such exams include one or more case studies (tabbed topic areas), each of which is followed by 4 to 15 questions. The question types for design exams and for Core Four Windows 2000 exams are multiple choice, build list and reorder, create a tree, drag and connect, and select and place. Depending on the test topic, some exams are totally case-based, whereas others are not.

Other Microsoft exams employ advanced testing capabilities that might not be immediately apparent. Although the questions that appear are primarily multiple choice, the logic that drives them is more complex than older Microsoft tests, which use a fixed sequence of questions, called a *fixed-length test*. Some questions employ a sophisticated user interface, which Microsoft calls a *simulation*, to test your knowledge of the software and systems under consideration in a more or less "live" environment that behaves just like the original. The Testing Innovations link at **www.microsoft.com/trainingandservices/default.asp?PageID=mcp** includes a downloadable practice simulation.

For some exams, Microsoft has turned to a well-known technique, called *adaptive testing*, to establish a test-taker's level of knowledge and product competence. Adaptive exams look the same as fixed-length exams, but they discover the level of difficulty at which an individual test-taker can correctly answer questions. Test-takers with differing levels of knowledge or ability therefore see different sets of questions; individuals with high levels of knowledge or ability are presented with a smaller set of more difficult questions, whereas individuals with lower levels of knowledge are presented with a larger set of easier questions. Two individuals may answer the same percentage of questions correctly, but the test-taker with a higher knowledge or ability level will score higher because his or her questions are worth more.

Also, the lower-level test-taker will probably answer more questions than his or her more-knowledgeable colleague. This explains why adaptive tests use ranges of values to define the number of questions and the amount of time it takes to complete the test.

Adaptive tests work by evaluating the test-taker's most recent answer. A correct answer leads to a more difficult question (and the test software's estimate of the test-taker's knowledge and ability level is raised). An incorrect answer leads to a less difficult question (and the test software's estimate of the test-taker's knowledge and ability level is lowered). This process continues until the test targets the test-taker's true ability level. The exam ends when the test-taker's level of accuracy meets a statistically acceptable value (in other words, when his or her performance demonstrates an acceptable level of knowledge and ability), or when the maximum number of items has been presented (in which case, the test-taker is almost certain to fail).

Microsoft also introduced a short-form test for its most popular tests. This test delivers 25 to 30 questions to its takers, giving them exactly 60 minutes to complete the exam. This type of exam is similar to a fixed-length test, in that it allows readers to jump ahead or return to earlier questions, and to cycle through the questions until the test is done. Microsoft does not use adaptive logic in this test, but claims that statistical analysis of the question pool is such that the 25 to 30 questions delivered during a short-form exam conclusively measure a test-taker's knowledge of the subject matter in much the same way as an adaptive test. You can think of the short-form test as a kind of "greatest hits exam" (that is, the most important questions are covered) version of an adaptive exam on the same topic.

Note: Some of the Microsoft exams can appear as a combination of adaptive and fixed-length questions.

Microsoft tests can come in any one of these forms. Whatever you encounter, you must take the test in whichever form it appears; you can't choose one form over another. If anything, it pays more to prepare thoroughly for an adaptive exam than for a fixed-length or a short-form exam: The penalties for answering incorrectly are built into the test itself on an adaptive exam, whereas the layout remains the same for a fixed-length or short-form test, no matter how many questions you answer incorrectly.

The biggest difference between an adaptive test and a fixed-length or short-form test is that on a fixed-length or short-form test, you can revisit questions after you've read them over one or more times. On an adaptive test, you must answer the question when it's presented and will have no opportunities to revisit that question thereafter.

Strategies for Different Testing Formats

Before you choose a test-taking strategy, you must know if your test is case study based, fixed length, short form, or adaptive. When you begin your exam, you'll know right away if the test is based on case studies. The interface will consist of a tabbed Window that allows you to easily navigate through the sections of the case.

If you are taking a test that is not based on case studies, the software will tell you that the test is adaptive, if in fact the version you're taking is an adaptive test. If your introductory materials fail to mention this, you're probably taking a fixed-length test (50 to 70 questions). If the total number of questions involved is 25 to 30, you're taking a short-form test. Some tests announce themselves by indicating that they will start with a set of adaptive questions, followed by fixed-length questions.

You'll be able to tell for sure if you are taking an adaptive, fixed-length, or short-form test by the first question. If it includes a checkbox that lets you mark the question for later review, you're taking a fixed-length or short-form test. If the total number of questions is 25 to 30, it's a short-form test; if more than 30, it's a fixed-length test. Adaptive test questions can be visited (and answered) only once, and they include no such checkbox.

The Case Study Exam Strategy

Most test-takers find that the case study type of test used for the design exams (70-219, 70-220, and 70-221) is the most difficult to master. When it comes to studying for a case study test, your best bet is to approach each case study as a standalone test. The biggest challenge you'll encounter is that you'll feel that you won't have enough time to get through all of the cases that are presented.

Each case provides a lot of material that you'll need to read and study before you can effectively answer the questions that follow. The trick to taking a case study exam is to first scan the case study to get the highlights. Make sure you read the overview section of the case so that you understand the context of the problem at hand. Then, quickly move on and scan the questions.

As you are scanning the questions, make mental notes to yourself so that you'll remember which sections of the case study you should focus on. Some case studies may provide a fair amount of extra information that you don't really need to answer the questions. The goal with this scanning approach is to avoid having to study and analyze material that is not completely relevant.

When studying a case, carefully read the tabbed information. It is important to answer each and every question. You will be able to toggle back and forth from case to questions, and from question to question within a case testlet. However, once you leave the case and move on, you may not be able to return to it. You may want to take notes while reading useful information so you can refer to them when you tackle the test questions. It's hard to go wrong with this strategy when taking any kind of Microsoft certification test.

The Fixed-Length and Short-Form Exam Strategy

A well-known principle when taking fixed-length or short-form exams is to first read over the entire exam from start to finish while answering only those questions you feel absolutely sure of. On subsequent passes, you can dive into more complex questions more deeply, knowing how many such questions you have left.

Fortunately, the Microsoft exam software for fixed-length and short-form tests makes the multiple-visit approach easy to implement. At the top-left corner of each question is a checkbox that permits you to mark that question for a later visit.

Note: Marking questions makes review easier, but you can return to any question by clicking the Forward or Back button repeatedly.

As you read each question, if you answer only those you're sure of and mark for review those that you're not sure of, you can keep working through a decreasing list of questions as you answer the trickier ones in order.

There's at least one potential benefit to reading the exam over completely before answering the trickier questions: Sometimes, information supplied in later questions sheds more light on earlier questions. At other times, information you read in later questions might jog your memory about Security Design facts, figures, or behavior that helps you answer earlier questions. Either way, you'll come out ahead if you defer those questions about which you're not absolutely sure.

Here are some question-handling strategies that apply to fixed-length and short-form tests. Use them if you have the chance:

- When returning to a question after your initial read-through, read every word again—otherwise, your mind can fall quickly into a rut. Sometimes, revisiting a question after turning your attention elsewhere lets you see something you missed, but the strong tendency is to see what you've seen before. Try to avoid that tendency at all costs.

- If you return to a question more than twice, try to articulate to yourself what you don't understand about the question, why answers don't appear to make sense, or what appears to be missing. If you chew on the subject awhile, your subconscious might provide the details you lack, or you might notice a "trick" that points to the right answer.

As you work your way through the exam, another counter that Microsoft provides will come in handy—the number of questions completed and questions outstanding. For fixed-length and short-form tests, it's wise to budget your time by making sure that you've completed one-quarter of the questions one-quarter of the way through the exam period, and three-quarters of the questions three-quarters of the way through.

If you're not finished when only five minutes remain, use that time to guess your way through any remaining questions. Remember, guessing is potentially more valuable than not answering, because blank answers are always wrong, but a guess may turn out to be right. If you don't have a clue about any of the remaining questions, pick answers at random, or choose all a's, b's, and so on. The important thing is to submit an exam for scoring that has an answer for every question.

At the very end of your exam period, you're better off guessing than leaving questions unanswered.

The Adaptive Exam Strategy

If there's one principle that applies to taking an adaptive test, it could be summed up as "Get it right the first time." You cannot elect to skip a question and move on to the next one when taking an adaptive test, because the testing software uses your answer to the current question to select whatever question it plans to present next. Nor can you return to a question once you've moved on, because the software gives you only one chance to answer the question. You can, however, take notes, because sometimes information supplied in earlier questions will shed more light on later questions.

Also, when you answer a question correctly, you are presented with a more difficult question next, to help the software gauge your level of skill and ability. When you answer a question incorrectly, you are presented with a less difficult question, and the software lowers its current estimate of your skill and ability. This continues until the program settles into a reasonably accurate estimate of what you know and can do, and takes you on average through somewhere between 15 and 30 questions as you complete the test.

The good news is that if you know your stuff, you'll probably finish most adaptive tests in 30 minutes or so. The bad news is that you must really, really know your stuff to do your best on an adaptive test. That's because some questions are so convoluted, complex, or hard to follow that you're bound to miss one or two, at a minimum, even if you do know your stuff. So the more you know, the better you'll do on an adaptive test, even accounting for the occasionally weird or unfathomable questions that appear on these exams.

Because you can't always tell in advance if a test is fixed length, short form, or adaptive, you will be best served by preparing for the exam as if it were adaptive. That way, you should be prepared to pass no matter what kind of test you take. But if you do take a fixed-length or short-form test, remember the tips from the preceding section. They should help you improve on what you could do on an adaptive test.

If you encounter a question on an adaptive test that you can't answer, you must guess an answer immediately. Because of how the software works, you may suffer for your guess on the next question if you guess right, because you'll get a more difficult question next!

Question-Handling Strategies

For those questions that take only a single answer, usually two or three of the answers will be obviously incorrect, and two of the answers will be plausible—of course, only one can be correct. Unless the answer leaps out at you (if it does, reread the question to look for a trick; sometimes those are the ones you're most likely to get wrong), begin the process of answering by eliminating those answers that are most obviously wrong.

Almost always, at least one answer out of the possible choices for a question can be eliminated immediately because it matches one of these conditions:

- The answer does not apply to the situation.
- The answer describes a nonexistent issue, an invalid option, or an imaginary state.

After you eliminate all answers that are obviously wrong, you can apply your retained knowledge to eliminate further answers. Look for items that sound correct but refer to actions, commands, or features that are not present or not available in the situation that the question describes.

If you're still faced with a blind guess among two or more potentially correct answers, reread the question. Try to picture how each of the possible remaining answers would alter the situation. Be especially sensitive to terminology; sometimes the choice of words ("remove" instead of "disable") can make the difference between a right answer and a wrong one.

Only when you've exhausted your ability to eliminate answers, but remain unclear about which of the remaining possibilities is correct, should you guess at an answer. An unanswered question offers you no points, but guessing gives you at least some chance of getting a question right; just don't be too hasty when making a blind guess.

Note: If you're taking a fixed-length or a short-form test, you can wait until the last round of reviewing marked questions (just as you're about to run out of time, or out of unanswered questions) before you start making guesses. You will have the same option within each case study testlet (but once you leave a testlet, you may not be allowed to return to it). If you're taking an adaptive test, you'll have to guess to move on to the next question if you can't figure out an answer some other way. Either way, guessing should be your technique of last resort!

Numerous questions assume that the default behavior of a particular utility is in effect. If you know the defaults and understand what they mean, this knowledge will help you cut through many Gordian knots.

Mastering the Inner Game

In the final analysis, knowledge breeds confidence, and confidence breeds success. If you study the materials in this book carefully and review all the practice questions at the end of each chapter, you should become aware of those areas where additional learning and study are required.

After you've worked your way through the book, take the practice exam in the back of the book. Taking this test will provide a reality check and help you identify areas to study further. Make sure you follow up and review materials related to the questions you miss on the practice exam before scheduling a real exam. Only when you've covered that ground and feel comfortable with the whole scope of the practice exam should you set an exam appointment. Only if you score 80 percent or better should you proceed to the real thing (otherwise, obtain some additional practice tests so you can keep trying until you hit this magic number).

If you take a practice exam and don't score at least 80 to 85 percent correct, you'll want to practice further. Microsoft provides links to practice exam providers and also offers self-assessment exams at **www.microsoft.com/trainingandservices/**. You should also check out **ExamCram.com** for downloadable practice questions.

Armed with the information in this book and with the determination to augment your knowledge, you should be able to pass the certification exam. However, you need to work at it, or you'll spend the exam fee more than once before you finally pass. If you prepare seriously, you should do well. I am confident that you can do it!

The next section covers other sources you can use to prepare for the Microsoft certification exams.

Additional Resources

A good source of information about Microsoft certification exams comes from Microsoft itself. Because its products and technologies—and the exams that go with them—change frequently, the best place to go for exam-related information is online.

If you haven't already visited the Microsoft Certified Professional site, do so right now. The MCP home page resides at **www.microsoft.com/trainingandservices** (see Figure 1.4).

Note: This page might not be there by the time you read this, or may be replaced by something new and different, because things change regularly on the Microsoft site. Should this happen, please read the sidebar titled "Coping with Change on the Web."

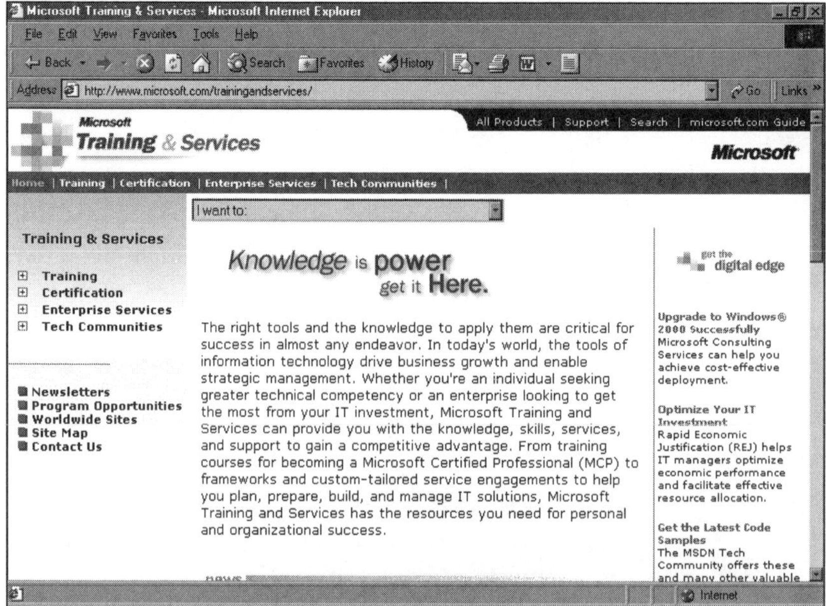

Figure 1.4 The Microsoft Certified Professional home page.

Other key military, government, and private sites you can consult for information about Security Design are as follows:

- *ftp://ftp.isi.edu/in-notes/rfcxxx.txt*—To use this URL, replace *xxx* with an RFC number
- *ftp://ftp.microsoft.com/*—Microsoft FTP Site for service packs
- *http://csrc.ncsl.nist.gov/topics/welcome.html*—National Institute of Standards and Technology Computer Security Resource Clearinghouse
- *http://ntbugtraq.ntadvice.com/*—NTBugTraq mailing list home page
- *http://web.mit.edu/is/help/mink/#overview*—The MIT Kerberos home page
- *www.alw.nih.gov/Security/security.html*—Advanced Laboratory Workstation System Computer Security Information page, CIT/NIH
- *www.armadillo.huntsville.al.us/*—The Fortezza Department of Defense home page
- *www.austinlinks.com/Crypto/*—Cryptography Archives page
- *www.boran.com/security/*—IT Security Cookbook
- *www.cerias.purdue.edu/*—Center for Education and Research in Information Assurance and Security page
- *www.cert.org/*—The Carnegie Mellon CERT Coordination Center
- *www.cryptography.com/resources/index.html*—Cryptographic Resources, Inc.'s Resource Library
- *www.cryptography.org/*—Cryptography.org's Crypto Archives page
- *www.cs.auckland.ac.nz/~pgut001/links.html*—Encryption and Security Related Resources Crypto-link farm
- *www.faqs.org/rfcs*—An Request For Comments search page
- *www.hideaway.net/index.html*—Hacker Libraries page
- *www.ietf.cnri.reston.va.us/*—The Internet Engineering Task Force home page
- *www.ietf.org/html.charters/ipsec-charter.html*—The Internet Engineering Task Force's page on IPSec
- *www.infosecnews.com/*—The InfoSecurity News home page
- *www.infosyssec.org/infosyssec/index.html*—Security Portal for Information Security Professionals
- *www.intelbrief.com/*—Intelligence Briefing; Computer Security page

- *www.iso.ch/search.html*—International Organization for Standardization Search Engine
- *www.microsoft.com/windows2000/upgrade/compat/default.asp*—Windows 2000 Hardware Compatibility List
- *www.nsa.gov/*—National Security Agency home page
- *www.nsi.org/*—National Security Institute's Security Resource Net page
- *www.pca.dfn.de/dfnpca/pki-links.html*—The PKI Page
- *www.pgp.com/*—Pretty Good Privacy home page
- *www.radium.ncsc.mil/tpep/library/rainbow/index.html*—Rainbow Series Library, Department of Defense page
- *www.sans.org/newlook/resources/glossary.htm*—National Security Agency Glossary page
- *www.setco.org/*—Secure Electronic Transaction LLC home page
- *www.vpnc.org/*—The VPN Consortium home page

Coping with Change on the Web

Sooner or later, all the information I've shared with you about the Microsoft Certified Professional pages and the other Web-based resources mentioned throughout the rest of this book will go stale or be replaced by newer information. In some cases, the URLs you find here might lead you to their replacements; in other cases, the URLs will go nowhere, leaving you with the dreaded "404 File not found" error message. When that happens, don't give up.

There's always a way to find what you want on the Web if you're willing to invest some time and energy. Most large or complex Web sites—and Microsoft's qualifies on both counts—offer a search engine. On all of Microsoft's Web pages, a Search button appears along the top edge of the page. As long as you can get to Microsoft's site (it should stay at **www.microsoft.com** for a long time), use this tool to help you find what you need.

The more focused you can make a search request, the more likely the results will include information you can use. For example, you can search for the string

```
"training and certification"
```

to produce a lot of data about the subject in general, but if you're looking for the preparation guide for Exam 70-220, "Designing Security for a Microsoft Windows

2000 Network," you'll be more likely to get there quickly if you use a search string similar to the following:

```
"Exam 70-220" AND "preparation guide"
```

Likewise, if you want to find the Training and Certification downloads, try a search string such as this:

```
"training and certification" AND "download page"
```

Finally, feel free to use general search tools—such as **www.search.com**, **www.altavista.com**, and **www.excite.com**—to look for related information. Although Microsoft offers great information about its certification exams online, there are plenty of third-party sources of information and assistance that need not follow Microsoft's party line. Therefore, if you can't find something where the book says it lives, intensify your search.

Security Overview

Terms you'll need to understand:

✓ Total cost of ownership (TCO)

✓ System security plan and audit

✓ Competency Model

✓ Information Technology (IT) security controls

✓ Risk management

✓ Encryption algorithms

✓ Hash function

✓ Message digest

✓ Digital signature

✓ Open Systems Interconnection (OSI) seven-layer model

✓ Department of Defense four-layer model

✓ Microsoft's four-layer model

Techniques you'll need to master:

✓ Identifying the major steps in risk management

✓ Applying the network reference models to security design

✓ Understanding the public/private key exchanges

✓ Identifying security attack modalities

✓ Mapping security protocols to the OSI Reference Model

New ideas are rare; most are repetitions of an old theme with slight twists and variations. When we view new concepts and "cutting-edge" technologies from a historical perspective, these ideas seem more familiar and easier to grasp. Recurring patterns help us immediately recognize common mechanisms. We visualize trends from these patterns and formulate a predictive model that helps us better understand trends and changes in information technology (IT). Many Windows 2000 concepts are actually built upon NT 4 core technologies and procedures. They are not a result of a radical mutation, but instead subtle shifts that lead to new forms of differentiation and specialization.

The Key Questions

You need to leverage your knowledge of NT4 security to develop an understanding of Windows 2000 security features. The procedural steps outlined in the following chapters will form a framework for efficient problem solving and reliable maintenance. Any approach to analyzing Windows 2000 security issues requires a broad, structured methodology because Windows 2000 distributed and network services are broad and relatively unstructured. Windows 2000 works in either a mixed legacy NT 4 domain model or in a native mode with Active Directory (AD) and Microsoft's version of Kerberos protocol. An enhanced Security Support Provider Interface (SSPI) now accommodates many distributed application services by supporting installable third-party security technologies. To efficiently analyze, compare, or design these systems, the security professional needs a flexible reference like the Open Systems Interconnection (OSI) model to add organizational structure to these interconnecting subsystems. Similarly, technical expertise is more easily acquired and maintained if similarities can be drawn quickly to well-known legacy systems. Procedural steps outlined in the following chapters will force you to systematically examine case studies, or real-world situations, to determine how to detect, protect, or correct a security vulnerability. Any security overview should ask the following questions:

- Who are the principal parties?
- What are the methods of exchange?
- What are the security objectives?
- What are the areas of risk?
- What are the security countermeasures?

This structured methodology will be applicable to both a system security audit (discussed in the "IT Controls and Corporate Objectives" section later in this chapter) or a Microsoft exam case study. It will help us identify, design, and troubleshoot security technologies as they relate to corporate objectives or a set of specific business rules. Furthermore, any methodology that makes it easier to identify sources of security risk in the planning stages of both distributed and network system security will continue to prove a valuable tool in the real world.

Required Technical Background

A major theme in Microsoft literature is the concept of total cost of ownership (TCO). The TCO, estimated at about four times the cost of a single workstation, includes:

- Cost of hardware/software
- Cost of system upgrades
- System maintenance
- System training
- Technical support

Of these cost components, system maintenance, training, and support vary the most. They are featured prominently in discussions of costs, benefits, and risk reduction. Other benefits less often cited but which are of similar significance and are more functional are streamlining workflow and increased productivity. This book is about achieving technical expertise in Windows 2000 security systems. The proper technical background when applied correctly impacts the most variable of the TCO cost components: productivity and the corporate "bottom line." This book is about achieving that technical expertise in Windows 2000 security systems. Thus, an effective system security plan is the synergy of three complementary factors:

- Appropriate security technologies
- Technical expertise for properly supporting and maintaining those technologies
- Proper social attitude and compliance of the user community

Experts seek out signs to help choose the most efficient direction toward some short-term objective or long-term goal. This book also uses Microsoft's Windows 2000 Competency Model to list those topics the exam candidate or security professional should give the closest scrutiny. The model ranks topics in security policy management, monitoring, planning, and administration in order of importance to specific job levels: IT executive, IT management, and IT workforce. The target audience of this book most likely has or will assume a role in IT management. The assumption in using this specific Competency Model is that if, in Microsoft's view, these topical areas rank high in required knowledge, they could be considered the most relevant areas on Microsoft certification examinations. It is also likely that these areas of expertise will be called upon most often for design, implementation, and support of security systems in the real world.

IT Controls and Corporate Objectives

In general, effective security management ensures confidentiality, integrity, and availability of information. It is both procedural and technical in nature. In fact, an organization's corporate security "culture" can sometimes be the critical factor in making security policy effective; firewall technologies are only as effective as the policy and administration that run them. You must thoroughly understand the fundamental relationships between corporate business objectives and IT security controls *before* you can formulate a system security plan or design a security infrastructure.

IT Security Controls

Corporate business objectives and IT security controls are found in departmental objectives in relation to some cumulative set of business rules or corporate business objectives. To formulate sound and reasonable policies, it is crucial to collect these departmental objectives with surveys. When you read these surveys, you will notice that specific themes define security concerns within a particular level of the organizational structure. The cumulative corporate business objectives determine the final implementation of a security system and how a company actually allocates financial resources.

Examples of IT security controls include:

- Availability of services or resources
- Optimized use of resources
- Compliance
- Reliability
- Integrity
- Confidentiality

These IT security controls can be categorized in more functional terms as preventing, detecting, and correcting breaches in security. For example, digital signatures prevent alteration or fabrication of information exchanged between two computer users on a network. One IT security control relevant here is the integrity of the message's content. If the receiver of the message detects some change in the message's content through comparison of hash values accompanying the message, the correct message can be re-sent. Security attack techniques might intercept and modify, or impersonate and fabricate, a message. Examples of security attack techniques include:

- *Brute force attack (or crack)*—One of the interception attack modalities. This type of attack applies all possible character combinations, one at a time, using the same encryption algorithm as the target from an appropriate character set to decrypt a password. The permutations involved limit the practicality of this attack method. A dictionary password attack, alternatively, uses a more limited list of dictionary words to either break the password or encrypt to the same one-way hash value used to authenticate a principal. The more sophisticated dictionaries offer mutation filters that change "idiot" to, for example, "1d10t", using the same word list.
- *Denial of service (DOS)*—One of the interference attack modalities. This type of attack overwhelms a service provider with legitimate requests for service beyond its operational capacity to service those requests in its intended manner. Normal use or management of the service provider is either prevented or totally inhibited. For example, a random crash of an application server is forced by a DOS attack following modification of logs showing evidence of penetration by an unauthorized, unauthenticated intruder.
- *Man-in-the-middle attack*—One of the impersonation attack modalities. In this type of attack, a consumer believes it is exchanging information *directly* with some other party when, in fact, the exchange is unknowingly passed through some intermediary intruder. An example of an active attack is when the intruding third party intercedes in the exchange on behalf of one of the conversing principals without the knowledge of the other. An example of a passive attack is when the intruding third party, masquerading as some legitimate service provider or other consumer, actively solicits information that is intended for the falsely portrayed legitimate party. The ability to actively solicit information distinguishes this attack from an interception attack modality.
- *Replay attack*—One of the impersonation attack modalities. This type of attack is an unauthorized, out-of-sequence retransmission of some previously intercepted service request or sequence of data. The replay attack is an attempt to actively impersonate an authenticated, authorized principal from whom the data stream was intercepted. Without appropriate IT security controls, such as using sequence numbers and timestamps to guarantee at least partial sequence integrity, the targeted service provider has no choice other than to respond to the request.
- *Spoof*—One of the impersonation attack modalities. This type of attack is an attempt to gain access or utilize some service as an authorized principal. This technique is often used as a legitimate network management tool to reduce

bandwidth consumption, especially across wide-area network connections. Often, routers and other network devices "spoof" replies from remote sites to decrease network traffic across slow or metered data links.

The attack techniques here could involve a combination of two different attack modalities—namely, interception to crack the password, then impersonation. A security attack is typically launched in three separate, distinct phases: reconnaissance, penetration, and then control. These different modalities cause security violations during various phases of a security attack that must be prevented, detected, or corrected.

Corporate Objectives

The corporate security objectives are often documented in a disaster recovery plan because the IT security objective of availability of services is a key security issue. The plan details how countermeasures will be implemented in response to some disaster or security incident. When you define a disaster recovery procedure, you implicitly make a policy statement that defines critical business assets. The disaster plan typically describes which areas, functions, or services must be reestablished before others and which assets need to be repaired or replaced first. It is necessary, though often quite difficult, to assess the risk of exposure to loss or misuse of these assets during some disaster or security disruption. For insurance and investment purposes, these probabilities are often converted to monetary value commensurate with the probability of loss. These costs are, in turn, compared to the benefit a capital investment would garner in securing the particular asset from risk. The formulation of any broad corporate policy of this nature requires the careful balancing of accessibility, security, investment, and profit. Thus, risk assessment supports a cost/benefit analysis of investment in each IT security control, as well as relative priority and importance of any one risk with respect to overall corporate objectives.

The case study exam format simulates actual interviews or survey responses. Learn to identify in these case studies or in actual interviews what are the IT corporate objectives and areas of perceived risk. Remember, however, that the success of an effective security design lies not just in its agreement with corporate business objectives, but also in technical support and employee compliance.

Physical and Logical Access

Security policies describe corporate roles and responsibilities; employee rights; and methods of management, review, and auditing. An effective policy is one that encourages employee awareness and commitment in supporting the corporate objectives; in effect, it defines, reflects, and fosters a positive corporate cultural attitude toward security in the organization. You must consider two key areas under the umbrella of effective security management: physical access and logical access to corporate assets and resources. Both areas require some form of security policy statement. The physical area includes:

- *Physical access to system resources*—Network and data communication equipment as well as removable storage devices must be removed from unauthorized employee access.
- *Backup, restore, and disaster recovery procedures*—These as well as the backup media must be in place.

Similarly, access to assets and resources through a network or standalone computer system also requires a security policy statement. This area of logical access includes:

- *Auditing and monitoring of system resources*—Tracking of logical access includes an audit of access to assets such as files and directories, the Registry, print services, and remote access.
- *Access through interactive or external network connections*—The ability to locally log on at a server console as compared to access to a server across a network.
- *Security management of users, groups, and resources*—The use of built-in instead of user-defined groups, the assignment of permissions and rights to different groups.
- *Domain account policies*—Password policies such as expiration, length, history, and intruder detection.

Notice the classification across a physical/logical dimension. For the purposes of analysis and study, try to determine a common dimension across lists of apparently related objects that helps associate and differentiate them from one another.

System Security Audits

Security objectives are defined on paper and implemented by a mixture of people with varying degrees of responsibility and hardware/software technologies with equally varying degrees of effectiveness. Superior security technologies can be totally compromised if a company administers procedures poorly. Conversely, the best administrative procedures will fail if a company improperly installs and maintains technology. Finally, comprehensive procedural planning as well as superior security technologies are subverted if the corporate culture or social practices foster noncompliance. It is a regrettable fact that security breeches are more likely to come from within an organization than from an outside source. Breaching security of an unauthorized area by an authenticated "rogue user" is an example of a security violation that uses an impersonation attack modality. These breeches may be intentional and a result of malice (with a clear aim to remove or destroy sensitive information), or they may be unintentional (due to poor training or inexperience with established procedures). A good security design detects, prevents, and corrects such breaches. It does not as much restrict as it directs "authorized" access; it should protect and facilitate legitimate use as transparently as possible, with as little required maintenance as possible and the lowest possible TCO.

An assessment of how well security controls detect, prevent, and correct breaches is called a *system security audit*, which consists of collecting background and support documentation, including:

- A disaster recovery plan
- Registration numbers
- License numbers
- The key network address
- Passwords
- Other background information about the IT organization

The company defines scopes of responsibility to determine key personnel, backup, chains of command, and communication procedures. Both technical and procedural security controls are reviewed, and findings are reported directly to the highest level of management.

Exam case studies may include comments by key personnel (such as the CEO, CFO, CIO, VP of Marketing, VP of Sales, and VP of HR) that state specific corporate objectives. List specific IT objectives as you read the case study. Look for keywords such as "confidentiality," "integrity," and "availability" when they are applied to users, business services, or corporate assets. When suggesting an appropriate response, remember to classify security technologies as primarily involved with prevention, detection, and correction.

Risk Management

Security must be part of a dynamic process rather than an infrequent static survey. Risk represents only the *perceived* possibility of suffering loss, denial of access, or interception of privileged information—not the actual event itself. In fact, both the probability that such a situation will occur and its impact can vary over time. Detecting risk, however, leads to correction, which leads to routine prevention.

Microsoft's five-step proactive risk management process can be condensed into the following three steps:

1. *Risk identification and analysis.* There is a need to identify a risk as both a risk condition that could occur and as a consequence of what might happen; this leads to better control (detection, prevention) and management (correction). The condition(s) leading to some probability that a risk can occur and the impact of it happening are incorporated into an action plan.

2. *Risk action planning.* Security strategies and business objectives are integrated into an implementation plan.

3. *Risk tracking and control.* The action plan is regularly monitored to assess its effectiveness, and risk management is subsumed under daily project management.

Security Requirements

Let's simplify Windows 2000 security by distinguishing two possibilities: the simplest one, a distributed security system dealing exclusively with security issues within the enterprise, and the more complicated possibility, an enterprise that deals with both an internal distributed system and external network security requirements resulting from Internet-access (which I will discuss in greater detail in the "Using Security Protocols" section later in this chapter). Use the three risk management steps listed previously in an analysis of a distributed security:

- *Security risks*—Identify both perceived risk probability and risk impact or consequence as described in the risk identification and analysis step of the risk management process
- *Security strategies*—Risk action plans as described in the risk action planning step of the risk management process
- *Security group descriptions*—Determine the mapping of users, groups, and group policies, the use of templates and need, if any, for user-defined "functional adaptations" of Microsoft's built-in categories
- *Group policies*—Management of Microsoft's Group Policy security features
- *Network logon and authentication strategies*—Administration of local, remote, and smart card logons
- *Information security strategies*—Management of secured information transmission and the identification of cost/benefits in the use of various forms of encryption, digital signatures, and trusts among Certificate Authorities (CAs)
- *Administrative policies*—Management, monitoring, and auditing of administrative and system-related tasks

Deployment of a Security System

To deploy an enterprise security system, follow these steps:

1. Identify security risks.
2. Plan the size and capacity of the system.
3. Formulate a document that details security policies and procedures.
4. Create a methodology to deploy your security technologies.
5. Train the support staff.
6. Plan and deploy equipment.
7. Identify user groups and their needs.

Notice that procedural tasks precede technical tasks and that security systems are deployed *before* user groups are identified and individuals are assigned user accounts. Microsoft recommends that you formulate a detailed plan using project methodology to deploy network security technologies. In the context of network security strategies, developing secured boundaries—referred to as "hardening the boundaries"—is essential because network traffic will reach beyond an enterprise's namespace. The most conservative network security strategy considers penetration of security from within the enterprise namespace just as likely as from outside it. Effectively deploying security technologies means that those technologies will work in as broad a security context as permitted by the corporate security objectives to maintain a practical TCO.

Strategic planning may or may not include quantitative and qualitative growth projections. In other words, you can have a healthy growth rate of IT resources without the need for Internet access. This would be a noteworthy and valid corporate business objective with a subtle but perhaps important effect on how the business implements a security policy. The corporate business objectives, not the consultant, determine the scope of IT within an enterprise.

Problems with Procedural Paradigms

The Microsoft paradigm is procedural in approach. It does not provide a framework within which to understand and apply security technologies in a systematic and organized way. You need to identify security risk areas in relation to the scope of a set of business objectives. Troubleshooting techniques need similar reference models so that you can isolate, define, correct, test, and retest security breaches. A methodology that identifies key components and, thus, areas of risk would be a valuable tool for analyzing and studying a security system. Isolating key components or features often reveals how a function relates to both physical and logical structure. Just as the study of animal physiology provides a rationale for many peculiar behaviors, you better understand functional adaptations in a business workflow when you explore the limitations in the underlying structure that caused it. For example, an IT workforce adopts superstitious behavior in performing one task on a "special" workstation because of poor training or poorly understood installation procedures. This favored machine becomes a workflow bottleneck because of little or no support for concurrent user access to enterprise resources.

Procedural paradigms mentioned in system documentation work best for software installation and administrative tasks; they do not help organize objects with common characteristics across similar security technologies. In recent years, programming languages have evolved from the procedural business languages of the 1970s to the contemporary object-oriented paradigms, profoundly affecting software engineering and especially quality assurance methods. Procedural approaches have been replaced by more structured, concept-oriented tools. Perhaps an object-oriented approach to designing and implementing security systems in Windows 2000 would offer similar advantages.

A security practitioner analyzes corporate business objectives to reveal functional adaptations of that particular corporate body. Although it's critical to understand both the underlying physical and logical IT structures, a client's corporate "culture" actually determines how, within the greatest strengths and weaknesses of its security policy, corporate business objectives are finally implemented. This "social" layer will interpret the policy statements and carry out all or part of the policy within the context of some group consensus. Once you have described the physical, logical, and social layers of an organization, you should systematically compile organizational data in the following order:

1. Classify relevant IT objects.
2. Map objects to the some layered network reference model.
3. Identify attack modalities—the "who," "where," and "when"—associated with these objects within a layered reference model.
4. Select appropriate security technologies to detect, prevent, or correct the impact and consequences of some identified risk.

A Microsoft Historical Perspective

The ability to classify animal and plant life comes from studying both anatomy and physiology in the real world. Many "new concepts" in Windows 2000 are as easy to classify based upon trends in information technologies over the last 25 years. The following historical trends focus on the logical progression of changes in features now available in Windows 2000. Beginning with the standalone machines in the early 1980s, several themes are noteworthy:

- User-related data requires a growing, disproportionate share of the Registry.
- Greater differentiation of "named objects" requires greater organization.
- More services run in their own process space in the operating system.
- Services are delegated to specialized servers.
- Specialization requires more specific functional management areas.
- Security information is more widely distributed across the enterprise.
- Distribution of security information improves performance and fault tolerance.

These themes help identify trends that will continue to affect the "anatomy" and "physiology" of IT systems in the future. Security systems are fundamental to the IT "body." As security professionals analyze a case study or listen to a CIO describe her IT security objectives, they must train themselves to recognize where structure supports function and where it forces functional adaptation. Especially in Windows 2000, most corporate business objectives are fully realized through the use of built-in structures or templates, further reducing the variable cost components of TCO: training, support, and maintenance.

Key Historical Trends

In the beginning, there was just a local machine with text-file scripts that initialized various software drivers and environmental parameters. The transition from standalone personal computer to workgroup, and from workgroup to domain, represented the first leap in specialization, specifically from disk operating system to network operating system. The fundamental structural change from a flat-file Registry in Windows 3.x to the hierarchical though nonrelational database in Windows 95 formed the substrate for all subsequent IT expansion and development.

Windows for Workgroups managed to carry the additional overhead of a bloated user.dat, but more scalable, networked resources required an evolutionary change in system architecture. Two especially significant characteristics of Microsoft software development have been the use of interface specifications and the abstraction of functional areas in the operating system and the network environment. Microsoft has proposed a four-layer model similar to one proposed in the late 1960s by the Department of Defense. Both Microsoft and DoD models, depicted in Figure 2.1, simplify the seven layers described in the International Organization for Standardization (ISO) Open Systems Interconnection Reference Model (OSI model). The layers in the Microsoft model are Application Programming Interface (API), Transport Driver (sometimes called "Transport

OSI Model	Department of Defense (TCP/IP) Model	Microsoft Model
Application Presentation Session	Application	Application Programming Interface
Transport	Transport	Transport Driver Interface
Network	Internet	Network Device Interface Specification
Data Link Physical	Network Interface	Physical

Figure 2.1 A comparison of reference models.

Device") Interface (TDI), and Network Device (sometimes called "Network Driver") Interface Specification (NDIS). The layers in the DoD model are Application, Transport, Internet, Network, and Interface.

We will use the twin themes of identifying boundaries through the definition of interface specifications and the abstraction and isolation of functional areas to discuss security systems throughout this book. By creating a layered architectural model that emphasizes boundary interfaces and specific functional areas, NT architecture can be described in terms of virtualized or abstracted components—for example, the Hardware Abstraction Layer (HAL) and the Local Security Authority (LSA). Microsoft has successfully applied a component object model to the network operating system itself.

Learn to cross-reference the three major layered architectural models: the OSI model, the TCP/IP (DoD) model, and Microsoft's four-layer adaptation (MS model). Use the Microsoft layered model to organize the hierarchical relationships across the protocols and services mentioned in documentation. Use the OSI model to map these protocols to physical/logical layers in network architecture.

The "new technology" of Windows NT not only supported multiple client service subsystems, but also centralized the user administration in one primary domain controller. This domain controller stored a hierarchical, nonrelational directory database that contains unique information about every authenticated user. This directory database is called the Windows Registry. The logon process required the user or principal to enter a name and password at their local machine, which, through the LSA, was somehow matched to stored information on some domain controller. The domain controller returned a token to the LSA authorizing the user to access services within the domain namespace.

Secondary backup units that supported the primary domain controller partially solved the inherent physical limitations of one machine in supporting user authentication. As a result, organizational systems scaled the number of users to within the primary domain controller's physical capacity. The increased responsibility of administering the directory database for the organization literally pushed other IT services off the domain controller onto other "member" servers in the domain.

In the NT 4 world, greater specialization of one IT object—the domain controller—led to differentiation of other kinds of servers, defined by the directory database, as member servers in that domain namespace. More users created a greater need for some logical organization. With server differentiation comes greater differentiation of services accessible to more users. Clearly, the constraint on increased users/services lies within the design of the primary domain controller and directory database; NT 4 reached its capacity at about 40,000 objects. Creating a Metabase in Internet Information Server 4, a separate directory database exclusively for Web services, was an interesting example of differentiation of structure and specialization of services. However, the Metabase object doesn't support scalability of users and services necessary to scale to a million-object enterprise namespace.

Active Directory

NT 4 system architecture supports a single primary domain controller as the definitive source of authentication for all users accessing a domain's resources and services. Copies of this directory database are replicated to a secondary, backup domain controller. The accessibility to this data store for logon authentication is thus balanced across all domain controllers. Although the security design offers a degree of fault tolerance, it is nevertheless constrained by the primacy of one definitive user accounts directory database. As you scale IT to the level of an enterprise, you reach limits in your ability to efficiently access/replicate one common, central store. Thus, as NT evolves, one can't expect primary domain controllers to multiply. One can, however, assume that security-related processes will further differentiate and specialize in some specific security service support. One can expect a more efficient distribution of user data, greater fault tolerance, and greater security associated with accessing these user stores given the fundamental role they play in consumer-to-provider interactions.

The hallmark of Windows 2000 is Active Directory Services (ADS), a single, consistent, relational database of objects in a uniform namespace scalable to the level of an enterprise spanning multiple domains.

Throughout this book, I use certain icons in the figures to denote specific Active Directory concepts; Figure 2.2 shows the icons and their descriptions. One product of ADS is greater granularity in permissions, not only across a broader ranges of objects and across a wider range of domains, but deeper into the object's attribute sets. Figure 2.3 depicts an AD forest of domain trees, organized into a layered structure of parent domains branching into child domains. Across the entire enterprise, one uniform interface stores information about millions of objects. With greater choices of "named" objects, you must seek greater control and organization of groups spanning across legacy flat NT 4 domain namespaces.

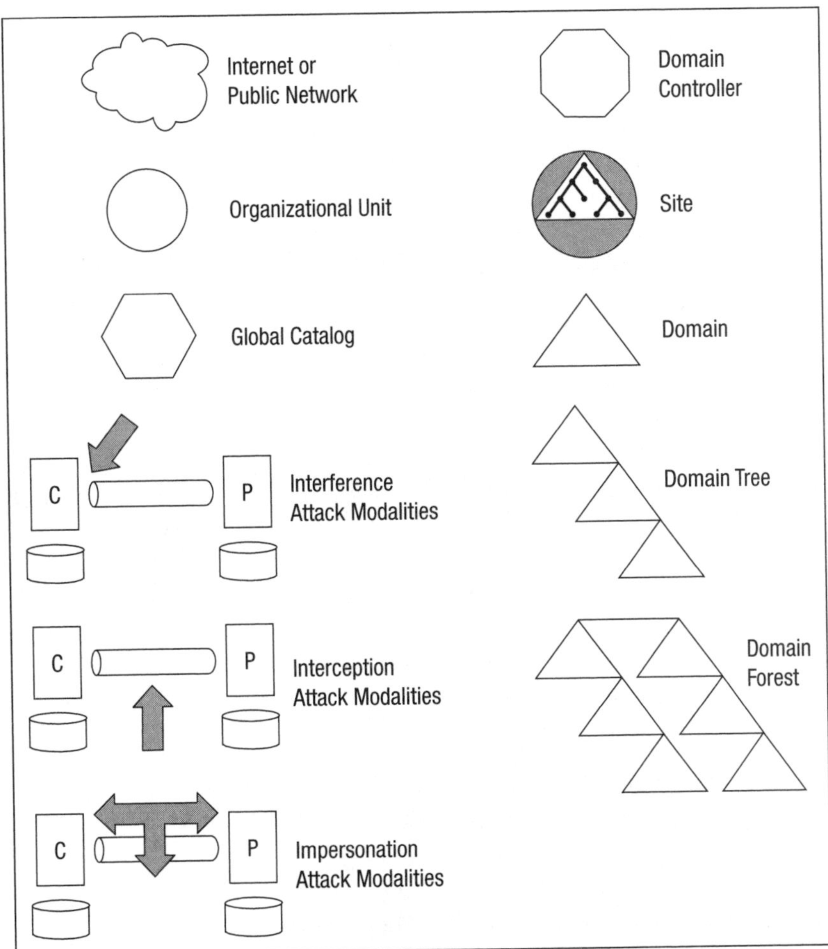

Figure 2.2 Commonly used icons and AD terms.

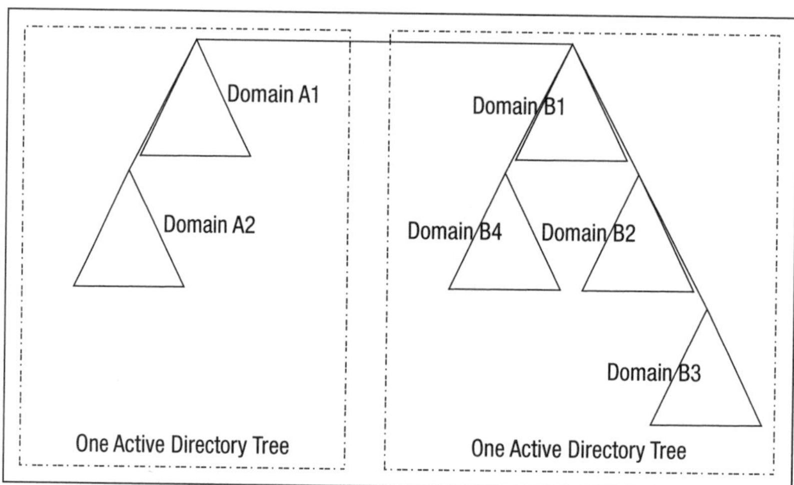

Figure 2.3 An example of an AD forest.

From a historical perspective, forces of differentiation lead not just to specialization, but also to the need for locating simple resources among specialty service providers. In fact, ADS provides a hierarchically arranged directory database and a mechanism to organize the objects within its namespace called the organizational unit (OU). Windows 2000, through its concept of group policies, can create and assign restricted "spheres of responsibility" across domain namespaces by using these logical OUs.

Group Policy usage and tools like OUs dramatically decrease the TCO of a Windows-based enterprise. Users and resource objects, now called *principals*, along with their rights and permissions, are mapped more closely to the way businesses operate, not by artificial constraints in hardware and system software. Microsoft describes ADS as "a single, consistent, open set of interfaces for performing common administrative tasks" that relates to named objects such as users, printers, and file resources across the enterprise. Resources are located in domains, trees, and forests. Just as with any other database, this hierarchical data store can be customized forest-wide through a central schema. ADS uses a multimaster replication model resulting in improved fault tolerance and accessibility; a complete copy of a common data store is replicated to every domain controller.

What is noteworthy here is that ADS is a directory service provider of information about named, network resources; ADS is not the directory database itself. In comparison to the practical 40,000-user limit of the flat NT 4 namespace, ADS will scale more than one million objects. The directory services it provides are a standards-based protocol called Lightweight Directory Access Protocol (LDAP). Using a nonproprietary protocol has security implications because a "well-known" interface allows access to directory stores. A stated goal of ADS is to provide a unified view of directories and namespaces regardless of location or operating system platform.

Given the huge capacity of ADS, Microsoft suggests that in Windows 2000, many enterprises can adopt a single domain model and further reduce their TCO. A single domain model is important in many security schemes.

Integrating Security Account Management

Much like with the Metabase, specialization of directory services has led to ADS and a host of other system, file, and Registry features that support a single namespace containing millions of objects. The greater need for authentication, authorization, and auditing (AAA) has led to the Kerberos protocol, public key infrastructure (PKI), and server differentiation of what are generically referred to as AAA servers. The Kerberos protocol builds on the limitations of the proprietary NT LAN Manager (NTLM) challenge/response authentication service. By adding a "multiheaded" gatekeeper, the NTLM authentication service has been replaced by a well-known, industry-standard design that efficiently delivers distributed security services within a native Windows 2000 environment. Single-user sign-on is enhanced through evolving APIs such as the SSPI, an adaptation of the *de jure* standard General Security Services API (GSS-API). Further scalability in authentication services leads to smart card logons and certificate mapping. In typical Microsoft tradition, backward compatibility rules implementation of system designs. LAN Manager and NTLM authentication servers will remain highly visible in most corporate environments for several years due to the integration of NT 4 and Windows clients. The pure Windows 2000 security system will *not* be the default configuration in most real-life scenarios.

You might assume that because of the increase in use of the Distributed Component Object Model (DCOM) in software development and the emphasis on software interoperability across non-Microsoft "cultures" (e.g., Novell, Unix, and Macintosh), a major Windows 2000 theme is a scalable organizational structure. Similarly, the process of authentication of users and authorization to use both services and resources will also change with the organizational scheme. The relational structure of the AD database in these AAA servers supports even greater granularity by storing more access control information. Just like the software engineer can develop programming objects that have associated methods and attributes, every object in the AD database, including the directory database itself, has associated with it a collection of access control entries (ACEs) that together form an access control list (ACL).

ACLs are either controlled by the system (system ACLs [SACLs]) or are user-defined Discretionary ACLs (or DACLs). Both provide a greater granularity of support in assigning permissions to objects like files, folders, printers, and the Registry than the hierarchical, nonrelational Registry found in NT 4. Such enhancements are necessary, for example, to authenticate and authorize remote users accessing the enterprise namespace. Security technologies included in Windows 2000, such as the PKI, offer a mechanism to secure mail and support new demands outside the boundaries of the enterprise. These security enhancements are discussed in the next chapter.

Physical Organization

Differentiation and specialization have occurred on the system side of the Registry. The local machine has evolved into virtual machine and client subsystems. The Windows 2000 enterprise, administering millions of objects, is still fundamentally a dichotomy of user and system data. The "physical" organization of sites may not reflect the "logical" organization of user objects and resources. Sites and domains still organize users and resources in a more physical dimension. With differentiation comes the need for enhancements in organization. Since the introduction of NT 4, there has been less emphasis on the individual user and growing administrative emphasis on groups. Group Policy spans both the physical and logical enterprise namespace. Workstation clients have names, printers have names, and files have names; all have ACLs.

A fundamental feature of a Microsoft domain model is that the system administrator can assign:

- Users to global groups
- Global groups to local groups
- Resource permissions to local groups

Windows 2000 builds on this schema but scales it to accommodate the enterprise; it places greater emphasis on the group and its policies than the legacy NT 4 domain model does. Group Policy Microsoft Management Console (MMC) snap-in dramatically expands upon the older System Policy Editor in NT 4. Whereas the legacy System Policy Editor specified both user and computer configurations, Group Policy, in association with the AD, centrally manages computers and users without additional administrative overhead. This topic is discussed in greater detail in Chapter 10. A more comprehensive, more accessible, more easily managed organizational structure with greater granularity at the object level has evolved. Tools such as MMC act as common, scalable administrative interfaces that allow you to add on tools such as the Security Template or the Security Configuration And Analysis snap-in to support both objects and policies.

Finally, specialization of individual component objects has also been scaled to accommodate the needs and breadth within *and* across enterprises. DCOM, in order to support increasing numbers of users *and* services, has forced differentiation of new kinds of inter-enterprise services (such as Microsoft Transaction Server, Microsoft Message Queue Server, and Distributed Transaction Coordinator) and has increased the need to both manage *and* audit the secured access to these services.

The majority of real-world corporate business objectives, and most likely the case studies in the Microsoft certification examination, will begin with e-commerce issues and will thus require you to analyze accessing services across enterprises. As suggested in the "A Microsoft Historical Perspective" section earlier in this chapter, you need to map business objectives to features that reflect recurring IT trends, not static system tools. Moore's Law states that because the number of transistors in integrated circuits has doubled every year since the integrated circuit was invented, the capacity to support data doubles approximately every 18 months. Technical experts must understand trends in order to efficiently map corporate business objectives to maintain or even reduce TCO.

The key characteristic across all Microsoft competency areas for IT management is that you must understand the benefits, impact, and rationale for Windows 2000 features and areas. It is likely that the commonly perceived ambiguity of exam questions is testing this particular competency. Identify and map business objectives to IT objects, trends, and current system features. Select an implementation using the most "effective" security technology at the lowest TCO.

A Layered Security Paradigm

Technicians, Microsoft Certified Systems Engineers (MCSEs), and network managers troubleshoot by systematically applying a generic paradigm:

1. Collect data about some event.
2. Isolate the event by identifying conditions and consequences.
3. Resolve the event.
4. Replicate and confirm the resolution of the event.
5. Document the incident, its consequences, and the fix.

Technical personnel rely on layered network-system models to isolate an event. Efficient troubleshooting identifies and isolates only one layer at a time in order to resolve and replicate that event. Replication is the critical step in this process; if you can re-create the event on demand, you identify, isolate, and control all conditions necessary and sufficient to create that event. Layer boundaries are critical in both troubleshooting and design because they define the scope of the event. Notice the similarities here between this troubleshooting methodology and risk management mentioned earlier in this chapter. Basic troubleshooting includes problem identification, an action plan, and resolution. Security controls identified in an organization's corporate objectives are identified and mapped to specific functional areas, layers or interfaces in Windows 2000. To resolve or troubleshoot a particular security incident, it is advantageous to have a generic schema that helps to identify required security components in relation to these areas.

You can consider workstations, member servers, and domain controllers as different "species" of computers with different Registry configurations that support different characteristic workloads—for example, client workstations, file servers, application servers, and domain controllers. Likewise, it might be useful to consider the client workstation as a consumer, and a server as a service provider. Based upon different workload characterizations, service providers offer services (for example, application servers) or resources (for example, files, printers, and so on). Thus, as the number of users/consumers increases, providers supporting both resources and services become more differentiated and specialized. Fundamental to all systems is the asset itself. A generic file server is a service provider; it provides files, an asset. The consumer seeks authentication in order to use services or retrieve resources that a host/provider offers; a consumer requests and accesses or retrieves a file. The domain controller or AAA provider supports the specialized security services of authentication, authorization, and auditing. Finally, a channel of communication or virtual pipe represents the physical connection or logical session that exists at some point in time between consumer and provider when services are requested or delivered. The pipe may not directly connect to the consumer or provider. Instead, it may require an interface layer, as did the old telecommunications model, which connected the session pipe to data terminal equipment (DTE) through some data circuit interface (DCE).

Figure 2.4 shows a security component schema. The benefit of the schema, originally borrowed from a telecommunications model, is that you can easily identify key security components within any OSI layer of a network. Reliance on the OSI model helps to strengthen your security design, analysis, and troubleshooting and force a systematic and replicable way to analyze security scenarios. Any object in the enterprise namespace having some account information and login username is a *principal.* This principal-to-principal (consumer-to-provider) schema thus supports comparisons of different security technologies at different OSI layers to help quantify the cost effectiveness of any security implementation.

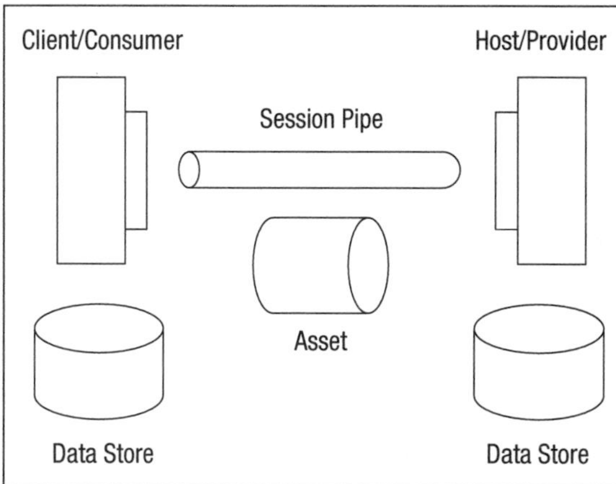

Figure 2.4 A consumer/provider interaction.

You can simplify all design scenarios as consumer/provider, provider/provider, or consumer/consumer interactions across a session pipe. Note that each component has a data store that may contain special security information used during the session. The simplest interaction involves a consumer, such as a client or user, who is requesting some asset (such as a file), from some provider (such as a file server).

Evaluating Risks

For the purposes of study and analysis, you must simplify the list of IT objectives and the many possible security exposures (any form of malicious program, denial of service attacks, spoofing, replay attacks, brute force attacks, and so on) that are detailed in numerous security references. In the real world, though, it is more advantageous to evaluate security designs in terms of generic kinds of security exposure, not in terms of security services. It is easier to conceptualize a denial of service, replay, or spoof directed at a service provider than discuss IT security control themes of availability and access. In fact, you can categorize security incidents as threats to one of the following:

- Users
- Assets
- Services
- Integrity of an object

You can determine the most effective security technologies by applying an attack modality to objects in your schema. Conceptualizing a security issue as an attack modality in this way helps to understand an issue and more readily translates that issue to the real world. Doing so helps to limit your scope of investigation and optimize your troubleshooting efforts when a security breach has occurred.

You can simplify the six IT security controls—namely, access, availability, integrity, authenticity, confidentiality, and nonrepudiation—by categorizing them into three attack modalities, each with an active and passive dimension. Figure 2.5 shows examples of three attack modalities staged against some service provider. In the remainder of the book, I will use this schema to explain security technologies at various levels of the OSI model. The three attack modalities are:

- *Interference*—Any form of security attack that renders an asset or service unavailable or unusable.
  - *Active*—An active interference attack specifically targets an asset or service with the programmed intention to either disable or destroy it. Examples of active interference attacks are classic boot sector viruses that rewrite the master boot record on a local hard drive or DOS attacks that overwhelm the capacity of a service provider, rendering it functionally useless.
  - *Passive*—Passive interference attacks, such as a virus, bacterium, or rabbit, do not target the asset or service directly but work to subvert accessibility through indirect activities. They are designed to exhaust all local resources and thereby prevent access to or use of an asset or service through indirect means.
- *Interception*—Any form of attack that covertly captures a data stream through either direct monitoring or redirection.
  - *Active*—An active interception attack intercepts a message flow and performs analysis of message content. Because the message content is known, the attack can include alteration or fabrication of data, which is

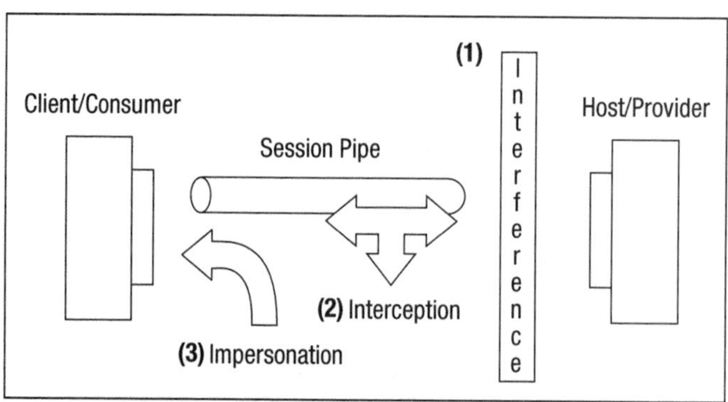

Figure 2.5 Applying attack modalities—three attacks on a provider.

then redirected to either subvert existing information or produce some unauthorized effect. An example is the unauthorized alteration of a DNS namespace.

- *Passive*—A passive interception attack intercepts a message flow and performs an analysis of the characteristics of the data stream, not its content. Examples are wire taps and network traffic analysis.

- *Impersonation*—Any form of attack that permits an intruding third party to intercede for one principal in the exchange of information or services without the knowledge of the other.
  - *Active*—An active impersonation involves a third party spoofing or faking the IP address of one of the principals. The spoof impersonates either principal online without the other's knowledge.
  - *Passive*—A passive impersonation does not directly target the session pipe or data stream but works indirectly to produce some unauthorized effect. A passive impersonation attack would involve the renaming of DNS namespace so that legitimate DNS lookup responses point to illegitimate hosts. Other forms of impersonation involve the creation of a secret trapdoor that allows unauthenticated, unauthorized access by a third party to system services.

A distinguishing factor between active and passive impersonation is the interactive nature and response time of the exchange of information between parties. An example would be a spoof logon screen requesting reentry of both username and password.

IT security controls like compliance are primarily procedural and attitudinal, so they cross attack modality boundaries. Similarly, many attacks include subversive techniques from all three modalities. Nevertheless, the classification scheme helps to identify areas of risk impact and their consequences. The different attack modalities and appropriate IT security controls for detection, prevention, and correction are summarized in Table 2.1.

Applying an attack modality to an asset, consumer, provider, or session pipe helps you identify the risk involved in losing accessibility to, the integrity of, or credibility in that particular object. Table 2.2 lists examples of security breaches within

Table 2.1 Three attack modalities and appropriate IT security controls.

Dimension	Interference	Interception	Impersonation
Active	Access control	Integrity	Authenticity
Passive	Availability	Compliance, nonrepudiation	Confidentiality

Table 2.2 Examples of security breaches.

Dimension	Interference	Interception	Impersonation
Active	Denial of service	Web page redirection	Spoof, replay, crack
Passive	Active viruses, bacteria	Wire taps	Trap doors, Trojan horse

the context of the three attack modalities. Security technologies need to support distributed application services in the context of e-commerce across enterprise borders. Especially outside the enterprise, authenticity applies to assets, consumers, and providers. Access control and integrity more clearly apply to asset providers. Confidentiality applies data flows through the session pipe between consumer and provider.

Familiarity with this schema helps you more readily:

1. Map the corporate business objectives to specific security objects within specific reference model layers.
2. Apply attack modalities to identify areas of security exposure.
3. Apply security technologies to detect, prevent, or correct any risk consequences.

This relatively simple analysis is useful when you are planning, troubleshooting, and building a security model. In the remainder of this book, you will use this security schema and these attack modalities to study and analyze security technologies. In Chapters 3 and 4, respectively, I discuss PKI and the Kerberos protocol at great length. In Chapter 5, you will apply this schema to design and analyze an actual network security plan. More important, though, is how to use the same simple schema at different OSI layers to correlate and compare different security technologies.

Documenting Nontechnical Procedures

Even though you can evaluate risks and apply security technologies, a critical part of a disaster recovery plan is thoroughly documenting nontechnical procedures associated with detecting, preventing, and correcting a security incident. Many times, the appropriate "paper trail" (compliance with a published auditing policy, the proper use of legal notices, proper disposal procedures, and so on) is carelessly overlooked or ignored. Sloppy administrative procedures sometimes undermine a company's ability to resolve a security incident. In Chapter 5, we will refine a network security policy and quantify the cost benefits/risk analysis so that financial decisions can be reached in an actual business context.

Using Security Protocols

I have already simplified designs by identifying scenarios that might deal just with distributed security within the enterprise. The unique factor facing network security issues is exposure to the Internet. Now, in addition to security threats to assets, services, and the integrity of objects, you have risks associated with impersonation from outside the enterprise namespace. For example, there are at least three active impersonation attacks:

- An unauthenticated person can impersonate or masquerade as a legitimate user (a *spoof*)
- An authenticated user (a *rogue user*) can access unauthorized areas
- An unauthenticated user (a *cracker* or *bogie*) can totally subvert security systems

Most corporate business objectives include e-commerce issues, so it's particularly relevant to understand the security ramifications of accessing services outside the enterprise. Chapter 3, which describes the PKI, and Chapter 4, which contains a discussion of the Kerberos protocol, deal with security issues that apply to both a distributed and Internet-aware security structure.

Expect the majority of case studies to include Internet access as a key security issue. It may be advantageous to first address distributed security concerns. You can address many network security issues by adding specialized servers (such as a proxy server), implementing security technologies (such as firewalls), and redesigning network topology (such as constructing a demilitarized zone—DMZ—within the enterprise).

Mapping Security Technologies

The hardening of layered boundaries applies more closely to adding and changing configurations at or below the TDI than above the TDI. The acronyms and services are overwhelming. When you categorize them by, for example, Microsoft interface layers, a clearer picture for study and analysis emerges. Typically, service providers occupy the API layer or are found at the API/TDI interface. Below the TDI, most security technologies are involved with either the session pipe itself or the data flow within the pipe. In fact, PKI, by definition, is neither a protocol nor a service provider; but rather a system of technologies that includes digital signatures and Certificate Authority service providers. Notice how the hierarchical listing in Table 2.3 maps to the seven-layer OSI model, with the Application layer (layer 7) corresponding to Microsoft's API layer, the Transport layer (layer 4) corresponding to the TDI, and layers 3 (Network) and 2 (Data Link) corresponding to NDIS. You can apply each technology to address specific attack modalities. It is obvious

Table 2.3 A hierarchical listing of key security protocols as they relate to the OSI and Microsoft models.

Layer Number	Layer Name (OSI)	Layer Name (Microsoft)	Security Protocols
7 6 5	Application Presentation Session	API	Secure Multipurpose Internet Mail Extensions (S/MIME); Kerberos protocol and other AAA servers; Proxy services; Secure Electronic Transaction (SET) service; IPSec: Internet Key Exchange Protocol (formerly ISAKMP/Oakley)
4	Transport	TDI	SOCKS (Sockets for Unix compatibility); Secure Sockets Layer/Transport Layer Security (SSL3/TLS1)
3	Network	NDIS	IPSec: Authentication Header (AH), Encapsulated Security Payload (ESP); packet filtering; Point-To-Point Tunneling Protocol (PPTP); Challenge Handshake Authentication Protocol (CHAP); Password Authentication Protocol (PAP); Microsoft CHAP (MS-CHAP)
2 1	Data Link Physical	Physical	PPP, L2TP, Hardware CSP

that implementing an effective security technology depends upon boundary interactions with other security technologies or server services.

Competencies

This chapter ends with a checklist of areas that Microsoft considers most relevant to anyone in a management role in the IT industry. What connotes technical expertise in this particular job role is always difficult to define. An objective of this book is that you will successfully pass the Microsoft Windows 2000 security exam, an area as widespread as the operating system itself. Even if you are not planning on taking a certification exam, the methodology and information in this book will offer valuable support in the analysis, design, and troubleshooting of Windows 2000 security systems. The areas Microsoft considers as requiring some competency are just as relevant to you as the certification exam candidate.

The Competency Model is a study guide that prioritizes topics in terms of their importance to particular IT support roles. Microsoft's list of required competencies are ranked from the lowest, 1, to the highest, 4. It is used in this book primarily as a checklist. As you review the various areas of study, you should note not only what is most significant, but also what is considered of lesser importance with regard to IT management. Unlike the competencies of the executive role, none of those for the management role received less than a 2 out of 4 ranking. In other words, all the areas listed in this section are relevant to the IT manager. You can assume that if these topics are considered relevant, they will somehow be included on a Microsoft examination.

Here is a list of the competencies and a description of each. These areas of competency are considered most relevant to an IT manager. Exam candidates should make certain they are thoroughly familiar with the topics listed prior to taking the security certification exam:

- *Security versus productivity issue*—This process requires that you maintain a balance between productivity and the security policy.
- *Security model*—This includes understanding the model's benefits, impact, and design rationale.
- *Compliance*—This IT objective, critical to the success of a security plan, is a procedural, legal, and social issue.
- Definition, rationale, and benefits of the following:
  - Single Sign-On capability
  - Active Directory
  - Security Configuration Manager
  - Remote access
  - Smart card infrastructure
  - IPSec protocol
  - Group policies
  - Access control lists
  - Public key
  - Certification server
  - Encrypting file system and asset protection
  - Kerberos 5

This book will discuss all topics included in the Microsoft Competency Model for Security but will focus especially on the areas Microsoft considers most relevant to IT management. One would expect that these areas are more likely to appear on a Microsoft certification exam and, therefore, require more than a casual understanding.

In the next few chapters, I will introduce more terms and concepts. Consumer-provider interactions will help you to conceptualize Windows 2000 security technologies. I will then apply these concepts to case studies. In addition, you will construct an actual network security plan using all techniques discussed in this chapter. As I discuss new technologies in subsequent chapters, I will introduce additional case studies to reinforce the Microsoft certification experience and security analysis in the real world.

Practice Questions

Question 1

Which of the following are components of TCO? [Check all correct answers]

- ❑ a. Cost of system upgrades
- ❑ b. System maintenance
- ❑ c. Cost of toner
- ❑ d. Technical support

Answers a, b, and d are correct. TCO (total cost of ownership) includes cost of system upgrades, system maintenance, and technical support. Cost of toner is not a component of TCO, so answer c is incorrect.

Question 2

An effective security plan is the synergy of which complementary factors? [Check all correct answers]

- ❑ a. Proper social attitudes in the user community
- ❑ b. A redundant array of independent drives (RAID) tower
- ❑ c. Technical expertise for proper support
- ❑ d. Appropriate security technologies

Answers a, c, and d are correct. Proper social attitude and compliance of the user community, technical expertise for proper support and maintenance, and the appropriate security technologies are all complementary factors. A RAID tower would most likely be included in a disaster recovery plan. Therefore, answer b is incorrect.

Question 3

Which of the following are examples of IT security objectives? [Check all correct answers]

- ❑ a. Confidentiality
- ❑ b. Training
- ❑ c. Integrity
- ❑ d. Firewall technology

Answers a and c are correct. Examples of IT (information technology) security objectives include confidentiality and integrity. Training is not a typical security objective. Therefore, answer b is incorrect. Firewall technologies are, in isolation, not security objectives. Therefore, answer d is incorrect.

Question 4

There are two categories of security policies:

Logical

Physical

Identify whether each of the following key security policies is logical or physical. Categorize each item under the proper heading.

Auditing and monitoring

Backup and restore procedures

Domain account policies

Security management of users, groups, and resources

The correct answer is:

Physical

Backup and restore procedures

Logical

Auditing and monitoring

Domain account policies

Security management of users, groups, and resources

Only backup and restore procedures in this list have a physical component—that is, access to either the physical tape backup unit or to the actual backup media set(s).

Question 5

Which of the following items are included in a system security audit? [Check all correct answers]

- ❑ a. Phone numbers of key personnel
- ❑ b. List of domain controller IP addresses
- ❑ c. Software license numbers
- ❑ d. Serial numbers of all printers
- ❑ e. Passwords
- ❑ f. Birth dates of key personnel
- ❑ g. Weekly backup tapes
- ❑ h. List of vendor telephone numbers

Answers a, b, c, d, e, and h are correct. A system security audit is a collection of all relevant background and support documentation including a disaster recovery plan. Telephone numbers to contact key personnel are important, but their ages aren't. Therefore, answer f is incorrect. Weekly backup tapes would not be an actual part of the audit. Therefore, answer g is incorrect.

Question 6

When you are compiling a list of corporate business objectives for a security plan, the Chief Information Officer will supply the most relevant information.

- ❍ a. True
- ❍ b. False

Answer b, false, is correct. Corporate business objectives reflect the business mission of the entire organization. The objectives usually are based upon a survey of many departments within the organization.

Question 7

Create an action plan for deploying an enterprise security system based upon the appropriate tasks listed below. Arrange all appropriate steps in the proper order.

Plan and deploy equipment.

Train your staff.

Plan for size and capacity of the system.

Create mandatory roaming profiles for all users.

Formulate a security policy and procedures document.

Identify user groups and their needs.

Identify security risks.

Create a methodology to deploy security technologies.

The correct answer is:

Identify security risks.

Plan for size and capacity of the system.

Formulate a security policies and procedures document.

Create a methodology to deploy security technologies.

Train your staff.

Plan and deploy equipment.

Identify user groups and their needs.

Note that the item "Create mandatory roaming profiles for all users" is not part of the action plan. The use of a mandatory or personal roaming profile might be documented in a comprehensive security policy statement, but it would typically be delegated to a system administrator or account operator.

Question 8

Interference, impersonation, integrity, and interception are all examples of security attacks.

❍ a. True

❍ b. False

Answer b, false, is correct. Interference, impersonation, and interception are examples of security attacks; integrity, on the other hand, is an IT objective.

Question 9

Which security protocol(s) are parts of the TDI layer in the Microsoft four-layer model? [Check all correct answers]

- ❑ a. Proxy services
- ❑ b. IPSec IKE protocol
- ❑ c. S/MIME
- ❑ d. SET
- ❑ e. All of the above
- ❑ f. None of the above

Answer f is correct. None of these protocols is part of the TDI layer. The four protocols listed are found in the API layer. Examples of TDI protocols are SOCKS, SSL3, and TLS1.

Question 10

The Microsoft Windows 2000 Competency Model for security can be used for what purpose? [Choose the best answer]

- ❍ a. A source of information about Windows 2000 features
- ❍ b. A selling tool
- ❍ c. A checklist
- ❍ d. A study guide

Answer d is correct. The Microsoft Competency Model helps prioritize topical areas for each role member, so it functions as a study guide. It also ranks topical areas as least to most relevant for IT executives, IT management, and the IT workforce. The Microsoft Competency Model is specific to security issues; it is not a source of information about Windows 2000 features. Therefore, answer a is incorrect. The model is neither a selling tool nor simply a checklist of topics. Therefore, answers b and c are incorrect.

Need to Know More?

McLean, Ian. *Windows 2000 Security Little Black Book.* The Coriolis Group, Scottsdale, Arizona, 2000. ISBN 1-57610-387-0. In addition to covering Windows 2000 security issues in a concise yet comprehensive manner, the author follows topical discussions with Immediate Solutions sections that explain, in a step-by-step format, how to implement the specific security techniques.

Murhammer, Martin W. et al. *TCP/IP Tutorial and Technical Overview, Sixth Edition.* Prentice Hall, Upper Saddle River, New Jersey, 1998. ISBN 0-13-020130-8. Part 2, "Special Purpose Protocols and New Technologies," contains information about security breaches, cryptography, firewalls, network address translation, and IPSec.

Search the TechNet CD (or its online version through **www.microsoft.com**) and the *Windows 2000 Server Resource Kit* CD using the keywords "competency", "security", "TCO", and "risk".

http://web.mit.edu/kerberos/www/dialogue.html offers a fictitious account that Bill Bryant wrote in February 1988 about the design of the Kerberos protocol as implemented in the MIT Athena project.

Public Key Infrastructure (PKI)

Terms you'll need to understand:

- ✓ Public key infrastructure (PKI)
- ✓ Symmetric/asymmetric encryption algorithm
- ✓ Cryptanalysis
- ✓ Hash function
- ✓ Message digest
- ✓ Digital signature
- ✓ Bulk data encryption
- ✓ Digital envelope
- ✓ Certificate Authority (CA)
- ✓ Microsoft Cryptographic Application Programming Interface (CAPI)

Techniques you'll need to master:

- ✓ Identifying the hierarchical organization of security-provided services
- ✓ Describing the differences between symmetric and asymmetric encryption algorithms
- ✓ Discussing major issues in key management
- ✓ Describing how Certificate Authority hierarchies are organized
- ✓ Discussing major issues in successful key deployment
- ✓ Summarizing the features in the PKI Suite
- ✓ Outlining CAPI-supported features
- ✓ Describing the standard certificate stores in a Certificate Authority

This chapter begins with a discussion of secret and public key encryption, which address issues of confidentiality and authenticity. The next topic, key management, is a critical issue for deployment of security controls across unsecured namespaces. This topic is especially relevant in the area of e-commerce, where authentication of some service provider and confidentiality of the information exchange is critical to completing a business transaction. Finally, the various components of the public key infrastructure (PKI) are outlined to provide a foundation for Chapter 9.

In Chapter 2, I described key questions relating to any security analysis—namely, who is involved, what is happening, what are the objectives, where are the risks, and what are the security countermeasures. I then proceeded to describe how I would deploy a security system based on a set of corporate security objectives. You should use these corporate objectives to establish assumptions, definitions, priorities, and goals. Within the scope of these corporate objectives, you should attempt to identify predisposing risk conditions as well as the ramifications of a risk's impact on the business organization and its operations. The structured organization of the OSI and Microsoft reference models are helpful for systematically examining the different layers of the network structure. You need to begin the identification process by reducing each risk situation to one of the following:

- *Three basic components*—Namely, a consuming agent (consumer), a service providing agent (service provider), and a virtual pipe (session pipe) through which a dedicated transaction occurs between the two principal agents.
- *One or some combination of any three basic security attack methods or modalities*—Namely, interference, interception, and impersonation.

The identification process, especially with regards to Windows 2000, requires a level of competency in understanding the rationale for both design and implementation of several security substructures. Unlike NT 4 with its simpler domain model and NT LAN Manager (NTLM) challenge/response security protocol, Windows 2000 incorporates security subsystems like PKI, Kerberos protocol, IP Security (IPSec), and several remote connectivity designs. These all require a basic understanding before even the simplest security scenarios and basic components can be applied for comparison studies. The Windows 2000 competencies stress the need to understand the rationale for both design and implementation issues, because subsystems like PKI and IPSec support multiple installable cryptographic service providers (CSPs) and security protocols (Authentication Header Protocol and Encapsulated Security Payload Protocol), respectively. The understanding of these core components ought to precede the development of an actual security plan so you can better assess methods and costs of deployment.

Thus, in this chapter, I will begin by applying the basic security scheme proposed in Chapter 2 to a real-life security scenario. Specific requirements and goals will be described in the context of a business. You will often observe that the deployment costs of any security countermeasure can be measured only in terms relative to corporate security objectives and an organization's total cost of ownership (TCO). In the next four chapters, more technology is discussed to better gauge the cost of deployment and TCO. In Chapter 8, I return to a scenario-based discussion and complete the steps in the deployment of a security system—namely, plan the size of the system, formulate a securities policy, and create a methodology for deploying a security system.

Applying the Basic Security Scheme

A consumer-provider system can be compared to two people speaking, and the security issues that arise in computer networks have counterparts in this example. In normal discourse, one person (the consumer) speaks directly to another (the provider), and each person can see and hear the other. There is no passive interference from outside sources. The speaker can see that the listener is paying attention; outside tasks do not actively interfere with the conversation. Similarly, the speaker can be reasonably sure that his or her words are communicated in the intended manner and that the conversation is not overheard. Finally, because one party sees the other, there is little question of active impersonation.

In a case study situation, compile a list of corporate business objectives before dealing with the technical issues of the data exchange. The consumer or service provider determines objectives for the exchange and establishes business rules that apply to how the exchange is conducted.

In this scenario, you can identify the following security components:

- Participatory roles as consumer and provider
- The session characteristics
- Relevant attack modalities based upon the security schema

How would the conversation change if one or both parties were threatened by outside forces seeking to learn about the exchanged information, interrupt the meeting, or discredit one or both parties in the exchange? IT security objectives would be established in anticipation of any one particular attack modality. Areas of risk and associated consequences of the attack would be systematically identified and evaluated in terms of the costs and benefits in this specific environment. Security breaches would be closed where appropriate. For businesses, the cost/benefits analysis, shaped by the business mission of the organization, becomes the security corporate objectives.

Table 3.1 A comparison of security objectives, controls, and countermeasure examples.

Corporate Security Objective	IT Security Control	Security Countermeasure
The picture ID card must be a credible source of authentication.	Authentication	Certificate Authority
The picture ID card cannot show evidence of tampering or forgery.	Integrity	HMAC or message digest
Both parties have agreed to keep the exchange of information confidential.	Confidentiality	Symmetric or asymmetric encryption
The location of the conversation is not prearranged but made known to the intended listener only moments before the scheduled meeting.	Authentication, confidentiality	Session secret keys
As the conversation progresses, the parties move in some random direction to further minimize the effectiveness of some long-distance listening device.	Authentication, confidentiality	Subsession secret keys

For example, possible corporate security objectives for the above meeting are described in Table 3.1. Some of these security countermeasures will be discussed in this chapter and in Chapter 4.

Encrypted Exchanges

Corporate security objectives delineate business needs both within and outside the boundaries of an enterprise. This chapter introduces terms and concepts that are the foundation for security technologies discussed throughout the remainder of this book. The concepts are fundamental to both distributed and network security designs. PKI is a collection of tools and technologies that provide a secured exchange of information within and outside an enterprise. These security technologies are a prominent feature in e-commerce activities, which occur every minute somewhere on the Internet. Confidence in the authenticity of speaker and listener as well as consumer and provider is fundamental to securely exchanging information and assets. That exchange's privacy or confidentiality is equally important. PKI verifies authenticity and confidentiality between parties in an electronic information exchange.

Three basic cryptographic technologies generate a security component:

- Symmetric key encryption algorithms
- Asymmetric key encryption algorithms

- Secured one-way hash functions or hash message authentication code (HMAC)

Each provides countermeasures against one or several attack modalities, as summarized in Table 3.2 and discussed in more detail later in this chapter.

If the scenario I described at the beginning of this chapter had included corporate business objectives, the most obvious theme to emerge would be the meeting's confidentiality. Then again, business objectives and the "corporate culture" dictate what is required. For example, especially rigorous efforts to establish authenticity of either party could, in fact, have been detrimental to the exchange's progress. More simply, proof of possession or verification without specific knowledge of a secret code might prove more expedient in a given situation. Thus, applying technologies is a balance among several factors: the security objectives, the cost and implementation of resources (including licensing of patented technology), the network proximity of parties, and the exchange's time frame.

Symmetric Key Encryption

If privacy is a security objective, encrypting messages using a single, secret key has been—and still remains—the most common method of securing the contents of a message transmitted between two parties. Figure 3.1 shows a symmetric encryption exchange.

In the figure, the sender uses a unique key composed of a string of characters to transform data (or *cleartext*) into some scrambled message (or *ciphertext*). This is the *encryption phase*. The receiver uses the same key to decrypt or unscramble the transformed data (or ciphertext) back into the original message (or cleartext). This is the *decryption phase*. When the encryption and decryption phases use the same key, both the key and the encryption process are described as *symmetric* or

Table 3.2 Three methods for authentication/integrity.

Feature	Symmetric Key	Asymmetric Key	Hash Function
Key management	Must be distributed	Publicly available	Not necessary
Execution	Fast	Slow	Fastest
Encryption	Just digital signature	Just digital signature	None
IT objectives	Authenticity, integrity, nonrepudiation	Authenticity, integrity, nonrepudiation	Integrity
Attack modalities	Interception, impersonation	Interception, impersonation	Interception, impersonation
Export restrictions	Yes	Yes	No

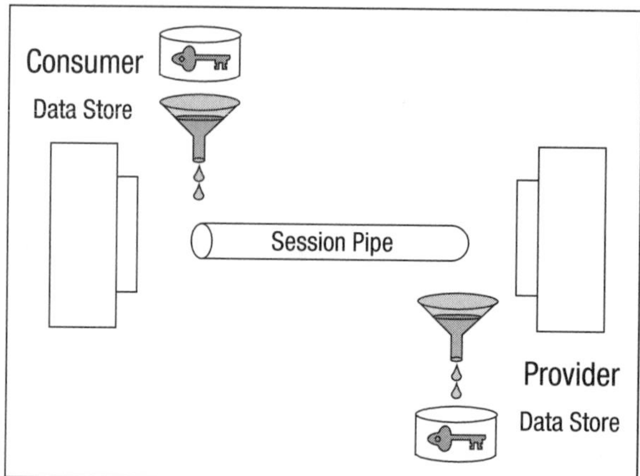

Figure 3.1 Applying symmetric encryption to a consumer/provider exchange.

conventional. In fact, the encryption algorithm and the ciphertext can both be publicly distributed. The guarantee of message confidentiality lies in the following:

- The secrecy of the symmetric key
- The length of the symmetric key

A strong encryption algorithm, by definition, cannot be used to generate a secret key even when the algorithm, ciphertext, and cleartext are known. In practice, however, as techniques to boost computational power—such as symmetric and massive multiprocessing (SMP and MMP, respectively)—improve, the resistance of a symmetric key to brute-force attack is decreasing.

The data encryption standard (DES) was developed in 1975 and standardized by American National Standards Institute (ANSI) in 1981. ANSI X3.92 uses 64 bits, a 56-bit key, and an 8-bit parity block. However, it is no longer considered secure because of its key length. A hardened version—called triple DES (TDES or 3DES), which uses three 128-bit keys—is available in a special upgrade High Encryption Pack as a Windows 2000 service pack add-on. You can also implement DES at the hardware level in the form of low-cost chips, especially for bulk encryption needs. However, using multiple keys in this algorithm increases the necessary computational time to generate the key. Nevertheless, symmetric key algorithms remain popular because you can implement them quickly. In Chapter 4, I will further discuss these encryption algorithms, along with such techniques as Cipher Block Chaining (CBC).

The following are prerequisites for symmetric encryption to work:

- Both parties must have the same symmetric key.

- The symmetric key must be secret—that is, known only to the intended parties.
- The encryption/decryption process must use a strong encryption algorithm.

Cryptanalysis

Going back to the security object schema shown in Figure 3.1, you can further refine the cryptographic operations performed on the message flowing through the session pipe. *Cryptography* describes how:

- The key is used in the symmetric or asymmetric encryption operation.
- The encryption operation—namely, substitution or transformation of a message's characters—is performed on the message before it enters the session pipe.
- The cleartext is encrypted, in blocks of bits or as individual bits.

Cryptanalysis is the interception and attempted recovery of a key or some specific cleartext from a secured exchange. *Passive interception* surreptitiously gathers any kind of information that flows through the pipe, such as traffic patterns and recurring blocks of encrypted code. Alternatively, an *active interception* attack uses a compromised secret key to reintroduce altered or newly fabricated information back into the session pipe. The method used to perform any cryptanalysis or code cracking depends on where the system security is breached; for example, copies of different cleartext can be captured in the data store prior to encryption, ciphertext can be intercepted in the session pipe, samples of known cleartext and its corresponding ciphertext can be captured through impersonation, and so on. Ciphertext interception through, for example, a network sniffer, typically provides just ciphertext, assuming that the attacker knows of the kind of encryption algorithm used. If the attacker does not have additional information about the nature of the cleartext source, such as file type, language, and so on, it is unlikely—though not impossible—that a key will be exposed. Success of a brute-force attack on any encryption algorithm is a function of the attacker's computing power and the encryption key length. In fact, Windows 2000 uses both the weaker DES 56-bit variation and the more hardened 3DES or TDES.

Statistical patterns in the traffic and recurring characteristics in the ciphertext flow increase the possibility that an attacker can decrypt ciphertext or discover a key. Once a session pipe is compromised, an attacker, through passive interception, will most likely scrutinize frequencies of pattern occurrence (e.g., a probable-word attack). To thwart statistical and structural analyses, you can convert cleartext blocks to ciphertext blocks (block cipher processes) so that there is a less predictable stream, eliminating the possible statistical regularities and pattern correlation.

Logically speaking, as the cost/benefit of uncovering a key increases, and/or the window of opportunity to use "cracked" ciphertext decreases due to the information's useful lifetime, the likelihood of an interception attack also increases. What is noteworthy, however, is that security attacks may not be motivated by logic. Nevertheless, because conventional symmetric encryption is computationally faster than asymmetric encryption, and because strong encryption algorithms are commercially available, symmetric encryption algorithms remain the most common security countermeasure to attacks against confidentiality or privacy.

Distribution Problems

If you look back at Figure 3.1, you can see that both parties share the secret key in the symmetric encryption method to exchange the encrypted information. Doing so is both a strength and a weakness. If the secret key is compromised, the secured exchange is breached. Issuing that key to some party, however, creates the opportunity for an on-demand, confidential virtual communication channel across public namespaces. Furthermore, frequently issuing a key to that same party shortens the time that secured information might be exposed to, for example, passive interception, if a key is compromised. Due to the computational speed of symmetric key distribution, it will always remain part of a comprehensive security strategy.

Distribution problems arise if the two parties are not within physical proximity. The most secure way to distribute a symmetric key is to deliver it physically. But in most case studies on an examination or in the real-world deal outside an enterprise, doing so is not a practical or cost-effective option. One alternative is to establish a specialized server, called a *key distribution center*, as a trusted third party to deliver keys (I will discuss this kind of server, which offers scalable authentication services that the NT 4 primary domain controller has been unable provide, in Chapter 4). A second alternative is to transmit the secret key in a secured fashion without the need for yet another secret key.

Asymmetric Key Encryption

Secret key distribution is a critical part of a comprehensive security plan, so a simple way to deploy those secret keys would be advantageous for a scalable network of distributed consumers and providers. The objective is to secure a session pipe between two parties to exchange confidential information. The process requires:

- A strong encryption algorithm
- A key that uniquely identifies the owner as a party to privileged data
- A key that can be distributed across unsecured namespaces

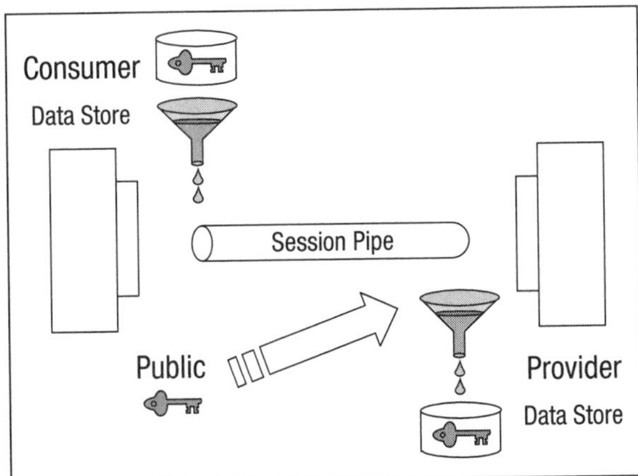

Figure 3.2 Applying asymmetric encryption to a consumer/provider exchange.

As shown in Figure 3.2, a possible solution is to break the key into two complementary parts: a private complement on the encryption side of the session pipe and another complement on the opposite decryption side. One complement key component, like the symmetric key, is secret; the other complement, like the strong encryption algorithm itself, can be publicly known. By definition, a strong encryption algorithm cannot be used to generate a key even when the algorithm, ciphertext, and cleartext are known. In a similar context, access to the cleartext, ciphertext, encryption algorithm, or the well-known, public key complement does not reveal the value of the private key complement. The advantage of two complementary but different—or *asymmetric*—keys is that you can publish or exchange the well-known public key across unsecured namespaces. The public key creates ciphertext that can be decrypted only by the complementary private key of the intended receiver.

Thus, asymmetric key encryption uses a set of complementary but different keys—one private and secret, the other public—and a strong encryption algorithm to securely exchange information across unsecured namespaces. The encryption algorithm requires greater processing time and hence is operationally slower than a symmetric key encryption scheme. The de facto public key standard, RSA (an acronym formed from the last names of the three inventors: Ron Rivest, Adi Shamir, and Leonard Adelman), uses asymmetric keys that are functions of two very large prime numbers. Unlike DES, which has a fixed-length key, RSA can continue to resist a brute force attack by increasing its key length. The ability to distribute a public key without compromising the integrity of a secret, private key is critical in the development of message confidentiality in distributed security systems. Public keys and asymmetric key encryption algorithms provide more scalable key management, confidentiality, authenticity, and nonrepudiation. However, asymmetric encryption algorithms are several orders of magnitude slower than symmetric algorithms, so they are not typically used for bulk encryption. In addition, they are more vulnerable than symmetric algorithms to cryptoanalytic or code breaking attacks. A good security design would thus use an asymmetric algorithm to establish a secured session (authentication and key transfer) and a symmetric algorithm for encrypting the message.

Active Interception

Asymmetric and symmetric encryption algorithms protect against any passive interception attack modality like wiretaps or traffic analysis. *Active interception* (surreptitiously modifying or fabricating exchanged data) requires a different form of protection. Possession of a secret key implies that you are the chosen participant in a secured exchange of information. But if the secret key is compromised and a message is modified, the integrity of the message will have been compromised unbeknownst to the receiving party. A countermeasure against active interception attack modalities requires authentication of the asset being exchanged. Implementing this security control is more complicated than passive interception countermeasures because this attack strategy raises questions regarding:

- Integrity of the asset
- Authenticity of the source
- Timing of the exchange

In general, if one assumes a secret key is secure, possessing that key and using it in the exchange of information implicitly authenticate the source and confirm the integrity of the asset exchanged. In fact, using a secret key in an exchange also supports claims of nonrepudiation, especially when a timestamp is included in the message. Timing issues for the most part are handled by the transport and network protocols. In fact, IPSec architecture uses sequence numbers instead of timestamps to protect against impersonation attack modalities.

However, sometimes, the receiver of some message or other asset needs to confirm not just the identity of the sender through a shared, secret key but something about the exchanged object itself. If corporate business objectives require separate corroborative evidence of authenticity and integrity, the company needs to implement independent countermeasures against active interception of an asset or message.

Authentication and Integrity Controls

You can apply a symmetric key to a message digest to generate an HMAC just before data is exchanged. This calculated HMAC block, like a checksum, is sent along with the asset to the receiving party. When the receiving party gets the asset or message, it applies its copy of the symmetric key to the asset and generates its own HMAC tag. If the two generated tags or message digests agree, the integrity of an asset or message was not compromised during the exchange process. I will further discuss these and similar topics in Chapter 9.

One-Way Hash Functions

The hash function or message digest takes a variable-length message and, like a meat grinder, converts it into a fixed-length output string or hash value. A mathematical algorithm, similar to but not the same as an encryption algorithm, generates a 128-bit to 256-bit number or message digest derived from the message contents when a hash value is created. There is no easy way to reconstruct the pieces of "meat" from the extruded meat "pâté" because the meat grinding is a one-way process. The identity of the meat, however, is uniquely defined by the contents of the generated pâté. Similarly, the hash value is considered an electronic fingerprint of the variable-length message. A good hash function is considered collision resistant when it's not very likely that two different variable-length messages will converge on the same hash value—a collision—no matter how small that hash output is.

This hash value or authentication block (which is independent of the message or content) can prove authentication through comparison. You can independently generate a second hash function when you receive either a message or a demand for verification, and compare the two authentication blocks. If one character in the message has changed since the message was created, you know the hash values are no longer identical and thus the authenticity of the message or asset is questioned. As shown in Figure 3.3, the receiver of a message compares the results of the second hash function to the hash value sent with the message. If the two values agree, the message has not been modified during the exchange.

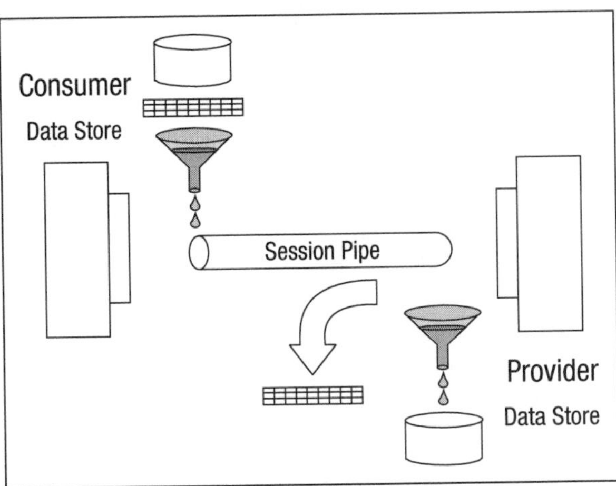

Figure 3.3 A hash function exchange.

The Windows 2000 Implementation

Microsoft uses two industry-standard cryptographic algorithms for creating message authentication code or digests—Message Digest 5 (MD5) and Secure Hash Algorithm (SHA-1)—to generate an HMAC. MD5 converts 512-bit blocks of cleartext to 128-bit-long tags. SHA-1 was designed for use with the Digital Signature Standard (DSS) by the National Institute of Standards and Technology (NIST) and the National Security Agency (NSA). It is slower than MD5 because it converts the same-size cleartext block into a larger, more secure 160-bit message digest.

Comparing hash values does not reveal the content of the actual message. For example, a personal banking or automatic teller machine (ATM) generates and compares hash values of the password keyed into its console with the personal identification number (PIN) it reads from the magnetic strip on the swiped smart card. If the two hash values agree, a transaction can proceed. The PIN password is never actually revealed in the authentication process. The NT LAN Manager (NTLM) challenge/response security service works in a similar way. The computational processing in encryption/decryption is, thus, eliminated. More significantly, information is never compromised because it is never revealed.

Sometimes, you can satisfy business objectives without using encryption. Generating asymmetric keys is more processor intensive and therefore slower than generating symmetric keys; using both encryption algorithms is slower than generating a hash number. In fact, when server workload or the processing of bulk messaging is an issue, it is not always necessary to encrypt a message. A message digest does not first have to be decrypted to prove authenticity.

Often, however, the hash function is keyed or encrypted to produce a digitally signed Message Authentication Code (MAC). As shown in Figure 3.4, the receiver can authenticate this digital signature by comparing his or her own generated hash number with the signed hash number from the sender using the receiver's copy of the shared, secret key. If a message were intercepted and modified during an exchange, the value of the signed, encrypted message digest would not necessarily be revealed. In a subsequent comparison of the two message digests, any discovered differences would indicate tampering.

Entity Authentication through Proof of Possession

One way the receiving party can determine the authenticity of the sending party is to send a cleartext challenge to that party. If the sending party possesses the private key complementing the public key that the receiving party is using to key the cleartext challenge, the sending party demonstrates proof of possession of that particular private key. The receiver initiates the exchange session and spontaneously creates the cleartext challenge, so impersonation attack modalities are not likely.

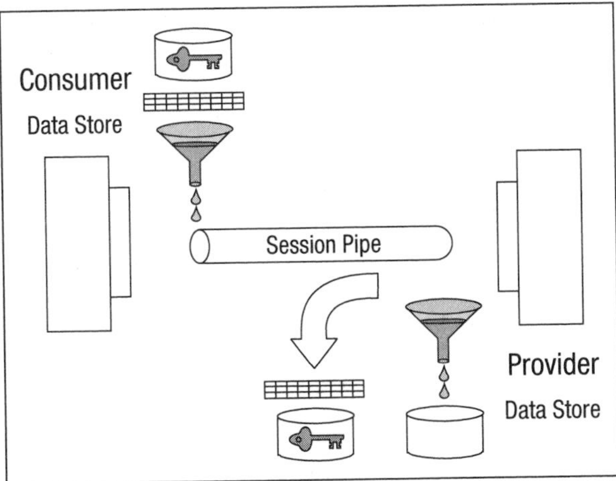

Figure 3.4 Applying a secured hash function or MAC to a consumer/provider exchange.

Secret Key Agreements

You can trade mutually complementary portions of secret keys using asymmetric encryption. Each participant creates and exchanges a random number encrypted with the public key of the other. The two random numbers are exchanged and, based on prior agreement, combined to form a secret, symmetric key that can be used henceforth in symmetric exchanges of information.

Bulk Data Encryption

Symmetric encryption algorithms are several orders of magnitude faster than asymmetric encryption. Furthermore, these encryption algorithms (like DES) can also be implemented at the hardware level in the form of low-cost chips for greater scalability and lowered total cost of ownership (TCO). The fundamental problem is the exchange of the secret key across the nonsecured channel. A secret key for the session encrypts the message. To compensate for the increased computational overhead of asymmetric encryption, only the session key is encrypted with the receiver's public key. Only the intended party can decrypt the public key to unlock the storage.

Digital Envelope

When two layers of encryption to protect a message are used, the resulting package is called a *digital envelope*. First, the message itself is encoded using symmetric encryption; then, the key to decode the message is encrypted using public encryption. Thus, only the key is protected with public-key encryption. Encoding this smaller block of data dramatically reduces the computational overhead associated with asymmetric encryption.

Certificates and Key Management Services

In many commercial exchanges, a signature provides the most common level of integrity and nonrepudiation. The three algorithms that support a digital counterpart to the written signature are:

- Hash-based signature
- DSS
- RSA signature

Hash signatures use a cryptographically secure hash function (such as MD5 or SHA-1) to produce a single value from the file. By hashing together the file and an appended a secret key, you generate a single value in the form of a tag or code block. The file is shipped with the authenticating code block (but without the secret key) to a second party, who also possesses the same secret key. The receiver adds the secret key and recalculates the hash value. If the hash values are identical, the signatures are valid. As mentioned earlier, using a hash signature requires less computational overhead than using other signature technologies. A disadvantage of this technique, however, is that you use conventional encryption. The shared, secret key must be distributed to all who are participating in the secured information exchange. The greater the number of participants in the secured exchange, the greater the number of secret keys exposed to possible attack, and the more likely any one secret key will be compromised.

Both DSS and RSA use an asymmetric encryption algorithm that solves the problem of distributing and storing keys. DSS, developed in conjunction with the NSA, is a signature-only system designed to avoid using encryption algorithms. In fact, although the U.S. government heavily restricts software that involves general encryption, security technology that exclusively provides an authentication function like DSS is openly exported outside the United States. RSA signatures, unlike those of DSS, can encrypt data as well as prove authenticity.

Making keys with longer-bit strings to resist attacks hardens both hash-based and public-key algorithms. Sharing a secret key doubles the possibility of a security breach when you are using hash-based algorithms. An asymmetric encryption algorithm is more secure than conventional symmetric encryption because, even though there are many published public keys available in an unsecured namespace, there is only one secret key for every public/private key pair. However, in a hostile environment, publishing a public key can also increase the probability of impersonation.

Digital Signatures

Distributing a public key solves the problem of exchanging the more computationally efficient symmetric, secret key used in conventional encryption algorithms. In addition, it offers a way to potentially authenticate parties exchanging messages. A *digital signature*, like an electronic fingerprint, uniquely identifies the package as originating from the party possessing the key that complements the easily accessible public key. Unfortunately, there is no guarantee—especially outside an enterprise's boundary—that the public key in use really belongs to the intended party. Active impersonation through forgery of a public key can be prevented only if some trusted authority vouches for that public key's authenticity.

A Certificate Authority (CA) is a certifying third party that vouches for the public key's authenticity. It applies its "universally" trusted digital signature to a public key and some ID of the key owner. This certificate is then made available much like the original public key. Now, however, the CA manages the key's distribution. The issued certificate conforms to the International Telecommunications Union (ITU) Telecommunication Standardization (ITU-T) X.509 version 3 standard, which I discuss in more detail in Chapter 7. The certificate contains the following:

- The public key of the key holder
- The certificate's date of expiration
- Detailed information about the holder of that key

Extensibility

Each certificate, although primarily invented to validate the authenticity of a public key, also has associated with it an extensible set of data fields. These certifications are similar to the access control lists (ACLs) associated with resources in the NT file system (NTFS); the extensible fields store an object's attributes much like ACLs contain access control entries (ACEs). The extensible fields delineate not only group membership but also object permissions. It is important to consider that a CA provides the following key-management services:

- Public operations for a consumer and quick access to a valid, authentic public key
- Privileged operations for a service provider and a certificate corroborating that provider's authenticity

Creating strong certification structures depends upon these extensible data fields and how both consumer and service provider use them. This concept as well as certification services will continue to be major trends in the future development of distributed security systems.

Certificates

Certificates contain the private key of a CA, which publishes its public key in the form of a root certificate. As long as the key holder has a certificate maintained by a CA, the CA's public key opens its digital certificate that corroborates the key holder's authenticity. An organization or provider installs the root certificate of some trusted CA outside the enterprise in a certificate data store. The private key in that root certificate is used to open and confirm certificates issued by the CA outside the enterprise to validate key holders. Likewise, a CA within an enterprise publishes its root certificate outside its boundaries. When properly installed within other organizations, the root certificate provides the private key that will open certificates associated with public keys of enterprise users and services.

CA Hierarchies

Typically, a hierarchy of authorities is deployed. As shown in Figure 3.5, Windows 2000 provides for both a root and subordinate CA. The root CA is the first CA in an organization and, hence, the most trusted when multiple CAs are deployed. The root certificate authority either certifies itself or secures certification from some worldwide commercial organization. A CA that is not a root CA is

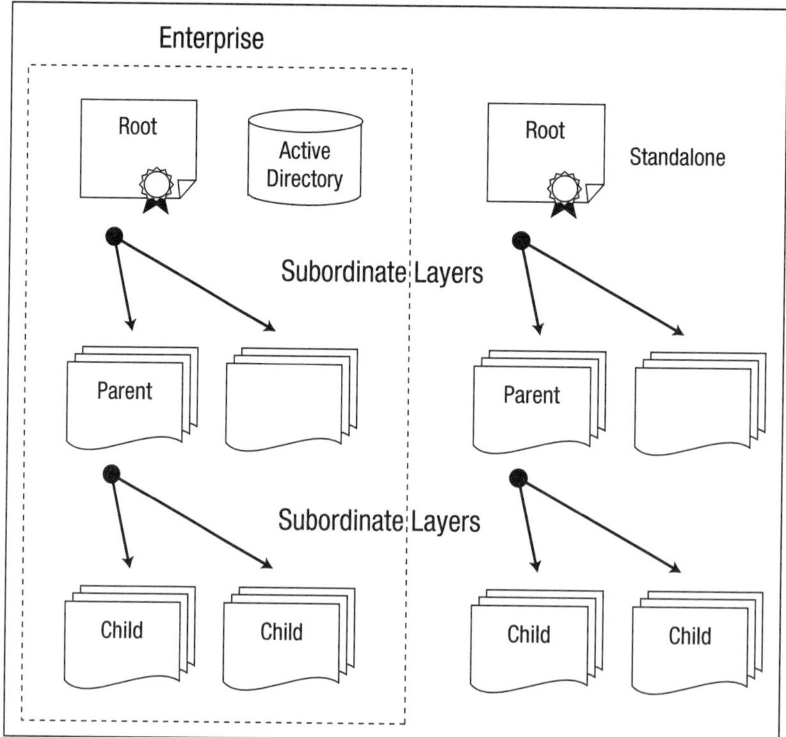

Figure 3.5 Certificate authority hierarchies.

subordinate to either the root or to another subordinate CA. A subordinate can issue its own certificates, but these are certified by its parent CA. A subordinate CA may act as a bridge that serves only to create certificates for other subordinate CAs. Finally, an enterprise CA is part of the Active Directory (AD); a standalone CA is not.

An organization might implement a hierarchy of CAs to achieve its corporate objectives. In fact, it is possible to have multiple CA hierarchies within an organization. Deploying multiple CAs offers:

- Structural support of organizational or administrative functions
- Separation of specific security technologies (e.g., smart card logons)
- Distribution of subordinate CAs on different sides of slow WAN links to facilitate access
- Redundancy and maintenance

Similarly, CA-based trust relationships can be created within or across organizations. An administrator can create a trust and select specific certificate purposes (such as client authentication, server authentication, time stamping, and so on) of that trusted CA. For example, to separate a specific security or administrative function, an administrator can configure a trusted root certificate authority to validate only certificates issued by a CA for smart card logons. Likewise, if two different organizations are subordinates under the same root CA, the two organizations implicitly trust each other. In addition to trust relationships and inheritance, Windows 2000 supports automatic certification enrollment defined through group policy at specific organizational levels.

The following factors can affect successful key deployment:

- Replication issues regarding authenticating information
- Verifying group policy and the effects of auto-enrollment
- Verifying certificate templates
- Effect of certificate revocation and certification revocation list (CRL) lifetimes
- Maintenance of CAs
- Certificate publisher's group membership

Providing Certificate Services

The CA's authority lies in the fact that it issues, renews, and revokes valid public key certificates for members of a specific user community. The community trusts the CA to validate the identity of the holder with a public/private key pair. The public key's authenticity lies in the credibility of the issuer of that certificate form. Auditing security, managing public keys, and maintaining the certification lists have become services of the certificate services provider. Because of these administrative roles, CAs maintain two databases: one that lists the certificate holders and one that lists the revoked certificates. The planned expiration as well as unplanned revocation of a certificate—published in a CRL—are parts of the provided certificate services.

Certificates are granted to and recognized by users of a specific community. The corporate business objectives usually define the criteria that requesters of this authentication must meet to receive certification by the CA. Thus, certificate authorities are policy independent. Likewise, a certificate can be requested and distributed through a variety of transport mechanisms. CAs are also transport independent. Certificate enrollment is standards based and uses message formats that support Public Key Cryptography Standards (PKCS) and the more recent Internet Engineering Task Force (IETF) Public Key Infrastructure X.509 (PKIX) draft standards. A CA typically accepts the PKCS #10 request package and issues an X.509 version 3 certificate in a PKCS #7 digital envelope. An exported certificate and key pair are encrypted as a PKCS #12 message. An Internet Architecture Board (IAB) draft standard called *Certificate Request Syntax* refines certificate enrollment.

The PKI Suite

Windows 2000 PKI is a suite of technologies and services that are relatively invisible to the consumer. Table 3.3 summarizes the standards that Microsoft included in its PKI suite.

Paralleling the historical theme of system architecture supporting increased scalability, PKI in Windows 2000 provides the security platform on which the Active Directory Services Interfaces (ADSI) can support million-user enterprises. It is noteworthy that these security technologies are nonproprietary and standards-based protocols. The goal of the ADSI, which I discuss in greater detail in Chapter 9, is to provide a unified view of directories and namespaces regardless of location or operating system platform. Windows 2000 PKI, the security platform for AD, reflects that theme.

In Figure 3.6, a user/consumer within the security context of logon services (provided by the NTLM domain/Kerberos protocol) uses network resources as defined by the organization and policies of AD.

Table 3.3 A summary of Windows 2000 PKI standards-based features.

Standard	Description
Authenticode	Digital signatures that verify software origin, authenticity, and integrity
Certificate Revocation List v2 (CRL)	Part of PKIX (X.509); cited in RFC 2459
IP Security (IPSec)	Support for network encryption at the Internet Protocol (IP) protocol layer
Personal computer/smart card	Specifications based on International Organization for Standardization (ISO) 7816 standards
Public Key Cryptography for Initial Authentication in Kerberos (PKINIT)	PK-based authentication using Kerberos 5
Public Key Cryptography Standards (PKCS)	Certificate message standards and formats
Public Key Infrastructure X.509 (PKIX)	IETF draft for interoperable PKI (RFC 2459)
Secure Sockets Layer (SSL) v3	HTTP-based authentication, integrity, and confidentiality
Server Gateway Cryptography (SGC)	Similar to TLS, this SSP requires a 128-bit session key and authorized CA certificates
Transport Layer Security (TLS)	Implemented by the SChannel SSPI along with SSL v3

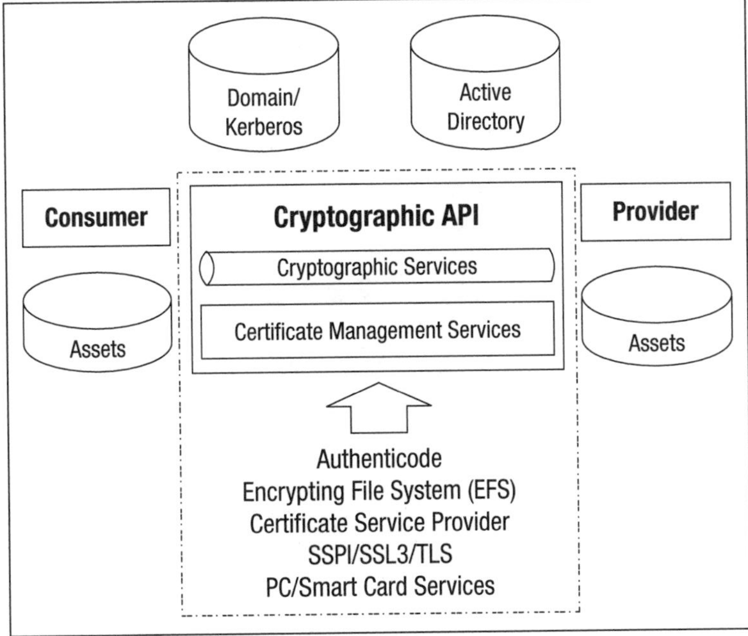

Figure 3.6 Microsoft PKI.

Microsoft CryptoAPI

To support exchanges between consumers (user/user) or consumers and providers—the generic scenario in this book—PKI provides services for the entire ranges of information technology (IT) security objectives in a distributed and scalable manner. Compatible with either legacy domain controllers or the Kerberos protocol, the Microsoft Cryptographic Application Programming Interface (CAPI) supports cryptographic service providers (CSPs) and certificate management services. The variety of services that CAPI supports is hierarchically shown in Table 3.4.

Security Support Provider Interface (SSPI) supports these primary security support provider protocols:

- *NTLM/Kerberos*—User authentication
- *SChannel security support providers*—Secured network exchanges
- *Server Gateway Cryptography (SGC)*—HTTP-based authentication
- *Distributed Password Authentication (DPA)*—Internet-based membership authentication

CAPI supports both cryptographic services and certificate management services. The Cryptographic Services layer must integrate with the domain administration/enterprise policy model as well as support potentially different providers of public-key algorithms. CAPI supports installable CSPs, each of which manages its own security material. Similarly, the certificate management services administer specific certificate stores or repositories for certificates and associate data in the "Providing Certificate Services" section earlier in this chapter. Table 3.5 shows standard certificate stores. Note that these certificate stores are logical representations of credentials available on a system-wide basis supporting authentication services in the AD namespace.

Table 3.4 CAPI-supported services.

Services	Description
Smart cards	User authentication
Authenticode	Origin and integrity; code-signing
SSPI	Security context management
DES hardware and RSA-based CSP	Encryption algorithms
EFS	Directory- and file-level security

Table 3.5 Standard certificate stores.

Certificate Store	Contents
ROOT	Self-signed CA certificates for trusted root CAs
TRUST	Certificate Trust Lists (CTLs) that describe the CA hierarchy
CA	Certification verification chains, including issuing CA certificates and intermediate CA certificates that show certification-verification chains
MY	User or computer certificates for the related private key
UserDS	Logical schema of the certificate repository stored in the AD

Global Encryption Policies

Even though security keys can be encrypted using different algorithms and technologies, the primary issue is key length. The most common commercially available encryption algorithms are provided by RSA, Inc., and use key lengths of up to 128 bits. However, encryption algorithms impact issues of national and international security. Different countries have restricted the importation/exportation of 128-bit encryption algorithms, whereas weak encryption systems using 40-bit keys are freely traded. Likewise, it is common for the banking industry to use DES products globally. Cryptography, formerly considered munitions, is now under the control of the U.S. Department of Commerce. Until 1999, the United States prohibited exportation of such software technology. France has even stricter licensing policies that control the marketing of cryptography in that country. A global policy has been proposed; it would create an international key-escrow system where copies of keys 128 bits or greater in length used by consumers and/or providers around the world would be stored. Access to these keys would be made available to authorities only through the written order of an international court.

Practice Questions

Question 1

Which of the following are encryption technologies? [Check all correct answers]

❑ a. Asymmetric key encryption

❑ b. Symmetric key encryption

❑ c. Hash function

❑ d. All of the above

Answers a and b are correct. Asymmetric key encryption and symmetric key encryption are encryption technologies. Hash functions convert a message to some hash value for comparison, not for decryption or reading, so answers c and d are incorrect.

Question 2

What factor guarantees message confidentiality?

❍ a. Proper social attitudes in the user community

❍ b. Length of the message

❍ c. Length of the key

❍ d. Authenticity of the sender

Answer c is correct. Length of the key guarantees message confidentiality. Proper social attitudes in the user community, length of the message, and authenticity of the sender do not guarantee confidentiality. Therefore, answers a, b, and d are incorrect.

Question 3

Confidentiality, using symmetric encryption, depends on what conditions? [Check all correct answers]

- ❑ a. Both parties have the secret key.
- ❑ b. Secret keys are secure.
- ❑ c. A strong encryption algorithm is used.
- ❑ d. The receiver has been authenticated.

Answers a, b, c, and d are correct. Symmetric encryption algorithms depend upon parties sharing the same secret key, ensuring that the security of that key has not been compromised, and using a strong encryption algorithm. Only the intended receiver has a copy of the shared secret key, so possessing the key is evidence of authenticity.

Question 4

What is the procedural order in using symmetric encryption to exchange a message? Arrange all appropriate steps in the proper order.

Create the message.

Apply your private key to the message.

Apply your intended receiver's public key to the message.

Send the message.

The correct answer is:

Create the message.

Apply your private key to the message.

Send the message.

In symmetric encryption, public keys are not used. Therefore, "Apply your intended receiver's public key to the message" should not be included in the ordered list.

Question 5

Which item correctly describes asymmetric encryption?

❍ a. The algorithm is faster than symmetric encryption.

❍ b. The algorithm is slower than both a hash function and symmetric encryption.

❍ c. The private key can be exchanged in an unsecured namespace.

❍ d. The public key must be protected from exposure to unauthorized parties.

Answer b is correct. The asymmetric encryption algorithm is slower than hash functions and symmetric encryption. Answer a is incorrect because asymmetric encryption is slower than symmetric encryption. The private key is kept in a secured data store, whereas the public key is published across unsecured namespaces. Therefore, answers c and d are incorrect.

Question 6

You should always use an asymmetric public key when performing bulk encryption to facilitate exchanges across unsecured namespaces.

❍ a. True

❍ b. False

Answer b, false, is correct. Asymmetric encryption requires greater computational resources and time to encrypt data; symmetric encryption is the method of choice when performing bulk encryption.

Question 7

What is the procedural order when you are receiving an asymmetric encrypted message? Arrange all appropriate steps in the proper order.

Open the message.

Apply your public key to the message.

Apply your private key to the message.

Apply the sender's public key to the message.

Apply the sender's private key to the message.

The correct answer is:

Open the message.

Apply your private key to the message.

The sender used your public key to encrypt the message, so only your private key will decrypt the ciphertext. Neither the sender's public nor the sender's private key will decrypt the message.

Question 8

Both symmetric and asymmetric encryption provide solutions to the issue of nonrepudiation.

❍ a. True

❍ b. False

Answer a, true, is correct. Unless the secret key is compromised, only an intended party can send or receive an encrypted message with a specific private key. Therefore, answer b is incorrect.

Question 9

What service(s) are supported by CAPI?

❍ a. CSPs

❍ b. DSS

❍ c. DES

❍ d. SSPI

❍ e. 3DES

❍ f. All of the above

❍ g. None of the above

Answer f is correct. CAPI (Microsoft Cryptographic Application Programming Interface) supports Cryptographic Service Providers (CSPs), Digital Signature Standard (DSS), Data Encryption Standard (DES), Security Service Provider Interface (SSPI), and triple Data Encryption Standard (3DES). All answers are correct, so answer g is incorrect.

Question 10

Your client develops software and wants to markedly improve its market share. It has added one new Windows 2000 server to a legacy NT 4 domain with two domain controllers and an application member server to improve production. You want to improve customers' confidence in the authenticity and integrity of the software that they purchase online from this company. What course of action should you suggest? [Choose the best answer]

- ❍ a. You suggest installing an enterprise CA.
- ❍ b. You suggest installing a standalone CA.
- ❍ c. You suggest contacting VeriSign or Thawte.
- ❍ d. None of the above.

Answer c is correct. The configuration stated in the question is a legacy domain model, so the servers will not use Active Directory Services (ADS). You can install only a standalone CA (Certificate Authority) in this environment. Answer b however, does not adequately address the stated objective to improve customer confidence in both authenticity and integrity. Although software certification by the developer will ensure integrity of the exchanged package, it does not address the level of trust in the authenticator, especially in a global market. The best answer is c, which is to seek authentication from some validating third party that has worldwide name recognition and reputation. Answers a, b, and d are not the best courses of action, so they are incorrect.

Need to Know More?

Stallings, William. *Network Security Essentials: Applications and Standards.* Prentice Hall, Upper Saddle River, New Jersey, 1999. ISBN 0-13-016093-8. This vendor-neutral overview of cryptography, system security, and network security applications describes and references the major security themes in a clear, technical style. Its balanced approach and broad range of topics offer a necessary perspective to texts specifically discussing Windows 2000 security design.

Search the TechNet CD (or its online version through **www.microsoft.com**) and the *Windows 2000 Server Resource Kit* CD using the keywords "DES", "CA", "Kerberos", and "PKI".

http://microsoft.com/windows2000/library/planning/security/pki.asp is the location of Microsoft's Windows 2000 White Paper, titled *Microsoft Windows 2000 Public Key Infrastructure,* originally posted in April 1999. This technical paper is the primary source of information for the Windows 2000 implementation of the public key infrastructure.

www.itl.nist.gov/fipspubs/fip46-2.htm is the location of the DES 1993 standard. *Data Encryption Standard 1993* specifies a cryptographic algorithm that federal organizations can use to protect sensitive data. To maintain the confidentiality and integrity of the information represented by the data, it may be necessary to protect data during transmission or while in storage.

Kerberos Security

Terms you'll need to understand:

- ✓ Kerberos protocol
- ✓ Authentication, authorization, and auditing (AAA) server
- ✓ Symmetric and asymmetric encryption algorithms
- ✓ Kerberos Authentication Service (AS) exchange
- ✓ AS request/reply
- ✓ Ticket-granting ticket (TGT)
- ✓ Kerberos ticket-granting service (TGS) exchange
- ✓ TGS request/reply
- ✓ Client/server (CS) authentication exchange
- ✓ Kerberos application request/reply
- ✓ Key Distribution Center (KDC)
- ✓ Hash function
- ✓ Cross-domain exchanges
- ✓ Security Support Provider Interface (SSPI)

Techniques you'll need to master:

- ✓ Describing the Microsoft Kerberos enhancements
- ✓ Describing the steps in the Kerberos AS exchange
- ✓ Describing the steps in the Kerberos TGS exchange
- ✓ Describing the steps in the Kerberos CS authentication exchange
- ✓ Describing the steps in cross-domain authentication of a service request

This chapter deals with the information technology (IT) security controls of authentication (who?) and authorization (what?). I begin by presenting an overview of the Massachusetts Institute of Technology (MIT) Kerberos protocol because it is the foundation for Microsoft's implementation of the protocol. Next, I discuss Microsoft's enhancements to the MIT Kerberos protocol. This information builds a foundation for the discussion of interoperability later in this chapter and a rationale for future enhancements in Microsoft's Multiple Authentication Architecture implemented through Security Support Provider Interface (SSPI), mentioned in Chapter 2. I then describe how Kerberos fits into the security protocol picture as a whole. Lastly, I describe common Security Support Providers (SSPs) that this interface supports: NT 4 NT LAN Manager (NTLM) and the Windows 2000 Kerberos authentication protocols. Chapter 7 discusses other supported SSPs: Secure Channel (SChannel) protocols.

This chapter also represents a turning point in how material is presented. As discussed in Chapter 1, my objectives are to prepare you for both simulated case studies on a Microsoft exam and real-life case studies. In Chapters 2 and 3, I introduced terms and definitions that provided the foundation for the fundamental IT security controls: authentication, confidentiality, and integrity. In this chapter, you will begin dealing with real-life problems you might encounter as an independent consultant.

MIT Kerberos: The Basis for Microsoft's Implementation

The Kerberos protocol, the default authentication protocol in Windows 2000, was proposed and first used in Project Athena conducted at MIT in the 1980s. The name "Kerberos" is a reference to the mythological three-headed dog that guarded the gates to Hades. The original proposed protocol in 1983 was to have provided the "triple A" services of authentication, authorization, and auditing (AAA). Of the three AAA services, MIT implemented only authentication services.

Goals and Requirements

The goals and requirements of the MIT Kerberos protocol are:

- Easy access that requires minimal information such as a username and password
- Strong authentication across an unsecured environment
- Scalability across a large, modular, distributed server architecture
- Reliable accessibility to security services in a scalable, distributed server architecture

- Prevention of an impersonation attack where one of the following occurs:
  - A legitimately authenticated user attempts to request unauthorized resources or services (a rogue user)
  - An outside intruder (a cracker or bogie) impersonates an authenticated, authorized user (a spoof)
  - An outside intruder gains unauthorized, illegitimate access to the network and obtains confidential information
- The Kerberos server itself is both physically and logically secured

Assumptions

The MIT Kerberos protocol makes several assumptions:

- *AAA servers are always accessible.* There is no countermeasure to interference attack modalities, specifically denial of service (DOS) attacks, where the AAA server is actively prevented from fully participating in legitimate exchanges with clients.
- *Secret keys are secured.* It is the responsibility of the principal (discussed later in this chapter) to store secret keys in a secure manner and to replace them as quickly as possible if a possible breach in that security occurs.
- *Symmetric keys are prone to attack.* There is no countermeasure to impersonation attack modalities, specifically password-guessing attacks where techniques are applied offline to solve the character combination in the secret key.
- *Timing is loosely synchronized.* There must be some clock-synchronization scheme across all participating network servers to differentiate slight discrepancies in timestamps from impersonation attack modalities such as replay attacks, where messages are intercepted and replayed out of temporal sequence to impersonate some authenticated principal or service.
- *Security identifiers (SIDs) are not reused.* Recycling of SIDs could evoke stale access control lists (ACLs), lists that describe how a user or group can manipulate properties of the specific resource object. An outdated ACL could permit new, potentially unauthorized consumers to have access to resources and services for which they have no authorization.

Components of the Protocol

MIT Kerberos uses a symmetric encryption protocol with appropriate data stores in some KDC. This encryption technique is discussed in Chapter 3. In Windows 2000 native mode, domain controllers (DCs) that run the Kerberos services are also referred to as KDCs. KDCs are discussed in more detail later in this chapter.

Kerberos security services can be divided into three exchanges, sometimes referred to as *subprotocols*. In this case, the term *protocol* refers to predetermined steps in any of the exchange procedures:

- *Authentication Service (AS) exchange*—The consumer requests authentication services in the form of a Kerberos Authentication Service Request (KRB_AS_REQ) from some AAA server. This consists of both the consumer's registered user ID and some encrypted preauthentication data that proves the knowledge of some secret key. The key response is a ticket-granting ticket (TGT) in the form of a Kerberos Authentication Service Reply (KRB_AS_REP).
- *Ticket-granting service (TGS) exchange*—The Kerberos client that is running on the workstation requests services in the form of a Kerberos Ticket-Granting Service Request (KRB_TGS_REQ). This request consists of a user ID, authenticator of that ID, targeted service provider, and TGT. The response is a Kerberos Ticket-Granting Service Reply (KRB_TGS_REP).
- *Client/server (CS) authentication exchange*—The Kerberos client that is running on the workstation requests services from a service provider in the form of a Kerberos Application Request (KRB_AP_REQ). This request consists of an encrypted authenticator, keyed with a session key common to consumer and provider, the TGS ticket, and a flag requesting mutual authentication. If the flag that indicates mutual authentication is set (during Kerberos configuration, not by the user), the service provider uses the session key to decrypt the time in the consumer's authenticator. The service provider then returns that time in a Kerberos Application Reply (KRB_AP_REP) to the consumer as a security control against a replay attack.

***Note:** The use of the term "protocol" or "subprotocol" to describe the separate Kerberos exchanges refers to the specific procedural steps that the ticket exchanges must follow, not to some packet design specification such as Transmission Control Protocol (TCP), User Datagram Protocol (UDP), or Internet Protocol (IP).*

Version 5 Enhancements

The current version of Kerberos, version 5, is a standards-based distributed security protocol described in Request For Comments (RFC) 1510 that uses a symmetric key to mutually authenticate servers/servers and clients/servers. Some significant Kerberos 5 enhancements described in RFC 1510 are as follows:

- *Replaceable encryption systems*—Ciphertext is tagged with an encryption type identifier to allow you to specify different encryption algorithms. Kerberos 4 uses only data encryption standard (DES).

- *Replaceable network protocols*—Network addresses are tagged, allowing you to specify different network address types. Kerberos 4 required exclusively IP, a part of the TCP/IP network protocol suite.
- *Standardized messaging*—All message structures in Kerberos 5 are unambiguously defined using Abstract Syntax Notation One (ASN.1) and Basic Encoding Rules (BER). Kerberos 4, which incorporated a "receiver makes right" philosophy, allowed a user to define the byte ordering in the message.
- *Time To Live (TTL)*—Timestamping includes explicit start and end times that permit arbitrarily long lifetimes for Kerberos validated program execution. Kerberos 4, which used an 8-bit field, counted five-minute units of time and thus imposed a maximum ticket lifetime of 21.25 hours.
- *Authentication forwarding*—In a scalable, distributed server architecture, to achieve efficient and transparent exchanges of services and information, it is necessary to be able to forward a service request on behalf of some consumer to other trusted service providers. Kerberos 4 did not allow this forwarding to occur.
- *Principal naming schemes*—Identifiers are multicomponent names that can accommodate as many components as are necessary to identify the principal. The naming convention follows the standard ASN.1 GeneralStrings. In the Unix culture, these identifiers are written exclusively in uppercase. In Windows 2000, they appear in all lowercase. Kerberos 4 did not support this standardized naming scheme feature.
- *Subsession keys*—The session key between consumer and provider is likely to be replayed often, so it is vulnerable to impersonation attack modalities. Both the consumer and service provider can renegotiate and exchange a secured subsession key with an especially short lifetime for one-time session exchanges. A new subsession key could be generated for each exchange. Kerberos 4 did not support this feature.

Microsoft's Implementation of Kerberos 5

The discussion of MIT Kerberos offers a historical perspective in which to better understand Microsoft's implementation of the Kerberos protocol. Microsoft's immediate objective was to leverage its well-established system of access authorization with a more scalable authentication protocol. As already mentioned, only one of the three heads—authentication—works in the MIT implementation. Microsoft has brought life to the remaining two heads of the mythological gatekeeper—authorization and auditing. In this section, I'll discuss the enhancements that Microsoft made to Kerberos 5, specifically in the use of public key infrastructure, ticket structure, and in providing security support services to the Active Directory (AD) through the KDC. I'll explain how the Microsoft process works by providing an annotated look at it. I'll also cover cross-domain authentication, delegation of authentication, account database, and Kerberos policy.

Public Key Infrastructure (PKI)

PKI, discussed in Chapter 3, differs from the Kerberos 5 protocol in that it uses an asymmetric encryption algorithm, which requires a pair of keys, and certificate-management services for authentication. Microsoft has enhanced MIT Kerberos 5 by incorporating public-key encryption in the authentication phase to support PC/smart card technology. The smart card offers an alternative password logon for domain authentication. These enhancements, described in an Internet draft of Public Key Cryptography for Initial Authentication in Kerberos (PKINIT), are examples of the flexibility of the Microsoft Cryptographic Application Programming Interface (CAPI) and the implementation of an installable CSP. PKINIT integrates transparently with the distributed authentication and authorization services of Kerberos and AD.

Ticket Structure

Kerberos protocol specifically adds a series of flags that can be set in an exchanged ticket, different time settings (start, expiration, and renewal), and a *nonce* (a random value used as a countermeasure against impersonation attack modalities during both the AS and TGS exchanges). These changes primarily increase the flexibility of the Kerberos structure and are specific countermeasures to impersonation attack modalities.

These flags, stored as a bit string in a 32-bit field, are significant in controlling message flow or, for example, in signaling the need for mutual authentication. In the exchange between consumer and service provider, not only can the principals negotiate the use of a subsession key for one-time encryption of messages, but they can also sequentially number each message that is exchanged. It is also noteworthy that the mutual authentication flag must be set when you are configuring Kerberos; the user cannot set it.

Other Enhancements

Microsoft has enhanced Kerberos 5 in several other ways:

- Microsoft relies heavily on extensible fields in the Kerberos tickets and its integration with the AD to manage additional credentials (such as global and universal group membership) to help determine authorization.

- Through the AD, Group Policy Objects (GPOs), and the use of Microsoft Management Console (MMC) snap-ins such as Local Computer Policy, you can easily implement system-wide audit and tracking policies.

In effect, Microsoft has, through integration with AD, added authorization and auditing, the two originally planned, but never implemented, Kerberos security services.

Microsoft's enhancements make possible the following characteristics of Windows 2000:

- *Efficient authentication of consumers and service providers*—The consumer presents credentials directly to a distributed architecture of service providers. Authentication no longer depends on repeated calls to some DC, so it is faster and impacts network bandwidth less than the recurring legacy NT 4 exchanges between the Local Security Authority (LSA) and the Security Accounts Manager (SAM) on the DC. Principal credentials are stored either on the client workstation in a data store called the *credentials cache* or in the "cloud" of the AD spread across every DC in the enterprise.
- *Mutual authentication of both principals in a distributed services environment*—The (security) down-level NT 4 domain model was conceived of in the context of a secure intranet architecture; neither services nor the server architecture were distributed. NTLM, the down-level security protocol, assumes that all servers are known and therefore authentic. The only unknown principal that requires authentication is the consumer who is logging in with some registered user ID and password. Kerberos challenges both principals in an exchange of information or services.

Microsoft uses the hierarchical concept of *up-level* (AD and Kerberos) and *down-level* (directory database and NTLM) in its seminars and technical literature. Remember that the default setup configuration is the deployment of Windows 2000 servers and legacy NT 4 DCs in an enterprise structure (a mixed mode organization). AD and Kerberos are not enabled in mixed mode by default; they are enabled in native mode.

- *Delegation of authentication*—NTLM uses local impersonation to access resources; it does not pass-through client data to support many service providers distributed across the enterprise. Kerberos uses a ticket for pass-through to a back-end server (a *proxy ticket*) to impersonate the client and support requests to distributed services on remote servers.
- *Scalable and easy trust management*—NTLM offers one-way trust relationships across domains; Kerberos establishes by default the more flexible two-way transitive trust relationship. This transitive trust structure supports the

building of chains or trees in which some parent domain spawns a child domain. Credentials supplied by some trusted authority can apply to all branches in the tree and—when the tree trusts other trees—to all trees in the forest.

- *Interoperability across heterogeneous platforms*—Kerberos is a standards-based protocol, and the Microsoft enhancements are part of an Internet draft recommended to the IETF. Therefore, Windows 2000 security is not only extensible but scalable to other networks that also use the Kerberos security protocol, specifically the Unix operating system.

KDC

The Kerberos protocol is physically mapped to a Kerberos client service that is running on some workstation supporting the consumer, some server supporting the service provider, and the trusted third-party Kerberos server service. This third-party intermediary is known as the KDC. In the Unix culture, it manages the database directory of all principals in the Kerberos realm. In the Windows 2000 culture, the KDC is integrated with AD, where principal records and credentials are stored, and the KDC runs as a service on the DC. The KDC manages, among other things, the collection of secret keys called *long-term keys*, derived from the user logon password. KDC functions are divided between the AS function (which issues authenticating TGTs) and the TGS function (which grants session tickets).

The KDC is thus implemented, along with Active Directory Services (ADS), as a domain service running on DCs throughout the enterprise. It uses AD as its directory database or data store and retrieves information about principals through the Global Catalog. These topics and access authorization are discussed in more detail in Chapters 6 and 7. Both KDC and ADS are started by and run in the trusted process space of the LSA. It is significant that neither service can be stopped. DCs in Windows 2000 are considered peers, so the AS and TGS functions of the KDC security service are redundant.

An Annotated Look at the Microsoft Process

Microsoft Kerberos services that run on the KDC are differentiated into two separate security functions: the AS and TGS functions. The actual authentication process is completed in one exchange of messages between a consumer and the AS portion of the KDC. Once the AS authenticates a consumer, the consumer does not have to exchange information again with the AS. A reusable "pass" or TGT is repeatedly presented to the now separate TGS function for new service requests.

Note: This single AS exchange feature of Kerberos both decreases bandwidth consumption and minimizes any exposure of exchanged security credentials. Even though the NTLM authentication protocol exchanges a hash value, not actual security credentials, for authentication purposes, it does require a new authentication exchange for each additional service a consumer requests during a logon session. The authentication portion of Microsoft's Single Sign-On (SSO) feature is actually just that—a one-time authentication exchange of information between consumer and KDC.

This TGT is stored for the consumer on the client workstation in the credentials cache. When the consumer presents an authentic copy of the TGT to the TGS, it generates and returns to the consumer a service-granting ticket that is presented to the service provider whenever a service request is made.

To securely exchange a plaintext message over an unsecured session pipe to the KDC/AS during the initial request for authentication, you send a hash function of the consumer's password to the KDC/AS. Here are the protocol steps in the exchange:

1. a. The LSA on the client, through WinLogon, queries the consumer for his or her user ID and converts it to a hash value that it stores in the credentials cache in a secured memory area. In native mode, the Kerberos client sends a copy of this hash, along with a TGS ID request for TGS services, to the KDC/AS (refer to Step 1a in Figure 4.1). This message, called KRB_AS_REQ, contains critical preauthentication data, typically a keyed timestamp encrypted with a symmetric key shared by the consumer and KDC/AS. This timestamp proves knowledge of the consumer's secret, long-term password to the KDC/AS.

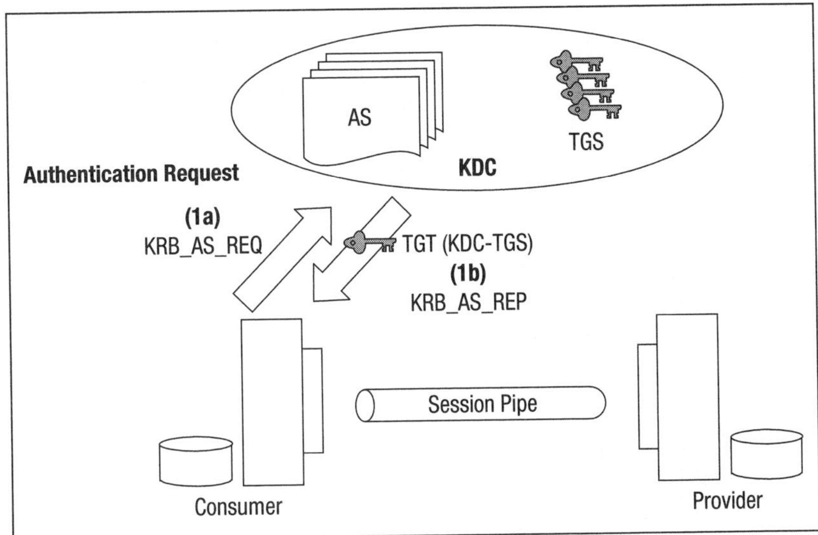

Figure 4.1 The flow of the Kerberos AS exchange.

b. The KDC/AS, upon validating the authenticity of the keyed timestamp, returns a TGT encrypted with a hash key derived from the user's archived password. The TGT is actually a timestamped digital envelope encrypted with a secret key shared by the KDC/AS and KDC/TGS. The KDC/AS also returns a secured session key specifically for the consumer using its copy of the secret, long-term password. In addition, a copy of the session key is included inside the TGT; it can be read only by the KDC/TGS to which the consumer directs his or her service requests. Both the ticket and session keys are encrypted with a hash derived from the consumer's password. It also contains the consumer's ID, the network address of the client on which the consumer is requesting service, and the TGS ID. This is the KRB_AS_REP (refer to Step 1b in Figure 4.1). Note the secret key, TGT (KDC-TGS), that is sent back to the consumer.

2. a. When the client receives this encrypted ticket, the client queries the consumer for his or her password. Using a hash key derived from the password, the client attempts to decrypt the incoming message. If the derived hash key can decrypt the ticket, the TGT is successfully recovered. The ticket includes a timestamp that indicates when it was issued and its lifetime or TTL (refer to Step 2a in Figure 4.2). The logon session key and the TGT are stored in the credentials cache. Using a copy of the stored TGT, the consumer requests a service-granting ticket from the KDC/TGS in a message called the KRB_TGS_REQ, which is encrypted with the secured session key (refer to Step 2a in Figure 4.2). This message

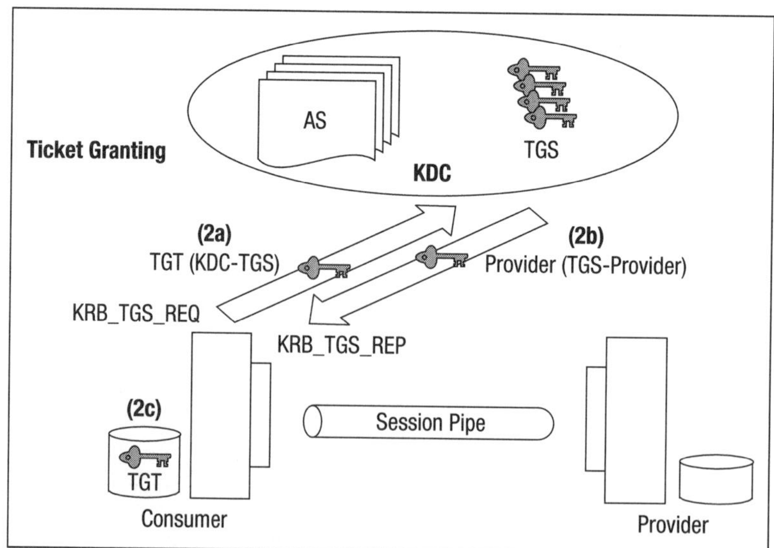

Figure 4.2 The flow of the Kerberos TGS exchange.

contains the consumer's name, a copy of the TGT, the ID of the targeted service provider, and an authenticator encrypted with the consumer's logon session key. The short-lived authenticator proves the identity of the consumer who is requesting the service at that moment in time. This proof is a countermeasure to an impersonator using a replay attack.

b. The KDC/TGS can verify the authenticity of the service request by decrypting its own TGS ID with a secret key that only it and the KDC/AS hold. It confirms the TGT's TTL. It compares the encrypted user ID and client network address with the incoming message. It decrypts the authenticator using its copy of the logon session key. If the user is authenticated, the KDC/TGS generates a service-granting ticket, the KRB_TGS_REP, for the requested service. It sends it back to the consumer with credentials, including the service provider ID and a new session key to be shared exclusively between the consumer and that targeted service provider. The service-granting ticket is encrypted with a secret key shared by the KDC/TGS and the service provider (refer to Step 2b in Figure 4.2).

c. The client receives the KRB_TGS_REP and, on behalf of the consumer, uses the logon session key to decrypt the new session key and the keyed service-granting ticket it will use for requesting the specific service. These credentials are also stored in the cache. The session keys, transferred to both consumer and service provider in a secured manner, create a secured session pipe for future exchanges of services (refer to Step 2c in Figure 4.2).

3. a. The consumer sends a KRB_AP_REQ that contains his or her user ID, a keyed authenticator, the service-granting ticket, and a preconfigured flag requesting mutual authentication to the service provider (refer to Step 3a in Figure 4.3). The authenticator is keyed with the new session key shared exclusively between the consumer and service provider. The service provider uses its secret key to decrypt the service-granting ticket and authenticate the consumer's ID. If the two coincide, the service provider determines whether the mutual authentication flag is set. If it is set, it uses the shared session key to encrypt the timestamp from the consumer's authenticator and returns it to the consumer in a KRB_AP_REP.

b. Upon receipt of the KRB_AP_REP, the client decrypts the returned timestamp and compares it with its cached copy to determine mutual authenticity. The session now proceeds using the shared secret key or a mutually agreed subsession key (refer to Step 3b in Figure 4.3).

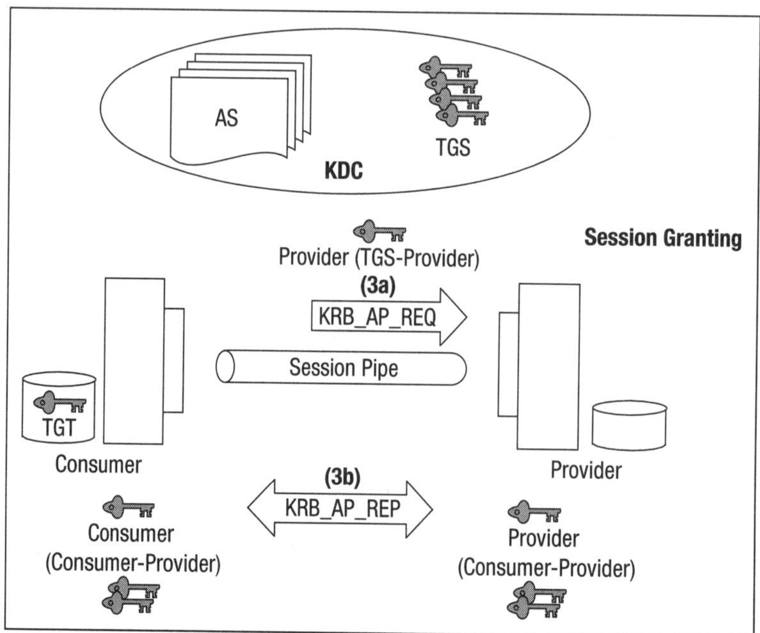

Figure 4.3 The flow of the Kerberos session-granting exchange.

The KDC/AS authenticates and authorizes the consumer. The ticket contains the network address of the client workstation on which the consumer has made his or her request. This prevents a spoof from some other client different from the workstation on which the request was originally made. The actual holder of the TGT who initiates requests for service is validated. To prevent reuse by some impersonator, the authenticator's TTL is for a very short period of time. Similarly, the service-granting ticket is symmetrically encrypted to prevent interception and alteration by all except the KDC/AS and the service provider.

Cross-Domain Authentication

Cross-domain authentication is the typical situation in a distributed server environment. A consumer requests services from some service provider in some other trusted domain. Figure 4.4 shows the more complex flow of exchanges in such a scenario. When you have multiple sites on different local area network (LAN) segments or subnets, you can arrange them in a hierarchical tree-like structure with a root domain (**examcram.com**) and child domains like **east.examcram.com**. If the domains are *well connected*—a term Microsoft uses to suggest that a reliable, high-speed connection interconnects the two domains—Windows 2000 transparently establishes a transitive, two-way trust that supports the sharing of TGTs across the domains. A transitive Kerberos trust is automatically created when you join a child

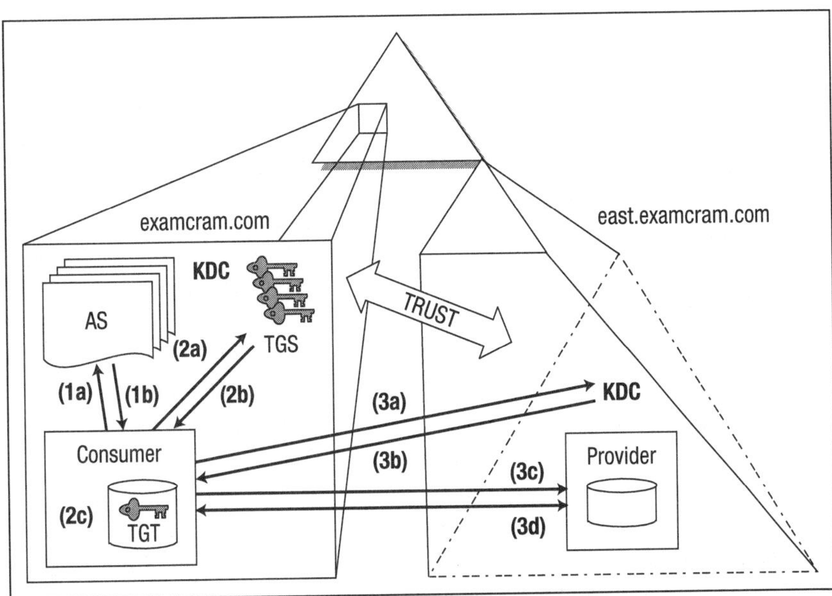

Figure 4.4 ExamCram Ltd. wants to expand its operations.

domain to a root or parent domain using the Active Directory Wizard (also referred to as DCPromo). The security relationships between parent and child domains are discussed in Chapters 9 and 10. You can define Kerberos policy in the default Domain Group Object in each domain.

The division of a KDC into two security services—AS and TGS services—is especially useful when services are distributed across domains or, in Unix terminology, Kerberos *realms*. KDCs in multiple Kerberos realms share a secret interrealm key, so their TGS components are, in effect, security principals in each other's realm. Referrals by local TGSs to some remote TGS provide session tickets to remote service providers; during their session, authenticated consumers can thus request a service anywhere in a Windows 2000 enterprise running in native mode.

Following authentication in Step 1 of Figure 4.4, the consumer in **examcram.com** needs services from a provider in **east.examcram.com**, a child domain. The consumer first requests a session ticket from its local TGS in the form of a KRB_TGS_REQ in Step 2. The local TGS first confirms the authenticity of the consumer. It then determines that the service provider is, in fact, not part of its local realm but, instead, is located in the child domain, **east.examcram.com**. Instead of replying with a session-granting ticket to a local service provider, the TGS issues the consumer a referral ticket to the TGS in **east.examcram.com** in Step 2c. This referral ticket is keyed with the secret interrealm key shared only by TGSs that trust each other. The consumer sends a request for services (KRB_AP_REQ) with the referral ticket to the KDC/TGS in **east.examcram.com**, as shown in Step 3a.

The remote TGS validates the referral ticket with its own copy of the interrealm key and returns a session ticket to the consumer that the remote targeted service provider can validate in Step 3c. If the service provider validates the session ticket, and if mutual authentication is flagged, it returns a key timestamp in the KRB_AP_REP to the **examcram.com** consumer to confirm its identity. Following successful completion of that exchange, the consumer can receive services from the provider in **east.examcram.com** over a secured session pipe, as shown in Step 3d.

Delegation of Authentication

In NT 4, services typically impersonated consumers when accessing other resources on the same client platform. The impersonation functioned within the security context of the consumer. This security context, however, could not be created on other servers that offered distributed services. Windows 2000, through Kerberos delegation, can, in fact, offer to other service providers on remote servers a proxy ticket and the security context of that ticket holder. This delegation of authentication is especially important in N-tier architectures and for when you are accessing Web service providers. For this delegation of authority to occur:

- All client platforms and service processes must be running native Windows 2000 in a Windows 2000 domain.
- The consumer's account must be enabled for delegation.
- The service provider's account must be enabled for delegation.

By default, principal account properties are not enabled for delegation. In addition to properly configuring these properties, you must also be aware that the account type under which the service provider runs is an issue. If the service provider runs under a domain user account, the Account Options list in the object's property sheet must indicate that the account is trusted for delegation.

Delegation of authentication can be implemented in two ways. The first way is that the consumer requests a service from some back-end server to which it has no direct access. The consumer then presents its proxy ticket to a front-end server.

If the consumer cannot determine or is not aware of the existence of some back-end server, he or she can instead present the front-end server with a TGT that can be used on the consumer's behalf to request services as needed. This ticket, generated from the consumer credentials, is called a *forwarded TGT*. Kerberos policy, discussed later in this chapter, determines whether you can implement either proxy tickets or forwardable TGTs.

Account Database

The data store that holds credentials and other related security information is provided as part of the domain's AD directory services. The AS portion of the KDC accesses this store to obtain credentials data that will authenticate consumers and build message components in the TGT. By definition, a principal is represented in this data store as an account object. Keys are attributes of these objects and are covered in more detail in Chapter 6. DCs are both KDC and AD servers, so they share replicas of the account database through a proprietary multimaster replication protocol over a secured channel. You can thus consider DCs as AAA servers that integrate the three IT security controls of authentication, authorization, and auditing in a somewhat amorphous cloud of services that span the boundaries of the enterprise.

Like other resources in the NT File System (NTFS), AD objects contain ACLs that delineate specific access permissions. The granularity for AD objects, however, is finer than that for files and folders; there are ACLs for each attribute associated with an AD object. Thus, with AD objects, you have greater control over access to account attributes. One of these attributes is the encryption key used to communicate with a consumer, a client computer, or service provider. Even though only the encryption key derived from the actual password (and not the password itself) is stored in the object, access is restricted to the account holder and processes such as the LSA with the Trusted Computer Base privilege.

On Windows 2000 clients, the credentials cache holds the tickets and keys obtained from the KDC. This secured area in volatile memory is protected by the LSA. Because of the sensitivity of the cache's contents, they are never paged to disk. Similarly, when you shut down the client machine or log in as a new principal, this cache is destroyed. The LSA calls upon the Kerberos SSP (discussed later in this chapter) to perform management functions related to tickets or keys. The Kerberos SSP, which runs in the security context of the LSA process space on the client machine, manages this cache.

Kerberos Policy

Kerberos policy, along with other account policies regarding password and intruder detection lockouts, is defined by the default domain GPO in Windows 2000. By default, the right to modify these settings is assigned to members of the Domain Administrators security group. Features such as mutual authentication and the use of proxy and forwardable tickets are determined by Kerberos policy here. The user cannot configure them. Local policies dealing with auditing, user rights, and other security options for the DC are defined in the default DC GPO. It is noteworthy that settings defined in the default DC GPO have a higher precedence for DCs than settings defined in the default domain GPO.

According to Microsoft documentation, Kerberos session tickets are sometimes called *service tickets* because session tickets are used to authenticate connections to services. Kerberos TGTs are called *user tickets* for the same reason; they authenticate connections to users. This confusing naming convention may change in future releases of the software. Some elements of the Kerberos policy include:

- Enforcement of user logon restrictions
- Maximum lifetime for the service ticket
- Maximum lifetime for the user ticket
- Maximum lifetime for user ticket renewal
- Maximum tolerance for computer clock synchronization

The KDC does not notify consumers when session tickets or TGTs expire; it does not maintain any record of these expiration times. If an expired session ticket is presented to the service provider, it returns an error message. The consumer must then request a new session ticket from the KDC for additional services.

Interoperability

A Windows 2000 design goal is for ADS to provide a consistent, uniform namespace for principals in the enterprise. Interoperability requires that the namespace accommodate objects outside the boundaries of the enterprise. Microsoft's implementation of Kerberos through SSPI (discussed later in this chapter) offers that promised seamless, out-of-the-box interoperability. Users can authenticate anywhere in an AD forest because the Kerberos authentication services in each domain trust the tickets issued by other KDCs in the forest. This is an example of the advantages of transitive trusts and their effect on simplifying domain administration.

When you are working from a Microsoft KDC to other Kerberos implementations, you will find several scenarios. The primary variables are:

- Kerberos services running on the client that requests authentication and services
- Kerberos services running on the KDC that provides those authentication services
- Targeted service providers that provide the requested services

Although implementation methods vary depending on how Kerberos technologies are implemented, they typically include the following scenarios:

- *Native mode*—Both principals use Windows 2000 Kerberos security; the Kerberos client exchanges information with a KDC.

- *Client configuration*—The Kerberos client is configured to access a particular KDC for authentication.
- *One-way trust*—A trust relationship has been established between a Microsoft domain and a non-Microsoft Kerberos realm such that tickets generated by one KDC are recognized and accepted by the other and its resource services.
- *Service account*—You can represent a non-Microsoft Kerberized service in a Windows 2000 domain by creating an AD service account object for that one specific service.
- *Account mapping*—When a trust exists between a Kerberos realm and a Windows 2000 domain, you can map non-Microsoft Kerberized accounts to Microsoft Kerberized account objects.

Non-Microsoft Kerberos clients can authenticate to a Windows 2000 KDC; conversely, Windows 2000 systems can authenticate to a KDC in a Kerberos realm. Windows 2000 client applications require General Security Services Application Programming Interface (GSS-API), on which SSPI is based, to run on non-Microsoft systems and authenticate to Kerberos server services. Non-Microsoft systems that are GSS-API compatible can authenticate on Microsoft Kerberos server services. Finally, both Microsoft and Kerberos 5 can establish cross-trusts and thus account mapping.

Kerberos and Alternative Protocols

This section discusses how Kerberos relates to and compares with the other SSPs available in Windows 2000. But first, let's look at the big picture, showing how the appropriate security service is negotiated as part of an exchange of information between a consumer and a service provider.

The Big Picture

Information exchanges occur between at least two parties that have named accounts; the parties have some account record and some logon password. Microsoft refers to these named accounts generically as *principals*. I typically use the generic scenario of a consumer and a service provider to identify a message flow. In the security schema used in Chapter 2, I assume that the two parties either exchange information or that one requests/delivers some service to the other. Every principal, by definition, has account information regarding its specific identity, group memberships, and some associated password in some data store. In a down-level, legacy NT 4 model, this is the directory database. The up-level, Windows 2000 platform integrates AD and Kerberos services to facilitate both the scalability of and accessibility to this data store.

A Windows 2000 DC could consequently be referred to as a generic *AAA server* because:

- AD-Kerberos security services together support authentication and authorization.
- Group Policy, as applied through the GPO, configures local and system-wide security settings.

Introducing cross-cultural terminology such as *principals* and *AAA servers* here will help you to see commonalties among security models (such as the AAA security models described in Chapters 7 and 8), regardless of operating system platform or "culture." For example, in the Unix culture, a Kerberos ticket is valid for only a finite time interval or *lifetime*. I interchange that term with the cross-cultural term *TTL* to help you grasp concepts more rapidly by drawing analogies with concepts you already understand.

The historical trend toward a Unix-style distributed server architecture model is apparent in the design trends of both Microsoft Windows 2000 and Novell NetWare 5 when compared to their earlier designs: NT 4.x/3.x and NetWare 4.x/3.x. Such a historical trend is suggested by:

- The adoption of standards-based security protocols such as Kerberos and Novell Directory Services (NDS)
- The adoption of a nonproprietary network protocol (TCP/IP)
- The adoption of scalable directory services such as AD and NDS
- The scalable enterprise support provided by the AD forest and NDS multiple trees

The use of cross-cultural terminology will enhance your understand of these evolving cultures in dealing with future issues of interoperability.

SSPs

A *security support provider* is fundamentally an installable library of security features. Windows 2000 can install several standards-based SSPs that provide distributed authentication services on any service provider. The three primary SSPs currently supported are:

- NTLM challenge/response protocol (discussed in more detail later in this chapter)
- Microsoft Kerberos (discussed in more detail later in this chapter)
- SChannel security protocols (discussed in Chapter 7)

Windows 2000 uses three other network SSPs to provide authentication services by using digital certificates, to authenticate users across the Internet:

- *Distributed Password Authentication (DPA)*—An Internet membership authentication protocol that is like triple Data Encryption Standard (3DES) in that it must be purchased as a separate add-in product. DES and its variants, like 3DES, are discussed in Chapter 3.
- *Extensible Authentication Protocol (EAP)*—Cited in RFC 2284 this extends the communication protocol Point-to-Point Protocol (PPP) to allow installable authentication services on both sides of the communication channel.
- *Public key-based protocols*—These are SChannel services specifically using public keys and are discussed in more detail in Chapter 7. They include Secure Sockets Layer (SSL) version 3, Transport Layer Security v1 (TLS1), and Private Communications Technology (PCT).

All the authentication services are implemented as separate SSPs working through a common interface—SSPI. This Win32 system API interface offers a uniform set of "hooks" on which current and future security providers can attach their technologies.

Principals in an exchange "negotiate" the use of a particular SSP, which, in turn, determines the use of a specific security protocol in the exchange.

SSPI, based on RFC 2078 and the standards-based GSS-API, provides multiple authentication architectural support for installable software or hardware cryptographic service providers (CSPs). Principals negotiate with SSPs for security services provided through these installable CSPs. Kerberos is the default SSP in Windows 2000 native mode.

Windows 2000 negotiations for a particular SSP are mediated by one of the many protocols defined by IETF: Security Negotiation Mechanism (SNEGO) for GSS-API (RFC 2478). Although Kerberos is the default SSP, SNEGO and SSPI extend the range of possible SSPs, allowing both future scalability and interoperability across current heterogeneous operating systems.

Of the SSPs discussed, Kerberos and the generic SChannel services focus primarily on authentication, integrity, and confidentiality. These technologies focus on the exchange of information through the session pipe as opposed to access management to resources or services. Authorization, alternatively, is based on a consumer's rights and the permissions associated with the requested resource; it is defined by specific attributes that either principal possesses.

As discussed previously, MIT Kerberos 5 does not provide authorization services; Microsoft enhanced MIT Kerberos 5 by integrating the Kerberos protocol with AD. Windows 2000 has leveraged a standards-based, well-known secured authentication protocol, Kerberos, with authorization services provided by the NT 4 legacy directory database using SIDs and ACLs. The NT 4 authorization system that manages these resources has not changed in Windows 2000. The SSPI uses a special pass-through SSP called *Negotiate* to match supportable security "levels" among its installable security providers, with those on the service provider to whom it has made a request. The Negotiate SSP applies the "strongest" available security services to the consumer/service provider exchange. In mixed mode, Negotiate may negotiate down-level to the NTLM challenge/response protocol and the directory database; in Windows 2000 native mode, Negotiate defaults to the Kerberos SSP. Microsoft designed Windows 2000 in native mode to seek the most restrictive security systems, typically Kerberos protocol.

To secure resources, there must be discretionary control over those securable objects. An object's security descriptor, a unique binary value, contains a discretionary access control list (DACL), and a system access control list (SACL). Activities associated with the use of many of these attributes can be audited. Both DACLs and SACLs are lists of individual access control entries that specify principal, specific rights that can be performed on the resource, as well as a description of how the right is activated. In addition to ACLs, the descriptor contains a listing of security attributes such as its SID and any associated group IDs. The SID is used to identify the principal or the group. A nonunique SID identifies the logon session.

NTLM Authentication Services

In Windows 2000, the basic NTLM exchange involves impersonation of a principal by using that principal's access token. A principal or consumer submits a request, with validating security identification data (including unique SIDs), to some provider for services. When NTLM authentication is used, passwords are never transmitted across unsecured namespaces. The principal and AAA server (DC) use a handshake method that encodes a random challenge. The principal encrypts random data that the challenging AAA server passes to it. If the AAA server can decrypt the random data, its challenge has been answered. Thus, passwords are never transmitted across unsecured channels.

When the LSA receives valid data, it generates an authorizing security access token based on the principal's SID. The provider, on behalf of the consumer, fulfills whatever requested services it can within the scope or security context of the issued token. The token's scope is limited by the resource's ACLs. An ACL, as previously described, is a list of individual access control entries (ACEs) that describe how a user, or more typically a group, can manipulate properties of the specific resource object. If the token's scope of authorization matches one or more specific ACEs, the service provider, on behalf of the consumer, performs the requested service. If any one ACE limits or denies a specific or required manner of manipulation, the provider is prevented from completing its task. For example, defining only the Read ACE in some ACL prevents a consumer from writing over that particular object. Thus, the security access token bestows authorization on its holder. Impersonation by operating system services is the most common method of providing distributed services to consumers in the enterprise. It is especially important that the token be exchanged in as secure a manner as possible in the scalable AD namespace.

Compared to Microsoft Kerberos, NTLM:

- Uses a slower one-way authentication process.
- Establishes trust relationships that are one way and nontransitive.
- Is proprietary and not standards based.
- Does not scale well.

Security services in Windows 2000 support scalable services through the use of impersonation; you can think of this as a form of distributed account authentication. The security services must also provide more flexible, transitive trust relationships to simplify administration while maintaining a major end-user feature: SSO.

Unlike with NT 4 and the security accounts manager, Windows 2000 security systems are integrated with directory services and hence are distributed system wide. The AD stores both account information and security policy in multilevel, hierarchical domain trees. With Kerberos protocol, trusts can be built across trees that are two way and transitive. Implicit relationships are established between parent domains and child domains. Finally, the granularity of security attributes has deepened within an object. In addition, because of AD, granularity now extends across logical organizational boundaries, transcending the legacy global groups, local groups, and users in the NT 4 domain model.

Note: NTLM is still necessary in Windows 2000 for establishing legacy one-way trusts with NT domains and the authentication of legacy or down-level NT 4 clients. In fact, the default installation is mixed node to accommodate Microsoft's current embedded customer base.

In a mixed-mode environment, NTLM authentication services are used instead of the Kerberos protocol.

Kerberos as an Installable SSP

Even though Kerberos protocol is the default provider of security features in Windows 2000, it is implemented as a dynamic link library (DLL). In fact, Microsoft has designed a security infrastructure that is truly extensible—SSPI.

This is where the Workstation service on the client communicates with an installed security service library, otherwise referred to as an SSP, to request services. The selection of any one specific DLL and hence a specific security protocol is negotiated between consumer and service provider. SSPI offers an API through which an extensible selection of these security libraries can be accessed. NTLM and the SChannel security protocols are, in addition to Kerberos, examples of security service libraries currently available as DLLs in Windows 2000. Figure 4.5 shows how SSPI supports multiple authentication protocols in addition to Kerberos security services.

When the key combination of Ctl+Alt+Delete (the Secure Attention Sequence) is pressed upon bootup, the Windows Logon (WinLogon) service is launched. It calls the LSA, which in turn loads both Kerberos and NTLM libraries using the Kerberos SSP by default. Negotiate, a pass-through SSP, seeks to establish up-level SSPs (like Kerberos) before falling back to down-level SSPs (such as NTLM). The consumer on the remote side of the session pipe determines which SSP is implemented based on the service provider ID it requests. If this were the logon sequence to a native Windows 2000 Server, the LSA, upon receiving a plaintext password from WinLogon, would do the following to subsequently secure session tickets through the TGS:

- Hash the password.
- Save a copy in the credentials cache.
- Forward a copy to the Kerberos SSP on the KDC for validation and a TGT.

Kerberos security services can be loaded as an instance within the security context of some user, by some process that requires, for example, the secured exchange of some messages. In fact, any system services and transport-level

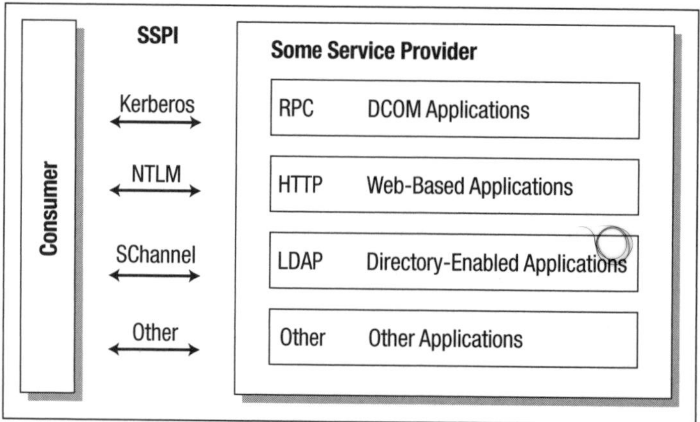

Figure 4.5 Security services available through SSPI.

applications can access any SSP through SSPI. The interface obtains authenticated connections based on the availability of SSPs and on the demands of the client/server applications that are attempting to establish a secure session.

As a security interface, SSPI contains methods that are called by applications running on the consumer side of the interface. For example, a consumer can send Kerberos credentials to a service provider using the SSPI method **InitializeSecurityContext** to generate a Kerberos Application Request message. The service provider responds with the SSPI method **AcceptSecurityContext,** which returns a Kerberos Application Response message back to the consumer. Once the consumer is authenticated, the LSA uses credentials in the consumer's ticket to build an access token on the service provider. It invokes the SSPI method **ImpersonateSecurityContext** to attach the token to an impersonation process thread to execute the service.

All Windows 2000 distributed services use SSPI to access the Kerberos SSP. A partial range of service requests involving Kerberos security includes:

- Print spooler services
- Common Internet File System (CIFS)/Server Message Block (SMB) file access
- Lightweight Directory Access Protocol (LDAP) queries in AD
- Intranet authentication to Internet Information Server (IIS)
- Remote management using authenticated remote procedure calls (RPCs)
- Certificate requests to the Microsoft Certificate Server

Table 4.1 summarizes the differences between NTLM and the Kerberos protocol.

Table 4.1 A comparison of NTLM and Kerberos.

Feature	NTLM	Kerberos
Scalability	No	Yes
Execution	Slow	Fast
Encryption	Secured hash	Symmetric key
Open source	No	Yes, standards-based
Trusts	One-way, nontransitive	Two-way, transitive
Mutual authentication	No	Yes

A Kerberos Case Study

Note: To expand on the topics discussed in this chapter and to allow you to practice working with case studies, I have provided an annotated case study here. Some of the later chapters in this book also have an annotated case study in the body of the chapter; each deals with the same company but involves different circumstances.

ExamCram Ltd.: Sharing Resources with Other Companies

ExamCram Ltd., a publishing company in AnyTown, Arizona, focuses primarily on developing and selling advanced technical training materials. ExamCram Ltd. works with a consulting firm company called MyCompany Inc., located in the same building as ExamCram Ltd.

MyPartner Inc., located in SomeOtherPlace, New York, works with MyCompany Inc. MyPartner Inc. and MyCompany Inc. have a long-term business alliance. Discussions about merging ExamCram Ltd. with MyCompany Inc. are in progress. At the moment, neither group of attorneys has arranged a meeting.

Company Goal

ExamCram Ltd. runs Windows 2000 AD. Its immediate objective is to understand how security policies will be written and deployed. Its stated goal is to develop scalable, security services that provide mutual authentication across unsecured, distributed server environments. In addition, confidentiality of information must be maintained at all times. There is a high incidence of impersonation attacks on the network, specifically where legitimate users are gaining access to unauthorized services. ExamCram Ltd. also wants MyCompany Inc. to share its network resources.

Take careful note of subtle nuances in a case study's stated goals or objectives. The inclusion of a single keyword that corresponds to an IT security control could radically change the proposed design or spoil the expected results. Some case studies actually state that a particular attack modality either has happened recently or is a specific risk outlined in the corporate business objectives.

Exhibit

Exhibit 1 shows a diagram that might accompany this case study on a Microsoft exam.

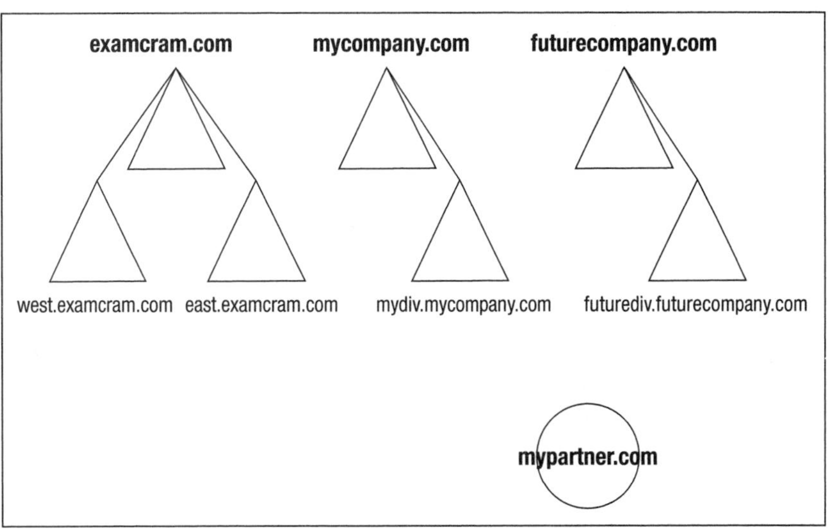

Exhibit 1 ExamCram Ltd. plans to expand operations.

Pay particular attention to depictions of AD trees, forests, OUs, and trusts. Remember that although Kerberos supports transitive, two-way trusts, you can still construct a one-way trust for security reasons.

Current LAN/Network Structure

All 100-client machines are running native mode Windows 2000 configured as a root domain with two child domains: **west.examcram.com** and **east.examcram.com**. Each system is connected to a 10Mbps hub through 10Mbps LAN cards, although Category 5 Unshielded Twisted Pair (UTP) cabling connects each system and hub in a star topology. The network protocol is TCP/IP.

MyCompany Inc. has 20 users running native mode Windows 2000 with a root domain, **mycompany.com**, and a child domain, **mydiv.mycompany.com**. Both trees, **examcram.com** and **mycompany.com**, are internally well connected.

Proposed LAN/Network Structure

The Network Manager from ExamCram Ltd. says, "Give me some examples of possible security relationships if we were to merge with MyCompany Inc. The companies are in the same building, so we can add another router and have them connected over a weekend. Show me how I can scale the security structure to support this merger and future acquisitions. By the way, I don't want any of MyCompany Inc.'s business partners using ExamCram Ltd. resources. In fact, the only heavy users of our resources will be the Sales division at MyCompany Inc. I don't want to hear these users complaining to our CEO."

Current WAN Connectivity

Both companies have T1 connections and use Internet access to communicate.

Proposed WAN Connectivity

No changes in the current structure are proposed at this time.

Design Commentary

No changes in the current structure are proposed at this time.

Current Internet Positioning

ExamCram Ltd. is registered as **examcram.com**. Its IP address is 201.101.1.1. MyCompany Inc. is registered as **mycompany.com** at IP address 198.2.4.6. Both companies use a Class C private network address range for their internal networks. The ExamCram Marketing group is in a separate domain, **east.examcram.com**, and uses 192.168.3.x/24; the group will have the greatest contact with Sales in the mydivision domain in MyCompany Inc.

Future Internet Plans

No changes in the current structure are proposed at this time.

Commentary

Figure 4.6 shows a diagram I would give the Network Manager of ExamCram Ltd. Compare this with Exhibit 1. In this annotated diagram, I show a variety of possible scenarios that will allow scalability (namely, **futurecompany.com**) and exclusivity (specifically, the one-way trust between **mycompany.com** and its own extranet business partner, **mypartner.com**).

Here is a brief explanation of what's in the figure:

- **examcram.com** and **mycompany.com** are roots of two separate trees in the same forest; they share a transitive, two-way trust.
- **west.examcram.com** and **east.examcram.com** are child domains under **examcram.com**; **mydiv.mycompany.com** is a child under **mycompany.com**.
- **east.examcram.com** trusts **mydiv.mycompany.com**; this is a one-way shortcut trust that improves performance by reducing hops and allows **mydiv.mycompany.com** users to access **east.examcram.com** resources easily. The Network Manager specifically stated that the greatest workload will come from this division, so this shortcut is important.
- **mypartner.com** is a business partner of MyCompany Inc. It shares resources with the MyCompany Inc. Sales department in **mydiv.mycompany.com**. This is a one-way, nontransitive trust, so users in **mypartner.com** have limited

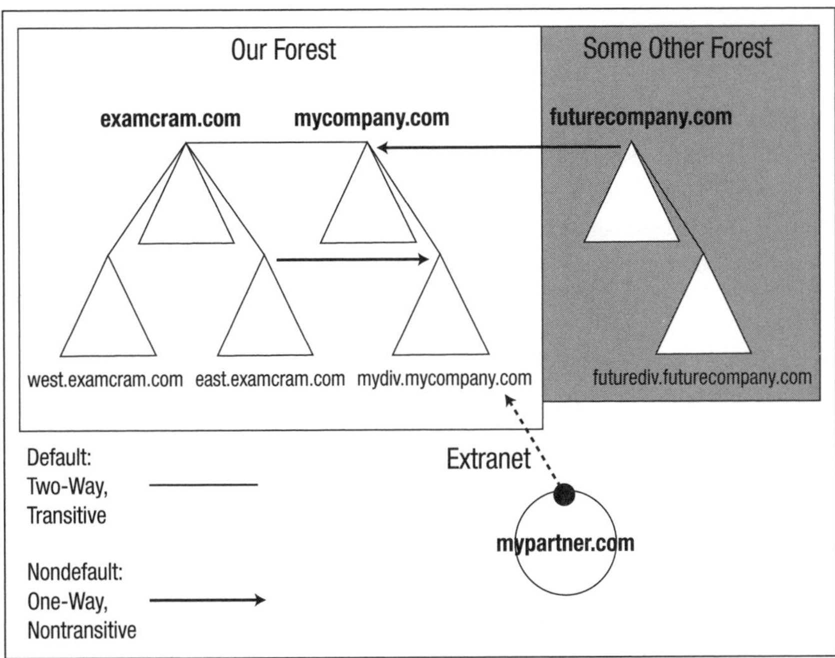

Figure 4.6 ExamCram Ltd. plans to expand operations.

access to the mydiv domain in MyCompany Inc. Users in **mypartner.com** cannot access ExamCram Ltd. resources.

- If a **futurecompany.com** tree were to merge with ExamCram Ltd., **futurecompany.com**'s domain users would, like those of **mycompany.com,** have access to all resources in both forests with a minimal amount of administrative maintenance. If, alternatively, **futurecompany.com** remains a root domain in its own forest, an explicit, one-way trust would allow **mycompany.com** domain users access to only **futurecompany.com** resources; access to any **futurecompany.com** child domains from **mycompany.com** or from its tree would not be allowed. Similarly, in a one-way trust, there would be no access from **futurecompany.com** into the ExamCram Ltd. forest.

Practice Questions

Case Study

4Sale, an online bartering company in ThatPlaceThere, North Dakota, focuses primarily on selling inexpensive, odd-lot items. 4Sale has recently merged forces with a smaller company, Got-a-Deal. Got-a-Deal rents space in the same office building. The corporate side of the merger has gone well, but the network infrastructure is under some reconsideration.

Current LAN/Network Structure

4Sale is presently running NT Server 4 on three machines:

- A primary domain controller
- A backup domain controller that serves as the Exchange (Simple Mail Transfer Protocol—SMTP) server
- A member server that is running IIS 4 (Hypertext Transfer Protocol [HTTP] server) and Proxy Server (packet filtering/caching/Network Address Translation—NAT)

All 100-client machines are configured in a single-domain model. The client systems are running Windows NT Workstation 4, with Office 97 being utilized as an applications package. Each system is connected to a 10Mbps hub through 10Mbps LAN cards running Category 5 UTP cabling in a star topology.

Got-a-Deal is undergoing changes to upgrade from its Ethernet bus topology, which uses coaxial cabling, to a more modern configuration. Got-a-Deal is using an NT Server in a 22-person-workgroup configuration as a file and print server. The network is stable but does not provide scalability.

Proposed LAN/Network Structure

4Sale would like to move forward towards Windows 2000 and develop its online barter/trading business. Some of the security features would help leverage development of its e-commerce plans and future corporate goals. In addition, 4Sale would like to improve the network's speed by implementing newer cards and hubs that support 100Mbps.

Got-a-Deal would also like to upgrade to Windows 2000 under a domain arrangement but has concerns regarding performance, deployment costs, maintenance, and training. The company will be hiring an in-house network engineer to be part of a newly formulated IT team that administers the resources of both companies. Got-a-Deal needs a faster network infrastructure in place within the next two months. It will depend on 4Sale for most of its network services.

Current WAN Connectivity

4Sale has a T1 connection to an Internet Service Provider (ISP) in OverHere, North Dakota. Got-a-Deal has 56Kbps dial-up networking connectivity through the same ISP.

Proposed WAN Connectivity

No changes are planned at this time.

Directory Design Commentary

Network Manager at 4Sale says, "We currently need personal password policies to be enforced and would like to retain as much control as possible over our portion of the directory."

Owner-Network Manager at Got-a-Deal says, "We would rather keep our password security at a minimum level, which will keep our current employees, some of whom we've had for five years, feel more comfortable about this merger of interests."

Current Internet Positioning

4Sale is registered as **4sale.com**. Got-a-Deal has been selling its goods through local companies and through the **4sale.com** Web site.

Future Internet Plans

No changes in the current structure are proposed at this time.

Company Goal with Windows 2000

4Sale has hired you as an outside consultant to get both companies up and running. You will try to accommodate each company's needs, but you've been given strict orders by 4Sale that there should be a higher level of control than what each company is individually proposing. You will help develop the standards and procedures that the newly formulated IT team will implement.

You have been told that 4Sale would like to utilize Windows 2000 AD by using the default schema that exists. 4Sale is expecting some growth and would like that growth to be facilitated through AD. It would also like to utilize some of the newer security features but does not understand all the possible options that will be available once Windows 2000 is implemented.

Question 1

Owner-Network Manager at Got-a-Deal says, "I've heard stories about how slow NT authentication runs on NT 4. I don't want my people turning on their machines in the morning and waiting 15 minutes. Why should I upgrade to Kerberos authentication on Windows 2000 when I have NT 4 anyway?"

Identify the two factors from the following list that you would use to formulate a reply:

PC/smart card technology

Kerberos

NT LAN Manager

SChannel

Next, group whichever of the following statements are applicable under the two headings you chose above:

Uses a slower one-way authentication process

Uses a faster authentication process

Is designed for distributed server architectures

Does not scale well

Is a proprietary standard

Is a standards-based protocol

The correct answer is:

- Kerberos
  - Uses a faster authentication process
  - Is designed for distributed server architectures
  - Is a standards-based protocol
- NT LAN Manager
  - Uses a slower one-way authentication process
  - Does not scale well
  - Is a proprietary standard

Question 2

Owner-Network Manager at Got-a-Deal says, "I'm still not convinced. I've done some more reading and it sounds to me like MIT Kerberos 5 supports the three key functions of authentication, authorization, and auditing. I think I am going to compile some pricing information about possible Unix operating systems."

What is your response? Is the Owner-Network Manager correct?

❍ a. Yes

❍ b. No

Answer b, no, is correct. Your client is misinformed. Microsoft's own implementation of Kerberos 5, not MIT Kerberos 5, integrates with Active Directory in Windows 2000 to deliver all three information technology security controls. In addition, when you compare Windows 2000 to other operating systems with regard to total cost of ownership, Windows 2000 provides both integrated, easy to manage services and a low total cost of ownership (TCO) as compared to other competitive operating systems.

Question 3

Owner-Network Manager at Got-a-Deal says, "I've been hearing about Unix and how Windows 2000 offers interoperability across the two system platforms. Explain to me how security works in native Windows 2000."

You need to first explain the specific Kerberos subprotocols.

There are three Kerberos subprotocols:

Client/server (CS) authentication exchange

Authentication Service (AS) exchange

Ticket-granting service (TGS) exchange

Identify the correct order of the three Kerberos subprotocols and group the following elements in the correct sequential order under their appropriate subprotocol:

The consumer requests a service-granting ticket.

The client requests service.

TGS returns the service-granting ticket.

The client requests a TGT.

The correct answer is:

Authentication Service (AS) exchange

The client requests a ticket-granting ticket.

Ticket-granting service (TGS) exchange

The consumer requests a service-granting ticket.

TGS returns the service-granting ticket.

Client/Server (CS) authentication exchange

The client requests service.

Question 4

Network Manager at 4Sale says, "I've been reading about the Unix implementation of Kerberos in magazines. Where can I go for more detailed information?"

You cite RFC 1510 as the source document for the protocol enhancements. You want to help the Network Manager, so you mention some of the major improvements. You also want to identify features that are not part of the specification. Which of the following are not Kerberos 5 enhancements as specified in RFC 1510? [Check all correct answers]

- ❑ a. Authentication forwarding
- ❑ b. Subsession keys
- ❑ c. A more flexible principal-naming scheme
- ❑ d. Replaceable network protocols
- ❑ e. Public-key authorization

Answers a, b, c, and d are correct. Authentication forwarding, subsession keys, a more flexible principal-naming scheme, and replaceable network protocols were all added with Kerberos version 5. Public-key authorization is part of the Public Key Cryptography for Initial Authentication in Kerberos draft proposal submitted to the Internet Engineering Task Force, not part of Request For Comments 1510. Therefore, answer e is incorrect.

Question 5

VP of Marketing at 4Sale says, "I am negotiating with **Mississippi.com**, the online bookstore, to provide us with banner space on its home page. I want to investigate how we can leverage its authentication systems."

Given 4Sale's plans for e-commerce, which Security Support Providers should you research for your next meeting?

- ❑ a. PPP
- ❑ b. DPA
- ❑ c. EAP
- ❑ d. PCT

Answers b, c, and d are correct. Distributed Password Authentication is used by online services for Internet membership authentication. Extensible Authentication Protocol enhances Point-To-Point Protocol by allowing installable authentication services on both sides of the communication channel. Private Communications Technology is one of the Secure Channel Security Support Providers along Secure Sockets Layer version 3 and Transport Layer Security version 1. PPP is a communications protocol. Therefore, answer a is incorrect.

Question 6

Network Manager at 4Sale says, "I can balance the authentication services load on my KDC by running just the TGS portion of the KDC on a separate domain controller."

Is this statement true or false?

- ❍ a. True
- ❍ b. False

Answer b, false, is correct. Both authentication services and ticket-granting services are functions of Key Distribution Center services. They can be neither separated nor shut down on the domain controller. The division of Authentication Service (AS) and ticket-granting service (TGS) function supports interrealm requests for session tickets, not load balancing.

Question 7

Network Manager at 4Sale asks, "Where are all the credentials like ticket-granting ticket or a service-granting ticket stored on the client computer?" [Choose the best answer]

- ❍ a. In the credentials cache in the LSA
- ❍ b. In the credentials subbranch in the Registry
- ❍ c. In the credentials cache in RAM
- ❍ d. In the credentials cache

Answer c is correct. Tickets and keys obtained from the Key Distribution Center are stored in a special area in volatile memory called the credentials cache. It is not located in the Local Security Authority nor in the Registry. Therefore, answers a and b are incorrect. Answer d is not as complete as answer c. Therefore, answer d is incorrect.

Question 8

Owner-Network Manager at Got-a-Deal says, "Give me an example of how native Windows 2000 lowers cost of maintenance and training."

Your client is concerned about TCO. Your discussions at the moment concern security, so you want to describe how Kerberos policy can be easily managed. Kerberos policy, defined in the default Domain Group Object, along with the password (length, expiration, and so on), IP security, and public key, includes what element(s)?

- ❍ a. Maximum service ticket lifetime
- ❍ b. Maximum TGT lifetime
- ❍ c. Maximum TGT renewal lifetime
- ❍ d. Maximum user ticket lifetime
- ❍ e. All of the above
- ❍ f. None of the above

Answer e is correct. Kerberos policy includes maximum service ticket lifetime, maximum TGT (ticket-granting ticket) lifetime, maximum TGT renewal lifetime, and maximum user ticket lifetime. Note that Microsoft calls the session key the service ticket and the ticket-granting ticket the user ticket. Use Microsoft's terminology to minimize confusion.

Question 9

Owner-Network Manager at Got-a-Deal says, "You are starting to convince me that deployment of Windows 2000 is a good business decision. But, if I did want to ever use the Unix platform, what are the important themes I should remember?"

You want to inform your client about key interoperability themes. Which theme is not relevant?

❍ a. Windows 2000 mode of operation

❍ b. Client configurations

❍ c. Organization and trust relationships

❍ d. Network protocol

❍ e. All of the above

❍ f. None of the above

Answer d is correct. Network protocol is not relevant in relation to interoperability themes. Answers a through c are all relevant with regard to interoperability, so they are incorrect answers. Windows 2000 must run in native mode for Kerberos to be the default security protocol; NT LAN Manager is a proprietary security protocol and does not work with other operating systems. Kerberos client services must run on a workstation for the security protocol to function. If trust relationships can be established, there are several ways two different systems can interoperate. Two possibilities are accounting mapping across the two systems; another is the possibility of cross-domain exchanges. Your client is not discussing legacy systems that might use proprietary network protocols.

Question 10

Considering the case study, what type of domain structure do you, as the consultant, visualize as an enterprise design with the lowest TCO?

❍ a. Two distinct forests with an extended trust connecting them

❍ b. An empty root domain with one domain in place and two OUs: one for 4Sale and one for Got-a-Deal

❍ c. One domain with the root **4sale.com** with a lower domain being **got-a-deal.4sale.com**

❍ d. One domain called **4sale.com** with two OUs: one for 4Sale and one for Got-a-Deal

Answer c is correct. This selection provides one of the solutions that would address the relevant concerns. For example, the company already has **4sale.com** registered and plans to continue with this naming convention for both companies when merged. Having two separate domains allows for distinct password structures, yet having 4Sale as the root still provides a way of implementing strong control. Another solution might have been an empty root with two distinct domains beneath, but this was not an option. Answer a is incorrect because it offers two distinct forests, and this provides a poor solution of unification and control. Answer b is incorrect because it offers an empty root, but then provides Organizational Units, which will not handle the issue of control over password security between the two locations. Answer d is incorrect for similar reasons as answer b; it provides a good root but does not allow for individual security policy control.

Need to Know More?

McLean, Ian. *Windows 2000 Security Little Black Book.* The Coriolis Group, Scottsdale, AZ, 2000. ISBN 1-57610-387-0. Chapter 4 details the subprotocols, tickets, and configuration of Kerberos policies.

Stallings, William. *Network Security Essentials: Applications and Standards.* Prentice Hall, Upper Saddle River, NJ, 1999. ISBN 0-13-016093-8. Chapter 4 discusses the Kerberos protocol and the rationale behind the development of the version 5 enhancements. Although this book deals specifically with the Unix operating system, it provides insights that are applicable to the Microsoft implementation of the security protocol.

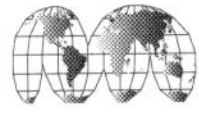

Search the TechNet CD (or its online version through **www.microsoft.com**) and the *Windows 2000 Server Resource Kit* CD using the keywords "Kerberos", "KDC", "SSPI", and "interoperability". This online source is Microsoft's most current collection of available technical bulletins and papers.

ftp://athena-dist.mit.edu/pub/kerberos/doc/krb_evol.lpt Here, you can find the following paper: Kohl, John T., B. Clifford Neuman, and Theodore Y. Ts'o, *The Evolution of the Kerberos Authentication Service.* In Distributed Open Systems, pages 78-94. IEEE Computer Society Press, 1994. This highly technical paper discusses the development of the protocol and goes into the mechanism of key exchanges. It is an excellent source for Unix style terminology and definitions as well as a comprehensive discussion of the limitations of version 4 of Kerberos. It presents solutions provided by version 5.

ftp://ftp.isi.edu/in-notes/rfc1510.txt Here, you can find the following paper: Kohl, John and B. Clifford Neuman, *The Kerberos Network Authentication Service (Version 5). Internet Request for Comments RFC-1510.* September 1993. This highly technical paper is the actual Internet RFC 1510 citation. This is how an Internet standards track protocol is specified for the Internet community and how technical requests for discussion and suggestions are solicited. It discusses improvements to the Kerberos protocol in version 5. It provides an overview and specification of version 5 of the protocol for the Kerberos network authentication system.

http://web.mit.edu/kerberos/www/papers.html#k5-papers This home page hosted by MIT contains citations and references to information about Kerberos and related systems. It includes papers and technical discussions of Kerberos 4, Kerberos 5, and variants and derivatives of Kerberos. Each section includes tutorials, papers, protocol specifications, proposed protocol extensions, a discussion of APIs, and other material. Some of these papers are the original documentation that was released in the early 1990s.

www.isi.edu/gost/gost-group/products/kerberos/ This is the home page for the Kerberos Network Authentication Service. This site is hosted by the Global Operating Systems Technology Group, an informal group consisting of faculty, staff, and students of the Computer Networks Division of the Information Sciences Institute of the University of Southern California. It lists Kerberos-related materials, projects, and software products such as Sesame and NetCheque. It also provides links to documentation on areas such as RFC 1510 revision, PKINIT, and Public Key Cross-Realm authentication (PKCROSS) open issues.

www.isi.edu/gost/publications/kerberos-neuman-tso.html Here, you can find *Kerberos: An Authentication Service for Computer Networks* by B. Clifford Neuman and Theodore Ts'o, reprinted, with permission, from *IEEE Communications Magazine*, Volume 32, Number 9, pages 33-38, September 1994. This well-written magazine article traces traditional authentication methods, discusses the use of strong authentication methods, and describes the Kerberos authentication system.

www.microsoft.com/windows2000/library/howitworks/security/kerberos.asp Here, you can find *Microsoft Windows 2000 Server White Paper—Windows 2000 Kerberos Authentication*. One of the Microsoft Windows 2000 resources under "How It Works," this paper provides a technical introduction to the Windows 2000 implementation of the Kerberos 5 authentication protocol. Starting with a nontechnical overview, it includes detailed explanations of important concepts, architectural elements, and authentication service features. The paper concludes with a discussion of interoperability with other implementations.

IP Security Architecture

Terms you'll need to understand:

- ✓ International Organization for Standardization (ISO) Open Systems Interconnection (OSI) Reference Model
- ✓ Symmetric and asymmetric encryption algorithms
- ✓ Hash message authentication code (HMAC)
- ✓ Data Encryption Standard (DES)-Cipher Block Chaining (CBC)
- ✓ Internet Key Exchange (IKE)
- ✓ Internet Security Association Key Management Protocol (ISAKMP)
- ✓ Oakley Key Determination Protocol
- ✓ Security association (SA)
- ✓ Tunneling
- ✓ Diffie-Hellman (DH) encryption algorithm
- ✓ Perfect Forward Secrecy (PFS)
- ✓ IP addressing scheme

Techniques you'll need to master:

- ✓ Describing different encryption techniques
- ✓ Discussing the impact of IP Security on total cost of ownership (TCO)
- ✓ Describing communication scenarios where IPSec enhances security
- ✓ Outlining the steps involved in deploying security protocols
- ✓ Listing the security services offered by IPSec security protocols
- ✓ Describing the components of IPSec policies
- ✓ Outlining the steps in a typical IPSec-secured exchange of information

Traditional network security draws analogies and terminology from the architecture of medieval castles and the way war was waged before field artillery was introduced. A long time ago, castles were built with high walls, moats, parapets, and drawbridges to thwart barbarian attacks. Terms like *bastion* (the strongest, most defensible part of a castle), and *choke* point (a narrow passage through which all traffic passes and can be monitored) are derived in part from the study of strategic warfare. Unfortunately, in the 21st century, sophisticated network attacks are more insidious than medieval battles. Although attacks are planned from outside the enterprise "walls," forces are now often unleashed from within the castle keep and its ring of authentication. Firewall technologies, secure routers, and foreign token authentication are ways to defend an enterprise from outside attack. The "hardened" bastion walls and moat, however, prove useless against an assault launched from within the boundaries of the enterprise. Unlike security technologies working at the Open Systems Interconnection (OSI) Application layer, Internet Protocol Security (IPSec) protects enterprise resources from both internal and external security breaches without increasing total cost of ownership (TCO); there are typically no extra costs for maintenance, training, or architectural changes.

IPSec, as defined by the Internet Engineering Task Force (IETF), uses two low-level, OSI Network layer security protocols: an Authentication Header (AH) and an Encapsulated Security Payload (ESP). AH provides source authentication and integrity; ESP offers confidentiality, authentication, and integrity. IPSec performs these services in such a way that only the principals know the key used in the information exchange. If the authentication data is validated while the exchange is taking place, the recipient of the message is assured that the information was not changed in transit.

Microsoft has enhanced IPSec by mixing asymmetric encryption algorithms with conventional symmetric cryptography and by providing automatic key management, which maximizes security and increases data throughput. Thus, information exchanges through the session pipe are guaranteed to be a combination of authentication, integrity, anti-replay, and (optionally) confidentiality. Working below the Microsoft Transport Driver (sometimes called "Device") Interface (TDI), IPSec provides the enterprise with a self-negotiating, transparent mechanism that supports strong network security.

IP and Security

With the proliferation of the Internet and the growing sophistication of users, IP as a network protocol has come under a variety of attacks. Table 5.1 lists some examples of IP attacks.

Table 5.1 Examples of IP attacks categorized by attack modality.

Involvement	Interception	Impersonation
Active	Connection hijacking: Active sessions (e.g., Telnet sessions) are seized.	IP (address) spoofing: Impersonation of an authenticated IP address.
Passive	Protocol analyzers (a.k.a. network sniffers): Information is captured in transit.	Data man-in-the-middle spoofing: Data is inserted into an active session pipe. An intruder between two parties can monitor and capture data.

The lack of protection at the OSI Network layer, although identified as a problem years ago, has never been addressed comprehensively because:

- Even though IP was designed for a distributed server architecture, the original architects did not anticipate how hostile the environment would become, nor the scale, number of participants, and sophistication of the user population.
- The IP protocol was not designed to provide any form of security services.
- Though designed to be an evolving protocol, IP clearly supports functions today for which it was never originally intended.

The stated objective of IP is to move data packets from one host computer to another on some network. No assumptions are made about what other computers or external devices are doing on the same network. When a third party intercepts and reads packets in realtime on that network pipe or on any data link, this activity (an example of a passive interception attack modality) is called *packet sniffing* or *eavesdropping*. In fact, Request for Comments (RFC) 1636 addresses architectural weakness in the Internet and recommends greater security for the exchange of information through the use of authentication and encryption. Susceptibility to passive interception varies with differences in protocol structure and the packet design. Table 5.2 compares the risk of a passive interception attack across different data links. It is obvious that most common channels that exchange information are highly susceptible to some form of attack.

The primary way to thwart interception and/or impersonation attack modalities is to encrypt the data stream. Several available methods are:

- *Link-level encryption*—This method is used in radio networking products. The packet stream is automatically encrypted upon transmission over unsecured channels and then decrypted at the receiving end.
- *End-to-end encryption*—This method is used in exchanges between encrypting routers. The packet stream is automatically encrypted upon transmission and then decrypted at the remote router.

Table 5.2 Potential of passive interception across various data links.

Data Link	Risk	Comments
Ethernet	High	This is a bounded, broadcast-based protocol. Protocol analyzers are common diagnostic tools.
Fiber Distributed Data Interface (FDDI) (token ring)	High	Ring networks, although deterministic with regard to the token path, still have packets pass through, on average, half the nodes in the ring before reaching their destination.
IP over cable TV	High	Physical access to the TV cable is necessary; packet streams passed through Radio Frequency (RF) modems are unencrypted.
Microwave and radio	High	This is an unbounded, broadcast-based protocol. Any radio receiver will intercept the transmission.
Telephone	Medium	Physical access to telephone lines is necessary; packet streams over high-speed modems are more difficult to tap because data is transmitted across many frequencies.

- *Application-level encryption*—Packet encryption is done at the OSI Application layer.

It is noteworthy that, similar to IP, Domain Name System (DNS), an important component in Windows 2000, was not designed as a secure protocol either. Both IP and DNS were designed primarily to move data as quickly and efficiently as possible. Neither IP nor DNS is assumed to support any form of authentication or other security service. However, many network designs commonly use hostnames and IP addresses for authentication purposes. This has led to many kinds of security vulnerabilities such as client flooding (impersonation of a DNS nameserver that overwhelms a client with invalid DNS lookup responses), bogus nameserver cache loading (another impersonation of a DNS server), and rogue DNS server attacks (actual modification of the DNS namespace). Although strategies exist to minimize these attack modalities (e.g., double reverse DNS lookups and firewall technologies), reliance on IP addressing or hostnames for authentication opens a breach in any security design.

Examples of IPSec Deployment

The increasing frequency of IP spoofing and other impersonation attack modalities has resulted in the recommendation that authentication and encryption be included in the next generation of IP: IPng or IPv6. Wide deployment of the

128-bit addressing scheme and other IPv6 features will take several years, so many OSI Network layer security enhancements have been designed for the current version (IPv4) as well. Most discussions of IPSec apply to both the current IPv4 datagrams and IPv6 packets. In fact, IPSec is already providing enhanced security in information exchanges across unsecured Internet namespaces in a variety of scenarios, such as:

- *Remote site connectivity*—An organization can leverage Internet connectivity yet maintain intranet security and secured channels of communication through Virtual Private Networks (VPNs), discussed in greater detail in Chapter 6.
- *Remote access*—The advantages of Routing and Remote Access Service (RRAS), using proper client software, over a dedicated telephone line are now available through remote dialup to Internet Service Providers (ISPs).
- *Extranet connectivity*—Key exchange and management as well as authenticity and confidentiality provide virtually on-demand secured connectivity with new business partners outside an organization's enterprise boundaries.
- *E-commerce security*—Online businesses demand security enhancements, especially in authentication, confidentiality, and the ability to establish secured session pipes. Reliable key exchanges across unsecured namespaces are a prerequisite for such security technologies.

Look for these deployment themes in either the "Objectives" or "Goals" section of exam case studies. IPSec is easier to implement than most other security technologies, which greatly enhances the security in the exchange of information and adds little to the TCO.

Building upon IPSec

IPSec provides comprehensive security management, including industry-standard encryption algorithms. These provide secured exchanges of information when TCP/IP is used on both ends of the session pipe between authenticated principals within the enterprise or across the corporate firewall. Microsoft's stated objective is end-to-end security strategies that prevent both external and internal attack modalities.

It is significant that IPSec comes with few or no deployment costs. Coordinating security at the Application layer of the OSI Reference Model is trivial because IPSec is deployed below the OSI Transport layer. Windows 2000 provides enterprise-wide protection and security subsystem safeguards that software applications automatically inherit. The encryption support of IPSec also extends to VPNs.

Advantages of IPSec include:

- *Full support for open industry (IETF) standards*—Interoperability is guaranteed by providing an open industry-standard alternative to proprietary IP encryption technologies.
- *Flexible security protocols and policies*—These policies can be implemented through easy-to-use Microsoft Management Console (MMC) snap-ins.
- *Transparency through flexible negotiation*—IPSec, invisible to both applications and users, is mediated through the IP Network layer with user intervention.
- *Authentication*—Both symmetric and asymmetric strong encryption algorithms block many interception attack modalities.
- *Confidentiality*—Information technology (IT) security controls that implement confidentiality prevent unauthorized access to data during exchanges.
- *Data integrity*—IP authentication headers and variations of hash message authentication code (HMAC) ensure data integrity during information exchanges.
- *Dynamic rekeying*—Dynamic rekeying during exchanges over unsecured session pipes thwarts most interception and impersonation attack modalities.
- *Secure end-to-end links*—Secure end-to-end links are provided for private network users within or across the enterprise boundary.
- *Easy implementation and centralized management*—Security policies and filters provide appropriate security levels while reducing administrative overhead and lowering TCO.
- *Scalability*—Security policies have a granularity that scales from a single workstation to the entire enterprise.

A historical theme shows the direct relationship between increased user demand for resources and services and a similar need for scalable security systems. The primary security concern in the NT 4 domain model was protection of resources from outside attack. With Active Directory (AD) now supporting distributed, enterprise-wide services, IPSec in Windows 2000 follows the Kerberos assumption (as discussed in Chapter 4) of *not making any assumption about authenticity*. IPSec protects information exchanges not just from outside attacks but from the more likely unauthorized rogue user inside the enterprise. Most technologies discussed in this chapter are invisible to the OSI Application layer and the user; they focus primarily on the packaging and exchanging of data below the OSI Transport layer and the analogous Microsoft TDI layer.

Industry Standards

Building on industry-standard cryptographic algorithms and security protocols, Windows 2000 is compliant with the latest IETF drafts proposed by the IPSec Working Group. IPSec, actually considered a protocol suite, provides not only an assortment of security techniques, but also a mechanism that negotiates, selects, and implements security services before engaging in a specific information exchange between two principals (such as a consumer and a service provider). Figure 5.1 uses a diagram published in RFC 2411 to show the interrelation among various IPSec component parts. It will serve as a reference model in the subsequent discussion.

Security Protocols

Secure Channel (SChannel) services at the OSI Transport layer provide, for example, security services to specific applications like browsers and Web applications. On the other hand, two other security protocols (AH and ESP) provide even lower-level security services of a similar nature. AH provides integrity, authentication, and anti-replay through partial sequence integrity checks by using an algorithm to compute a keyed message hash (HMAC) for each IP packet. AH does not offer confidentiality as a security service. ESP offers the same services as AH as well as provides confidentiality using the Data Encryption Standard (DES)-Cipher Block Chaining (CBC) algorithm, described in the "Encryption Techniques" section later in this chapter.

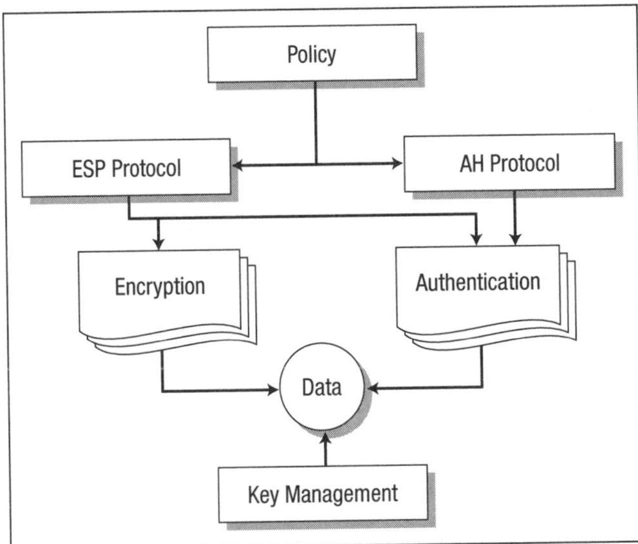

Figure 5.1 A modified IPSec overview from RFC 2411.

IPSec provides authentication, integrity, and confidentiality on both sides of a session pipe at the OSI Network layer, whether inside or outside a corporate firewall. Table 5.3 summarizes AH and ESP. ESP offers selectable features (e.g., encryption can be selected independent of authentication), so it is listed as two distinct variants of the same protocol.

The IPSec suite, as implemented in Windows 2000, is divided into AH, ESP, and Internet Key Exchange (IKE). IKE—the mechanism for exchanging keys between parties to ensure authenticity, integrity, and confidentiality—is further subdivided into two protocols:

- Internet Security Association and Key Management Protocol (ISAKMP)
- Oakley Key Determination Protocol

ISAKMP and Oakley are discussed in more detail in the "Key Management Protocols" section later in this chapter.

IPSec Architecture

In order for two client workstations to establish an IPSec connection, they must negotiate and agree on some arrangement of encryption algorithms, key generation methods, and security protocols. This arrangement is a Security Association (SA) between the two clients. ISAKMP defines the framework in which these security associations are established. Both SA and tunneling are two important concepts in IPSec architecture.

SA

An SA is a logical connection between two IPSec systems that defines, in unidirectional terms, the specific security protocol to be used when datagrams are passed to some destination IP address. This security descriptor or vector assumes one of two modes depending on the selected security protocol: transport or tunnel. SAs describe one-way relationships, so a bidirectional session pipe requires

Table 5.3 A comparison of IPSec security services by protocol.

Protocol	Access Control	Integrity	Authentication	Partial Sequence Integrity*	Confidentiality
AH	Yes	Yes	Yes	Yes	No
ESP (encryption only)	Yes	No	No	Yes	Yes
ESP (encryption plus authentication)	Yes	Yes	Yes	Yes	Yes

** The rejection of packets not in sequence protects against replay attacks.*

two SAs, one for each of the two directions. An SA indicates in which direction a specific security protocol carries a specific encryption service in the session pipe. An SA indicates only one security service carried by one protocol in one direction at one time.

When a session pipe carries two protocols, the SAs form an SA bundle. These SAs do not necessarily have to have the same destination IP address or target. One SA vector in an SA bundle, in other words, might specify that the AH protocol is supported up to a corporate firewall; another SA vector in the same bundle would extend ESP directly to some host behind that same firewall. Information about the SA vector, such as its source, destination, and whether it is inbound or outbound, is contained in some kind of security policy database. This data store assumes the form of an ordered list of policy entries separated according to inbound/outbound directions.

Tunneling

Tunneling or encapsulation consists of conceptually wrapping one packet inside another. A new header, in fact, is attached to the front of some existing datagram. This functionally changes the original packet header into a "data" payload of that leading or "encapsulating" header. Tunneling is a common technique used to carry some "unintelligible" protocol datagram over a network that does not "understand" that particular protocol directly. It is common practice, for example, to encapsulate Network Basic Input/Output System (NetBIOS) or Internet Protocol Exchange (IPX) in IP for transmission over a local area network (LAN)/wide area network (WAN) link. Using IPSec, you can hide the internal addressing scheme of a private network because the encrypted packet carrying that data is encapsulated in another IP datagram. Packets exchanged across hostile or unsecured namespaces in this way are never actually read; they remain payloads of other IP packets.

IPSec tunneling was originally designed for Mobile IP (RFC 2003), where a mobile host uses its home IP address for all transmissions regardless of its attachment to a remote network or foreign subnet. This topic is discussed in further detail in Chapter 6.

Encryption Techniques

Microsoft uses the following industry-standard cryptographic algorithms and authentication techniques:

- Diffie-Hellman (DH)
- Variations of HMAC
- DES-CBC

DH

The DH technique is a public-key algorithm invented by Whitfield Diffie and Martin Hellman. It allows two communicating principals to negotiate the sharing of a secret key over an unsecured namespace. DH is initiated when the two entities begin exchanging public information. Each entity combines the other's public information along with its own secret information to generate a shared-secret value.

HMAC

HMAC is a secret-key algorithm that provides integrity and authentication, and thus offers a defense to impersonation attack modalities. Authentication using keyed hash produces a digital signature for the packet that the receiver can verify. If the message changes in transit, the hash value is different and the IP packet is rejected. Message Digest 5 (MD5), sometimes referred to as HMAC-MD5, is a hash function that produces a 128-bit value. Secure Hash Algorithm (SHA), developed by the National Institute of Standards and Technology (NIST) and published as a federal information processing standard (FIPS PUB 180) in 1993, is a hash function that produces a 160-bit value. It was revised in 1995 as FIPS PUB 180-1, or SHA-1. Although somewhat slower than HMAC-MD5, SHA-1 is more secure.

DES-CBC

DES involves CBC, a secret key algorithm used for confidentiality. This key algorithm is a generated random number used with the secret key to encrypt the data.

IPSec uses state-of-the-art cryptographic algorithms. The term *transform* is used to describe the specific implementation of an algorithm by an IPSec protocol. For example, when ESP invokes the DES algorithm, it is commonly called the ESP DES-CBC transform.

Key Management Protocols

Windows 2000 supports the standards-based protocols published by the IETF. IPSec complies with the latest IETF proposals, which include the ISAKMP/Oakley drafts. IPSec implements ISAKMP using the Oakley key determination protocol, which allows for dynamic rekeying.

ISAKMP

An SA must be established before IP packets can be transmitted. It is defined by a set of parameters that describe the security services and techniques, such as keys, that a security protocol uses to protect the exchange of information. An SA must be established between two principals using IPSec. ISAKMP defines a common, generic framework to support the establishment of these security associations. It does not define any one encryption algorithm, key-generation method, or security protocol.

Oakley

Oakley, a key determination protocol, uses the DH key exchange algorithm and supports Perfect Forward Secrecy (PFS). PFS ensures that if a single key is compromised, it permits access only to data protected by a single key. It does not reuse the key that protects communications to compute additional keys, nor does it use the original key-generation material to compute another key.

TCO

The principle of least privilege states that a (security) system is most robust when it is structured to demand the least privilege from its components. RFC 1636, as mentioned earlier in this chapter, suggests that the principle of least privilege might be in contradiction to the principle of least cost. Corporate security objectives very often fail to balance security needs, such as data protection, with the high costs of implementation and maintenance. In fact, the cost of a properly administered security policy—namely, the recurring costs of software upgrades, training, and cryptographic key management—typically exceeds the capital investment in original hardware. These recurring cost items are all variable components of TCO.

IPSec is a protocol suite that does not force the same investment of time or money as other security technologies, especially those working at the OSI Application layer. When correctly implemented, it is designed for interoperability because it is application independent. It does not affect networks or host machines that do not support it. It is fully compatible with IPv4 and will accommodate new cryptographic algorithms as they become available. It is a mandatory component of IPv6. In terms of TCO, IPSec is probably the most cost-effective security subsystem.

Software Upgrades

IPSec is deployed at the transport level, so it is transparent to software applications. These applications inherit the security without code modifications. Network-level security provides immense savings by eliminating the need for the upgrade of software applications to accommodate changes in the security structure.

Training

No user training is required because IPSec is transparent to users; this expense is eliminated.

Cryptographic Key Management

Manual key management, the regular changing of cryptographic keys, becomes extremely time-consuming and prone to intentional or unintentional noncompliance. Keys or passwords are often not changed or are changed on only some computers, in direct violation of corporate security policy. Windows 2000 IPSec, however, automatically handles key management and eliminates the maintenance costs associated with manual key management. TCO is lowered while compliance issues and stronger security are guaranteed across the enterprise.

Deployment Strategy

Windows 2000, through its selection of security protocols, provides scalable, enterprise-wide information security at a low TCO. There is both greater flexibility and granularity in security, permission management, and system-wide administration and policies as compared to earlier versions of NT. Security policies can be applied hierarchically, across the enterprise, or at the level of a single user, workstation, or group; there is minimal administrative overhead, redesign, or retraining. Furthermore, internal application programming interfaces (APIs) like the Security Support Provider Interface (SSPI) and the Cryptographic API (CAPI) provide extensible software interfaces that will accommodate future installable security libraries with minimal changes to the OSI Application layer.

I will go into greater detail about building a network security policy in Chapter 8. In brief, an administrator performs several steps in deploying security protocols:

1. Analyze the kind of information exchanged.
2. Create communications scenarios.
3. Determine security needs for each scenario.
4. Build the specific security policies.

Analyze Information

All information sent over networks or over the Internet is subject to, at the very least, interception attack modalities, including examination and modification. An administrator can determine which kinds of information are most valuable and what communications scenarios are most vulnerable.

Create Communications Scenarios

Organizations often follow specific, predictable operational steps in their business processes or information workflows. For example, a remote sales office sends daily business data to one of several different data stores in a centralized home office. Each communications scenario (e.g., operations information to a warehouse, daily payroll data and new hires to Human Resources, contracts to the Legal department) has different IP security policies associated with the confidentiality of the data. A policy needs to state, for example, that all communications to and from the HR department must be authenticated and confidential. Furthermore, required security levels will change, depending upon the sensitivity of exchanged information, operational procedures, and the relative vulnerability of the data link. IPSec configuration and deployment also relates to AD and Group Policy. You build a policy that can be applied to a forest, a tree, a domain, or a single computer, based on some scenario, in order to deploy IPSec in your enterprise.

Determine Security Levels

As with any security technology, it is necessary to adjust to changes in network infrastructure, the nature of the information exchanged, its level of sensitivity, and the vulnerabilities of the session pipe through which the message is sent. You need to assess the value of a resource in terms of its loss or unavailability over the short, medium, and long term, and categorize security levels based on an assessment of this loss. For example, information that could cause irreparable damage to your organization if it were publicly disclosed should be kept the most secured. Windows 2000 wizards and MMC snap-ins simplify the addition or modification of security options in any one security policy. For example, the IP Security Rule Wizard assists you in building a security rule that will control how and when security techniques are deployed based on a user-defined IP filter list. The wizard helps you compile a collection of actions that are activated when specific, user-defined criteria in this filter list, such as packet source, destination, and type, are met. These actions include IP tunneling attributes, authentication methods, and filter actions.

Build Security Policies

An administrator using Windows 2000 wizards and MMC snap-ins configures security attributes into what are called *security policies*, collections of associated negotiation policies and IP filter lists. Probably the simplest way to view the default IP security polices is in the IP Security Policy Management MMC snap-in.

During daily exchanges of information, negotiation policies determine the appropriate security services for any one particular communication scenario. Each negotiation policy sets multiple security methods so that appropriate security services are chosen. If the first method is not acceptable for the security association, the ISAKMP/Oakley negotiation service continues to look for a service until it finds one that it can use to establish the association.

An IP security policy can be assigned to the default domain policy, the default local policy, or a user-defined, customized local policy. During the logon process, computers automatically load these security policies. This lowers TCO by eliminating the need to configure or maintain each individual machine. Each security policy may contain one or more security rules, which are in turn related to filter lists and filter actions.

Rules, Filter Lists, and Filter Actions

A rule has six components:

- *IP filter list*—Target packets are defined by IP type or address with this rule
- *Filter actions*—Specific actions—namely, permit, block, and negotiate—are triggered when the target packet matches filter criteria in the filter list.
- *Security methods*—Computers secure an exchange of information using a high, medium, and custom method. The high method, which uses ESP, applies confidentiality (encrypted), authentication (authentic), and integrity (unmodified) security controls. The medium method, which uses AH, applies only confidentiality (encrypted) and integrity (unmodified) controls. The data in the medium method is not encrypted. The custom method allows the user to define an integrity algorithm without encryption, integrity with encryption, and session key settings.
- *Authentication methods*—This rule defines how trust is established between computers. Either the Windows 2000 default (Kerberos v5), a X.509 digital certificate from some specific certificate authority (CA), or a secret, preshared key can be specified. If a method cannot be negotiated, the next method in the list will be applied in descending order.
- *Tunnel settings*—This rule includes specification of transport or tunnel mode. Transport mode is the default method that provides end-to-end security between consumer and service provider on the same network, RAS, or intranet routers. It is not, however, recommended for exchanges of information across unsecured namespaces like the Internet. Tunnel mode is appropriate for information exchanges outside the boundaries of the enterprise. This topic is covered in Chapter 6.
- *Connection types*—This rule specifies whether network traffic will pass over all networks, the local area network, or remote access connections.

Security rules are applied to target computers matching specific criteria in an IP filter list. The filter list defines specific network traffic to which specific rules will apply. Filtering allows Windows 2000 to apply different security policies to different target machines. This filtering can include source and/or destination IP addresses; either individual host clients, network IDs, or subnet IDs that represent a scope of host IP addresses; or a specific DNS name. It also allows screening of the

IP protocol type—e.g., exterior gateway protocol (EGP), Internet Control Message Protocol (ICMP), host monitor protocol (HMP), and so on—and IP protocol port. By default, all IP or ICMP traffic—primarily Packet Internet Groper (Ping) packets—is targeted for IPSec rules. IP filters determine which actions to take, based upon the destination and protocol of individual IP packets.

A specific filter action is applied to a connection when communications are established through any of the filtered addresses or protocols. The default or customized action is then triggered. Actions are applied in the order in which they are listed. If an action cannot be negotiated, the next action in the list will be applied in descending order.

The three filter action options are:

- *Permit*—No IP security is applied to exchanges of information.
- *Block*—All packet traffic specified in the filter list is rejected.
- *Negotiate Security*—All packet traffic specified in the filter list must negotiate a compatible security protocol.

IPSec Policies

An IPSec policy is thus composed of IP security rules, IP filter lists, and IP filter actions. There are three built-in IPSec policies:

- *Client (respond only)*—Communications are normally unsecured. The default response rule is applied to secure connections that request security. Only the requested protocol and port traffic are secured.
- *Secure Server (require security)*—Secured connections must use Kerberos protocol for the exchange of information. Unsecured incoming packets from untrusted clients are rejected.
- *Server (request security)*—Secured connections are always requested but do not need to use Kerberos protocol for the exchange of information. Unsecured communications with untrusted clients are allowed. There is also an option to accept unsecured communications but respond with IPSec and thus negotiate a secured channel.

IPSec can significantly impact the flow of data. Although the built-in Server policy is IPSec aware and seeks the more preferred secured connection, it is flexible enough to exchange information with non-IPSec principals in the common Windows 2000 mixed-mode environment. Secure Server policy in a mixed-mode environment can cause major disruptions in the flow of services; those services that unsuccessfully negotiate security policies will fail to execute.

A typical exchange of information using IPSec occurs as follows:

1. A consumer sends a message to a service provider.
2. The consumer's IPSec driver attempts to match the outgoing packet's address or the packet type against the IP filter list.
3. The IPSec driver notifies ISAKMP to initiate security negotiations with the service provider.
4. The service provider's ISAKMP receives the security negotiations request.
5. Both principals initiate a key exchange, establishing an ISAKMP SA and a shared secret key.
6. Both principals negotiate the security level for the information exchange, establishing both IPSec SAs and keys.
7. The consumer's IPSec driver transfers packets to the appropriate connection type for transmission to the service provider.
8. The provider receives the packets and transfers them to the IPSec driver.
9. The provider's IPSec uses the inbound SA and key to check the digital signature and begin decryption.
10. The provider's IPSec driver transfers decrypted packets to the OSI Transport layer for further processing.

The IPSec security suite operates below the Transport layer, so neither application software nor user is aware of the additional security steps dealing with authentication, key exchanges, and encryption during the transmission of data. Routers and switches, in addition to workstations, ignore IPSec packet information. To ensure compatibility in heterogeneous environments, Windows 2000 IPSec-aware clients send data packets without encryption to non-Windows 2000 clients. Firewalls, security gateways, and proxy servers, however, require special configuration to avoid rejection of packets because they read and sometimes alter parts of the packet as it travels from its source to its destination—that is, end-to-end. Some devices, such as firewalls, translate the network addresses as they forward a packet from an external network to an internal network. Other times, the device will alter a header in a packet. In both cases, this network address translation (NAT) process either rejects the packet or causes the packet to fail an integrity check at its destination. Another problem with IPSec is in the exchange of key and dynamic rekeying between two parties that have their addresses translated; the outside party never really "knows" the IP address of the internal party, so the key exchanges to an "authentic" address always fail. These issues limit the use of IPSec, especially across public networks.

An IP Security Architecture Case Study

ExamCram Ltd.: Considering Network Layer Security Solutions

ExamCram Ltd., a publishing company in AnyTown, Arizona, primarily focuses on developing and selling advanced technical training materials. The Legal department at ExamCram Ltd. is expanding operations as the company accepts more clients. MyCompany Inc. does business with ExamCram Ltd. and is located in the same building.

Current LAN/Network Structure

All 100 client machines are configured in a single Windows 2000 root domain. The client systems are running Windows 2000 Professional, with Office 2000 being utilized as an applications package. Each system is connected to a 10Mbps hub through 10Mbps LAN cards, although Category 5 Unshielded Twisted Pair (UTP) cabling is connecting each system and hub in a star topology.

A centralized Legal department requires that communications:

- Within the department be secure but not confidential
- Between the Legal department and other departments within the organization be both secure and confidential

The Legal department runs on network 192.168.2.0/24. A network outside the department runs on 192.168.3.0/24.

MyCompany Inc. has 22 Windows 2000 Professional computers in a single child domain. The client systems are running Office 2000 as an applications package. Each system is connected to a 10Mbps hub through 10Mbps LAN cards, although Category 5 UTP cabling is connecting each system and hub in a star topology. A professional IT person administers the network.

Proposed LAN/Network Structure

No changes in the current structure are proposed at this time.

Current WAN Connectivity

No changes in the current structure are proposed at this time.

Proposed WAN Connectivity

No changes in the current structure are proposed at this time.

Design Commentary

It is assumed that IPSec is applied to all communications initiated by the Legal department. The VP of Sales at ExamCram Ltd. says, "We need to have our contracts signed, sealed, and delivered as quickly as possible to beat our competition. I don't want good authors getting away from us."

Current Internet Positioning

ExamCram Ltd. is registered as **examcram.com**. The Marketing department is registered as **mrkt.examcram.com**. MyCompany Inc. is registered as **mycompany.com**.

Future Internet Plans

No changes in the current structure are proposed at this time.

Company Goal

The only concern at the moment is the Legal department. All legal correspondence is considered top secret. Only top management and the Legal department need to know the actual terms of a book contract.

Commentary

Figure 5.2 shows the implementation plan, which is as follows:

1. Create a security policy in the IPSec Security Polices on Active Directory node in your MMC snap-in, which is assigned to the default domain policy with the following two negotiation policies and IP filters:

    - *LegalPol1*—Provides confidentiality for all communications outside the Legal department. Under Edit Rule Properties, in the Security Method, select High (ESP). The caption reads: Data Will Be Encrypted, Authentic, And Unmodified.

    - *LegalPol2*—Provides authentication and integrity for all communications within the Legal department. Under Edit Rule Properties, in the Security Method, select Medium (AH). The caption reads: Data Will Be Authentic And Unmodified, But Will Not Be Encrypted.

2. Create an IP filter associated with one of the negotiation policies listed in Step 1. The Legal department runs on network 192.168.2.0/24. A network outside the department runs on 192.168.3.0/24.

    - *LegalFilt1*—Is for communications outside the Legal department and is associated with LegalPol1. The filter's source IP address is 192.168.2.0/24, its destination IP address is 192.168.3.0/24, and its protocol type is ALL.

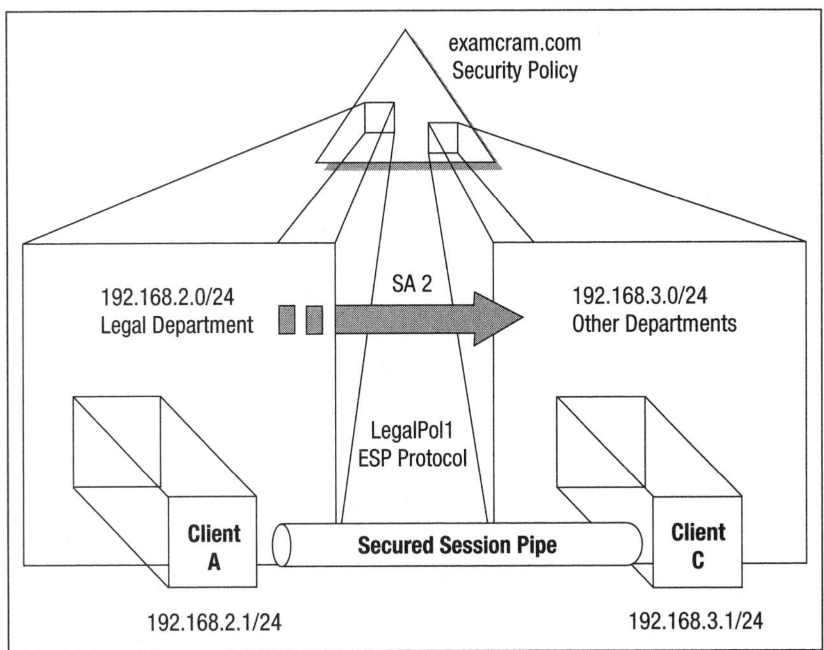

Figure 5.2 An example of IPSec deployment.

- *LegalFilt2*—Is for communications within the Legal department and is associated with LegalPol2. The filter's source IP address is 192.168.2.0/24, its destination IP address is 192.168.2.0/24, and its protocol type is ALL.

For communications outside the Legal department, both source and destination IP addresses are checked against the IP filters in the legal security policy. The IPSec level for the communication is determined by the associated negotiation policy assigned to an IP address range in the filter list.

For example, if a client in the Legal department with 192.168.2.1/24 as an IP address sends data outside the department, LegalFilt1 is triggered. The communication is sent according to the security level that LegalPol1 specifies. Thus, the authentication, integrity, and confidentiality IT security controls are applied using the ESP protocol to the information exchange, as you saw in Figure 5.2.

Practice Questions

Case Study

4Sale, an online bartering company in ThatTherePlace, North Dakota, primarily focuses on selling inexpensive, odd-lot items. The merger between 4Sale and Got-a-Deal has been finalized, and both companies have merged office space in the same office building.

Current LAN/Network Structure

4Sale is presently running Windows 2000 Server in native mode. One member server supports Exchange, and another member server is running Internet Information Server (IIS) 5, and Proxy Server 2. All 100 client machines are configured in a single domain model. The client systems are running Windows 2000 Professional, with Office 97 being utilized as an applications package. Each system is connected to a 10Mbps hub through 10Mbps LAN cards running Category 5 UTP cabling in a star topology.

Got-a-Deal has undergone changes. It is running all 22 client machines in a single child domain under the 4Sale root domain. The client systems are running Windows 2000 Professional, with Office 97 being utilized as an applications package. Each system is connected to a 10Mbps hub through 10Mbps LAN cards running Category 5 UTP cabling in a star topology. These hubs are on the same backbone as 4Sale but have a different subnet.

Proposed LAN/Network Structure

4Sale is developing its online barter/trading business through business alliances. It wants secure communications among specific departments. For example, the exchange of bids must be authenticated and kept confidential.

Current WAN Connectivity

4Sale has a T1 connection to an ISP in OverThere, North Dakota. Got-a-Deal has 56Kbps dial-up networking connectivity through the same ISP.

Proposed WAN Connectivity

No changes are planned at this time.

Directory Design Commentary

The Network Manager at 4Sale says, "We want to establish a firm security foundation that will be application independent. Our major IT concern is confidentiality within the company. In the future, I will be coming back to you with questions about remote connectivity."

Current Internet Positioning

4Sale is registered as **4sale.com**. Got-a-Deal has been selling its goods through local companies and through the **4sale.com** Web site.

Future Internet Plans

No changes in the current structure are proposed at this time.

Company Goal with Windows 2000

4Sale puts you on retainer. You will spend most of your time answering questions to help top management compile the company's long-term objectives.

Question 1

The CEO of 4Sale tells you, "We need security, but I don't want to overspend on technology." What TCO component is affected by deploying IPSec? [Choose the best answer]

❍ a. Software upgrades

❍ b. Training

❍ c. Hardware

❍ d. All of the above

❍ e. None of the above

Answer e is correct. IP Security works at the OSI Transport layer. Software upgrades, training, and hardware are not directly affected. In other words, IPSec adds features like strong encryption without affecting the TCO specifically in terms of software upgrades, training, and hardware. Therefore, answers a, b, and c are incorrect. A feature like manual key management is an example of what is affected during deployment of IPSec; in other words, its maintenance is eliminated.

Question 2

The Network Manager at 4Sale asks, "From a technical point of view, what do I gain from using IPSec?" [Check all correct answers]

❑ a. Dynamic suballocation

❑ b. Confidentiality

❑ c. Flexible security protocols

❑ d. Flexible negotiation

❑ e. Data integrity

Answers b, c, d, and e are correct. Confidentiality, flexible security protocols, flexible negotiation, and data integrity, along with dynamic rekeying of sessions, are all advantages of IPSec. Dynamic suballocation applies to storage. Therefore, answer a is incorrect.

Question 3

The Network Manager at 4Sale asks, "How does IPSec actually work?" List the following elements in the correct sequential order:

Secured packets are exchanged.

The consumer's IPSec driver matches the outbound IP address to the filter list.

Security association is established.

The consumer's IPSec driver notifies ISAKMP to initiate security negotiations.

The service provider's ISAKMP receives the request and initiates the key exchange.

The correct answer is:

The consumer's IPSec driver matches the outbound IP address to the filter list.

The consumer's IPSec driver notifies ISAKMP to initiate security negotiations.

The service provider's ISAKMP receives the request and initiates the key exchange.

Security association is established.

Secured packets are exchanged.

Question 4

The Network Manager at 4Sale asks, "I mentioned to you my long-term plans to connect to other locations throughout the country. How does IPSec help us get closer to that goal?" Select the scenarios that would benefit from IPSec. [Check all correct answers]

- ❑ a. Remote site connectivity
- ❑ b. Remote access through TCP/IP
- ❑ c. Extranet connectivity
- ❑ d. All of the above

Answer d is correct. Remote site connectivity, remote access through Transmission Control Protocol/Internet Protocol, and extranet connectivity would all benefit from IP Security.

Question 5

The Network Manager at 4Sale says, "I've been reading *MCSE Windows 2000 Security Design Exam Prep*. I think I understand now: IPSec, like Kerberos, assumes that servers in the enterprise are authenticated; only the sender in a message exchange needs to be authenticated." Is the Network Manager correct?

❍ a. Yes

❍ b. No

Answer b, no, is correct. The Network Manager is incorrect. Neither IP Security nor Kerberos makes any assumptions about the authenticity of machines in the enterprise. Keys expire and need to be renewed. Also, the recipient of a message requests verification of the sender's authenticity when the mutual authentication flag is set during the setup of Kerberos policy.

Question 6

The Network Manager at 4Sale asks, "How do I organize IPSec's suite of protocols to better understand what each one does?"

List the components and subcomponents of the IPSec suite. Create an ordered list of only the appropriate components/subcomponents, and group each subcomponent under the correct component.

Internet Key Exchange

Oakley Key Determination Protocol

Internet Security Association

Key Management Protocol

Encapsulated Security Payload

Authentication Header Protocol

Security protocols

The correct answer is:

Security protocols

Authentication Header Protocol

Encapsulated Security Payload

Internet Key Exchange

Internet Security Association

Key Management Protocol

Oakley Key Determination Protocol

Question 7

The Network Manager at 4Sale says, "Let me know whether I have this straight. An example of tunneling is simple: A data packet is encapsulated in a network protocol and exchanged across unsecured namespaces. Nothing else." Is the Network Manager correct?

- ❍ a. Yes
- ❍ b. No

Answer a, yes, is correct. The Network Manager is correct. Tunneling occurs at the Open Systems Interconnection (OSI) Network layer when one protocol datagram or packet is "wrapped" or encapsulated in another. You can tunnel packets without encrypting them.

Question 8

The Network Manager at 4Sale asks, "When I build security policies, what protocols do I need to know about?" You tell him he needs to be aware of OSI Network layer protocols. Which of the following are such protocols? [Check all correct answers]

- ❑ a. Authentication Header Protocol
- ❑ b. Authentication Header Payload
- ❑ c. Encapsulated Security Protocol
- ❑ d. Encapsulated Security Payload

Answers a and d are correct. The correct names are Authentication Header Protocol and Encapsulated Security Payload. Therefore, answers b and c are incorrect.

Question 9

The Network Manager at 4Sale asks, "When I build a security policy, it asks me to choose between AH and ESP. What security services does AH provide?" [Check all correct answers]

- ❏ a. Access control
- ❏ b. Integrity
- ❏ c. Authentication
- ❏ d. Partial sequence integrity
- ❏ e. Confidentiality
- ❏ f. All of the above
- ❏ g. None of the above

Answers a, b, c, and d are correct. Authentication Header (AH) provides access control, integrity, authentication, and partial sequence integrity. Because AH doesn't offer encryption, it doesn't provide confidentiality. Therefore, answer e is incorrect, as are answers f and g.

Need to Know More?

Garfinkel, Simson and Gene Spafford. *Practical Unix and Internet Security, Second Edition.* O'Reilly & Associates, Sebastopol, CA, 1996. ISBN 1-56592-148-8. Chapter 16 provides a very general, nontechnical discussion of IPSec. The authors briefly discuss link-level and end-to-end encryption in the context of TCP/IP networks. Chapter 17 deals specifically with TCP/IP services.

Murhammer, Martin W. et al. *TCP/IP Tutorial and Technical Overview, Sixth Edition.* Prentice Hall, Upper Saddle River, NJ, 1998. ISBN 0-13-020130-8. Section 5.5 provides a technical review of IPSec architecture, the various protocols, the combination of IPSec protocols, and IKE. Section 5.4, Network Address Translation and NAT Limitations, is especially relevant in a discussion of incompatibilities within the IPSec suite. This book describes these protocols from a Unix perspective but is relevant to Windows 2000 topics.

Shinder, Thomas W., Debra Littlejohn Shinder, and D. Lynn White. *Configuring Windows 2000 Server Security.* Syngress Media, Inc., Rockland, MD, 2000. ISBN 1-928994-02-4. Chapter 7 provides an excellent discussion that begins with network encroachment methodologies. The authors provide a comprehensive and technical discussion of IPSec architecture. They conclude with sections on how to evaluate levels of security, build rules, and configure policy.

Stallings, William. *Network Security Essentials: Applications and Standards.* Prentice Hall, Upper Saddle River, NJ, 1999. ISBN 0-13-016093-8. Chapter 6 provides a detailed and technical discussion of the IPSec protocol suite. There is also a section on key management. This text discusses the protocols from a Unix perspective. Nevertheless, most topics are relevant in the Windows 2000 environment.

Search the TechNet CD (or its online version through **www.microsoft.com**) and the *Windows 2000 Server Resource Kit* CD using the keywords "IPSec", "AH", "ESP", "DES", and "SA".

www.faqs.org/rfcs/ This is the RFC search page. Relevant RFCs found at this site include:

RFC 2401: An overview of a security architecture. This memo specifies the base architecture for IPSec-compliant systems. Replaces RFC 1825.

RFC 2402: Description of a packet authentication extension to IPv4 and IPv6. This memo describes the IP Authentication Header (AH) used to provide connectionless integrity and data origin authentication for IP datagrams, and to provide protection against replays. Replaces RFC 1826.

RFC 2406: Description of a packet encryption extension to IPv4 and IPv6. This memo describes the Encapsulated Security Payload (ESP) header that is designed to provide a mix of security services in IPv4 and IPv6. Replaces RFC 1827.

RFC 2408: Specification of key management capabilities. This memo describes a protocol utilizing security concepts necessary for establishing Security Associations (SAs) and cryptographic keys in an Internet environment.

www.ietf.cnri.reston.va.us/html.charters/ipsec-charter.html This is the IETF's IPSec Web site. It offers links to draft papers and RFCs related to IPSec.

www.microsoft.com/windows2000/library/howitworks/security/ip_security.asp This site offers the Windows 2000 Server White Paper, *IP Security for Microsoft Windows 2000 Server*. This technical paper provides a clear overview of IPSec as well as a scenario that describes in general terms how security policies are configured. It supplies many of the terms associated with this particular security suite and thus provides a good introduction to this area.

Remote Connectivity Issues

Terms you'll need to understand:

- ✓ Network Address Translation (NAT)
- ✓ Secure Sockets Layer/Transport Layer (or Level) Security (SSL/TLS)
- ✓ Hypertext Transfer Protocol (HTTP)
- ✓ Secure Hypertext Transfer Protocol (S-HTTP)
- ✓ Virtual Private Network (VPN) client
- ✓ VPN server
- ✓ Tunneling protocol
- ✓ IP Security (IPSec) protocol suite
- ✓ Security Parameter Index (SPI)
- ✓ Tunneled data
- ✓ Firewall technologies
- ✓ Demilitarized zone (DMZ)
- ✓ Screened-host architecture
- ✓ Screened-subnet architecture

Techniques you'll need to master:

- ✓ Describing how different IPSec components support remote access
- ✓ Understanding the basic remote access deployment scenarios
- ✓ Describing different tunneling modes
- ✓ Discussing feature differences in VPN-related security protocols
- ✓ Describing the three general firewall topologies

In this chapter, I explore the technologies used to exchange information with remote sites. The topic of remote connectivity begins with a discussion of Virtual Private Networks (VPNs). Microsoft has integrated VPN solutions with Routing and Remote Access Service (RRAS) because of the critical role this technology plays in supporting telecommuting, the designs of remote branch office enterprises, and off-site enterprise partnerships. This form of remote connectivity uses a secure tunneled connection within which only authenticated messages are exchanged. This chapter discusses several protocols emphasizing the OSI Link Layer and end-to-end security, including Layer 2 Tunneling Protocol (L2TP) and Point-To-Point Tunneling Protocol (PPTP). I also discuss a variety of topologies that involve the transmission of secured information over an unsecured namespace.

The chapter describes in greater detail IP Security (IPSec) and other security protocols associated with VPN, providing the critical security controls: encryption, authentication, and integrity. L2TP and IPSec together provide strong security solutions. IPSec, discussed in Chapter 5, is especially relevant in discussions of information authenticity and confidentiality, not just in an e-commerce scenario but also in daily interoffice communications.

Then, I discuss three general firewall architectures in the context of remote connectivity. This topic provides a foundation for Chapter 7. Finally, this chapter ends with a variety of VPN scenarios that show various remote access features of Windows 2000.

An Overview of VPN

A VPN is created when a private channel, extended typically across an unsecured public network like the Internet, connects two computers. The private communication channel creates, in effect, a "virtualized network" within which both these computers can work. From the consumer's viewpoint, this virtual network provides the same functionality found within the physical boundaries of the enterprise by delivering point-to-point private data links through a private tunnel. Figure 6.1 shows a VPN for ExamCram Ltd. A client workstation in **east.examcram.com** connects with a client workstation in **west.examcram.com** across the Internet. The connection travels through a tunnel that extends from client to server (more commonly referred to as end to end). The nature of the internetwork is irrelevant to both consumers, neither of which can tell the difference between a VPN connection and a physical connection to another workstation across the room. VPN connections may sometimes be appropriate between, for example, subnets on the same local area network to provide strong authentication and confidentiality.

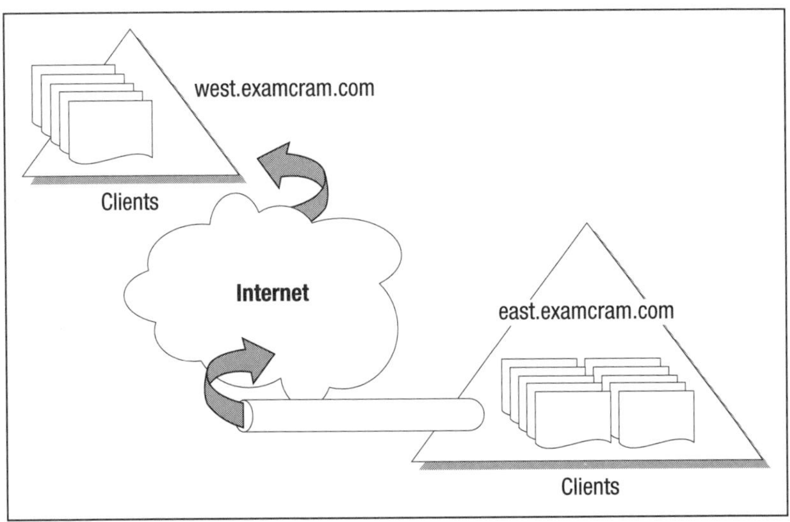

Figure 6.1 Representation of a virtual private network.

Before I can delve into the topic of VPNs, I need to give you a little background. This section provides the technical foundation for the rest of the chapter. I then go on to discuss tunneling and Network Address Translation (NAT).

Security Protocols

Windows 2000 supports the following new security protocols that verify a user's security credentials when connecting to network services:

- *Layer 2 Tunneling Protocol (L2TP)*—Discussed in the "VPN Security Protocols" section later in this chapter, this OSI Link layer protocol is a combination of PPTP and Layer 2 Forwarding (L2F, described in RFC 2341) and was originally created by Cisco Systems.
- *Extensible Authentication Protocol - Transport Layer (or Level) Security (EAP-TLS)*—The EAP protocol (RFC 2284), especially with TLS (RFC 2246), supports two-factor authentication through application programming interface (API) extensions and uses Message Digest 5 (MD5) as an encryption method.
- *Bandwidth Allocation Protocol (BAP)*—This control protocol enhances the ability of Point-To-Point Protocol (PPP) Multilink Protocol to bundle multiple physical connections in a single virtual connection of greater bandwidth.
- *Remote Authentication Dial-In User Service (RADIUS)*—A vendor-independent distributed user authentication service and dial-in security solution (RFC 2058 and 2138).

These security protocols lend support to legacy NT 4 authentication protocols such as PPTP, Password Authentication Protocol (PAP), Challenge Handshake Authentication Protocol (CHAP), Microsoft Challenge Handshake Authentication Protocol (MS-CHAP), and Shiva Password Authentication Protocol (SPAP, used in mixed environments that support Shiva LAN Rover software). Most noteworthy of the legacy protocols is PPTP, which was originally created by the PPTP Industry Forum. I will reference different components of the IPSec protocol suite, discussed in Chapter 5 of this book and described in RFCs 2401-2409, throughout this chapter.

Basic Remote Access Models

Windows 2000 supports three basic remote access models for a networked enterprise:

- Transport layer security technologies
- Private or trusted network infrastructures
- End-to-end network security

Many in the computer industry consider these three models to be examples of VPNs, but Microsoft has a more restricted view of VPNs, especially in relation to Windows 2000, which I will also address.

Transport Layer Security Technologies

Secure Sockets Layer/Transport Layer Security (SSL/TLS), Unix Sockets (SOCKS), and Secure Hypertext Transfer Protocol (S-HTTP)—among others—provide security to applications interfacing directly with the OSI Transport layer. SSL/TLS applications are typically written for the personal computer market and tend to scale poorly because of the specificity in their design. SOCKS, developed for the non-Windows market, is an authenticated firewall traversal protocol that provides both extensible authentication for distributed server architectures and sufficient granularity to control authorization of inbound/outbound transport sessions. SSL/TLS and SOCKS are complementary services that provide Transport layer security within VPNs and extranets. S-HTTP is an extension to the HTTP protocol that supports secured exchanges of information. SSL/TLS and S-HTTP use different technologies. SSL/TLS creates a secure connection by authenticating two computers; S-HTTP secures the transmission of individual messages.

Private or Trusted Network Infrastructures

Companies that physically deploy internal or outsourced data communication infrastructures for wide area networks (WANs) achieve their security objectives through true physical isolation. This method of deployment, however, does not avoid the problems common to other forms of deployment (such as passive interception or impersonation). Once the capital investment is made, though, these private infrastructures are less likely to adapt to newer technologies or to provide the plasticity necessary to cope with future business objectives. This is because these infrastructures are typically expensive physical devices with structural limitations to installation, modification, extensions, and scalability, not to mention the training needed to maintain them. There is thus a twofold disadvantage to this kind of security deployment method: First, just like other technology, the investment experiences almost immediate obsolescence once it is deployed, and second, the cognitive dissonance experienced by management over the perceived return on investment increases in relation to the total cost of the infrastructure.

End-to-End Network Security

Security systems working end to end are a more functional approach to deployment than a private, physical infrastructure because the end-to-end systems transparently negotiate appropriate technologies and protocols from installed support services at each layer of the network. One example of end-to-end remote connectivity is when a person telecommuting from home or working on the road transmits data over a dedicated private link directly to some corporate server. The dial-up networking technology on the telecommuter's machine establishes secure connections with the branch office VPN server just as easily as employees communicating from one end of the office to another. The possible support service selections are controlled by remote access policies, which simplifies administration and maintenance. This approach to security is more centered on the network infrastructure (that is, more network-centric) and adopts a more restricted use of the VPN category as a support technology that provides security services across a public or untrusted network infrastructure.

VPN and RRAS

Although many in the computer industry consider the three models just mentioned to be distinct VPN categories, Windows 2000 integrates a secured end-to-end remote connectivity solution within its operating system design. It incorporates VPN into its RRAS and refines the definition to include:

- Any secured access from some remote client to some gateway through a public (Internet) infrastructure or within some private or outsourced one
- Any secured gateway-to-gateway connections across public, private, or outsourced networks

With the service integrated, both IPSec and Active Directory (AD) directory services provide the foundation for secured access to enterprise resources. Thus, remote access services have been fully incorporated into the network operating system and can benefit from centralized administration and policy-managed control.

Tunneling

A *VPN client* (for example, a remote user or consumer) connects to a *VPN server* (some service provider) through a *tunnel* (session pipe) using a *tunneling protocol*. *Tunneling* is a technique where a data packet is transferred inside the frame or packet of another protocol and thus uses the infrastructure of one network to travel across another network. Data packets are called the *payload*. The tunneling protocol encapsulates the data frame by appending an additional header on the front of the tunneling protocol's data packet. The new header provides routing information and conceals the true nature of the payload. The encapsulated packets are routed between tunnel endpoints over some other network. The logical path along which the encapsulated packet is routed is called the *tunnel*. At the end of the tunnel, the encapsulated payload is stripped of its wrapper and is forwarded to its final destination. Tunneling describes the entire process: encapsulate the data packet at the source, transmit the data packet through the tunnel, and unencapsulate the data packet at the destination.

When confidentiality is required, you need a private tunnel. To emulate that private link, you encrypt the packet for confidentiality before encapsulating it. Then, if some third party intercepts a packet in transit, that party would not be able to decipher the message. The private link in which encrypted data is encapsulated and transmitted is the VPN connection. When you create and send data without encryption, you are using a tunnel but not a VPN connection.

Note: A VPN connection sends encrypted data through the tunnel. If the data must be encrypted, the connection must be private.

Both the tunnel client and tunnel server must use the same OSI (Open Systems Interconnection) Layer 2 Data Link or OSI Layer 3 Network-based tunneling protocol. When an OSI Layer 2 protocol is used, frames are exchanged between client and server; packets connote an OSI Layer 3 exchange. Both PPTP and L2TP, working with frames at OSI Layer 2, create tunnels that are similar to sessions between the two endpoints. The tunnel and various configuration variables (such as address assignments, encryption, and compression variables) are negotiated. In addition, the L2TP over IP uses User Datagram Protocol (UDP) port 1701 to send control messages that provide tunnel maintenance.

There are two kinds of tunnels:

- *Voluntary tunnels*—When a client or a user requests to be a tunnel client, you can configure and create a voluntary tunnel where the client is the tunnel endpoint.
- *Compulsory tunnels*—With a compulsory tunnel, some device other than the client, such as a VPN-capable dial-up access server, is the tunnel endpoint

and acts as the tunnel client. Such an endpoint is commonly known as a Front End Processor (FEP) in PPTP, an L2TP Access Concentrator (LAC) in L2TP, or an IPSec gateway in IPSec. An FEP must be able to support and negotiate establishing a tunnel when a client attempts to connect to it.

A virtual interface on which all VPN connections are made is created when a VPN server is configured. Both the client and server interfaces must have IP addresses assigned. The VPN server can obtain either statically assigned or DHCP (Dynamic Host Configuration Protocol)-leased IP address ranges for all VPN clients.

NAT

NAT reassigns the private IP addresses of, usually, a small number of client machines inside a network to published—and therefore accessible—IP addresses on the Internet. The internal, typically nonrouteable IP addresses are translated to a scope or range of IP addresses from a pool that the NAT administers. An advantage of using a NAT is that fewer published or officially assigned IP addresses are required because the NAT can reuse the same IP addresses at different times. Another advantage is security; the internal IP address ranges are never made known outside the enterprise.

A disadvantage of NATs is the size of the pool; the number of addresses in the NAT's assignable pool limits the number of concurrently used addresses. Other disadvantages arise from the inability of some protocols (such as L2TP and IPSec) to pass-through the translation process. The Internet Key Exchange (IKE) protocol, a component of the IPSec security suite, does not function properly when actual IP source or destination addresses are unknown. Thus, both L2TP/IPSec and IPSec tunnel mode (discussed later in this chapter) cannot engage in the automated exchange of keys across a NAT. The Internet Engineering Task Force (IETF) IPSec workgroup is currently working on correcting these and other incompatibilities.

VPN Security Protocols

Among the authentication protocols mentioned at the beginning of this chapter, several protocols are categorized by Microsoft specifically as VPN tunneling protocols—namely, PPTP and L2TP, based on PPP or IPSec. Although these specific protocols generally perform the same functions and are considered competing technologies, each offers different features particularly suited for different situations. You must therefore consider what features each protocol offers in relation to design goals before you choose which one to deploy.

Design Considerations

When planning VPN deployment, especially across a public network, security protocol features must be evaluated in terms of the three design approaches to the exchange process:

- Addressing each intermediate node link to link between the source and destination
- Viewing the deployment from end to end
- Dealing with security controls at the OSI Application layer

Now, I'll discuss PPP, PPTP, L2TP, and IP Sec in terms of these design considerations.

PPP

PPP is a widely supported communication protocol, so it benefits from multiprotocol support from such diverse network architectures as Novell Internet Protocol Exchange (IPX) and Apple (AppleTalk). PPP also offers a wide range of user authentication options that support smart card authentication, including CHAP, MS-CHAP, MS-CHAP2, and EAP. As mentioned earlier in this chapter, Microsoft implements PPTP and L2TP with EAP-TLS, a strong authentication protocol based on public key certificates. The TLS component is used for two-factor authentication technologies like smart cards.

PPTP

PPTP is a common protocol for both client-to-gateway and gateway-to-gateway VPN scenarios. PPTP not only passes through NATs but also supports mutual authentication based on consumer passwords and encryption keys. Thus, PPTP is inexpensive to install and simple to maintain. It uses a Transmission Control Protocol (TCP) connection for tunnel maintenance and Generic Routing Encapsulation (GRE) encapsulated PPP data frames for tunneled data. Payloads can be both encrypted and compressed.

L2TP

L2TP is a mature IETF standards-based protocol. PPP packet frames are encapsulated in L2TP for transmission across a variety of network and communications protocols like IP, X.25, Frame Relay, or asynchronous transfer mode (ATM). It was specifically designed for client-to-gateway and gateway-to-gateway connections with broad tunneling and security interoperability. L2TP has wide vendor support because it addresses the IPSec shortcomings of client-to-gateway and gateway-to-gateway connections.

L2TP tunneled in IP using UDP port 1701 is used as the VPN tunneling protocol over the Internet for tunnel maintenance. Compressed or encrypted PPP frames encapsulated in L2TP also use UDP to transmit tunneled data. L2TP tunnels appear as IP packets, so IPSec transport mode provides authenticity, integrity, and confidentiality security controls.

A security design calling for the encapsulation of an L2TP packet in IPSec leverages the authentication and encryption security controls of the IPSec wrapper with the protocol interoperability of the PPP payload. This combination is commonly referred to as L2TP/IPSec.

Microsoft recommends the L2TP/IPSec combination as the best multivendor, standards-based client-to-gateway VPN solution.

IPSec

As mentioned in Chapter 5, the IPSec protocol suite consists of two security protocols—Authentication Header (AH) and Encapsulated Security Payload (ESP)—and key management provided by a variety of mechanisms and features. To review, the two protocols provide varying amounts of security services; ESP provides encryption and a combination of encryption and authentication, whereas AH provides just authentication. A security association (SA) between the sending and receiving parties provides access control based on the distribution of a cryptographic key and traffic management relative to these two protocols. This SA is either one one-way relationship or two one-way relationships in complementary directions. A Security Parameter Index (SPI) uniquely distinguishes each SA from other SAs.

IPSec is controlled specifically by a security policy of both sender and receiver and one or more SAs negotiated between them. The security policy consists of a filter list and associated actions. If some packet's IP address, protocol, or port matches the criteria, a specific security action is applied.

Key management involves the manual or automatic determination and distribution of secret keys between sender and receiver for both AH and ESP. The default protocol, referred to as IKE and previously known as ISAKMP/Oakley, supports automated SA negotiations and the automatic generation of keys. Internet Security Association and Key Management Protocol (ISAKMP) generically defines the management of SAs and keys. Oakley Key Determination Protocol uses public key encryption (sometimes referred to as the Diffie-Hellman encryption algorithm) to exchange and update key materials for the SAs.

IPSec Tunnel and Transport Modes

IPSec is deployed in *tunnel mode*—in which one packet is encapsulated or tunneled in another—or *transport mode*, which secures the packet exchange from end to end, source to destination. IPSec tunnel mode is used primarily for link-to-link packet exchanges between intermediary devices like routers and gateways; transport mode provides the security service between the two communicating endpoints.

IPSec provides different security controls by using the two protocol packet types:

- *IP 50 (ESP) packet type*—Offers authentication, integrity, and confidentiality
- *IP 51 (AH) packet type*—Offers authentication and integrity

Either mode can employ ESP or AH packet types. Both modes require that the two clients engage in a complex negotiation involving the IKE protocol and PKI certificates for mutual authentication.

IPSec tunnel and transport modes as well as L2TP/IPSec encounter incompatibility issues when dealing with NATs. Neither L2TP/IPSec nor IPSec tunnel mode functions when the IKE protocol is used across a NAT. Microsoft is actively encouraging the development of IPSec Remote Access (IPSRA) solutions for this IKE compatibility problem as well as integration with DHCP and other IETF standards for extensible authentication using EAP and General Security Services API (GSS-API).

Microsoft recommends that you choose PPTP in scenarios that require NAT-capable VPN connectivity or where security that requires IPSec or PKI is not a major factor. It supports mutual authentication based on passwords and encryption keys.

Security Protocols Compared

PPP is actually a set of standardized authentication protocols (RFC 1334) that support interoperability among the various kinds of remote access software available. Thus, we can discuss a general PPP dial-up sequence in which various operations, including link configuration and authentication, are performed following the initial connection to some remote PPP server from some PPP client machine. Technical differences among the authentication protocols discussed in the previous sections are summarized in Table 6.1.

Table 6.1 Feature differences among network security protocols.

Feature	PPTP	L2TP	L2TP/IPSec	IPSec Transport	IPSec Tunnel
Consumer authentication	Yes	Yes	Yes	Under development[1]	Under development[1]
Client authentication	Yes[2]	Yes	Yes	Yes	Yes
Packet authentication	No	No	Yes	Yes	Yes
Encryption	Yes	Yes	Yes	Yes	Yes
PKI support	Yes	Yes	Yes	Yes	Yes
NAT capable	Yes	Yes	No	No	No
Multiprotocol support	Yes	Yes	Yes	No	Under development[1]
Dynamic tunnel address assignment	Yes	Yes	Yes	N/A	Under development[1]
Multicast support	Yes	Yes	Yes	No	Yes

[1] *Support is under development by the IETF IPSec working group.*

[2] *The user is authenticated when used as a client VPN; the machine is authenticated in a gateway-to-gateway connection.*

You should be able to arrange components (for example, PPP client, PPP server, RADIUS server, Web Server, Domain Controller) and protocols (for example, TCP/IP, PPP, L2TP, L2TP/IPSec) in some logical order and then connect components with the appropriate protocols. Not all components and protocols will be relevant in the context of the specific situation.

VPN Support

Microsoft currently says that IPSec tunnel mode by itself is a poor choice for most client-to-gateway VPN solutions. Although interoperability problems exist, gateway-to-gateway solutions are functional in tunnel mode. On the other hand, IPSec transport mode effectively delivers end-to-end authenticity and encryption within the network. In client-to-gateway and gateway-to-gateway VPN situations, user authentication and internal address configuration are critical but problematic because most aspects of this part of the VPN technology are either proprietary to the IPSec specifications or are weakly adopted extensions of them.

Note: The IETF IPSec working group is currently developing user authentication and internal (NAT) address features in both tunnel and transport modes. Microsoft has not announced plans to provide IPSec to legacy NT 4 or Windows 9x.

Windows 2000 includes L2TP/IPSec support for packet encryption from client-to-gateway or gateway-to-gateway scenarios and has tested interoperability with a variety of vendor-implemented VPN scenarios. Microsoft supports

L2TP/IPSec only on Windows 2000; it has not announced plans to bring this protocol to legacy operating systems like NT 4 or Windows 9x.

Windows 2000 includes PPTP support for password-based and public-key authentication (the latter through EAP) for both client-to-gateway and gateway-to-gateway configurations across most Windows operating system platforms, including down-level systems like NT 4 and Windows 9x.

Table 6.2 compares network security protocol differences among various VPN connection types.

VPN Management Policies

When an enterprise deploys a remote networking solution, it supports controlled access to resources and assets such as information. This access is provided by both roaming and remote users. In an enterprise, remote offices are just as common as remote users and assume a similar role. The remote local area network (LAN) connects to and shares resources; whether it's doing so across the internal enterprise or an unsecured network like the Internet, the same security controls are necessary because the security demands are the same. Thus, a VPN solution must provide:

- User authentication and auditing
- Address management
- Data encryption
- Key management
- Multiprotocol support

Remote Access Policy Management

In addition to the issues of encryption, Windows 2000 provides an extensive set of administrative policies in both the client-to-gateway and gateway-to-gateway scenarios. These access policies control consumer remote access to network

Table 6.2 VPN effectiveness of the network security protocols.

Connection Type	PPTP	L2TP	L2TP/IPSec	IPSec Transport	IPSec Tunnel
End-to-end (no NAT)	Good	Good	Good	Good	Good
End-to-end (NAT)	Good	Good	Not good	Not good	Not good
Client-to-gateway	Good	Good	Good	Good	Not good
Gateway-to-gateway	Good	Good	Good	Good	Fair

resources through dial-up connections (RRAS), PPTP, and L2TP/IPSec connections. Access and authorization are granted or denied based on a variety of factors, including user ID calling/called station ID, day and time restrictions, TCP/UDP port number, tunnel type, encryption level, and so on. It is noteworthy that these policies are available in both native mode using the AD environment and mixed mode using a legacy NT 4 PDC directory database through the RADIUS protocol. A RADIUS server can also provide proxy services where authentication requests are forwarded to other RADIUS servers in remote locations. Internet Service Providers (ISPs) use this design to provide uninterrupted support services to roaming subscribers. Finally, RADIUS provides call-accounting services for auditing.

Other remote access policy management issues involve the design and placement of calling and answering routers, especially when dealing with a persistent branch office connectivity scenario. If a VPN answering router is deployed to support some remote branch office, it should be dedicated to remote access services and, depending on business needs, typically supports 24/7 access to the local network. VPN calling routers, on the other hand, do not require that guaranteed level of service. Consider hardware, maintenance, and support issues when formulating your remote access policy.

Client Management

The IPSec suite as well as security systems like Kerberos and PKI depend on AD for the definition of security policy. Windows 2000 by default installs the PPTP, L2TP, and IPSec protocols. Client configurations are accomplished in two ways:

- *Client side*—The New Connections Wizard guides the user through a series of dialog boxes to configure the client machine.
- *Administration side*—The Connection Manager Administration Kit and Connection Point Services deliver customized remote access configurations for both direct-dial and VPN client installations.

Firewall Technologies

Windows 2000 divides its security into distributed security within the enterprise and network security, which extends outside the enterprise perimeter. The simplest way to protect a computer system is through physical isolation from outside agents. However, electronic commerce and the need for remote access for mobile computing have forced the opening of the enterprise to outside forces and a hostile unsecured environment. Physical isolation is all but impossible in most network situations. One compromise approach is to allow partial connectivity through some managed bidirectional control or choke point. With this solution—as with a medieval castle—traffic moving to and from the interior of the fortress is forced through a narrow gate with extra-thick walls called the bastion. This heavily fortified central gateway can be closed and defended against attack. The gateway itself is not the security device; it provides an especially defensible setting that complements the military forces housed within the stronghold. Firewall technologies do not replace network security systems; they complement already hardened technologies.

Thus, firewall technologies separate the internal, distributed security network from outside, external namespaces like the Internet. Quite often, a specific topology called a demilitarized zone (DMZ), which physically separates data packet flows, is deployed. This middle area is designed to break the physical continuity between internal data packets and external ones. Just as a brick wall that separates office suites or apartments in large buildings retards or prevents the spread of fires, firewalls can limit network damage through physical containment.

Firewall Components

Firewall technology consists of chokes and various gates. *Chokes* are computers or communication devices that selectively restrict data flows among networks. Although these are often implemented using relatively expensive routers, a simple alternative is a multihomed server built using any computer with two or more network interface cards (NICs). This type of server is inexpensive to install and easy to implement.

Gates, such as packet filter routers and proxy servers, are specially designed software, devices, or computers that handle one or more firewall services or functions. A single computer designated to handle all firewall services is called a *bastion host*. Alternatively, one or more gates that support different functions are positioned inside a middle area or DMZ, as mentioned earlier in this chapter.

Packet Filter Routers

A *packet filter* is a device that examines a datagram or packet for some predefined contents; it is typically a router. Normally, this function is performed at some external router that interfaces with some other network or specifically the Internet. Packet filters work at the OSI Data Link, Network, or Transport layers. Therefore, any implementation requires that you formulate a policy and configure the filter to recognize inbound/outbound IP addresses or TCP/UDP source/destination ports.

Proxy Servers

These service providers act as intermediaries between the host machines within the enterprise and the hosts outside the enterprise namespace. The proxy server plays a significant role in managing IP address ranges by effectively replacing internal address ranges with its own address. This feature, NAT, provides significant protection from the outside attacks by, in effect, hiding the internal network address ranges from outside view. At the same time, it disrupts security protocols that authenticate to those internal addresses from the outside. This topic is discussed in more detail in the "Basic Remote Access Models" section earlier in this section and in Chapter 5. Its caching services improve response time for repeatedly requested Internet information, reduce the need to download material from remote Internet hosts, and reduce the amount of traffic on the Internet. Instead of filtering packets or protocol types, you can achieve higher-level filtering more logically by combining the use of specific Uniform Resource Locators (URLs) with domain names. In addition, you can permit or deny the passage of URL pattern matching, domain names, and host names through the proxy gate. Finally, some applications such as browsers are specifically configured to work exclusively through proxy servers to further control the flow of data to and from the enterprise.

Proxies come in two basic forms:

- *Circuit-level gateway*—Working at the OSI Transport layer, this separates the end-to-end TCP flow of packets by acting as a forwarding agent. The internal host sends its packet to the circuit-level gateway, and the packet is forwarded to the outside target from the gateway. The gateway, in relaying the packets across its own isolated address space, can apply filter rules regarding inbound/outbound TCP/IP addressing.
- *Application-level gateway*—Also called a proxy server, this relays OSI Application-level protocol traffic such as Simple Mail Transfer Protocol (SMTP), HTTP, and File Transfer Protocol (FTP) services. The filtering is application specific, so the application clients must be configured to access the gateway. This type of gateway is more secure than a packet filter gateway because Application-level gateways scan for specific applications, not IP addresses and TCP/UDP port numbers. Alternatively, these gateways add processing overhead to each transmission because all traffic must be examined and then forwarded to its target destination.

Firewall Architectures

A key to good firewall design is to create one choke point through which all outbound and inbound traffic must pass. This single portal, especially when isolated within a separate subnet, offers a defensible embattlement as well as an easily administered focal point for the deployment of network authentication, authorization, and auditing (AAA) services.

It is a conservative assumption that, given enough time and processor/memory firepower, someone will find a method to circumvent *any* firewall technology or topology. However, a well-designed multilayered security system offers sustainable resistance to any attack long enough to do the following:

- ➤ Detect and implement some corrective actions.
- ➤ Exhaust, at least temporarily, the attacker's resources long enough to implement some corrective actions.

You cannot truly deter an attack because, ethically speaking, there is no acceptable counterattack or form of retaliation outside of some form of legal prosecution. In practical terms, there is only a sustainable defense. You should view with suspicion any suggestion that an attack is unlikely due to some cost/benefit or "logical" argument; the motivation behind a security attack may have little to do with either practicality or logic.

Firewall architectures or choke point designs generally assume one of three topologies: packet filter, screened-host, and screened-subnet architectures.

Packet Filter Architecture

The packet filter topology is the most common option and the simplest. It uses a router as both a firewall component and outside, or external, network interface. The router, acting as a choke, relays inbound and outbound packets after inspecting packet IP addresses and TCP/UDP port numbers. Advantages of this option are its cost-effectiveness and low maintenance. Disadvantages include a lack of auditing features, vulnerability as a single-line-of-defense firewall strategy, and the success of the filter rules in rejecting rogue (authenticated but unauthorized) or bogus (unauthenticated) packets. Attacks to a packet filter router include:

- ➤ IP address spoofs that impersonate legitimate source IP addresses
- ➤ Source routing attacks in which specific routes across source-routing bridges are specified in an attempt to bypass inspection
- ➤ Tiny fragment attacks that circumvent the TCP filtering rules by sending illegally sized packets

Figure 6.2 shows a packet-filtering router architecture.

Screened-Host Architecture

This topology uses a computer (the host) as a gateway behind the packet-filtering (screening) external network interface. Figure 6.3 shows a screened-host architecture with a single-homed bastion.

A single-homed host or server has only one NIC and one IP address. When more than one NIC is added to the screened-host firewall, the bastion is considered a dual-homed (or multihomed) host or server. These servers are also sometimes

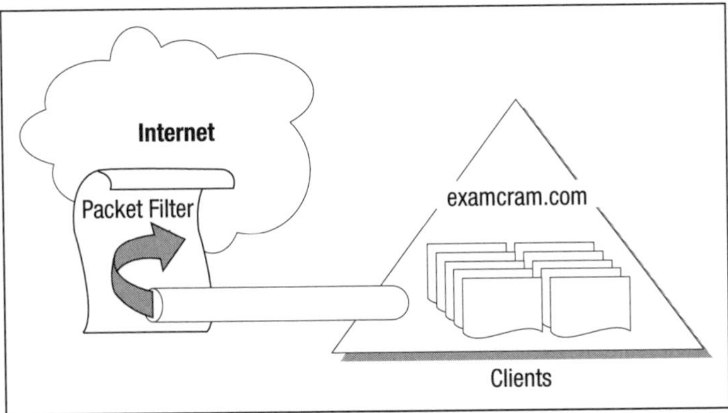

Figure 6.2 A packet-filtering (screening) router.

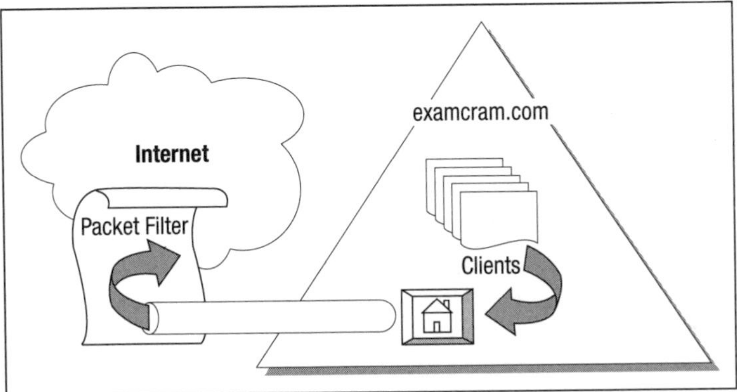

Figure 6.3 A screened-host (single-homed server) firewall.

called *dual-ported hosts*. IP packet forwarding must be disabled so that rules and policies determine which packets are relayed across the two or more NIC cards and the IP subnet spaces. Similarly, network users should be prevented from logging on to this server. Figure 6.4 shows a screened-host architecture with a dual-homed bastion.

The packet filter sends inbound packets directly to the bastion host and, similarly, accepts only outbound traffic from the bastion host. Thus, the bastion host is a choke point through which all outbound traffic must be directed. In addition to serving as a circuit-level gateway, the bastion typically functions as an Application-level gateway behind which externally accessible SMTP and HTTP application service providers can, in effect, hide. Advantages of dual-homed servers include a more sophisticated firewall technology than single-homed servers because the bastion, physically separate from the packet filter, also supports circuit-level and Application-level gateway services. The firewall now

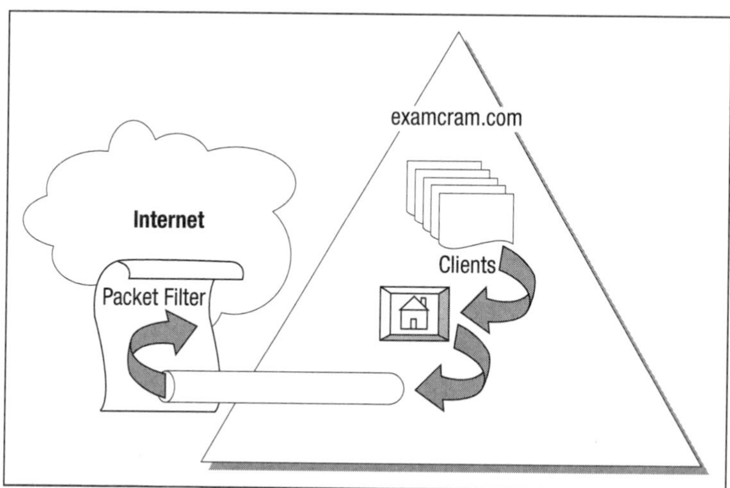

Figure 6.4 A screened-host (dual-homed server) firewall.

has a second line of defense that is technologically different from the first line of defense (the packet filter). With the addition of a multihomed server, the physical separation of IP address ranges adds a further level of complexity and hides the internal IP address ranges, thwarting, for example, the spoofing that can defeat a packet filter. Disadvantages of a bastion include increased cost, increased overhead, and reduced performance (as compared to packet filters) because packets must pass through at least two distinct firewall layers. With the increase in rules and policies, users typically experience a decrease in provided services. For example, policies may disallow some online services such as inbound Telnet.

Screened-Subnet Architecture (DMZ)

The last and most secure design is to isolate a subnet between two screening packet filters. Figure 6.5 shows a picture of this topology.

In this DMZ located between the two packet filters, the multihomed bastion host supports client-level and Application-level gateways. In addition, however, the externally accessible application service providers (such as SMTP, FTP, and HTTP servers) are deployed in this subnet. Both external and internal screening packet filters direct inbound and outbound traffic, respectively, through the bastion host. Application servers must also direct their traffic through the bastion because the external packet filter rejects outbound packets from any other source. Advantages of the DMZ architecture include three distinct lines of defense; two perimeter packet filters and one multihomed bastion. The DMZ physically separates the internal network from the outside world. The bastion host is not only a choke point for both inbound and outbound traffic but also effectively conceals private IP address ranges. Neither inbound nor outbound packets can bypass this

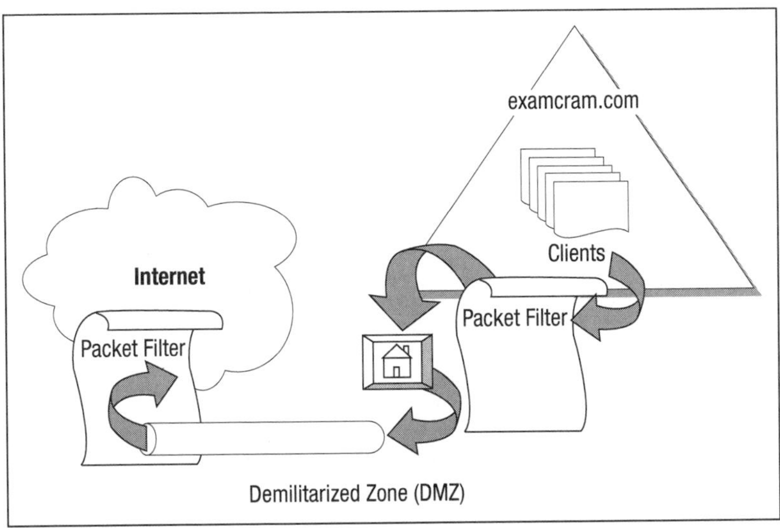

Figure 6.5 A screened-subnet firewall (DMZ) architecture.

security topology, so no a priori assumptions are made regarding the possible staging area for some security attack.

Of the three firewall architectures—packet filtering, screened hosts, and screened subnets—the screened-subnet firewall (or DMZ) topology is the most secure and makes the fewest assumptions regarding the origins of a security attack.

Firewall Policies

Just as with any other security technology, policy precedes implementation. Corporate objectives must define what will pass and what will be blocked at the firewall choke point for both inbound and outbound data. These rules, like IP filters (defined in Chapter 5), determine how the firewall mechanism operates. The firewall operates according to one of two basic strategies:

- *Default permit*—What is not expressly prohibited is, by default, permitted.
- *Default deny*—What is not expressly permitted is, by default, prohibited.

The two strategies differ primarily in the degree of management; a default permit strategy requires that you explicitly list hosts or protocols that are considered security threats; otherwise, it offers a relatively open gateway to and from the enterprise namespace. Alternatively, a default deny strategy enables pass-through only upon request for that passage case by case; it requires much more management but is more conservative in its restrictive approach to the data flows. It is noteworthy that the default deny strategy errs administratively on the side of greater, more restrictive, security. This is, however, a safer defensive posture when an enterprise borders on any public network, including the Internet. Even the most restrictive firewall policies are not panaceas, nor should you view them as turnkey security solutions when defending a network from any attack modality.

Firewall technologies and IPSec can be considered first-line defenses in securing the enterprise from a hostile assault. It is important to realize that these technologies can be deployed without any assumption regarding from which direction the attack will take place—from outside or inside the secured enterprise namespace.

Positioning firewalls at network choke points can:

- Block access to specific Internet sites by host address, address range, or protocol type (for example, FTP or Telnet).
- Audit inbound and outbound data flows or protocol type; an example is corporate-sanctioned passive interception or eavesdropping.
- Provide the basis for secured information exchanges across unsecured namespaces using a VPN.
- Simplify the authentication process within an especially secured subnet within the enterprise namespace.

Practice Questions

Case Study

4Sale, an online bartering company in ThatTherePlace, North Dakota, focuses primarily on selling inexpensive, odd lot items. A merger between 4Sale and Got-a-Deal has been finalized and both companies have merged office space in the same office building. The corporate side of the merger has gone well and the staff is fully adjusted. The IT department, though well staffed, still needs your help.

Current LAN/Network Structure

4Sale is presently running Windows 2000 Server in native mode; one member server supports Exchange, whereas another is running Internet Information Server 5 and Proxy Server 2. All 100 client machines are configured in a single-domain model. The client systems are running Windows Professional, with Office 97 being utilized as an applications package. Each system is connected to a 10Mbps hub through 10Mbps LAN cards running Category 5 UTP cabling in a star topology.

Got-a-Deal is running all 22 client machines in one child domain under the 4Sale root domain. The client systems are running Windows Professional, with Office 97 being utilized as an applications package. Each system is connected to a 10Mbps hub through 10Mbps LAN cards running Category 5 UTP cabling in a star topology. These hubs are on the same backbone as 4Sale but have a different subnet.

Proposed LAN/Network Structure

4Sale is developing its online barter/trading business through business alliances. It is now investigating the use of remote access for employees and secured private networks for branch offices and business alliances.

Current WAN Connectivity

4Sale has a T1 connection to an ISP in OverHere, North Dakota. Got-a-Deal has 56Kbps dial-up networking connectivity through the same ISP.

Proposed WAN Connectivity

No changes are planned at this time.

Directory Design Commentary

Network Manager at 4Sale says, "We are negotiating with several companies on the West coast. How can we give them limited access to our network?"

Current Internet Positioning

4Sale is registered as **4sale.com**. Got-a-Deal has been selling its goods through local companies and through the **4sale.com** Web site.

Future Internet Plans

No changes in the current structure are proposed at this time.

Company Goal with Windows 2000

4Sale has put you on retainer and has given you strict orders that there should always be a higher level of control than what any one department or division individually proposes. You continue to help develop the standards and procedures that the IT department will implement.

Question 1

Considering the case study provided, what issue might be a major concern if you want to use L2TP/IPSec? Give a simple answer that emphasizes the key points of the case study.

- ❍ a. UDP filtering policy
- ❍ b. Authentication and encryption
- ❍ c. Client-to-gateway connections
- ❍ d. All of the above
- ❍ e. None of the above

Answer d is correct. Answer a is correct because Layer 2 Tunneling Protocol tunneled in Internet Protocol uses User Datagram Protocol port 1701 for tunnel maintenance. Answer b is correct because compressed or encrypted Point-To-Point Protocol frames are encapsulated in L2TP; IP Security provides authenticity, integrity, and confidentiality. Answer c is correct because L2TP was specifically designed for client-to-gateway connections. Because all the answers are correct, answer d is the best choice.

Question 2

Network Manager for 4Sale asks, "If we install a proxy server, what protocols can we use?" You must consider the impact of Network Address Translation (NAT) in answering this question. Which protocols can pass through a NAT? [Check all correct answers]

- ❑ a. PPTP
- ❑ b. L2TP/PPP
- ❑ c. IPSec transport mode
- ❑ d. IPSec tunnel mode

Answers a and b are correct. PPTP and L2TP/PPP can both pass through a NAT, so they can be used in conjunction with a proxy server. IP Security, because of incompatibilities with the automated exchange of keys, does not function properly when network addresses are translated. Therefore, answers c and d are incorrect.

Question 3

Network Manager for 4Sale asks, "Do I have to leave the RRAS server up all the time?" For future growth projections, distinguish between answering routers (RRAS servers enabled for VPN) and calling routers or local RRAS servers that are calling, for example, a home office. Choose the correct statements from the following options.

- ❑ a. Answering routers must be dedicated.
- ❑ b. Calling routers must be dedicated.
- ❑ c. Answering routers do not have to be dedicated.
- ❑ d. Calling routers do not have to be dedicated.

Answers a and d are correct. Answering routers must be dedicated, and calling routers do not have to be dedicated. Answer b is incorrect because it doesn't matter whether the calling router is dedicated. A client or calling router makes requests either on demand or on a fixed schedule. The answering router however, must be accessible 24/7 to handle incoming requests. Answer c is incorrect because answer a is correct.

Question 4

Network Manager says, "What configuration provides the least exposure to internal IP address ranges?" The Network Manager is asking several question at once. He mentions internal IP addresses, which suggests that there are external and internal addresses. This, in turn, implies the use of a NAT, which implies that the VPN is located in such as way that it protects the integrity of the internal network addressing scheme.

Place the following in their proper order to indicate the flow of a packet through a firewall. Start at the highest level and work toward the bottom, with the bottom being the strongest applied.

External source

Bastion server

External packet filter router

Internal network

VPN server

Internal packet filter

The correct order is:

External source

External packet filter router

Bastion server

VPN server

Internal packet filter

Internal network

Question 5

Network Manager for 4Sale says, "What is the most flexible protocol that can be both encrypted and compressed?"

❍ a. L2TP

❍ b. PPTP

❍ c. Both are the same in terms of encryption and compression

❍ d. Neither can be encrypted or compressed

Answer a is correct. Layer 2 Tunneling Protocol is the most flexible protocol that can be both encrypted and compressed. Although both Layer 2 Tunneling Protocol and Point-To-Point Tunneling Protocol use Transmission Control Protocol connections for tunnel maintenance and generic routing encapsulation (GRE) to encapsulate Point-To-Point Protocol frames for tunneled data, they are not the same in terms of encryption and compression. PPTP is not as flexible as L2TP because PPTP requires IP, whereas L2TP requires only that tunnel media provide point-to-point connectivity. PPTP supports only a single tunnel, but L2TP allows the use of multiple tunnels. L2TP uses 4 bytes of overhead when compression is enabled; PPTP uses 6. L2TP alone provides tunnel authentication; PPTP does not.

Question 6

Network Manager of 4Sale says, "We have a static IP address on the Internet. In simple terms, what kinds of scenarios are we talking about for remote access for our offices and staff?" You want to suggest no more than three scenarios. The Network Manager suggests two. The best two scenarios to use in this conversation with the Network Manager are:

Remote access for employees

Persistent branch office

Place the following items in the appropriate scenarios (the design flow is from the remote client end coming into the 4Sale internal network):

VPN calling server

VPN client

VPN answering server

T1

Internet cloud

ISP

The correct answer is:

Remote access for employees

VPN client

ISP

Internet cloud

VPN answering server

Persistent branch office

VPN calling server

T1

ISP

Internet cloud

VPN answering server

Question 7

Network Manager of 4Sale says, "If we really involve ourselves in remote access, is there a scalable approach that might incorporate long-term management features like auditing and accounting?" You need to discuss RADIUS. What is its key feature?

❍ a. Ability to authenticate users through methods other than Windows 2000

❍ b. Support for multiple VPN and/or RRAS servers configured with a common policy

❍ c. Centralized call-accounting services

❍ d. Proxy service to forward authentication

❍ e. All of the above

Answer e is correct. Remote Authentication Dial-In User Service offers the ability to authenticate both Windows 2000 and non-Windows users, support for multiple Virtual Private Network and/or Routing and Remote Access Service (RRAS) servers configured with a common policy, centralized call-accounting services, and proxy service to forward authentication to other RADIUS servers.

Question 8

Network Manager for 4Sale says, "What are the advantages of using Layer 2 protocols?" You want to explain that Layer 2 protocols inherit authentication methods from PPP. Which of the following authentication methods are inherited? [Check all correct answers]

❑ a. PAP

❑ b. CHAP

❑ c. SPAP

❑ d. EAP-TLS

Answers a, b, c, and d are correct. Microsoft Virtual Private Networks support all these Data Link layer (OSI Layer 2) authentication protocols. PAP (Password Authentication Protocol), a weak method, uses a clear-text authentication scheme. CHAP (Challenge Handshake Authentication Protocol) does not transmit the actual password and is thus a stronger scheme than PAP. Remote consumers use a Message Digest 5 hash of their credentials in response to a challenge by a network access server. SPAP (Shiva Password Authentication Protocol) is used in mixed environments that support Shiva Local Area Network Rover software. Finally, EAP-TLS (Extensible Authentication Protocol - Transaction Level Security) is a Microsoft implementation of a strong authentication method that uses public-key certificates.

Need to Know More?

Garfinkel, Simson and Gene Spafford. *Practical Unix and Internet Security, Second Edition.* O'Reilly & Associates, Sebastopol, CA, 1996. ISBN 1-56592-148-8. Chapter 21 of this book contains a detailed discussion of firewall technology. Chapter 22 discusses wrappers and proxies, as well as SOCKS. A separate section offers a 90-page discussion on how to handle security incidents. Although this book is specifically about the Unix architecture, these sections are well written and relevant to Windows 2000.

McLean, Ian. *Windows 2000 Security Little Black Book.* The Coriolis Group, Scottsdale, AZ, 2000. ISBN 1-57610-387-0. The author discusses VPNs in Chapter 11 and follows topical discussions with "Immediate Solutions" sections that explain, in a step-by-step format, how to implement the specific security technique. Chapter 11 concisely discusses how to configure VPN servers and clients. This book is designed primarily as a quick reference and resource for immediate solutions to problems that you encounter in the field.

Murhammer, Martin W., et al. *TCP/IP Tutorial and Technical Overview, Sixth Edition.* Prentice Hall, Upper Saddle River, NJ, 1998. ISBN 0-13-020130-8. Part 2, "Special Purpose Protocols and New Technologies," contains information about security breaches, cryptography, firewalls, NAT, and IPSec. This book, though written from a Unix perspective and focusing on both transport and network protocols, describes many security aspects in great detail. Most topics are relevant to the Windows 2000 environment.

Search the TechNet CD (or its online version through **www.microsoft.com**) and the *Windows 2000 Server Resource Kit* CD using the keywords "VPN", "PPTP", "L2TP", and "EAP". This is Microsoft's definitive online resource for technical papers and bulletins.

www.microsoft.com/ISN/ind_solutions/virtual_private_networking.asp?RLD=90 This is the home page for Microsoft Internet Services Network, a subscription service. It offers featured articles, technical and strategic white papers, and downloads like the Internet Services Connection for RAS, Commercial Edition. This is a subscription service. When using this or other technical resources, I strongly recommend that you disregard papers that refer to Windows 2000 as NT 5 or papers that are more than a year old. Using the NT 5 abbreviation suggests that the material is seriously dated and might misrepresent or inadequately describe actual Windows 2000 features and configurations.

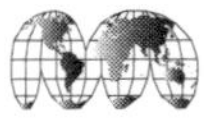

www.microsoft.com/windows2000/library/howitworks/communications/remoteaccess/vpnoverview.asp This is the location of Microsoft's Windows 2000 White Paper, titled *Virtual Private Networking: An Overview,* originally posted in April 1999. This paper describes VPN technology used on Microsoft Windows 2000 Server and provides an overview of VPNs, describing basic requirements and key technologies that permit private networking to be provided over public internetworks.

www.vpnc.org/ietf-ipsec is the Virtual Private Network Consortium (VPNC) Web site. This home page points to many important collections of material that relates to VPN and IPSec. It also offers RFCs and Internet drafts on related topics. Tables describe many features supported by VPNC's members in their software and hardware. There is a section on interoperability issues and a separate section on VPN terms, which is particularly useful when you are learning relevant terminology that pertains to remote connectivity issues.

Other Network Issues

Terms you'll need to understand:

- ✓ Principals
- ✓ UUEncoding
- ✓ Secure Channel (SChannel) security protocols
- ✓ Secure Hypertext Transfer Protocol (S-HTTP)
- ✓ Application Specifications For Windows 2000
- ✓ Secure Multipurpose Internet Mail Extensions (S/MIME)
- ✓ Fortezza Crypto Card technology
- ✓ Lightweight Directory Access Protocol (LDAP) version 3
- ✓ Meta-directory
- ✓ Directory consolidation technologies
- ✓ Active Directory Connector (ADC)
- ✓ Microsoft Directory Synchronization Services (MSDSS)
- ✓ Certificate practices statement

Techniques you'll need to master:

- ✓ Deploying security methods for intranet, Internet, and extranet Web sites
- ✓ Describing different Internet Information Server (IIS) authentication security methods
- ✓ Describing Secure Sockets Layer (SSL) in combination with X.509 v3 client certificates
- ✓ Describing differences between e-commerce and intranet connectivity issues
- ✓ Developing strategies for consolidating directory services

This chapter shows you how to configure and use Internet Information Server (IIS) and Secure Sockets Layer (SSL). With the default installation of IIS as part of the Windows 2000 operating system, Web security is not only relevant in real life but also figures prominently in any series of case studies that Microsoft will present in an examination setting. As I explain later in this chapter in the context of identity management, the Windows 2000 enterprise goes far beyond what the legacy NT 4 domain model would typically support.

The basic dichotomy of distributed and network security services, as described in Chapter 6, was useful in the NT 4 domain model to determine the initial scope of a security plan. With the integration of Web access and remote access in Windows 2000, however, an enterprise scenario now includes many forms of network connectivity outside the boundaries of the enterprise. You will see that the Internet and remote connectivity radically change the scope of your enterprise as well as its security requirements. I will distinguish these different service areas with regard to control and responsibility as well as design and deployment; each kind of connectivity contributes specific costs and benefits to the total cost of ownership (TCO).

Historical trends cited in Chapter 2 suggest a gradual differentiation in the distributed server architecture with increased specialization. I use Chapter 8 to describe how the boundary of distributed services inside an internal network is dissolving and how the dichotomy of distributed and networked services is losing significance in the Windows 2000 enterprise. In an Active Directory (AD) of over a million objects, there is, in relative terms, literally a universe of resources from which a consumer can request services. In Chapter 2, I describe the primary information technology (IT) security controls: identification, authentication, and authorization. In a corporate environment, identification is restricted to a limited namespace of known users or principals. However, you should pay more immediate attention to authentication and authorization, because both form the substrate on which all exchanges of digital information are made. In the AD of over a million objects, identification must come first. Confidentiality and non-repudiation always complement these primary security controls. The last two sections of this chapter, "Permission Management" and "Identity Management," suggest important developmental trends that Microsoft claims, are already works in progress. The discussion of these technologies and trends in Chapter 8 will help you design a security infrastructure that accommodates the breadth of Windows 2000 enterprise services, heterogeneous environments that demand interoperability, and the constantly evolving forces that drive e-commerce and network connectivity.

IIS 5

In Windows 2000, IIS 5 provides a scalable environment for hosting Internet, intranet, and extranet Web sites. Services include access to virtual servers, virtual directories, or published documents. Granting a request for IIS services depends upon passing sequentially through four separate security control layers:

1. *Internet Protocol (IP) address and domain name security*—Access based on network address or domain name regardless of group membership.
2. *IIS authentication security*—Access based on authentication method regardless of group membership.
3. *IIS permissions*—Access determined on the basis of Web-clients assigned permissions to published resources regardless of group membership.
4. *NT File System (NTFS) security permissions*—Access to physical data stores is determined by the access control list (ACL) of the specific resource. The ACL provides greater granularity in control than IIS permissions, specifically in differentiating group membership. The other three methods apply to all consumers regardless of group membership.

Note: IIS 5 uses two layers of access control: Web (IIS) permissions and NTFS permissions. The Web permissions define how the web clients accesses resources; NTFS permissions define how individual accounts access server resources

Network Addressing and Domain Name Security

By configuring IP address ranges or Domain Name System (DNS) domain names, the IIS server grants or denies access to resources. This gross, low level security setting acts as a gate that controls access to all resources exclusively on the basis of network addressing as opposed to a more granular control based on user identity or group membership. Methods for configuring these security restrictions vary depending on the kind of resource:

- *To configure virtual servers, directories, or subdirectories*—Right-click on the object's node in the Internet Services Manager and select Properties|Directory Security|Edit.
- *To configure file restrictions*—Right-click on the object's node in the MMC and select Properties|File Security|Edit.

Similar to firewalls, the restrictions with regard to the network addresses and domain names are based on one of the following basic strategies:

- *Default permit*—That which is not expressly prohibited is, *by default*, permitted.
- *Default deny*—That which is not expressly permitted is, *by default*, prohibited.

For example, by applying the principle of least privilege ("only enough access to get the job done"), the *default deny* strategy prohibits all external, public network access except for access expressly permitted, such as traffic to and from a business partner's extranet. Similarly, only the traffic from one particular subnet in an intranet is allowed access to some virtual directory; all other traffic is denied.

IIS Authentication Security

Four IIS authentication schemes are available:

- *Anonymous access*—An Everyone user category that allows access to all resources.
- *Basic authentication*—A valid Windows 2000 user account and password are required to request services.
- *Digest authentication for Windows domain servers*—Valid only in Windows 2000 domains. With an Internet Explorer browser version 5 or higher, a password's hash value (rather than the password itself) is transmitted across a network, firewall, or proxy server.
- *Integrated Windows authentication*—An example of Single Sign-On (SSO) where authentication of an account during the logon process is transparently applied during subsequent requests for service and access to resources. Integrated Windows authentication uses a cryptographic exchange between browser and server to confirm the user.

You should use Integrated Windows authentication only when anonymous access is disabled or anonymous access is denied because the Windows file system permissions require a user to provide logon information before a connection can be established.

Access control extends to all Web content, virtual servers (individually hosted Web sites), virtual directories, and physical subdirectories and their contents on the host Web server. A default authentication setting for all virtual servers (Web sites) on a physical Web server can be applied through Computer Management in Administrative Tools. Under Internet Information Services, in the WWW Service Master Properties dialog box as well as an Inheritance Overrides option, which allows some virtual servers to have their own authentication methods independent of default settings. By default, all virtual servers inherit settings in the WWW Service Master Properties dialog box.

Anonymous Access

Upon installation, IIS creates an Internet Guest account, IUSR_*Servername*, where *Servername* is the machine name of the physical Web server. This account is a member of the Guests local group (assuming IIS services are running on a member server), has a nonexpiring password that cannot be changed, and has been assigned the user right to Log On Locally. By default, Allow Anonymous Access is enabled on the Authentication Methods dialog box. Regarding deployment strategies, this setting is acceptable in the following scenarios:

- For Web sites that are low-risk, public Internet areas
- Within an intranet, where this account simplifies administration

IUSR_*Servername* is a member of the Guests group, so this account inherits any changes to rights or permissions made to that group during or sometime after installation of the Web server. You should periodically test the security scope of this group account with respect to outside Internet connectivity.

Basic Authentication

Basic authentication is the standard Hypertext Transfer Protocol (HTTP) user authentication method that most browsers support. Any consumer who requests Web services encounters an Enter Network Password dialog box that requests a username and password. An intruder detection feature is associated with the dialog box; after three unsuccessful attempts, an error message (401.1 Unauthorized Logon Failed) is returned to the consumer.

This form of authentication, however, is not secure because the username and password are encoded using a technique called *UUEncoding*, which translates the message into an easily decipherable string of American Standard Code for Information Interchange (ASCII) characters. This encoded string is placed in the HTTP Get Request Packet and sent to the server that provides the Web services. You can strengthen basic authentication, however, by combining it with SSL encryption to provide a secure method of authentication in heterogeneous environments. The disadvantage, however, is that the stronger encryption negatively impacts on server performance.

Regarding deployment strategies, basic authentication is useful in the following situations:

- Where security is low and non-Windows authentication is required
- Where browsers do not support integrated Windows authentication methods (discussed shortly)

- In extranet scenarios where security is needed and the information can be considered confidential but has no security classification (sensitive but unclassified—SBU—as discussed in Chapter 8).

Digest Authentication

Though not an Internet standard and currently supported only by Internet Explorer version 5 while accessing a Windows 2000 domain controller (DC), digest authentication (RFC 2069) improves upon basic authentication by passing the security credentials in a hashed format. A Windows 2000 domain must be specially configured to use digest authentication, as follows:

- The Web server must be running IIS 5 and must be in a Windows 2000 domain.
- The Save Password As Encrypted Clear Text must be enabled in the User account property sheet in the AD Users And Computers MMC snap-in.

Regarding deployment strategies, within a Windows 2000 intranet, this method provides greater security than basic authentication. It is a hashed value, so it passes through firewalls and proxy servers.

Integrated Windows Authentication

This method is the most secure of the authentication schemes because the consumer exchanges encrypted packets with the server. At no time is the actual password exchanged. Although all Microsoft browser software versions 2 or higher support this authentication method, no version of Netscape Navigator does. SSO depends upon which Windows platform you use to access the IIS server:

- *If you are a Windows 2000 domain user*—All exchanges involving the Web server are transparent. The only requirement here is that the initial authentication has taken place.
- *If you are requesting services from a non-Windows 2000 system*—The Enter Network Password dialog box is displayed. The initial authentication must again take place before Web-related services are rendered.

Regarding deployment strategies, with integrated Windows authentication, it is necessary to enforce the appropriate account policy, especially regarding passwords, through the Domain Security Policy MMC snap-in. With the policy in place and a written network security policy distributed to all users, this method is appropriate in high-security situations where domain users access Web resources. Similarly, both Windows 2000 and 98 clients benefit from SSO.

Combination Authentication Methods

If you use the Anonymous account in combination with some other authentication method, such as basic or integrated authentication, anonymous access to the resource is attempted first. If, for whatever reason, this access attempt fails (see the "IIS Permissions" and "NTFS Permissions" sections coming up shortly), a second, stronger authentication method that requires a username and password is used. In other combinations, integrated Windows authentication has precedence over all other methods.

IIS Permissions

The Web server can control access to the resources it hosts through global security settings for each object. These settings, done through the property sheets within the Context menus of the specific objects, affect access regardless of group membership. Access permissions such as Read, Write, and Execute, which involve exclusively running scripts or both scripts and executables, are enabled for a virtual directory through these settings. Conversely, you can configure a condition where no executables are allowed to run in a directory.

Combining NTFS and IIS Permissions

The access to physical directories and files on the Web server is based on how you configure NTFS. This access method, available only if the storage medium is formatted using NTFS, allows granularity that is unavailable with any of the other methods described in the "IIS Authentication Security" section earlier in this chapter. You can assign different permissions on the basis of user and group. This topic is discussed in greater detail in Chapter 9.

Regarding deployment strategies, always confirm that the Everyone group has been removed from ACLs on any virtual directories or Web pages. Assign the built-in Users group Read access permission to the specific sites. To minimize administration, consider a policy that what is not expressly prohibited is permitted (default permit). Restrict access by assigning problem users to a No Access group, which overrides the individual's effective permissions to the resource.

A more secure strategy than using NTFS permissions alone is to combine NTFS with IIS permissions. A possible strategic combination would be to assign IIS Read permission for directory browsing, NTFS Read permission to a local Users group, and Full Control to a local Administrators group. Using an NTFS No Access permission would deny access to any user or group to even browse the directory. In such a situation, explicitly denying access overrides permissions that explicitly grant access. Also apply the rule of least privilege, where access is allowed only to resources necessary and sufficient to complete the assigned job function. You should enable the execution of scripts as opposed to binary executables to control a user's range of activities in or outside the accessible virtual directory.

Other Security Methods

Besides the security methods mentioned previously, there are three other noteworthy methods of securing IIS servers, as follows:

- Disabling services, protocols, and bindings
- Disabling directory browsing
- Logging and auditing

In this section, I discuss each one in turn.

Disabling Services, Protocols, and Bindings

Disabling services, protocols, and bindings offers you several benefits. When you disable unnecessary services, you immediately see an increase in performance because of the decrease in demands on system resources. If a service or protocol is not available, a mistake in configuration that might otherwise impact performance is less likely to occur. However, the most important detail in disabling services is to minimize access to resources that an intruder might exploit in a security attack.

Regarding deployment strategies, by disabling the Server service on a dedicated Web server, you stop supporting shares, a potential point of entry to your Web server. Make certain, however, that you understand *all* dependencies that exist among services before you take such an action. A less radical strategy is to build a multihomed server with a second network interface card (NIC) (see the discussion of firewalls in Chapter 6). This design not only helps secure the Web server and your internal network but can segregate services on either the internal or external networks via the two network interfaces. Similarly, if you unbind or eliminate unnecessary protocols on either one of these two NICs, you not only improve the efficiency of your protocol stack, but you also minimize configuration errors in some network or system setting.

If the Server service, which uses the Server Message Block (SMB) protocol, is allowed to function over the Internet, you are in violation of the Microsoft licensing agreement that applies to the SMB protocol; you need to obtain additional licensing for Windows 2000 Server.

Disabling Directory Browsing

It is especially important to disable the ability to browse directories in a virtual server, virtual directory, or folder. This is one of the IIS permissions, mentioned earlier in this chapter, that you can configure through the property sheets within the Context menus of the specific objects. Make certain that the checkbox control for Directory Browsing Allowed is clear (disabled).

Logging and Auditing

One of the least expensive and probably most important tools in securing your IIS server is logging all IP activity. Both baseline and regular monitoring provide diagnostic tools to help analyze typical workloads, as well as indicate unusual external and internal activity. Periodic review of logs should include monitoring authenticated users, especially those making frequent visits to unusual internal areas. Such atypical behavior could indicate some security breach in your internal network. In fact, the combination of IIS logging with NTFS auditing and the Everyone group provides the most comprehensive security view of your Web server.

Auditing successful and failed logons and logoffs provides information about users and possible intruders, respectively. The failure of File And Object Access can similarly alert you to attempts to use unauthorized resources. Although using auditing impacts your system performance, the benefits of detecting an attack early can easily outweigh the performance penalties. You must remember, though, that to detect a breach in security, you must systematically review logs on a timely and consistent basis.

Secure Channel (SChannel) Protocols

In Chapter 2, I used the generic scenario of consumer and service provider to describe the various attack modalities. In the context of a Web server like IIS, we can again focus on the possible targets of a security attack, namely:

- Client browser
- Web server
- Traffic through the session pipe

The issue of traffic security rests upon authentication of client browser (consumer), Web server (Hypertext Transfer Protocol (HTTP) service provider), and the connection between the two, especially across public networks. Collectively, the issue of traffic security rests on a secure end-to-end service. The security of that service begins with confirming the authenticity of the two ends followed by securing the session between them. Both SSL and Transport Layer Security (TLS) protocols rely on public-key–based authentication and session key negotiations. They are associated with another common security protocol, Secure Hypertext Transfer Protocol (S-HTTP), although they operate at the Open Systems Interconnection (OSI) Transport layer (discussed in the "Transport Layer Security Technologies" section in Chapter 6) and have a different security focus. S-HTTP secures the transmission of individual messages; SSL/TLS creates a secure connection by authenticating two computers. This section describes how that is done.

SSL3/TLS1

Originally developed by Netscape, SSL3 allows you to encrypt information between a browser client and a Web server by using public key cryptography (see Chapter 4) and digital certificates (see Chapters 3 and 4). TLS, published as Request for Comments (RFC) 2246, represents a common proposed standard that incorporates SSL3 features. Though the two protocols are functionally the same, architectural differences between them are significant enough to raise interoperability issues. TLS1, however, can negotiate back down to SSL3. When used in conjunction with a browser, SSL/TLS, and a secure protocol designated as S-HTTP, use Transmission Control Protocol (TCP) to provide a secured end-to-end pipe between consumer and service provider. (Enterprise Integration Technologies developed S-HTTP in 1995.)

Deployment of SSL

A typical SSL session between a consumer and a Web server occurs as follows:

1. A certificate is issued to the Web server and installed on the Web server.
2. SSL is enabled on a virtual server or directory on that Web server using the Directory Security panel in the specific object's property sheet.
3. You must have stored on your browser a Certificate Authority (CA) certificate that contains the CA's public key to decrypt issued certificates.
4. You access the SSL-enabled virtual server using a secured Uniform Resource Locator (URL) such as **https://myweb.mysecuredserver.com** across TCP. You then encounter a security alert message that notifies you that you are about to view pages over a secured connection. If you do not have a copy of the CA's public key, a message saying the certificate issuer is untrusted appears. At this point in the exchange, you can install the CA certificate in the trusted root (certificate) store in your browser using the Certificate Import Wizard.
5. When your browser can read the server's digital certificate, the session pipe between you and the SSL-enabled Web site is established, keys are exchanged, and the encryption of information provides secured data.

Certificate Services

A *digital certificate* is a text file issued by some trusted certificate service provider (or Certificate Authority—CA) that corroborates the identity and credentials of the application or consumer. It usually also contains the public key in a digital envelope encrypted with the CA's private key. In fact, the only requirement of a CA is that it accurately bind security credentials to a public key. The authority of a CA is based on the namespace from which the identifying credentials are chosen. The CA must guarantee that all the security attributes that make up the credentials are accurate and that the list of endorsed account names are current. Only the CA's public key decrypts the envelope, so you can be confident that the certificate is authentic and unaltered.

The CA is a trusted service provider and is very often an outside third party such as VeriSign (**www.verisign.com**) and its subsidiary, Thawte (**www.thawte.com**). VeriSign provides global enterprise certificates, whereas Thawte caters to the global small-business market that requires entry-level SSL solutions. VeriSign, for example, offers a Class 1 certificate, which requires filling out an application form, through a Class 3 certificate, where credentials are notarized. A CA documents its practices in a certification practices statement. IIS can use third-party services or Microsoft Certificate Services, discussed later in this chapter, as an internally managed, private provider of these certificate services.

Certificates play an important role in Windows 2000 by providing three IT security controls: integrity, confidentiality, and nonrepudiation. These were briefly discussed in Chapter 2 and are involved in the Encrypting File System (EFS) (discussed in Chapter 9). These controls are a critical component of smart cards (discussed in Chapter 12), and you need them when verifying the parties in Web exchanges. The certificate identifies and encrypts information exchanged between consumer and service provider. It contains the holder's public key; an expiration date; and credentials about the holder such as name, address, and so on.

These certificates are widely used throughout the enterprise and are thus a critical component of Windows 2000 public key infrastructure (PKI), which runs transparently in the OSI Application layer. In general terms, a client (client digital certificate), a server (server digital certificate), and an application (application digital certificate) are all considered authentic principals because the same trusted CA corroborates their credentials. The first CA installed in an enterprise is called the *root CA*; it signs its own site or CA certificate. Certificates are issued to many objects in the enterprise, including:

- EFS Recovery Agent
- Basic EFS
- DCs

- Web servers
- Client machines
- Users
- Subordinate CAs
- Administrators

Certificate Server Tools

A Certificate Server provides several services: administration (creating certificates), logging (tracking requests for certificates), and revocation (maintaining lists of revoked certificates). Both Internet Explorer version 2 or higher and Netscape Navigator version 3 or higher support these certificates. A database logs the life cycle (the request, issuance, and revocation) of each certificate. The Certificate Services Manager MMC provides certificate services. There are four nodes, located under the root certificate authority, in the Certificate Authority MMC snap-in:

- Revoked Certificates
- Issued Certificates
- Pending Certificates
- Failed Certificates

Deploying Security for Distributed Services

You can address network security in general and Web security in particular at several OSI layers. One strategic approach is to deploy security technologies at the OSI Network layer by using IP Security (IPSec), discussed in Chapter 5. These gross, low-level techniques screen traffic flowing through the session pipe on the basis of network address schemes. Another more focused approach is at the OSI Transport layer using SSL/TLS technologies. Both are application independent and transparent to the consumer. An example of an OSI Application layer technique would be the use of S-HTTP.

Yet another category of technologies is application specific and therefore most readily customized to any specific business or user need. Assuming proper installation and administration, this last category of technologies provides high security protection because the technologies have been customized to a specific set of conditions. At the same time, because they are customized, they are the least adaptable of the technologies to changes in those conditions. Even a slight change can totally compromise what was a strong security infrastructure. Application-specific systems therefore incur greater administrative costs than security at lower network levels such as SSL/TSL and IPSec because of their need for maintenance and support. In a distributed services environment, you will see a mixture of all three strategies that each add their own individual costs and benefits to the TCO.

SSL in Windows 2000

The use of SSL/TLS, as a multivendor standard, to provide security services for distributed applications will remain an efficient and common practice because it provides authentication services. The application itself handles authorization. However, SSL/TLS cannot by itself support a Windows 2000 logon because it does not provide credentials to determine a user's levels of authorization. It needs help from AD directory services.

When Microsoft Certificate Services creates a digital certificate, an extended attribute field contains the special credentials called the User Principal Name (UPN). You can use this field to locate the account records in AD. When these records are located, authorization information is returned to the server. Similarly, if the certificate is from a third-party CA, the issuer's and holder's names are used as lookup keys to search the AD account database for security credentials. In the latter case, however, you must do some mapping of the issuer's and holder's name to valid account records for an association to take place.

The primary differences between SSL/TLS and Kerberos arise when you compare application-level security with networking security systems. SSL/TLS use public keys as opposed to directly or indirectly shared Key Distribution Centers (KDCs) across domains or realms. SSL/TLS scales more efficiently than Kerberos and can work in heterogeneous environments. The Kerberos protocol is more efficient than SSL/TLS in a homogeneous environment and is the default protocol in a Windows 2000 enterprise. Web-based applications determine their own authorization, so the need for AD directory services is actually redundant; SSL/TLS remains the security technology of choice in these situations.

Application Standards and Policies

It is important to remember that a secured enterprise doesn't remain secured; it grows and changes over time. General-purpose security technologies like IPSec and SSL/TLS provide wide-spectrum solutions without administrative overhead; secure applications provide granularity and a narrow security scope without administrative overhead. Applications that have security-enabled features integrate well with Microsoft's SSO theme for authenticated network connections. The

Application Specifications For Windows 2000 defines these technical requirements to earn the Certified For Microsoft Windows logo. Using secure applications that conform to this specification is an important factor in controlling an organization's TCO. The minimum requirements for a secure application include support for:

- Running on Windows 2000 servers
- Use of Kerberos and support of SSO
- Use of client impersonation to support access control mechanisms using permissions and security groups
- Application services run by using more limited service accounts rather than full privileged local system accounts

Although the Microsoft specification does not state the need to properly design the application so that it provides services as originally designed, I discuss this need in Chapter 8. If there is a design issue in some application component caused by faulty logic or some unusual boundary condition that in turn causes a buffer overflow, you will eventually discover it. You must anticipate that some intruder will exploit any security weakness in the enterprise to gain access to the security context within which the application runs. Although outside the Microsoft specification, these subtle design weaknesses compromise the strongest security infrastructures because they remain relatively invisible until *after* the security attack has been launched.

Authenticode

A way to control the deployment of software components and applications is by using Authenticode, Microsoft's digitally signed technology that works through Internet Explorer. A network policy statement is hardened when it prohibits the execution of any software component or application, especially one downloaded from a foreign Internet site. Authenticode allows developers to digitally sign an application using the standard X.509 public key certificate (see Chapter 3). Any consumer can verify not only a developer's identity but also the integrity of the downloaded package. You can use Microsoft Certificate Services to issue digital certificates to application software prior to distributing them through an intranet or enterprise. Creating these digitally signed packages and using administrative kits such as those for Internet Explorer, Outlook, and Connection Manager impact administration and maintenance of remote users and TCO tremendously. You can enable Authenticode-based screening for trusted digital signatures in Internet Explorer and then lock them down through the Group Policy snap-in in MMC. Group Policy is discussed in Chapter 10.

Secure Multipurpose Internet Mail Extensions (S/MIME)

Another significant Internet draft that uses X.509 digital certificates and public key technology is an enhancement of the traditional email format standard, MIME, specified in RFC 822. S/MIME provides open-standard interoperability at the OSI Application layer among third-party secure email applications. Significant features of S/MIME are:

- Signed receipts that provide proof of delivery to the message originator
- Security labels that you can use for access control
- Secured mail lists where a mail list agent handles the administrative overhead

This technology provides for data integrity, authentication, and nonrepudiation, all features that PKI typically provides. In addition, senders can encrypt email messages to provide confidentiality. An example of a hardware solution that provides secured email exchanges is Fortezza Crypto Card technology. This security technology, originally developed by the National Security Agency for Department of Defense (DoD), has been incorporated into the Defense Message System (DMS) especially for SBU information. Another security technology that offers similar security services is Pretty Good Privacy (PGP), but it was not developed by, nor is it under the control of, any governmental agency or standards organization.

Permission Management

In a corporate environment, identification is simplified because it is restricted to the universe of known principals in the organization. Security is also simplified; you are either "known" or "unknown." Most IT security controls begin with the assumption that you are known and focus on proving that you are who you say you are. As enterprises scale to cover entire geographical continents and as a hierarchical AD structure composed of over a million objects replaces the flat domain model of NT 4, identity will become another major issue. This section and the "Identity Management" section at the end of this chapter discuss these issues and future trends in the context of Microsoft's current works in progress.

Within the enterprise, authentication, authorization, and auditing come before permissions are granted and services are rendered. When I expand my enterprise borders to include distributed services on the Internet, identification becomes a major focus of permission management. Web services, especially in a public network or e-commerce scenario, are all fundamentally based on identification.

In Chapters 9 and 10, I discuss in great detail how to handle permission management within the enterprise or any intranet. This chapter deals with various network issues, so it is appropriate to mention a few topics that relate to e-commerce and Web services. As already mentioned, identity management is a key issue. If the identity of the consumer is somehow validated, permissions will most likely flow out of specific distributed application software that is designed to deliver predetermined services. How you build, install, and manage the software dictates the scope of security. E-commerce security issues between consumer and service provider were compiled in the Secure Electronic Transaction (SET) specification that MasterCard and Visa originally proposed in 1996. This suite of security protocols and formats is based on data exchanges between a consumer, a merchant, and a host of service providers, all separated into independent yet codependent transactions that are coordinated over both time and space.

In addition to the need for a secure session pipe, trust between parties, and confidentiality, security controls must extend to transaction integrity. Any one transaction includes secure exchanges between customer/cardholder, vendor/merchant, bank/issuer, and payment acquirer. Other intermediate agents (such as a payment gateway) could be involved. Permission management is integrated here with transaction management divided across several different parties into purchase request/response, payment authorization, and payment capture. Although the full details of this simplified e-commerce event are beyond the scope of most case studies (especially those presented in an exam environment), this scenario is one a consultant will encounter in real life. It requires specialized and detailed knowledge, not just of Windows 2000 security subsystems, but also of the specific objectives and rules of the e-commerce business involved.

It is significant that although the design and security requirements of e-commerce exchanges are radically different from intranet/extranet network connectivity issues, the security solutions are based on the same technologies outlined for intranet exchanges.

Identity Management

In Chapter 2, I suggested that it would be useful to view current IT trends from a historical perspective. I will now outline how to construct a security plan for a Windows 2000 environment. The focus of this plan, however, is not on complex technical aspects but rather on architectural layers and the issue of identity management.

Any IT enterprise is fundamentally a heap of resources and a collection of information about the people that can use it. Software applications connect people to resources, or resources to other resources, to provide useful information functions or services. In previous chapters, I often replaced the term *user* with *consumer*, and *server* with *service provider*, to emphasize a more functional relationship between these two named entities. Scalable network operating systems like Windows 2000 require dedicated services to administer the credentials that identify legal member entities in its namespace. Microsoft now uses standards-based directory services that offer a uniform application interface, providing identity management that handles a variety of identity issues, such as:

- *SSO*—SSO initiatives manage object name, security password, and user rights across the entire enterprise namespace. This is an important Microsoft theme.
- *Global address book services*—Address book services synchronize collaborative or communicative information, especially across electronic mail systems.
- *"Hire & fire" scenarios*—This category deals with propagation issues of a newly hired or terminated employee's access permissions to company resources and services.
- *E-commerce applications*—Web-based applications require identity management, including the use of digital certificates that authenticate extranet partners and users outside the enterprise namespace.

Historical trends suggest that as namespaces expand and merge in a distributed server architecture, the need to manage distributed identity datastores will increase. Interoperability issues have already forced the migration of major operating systems like Novell and Microsoft to adopt a common standards-based protocol, Lightweight Directory Access Protocol (LDAP). In addition to maintaining account records and security credentials, directory services need to provide housekeeping services that manage duplicated information and issues of referential integrity across many different datastores throughout their namespaces.

Requirements for Identity Management

The goal of having one single, uniform enterprise directory that holds an organization's universe of principals and their associated security credentials does not seem achievable for a variety of reasons. Boundaries in a namespace will always exist; political, technical, and functional divisions will never totally disappear. Thus, at least for the foreseeable future, heterogeneous identity data in scattered locations throughout the enterprise will be a common occurrence. Furthermore, some datastores will either never be exposed or will never be accessible to a directory services interface. Issues of redundancy and referential integrity due to stale ACLs or other drifts in timestamp synchronization used, for example, in the exchange of secret keys, will also be common. In fact, one might predict that any centralized or composite view of credentials across identity datastores will be increasingly unlikely because of the increasing trend in distributed services.

Directory services and identity management are at the heart of the Windows 2000 enterprise. Therefore, to make the identity data accessible, you need a compromise strategy to transparently link disparate directory datastores in some easily managed way. This compromise approach must provide:

- *Connectivity*—The negotiation of secured exchanges of identity data includes interfacing with heterogeneous directory service providers, datastores, repositories, warehouses, and application programming interfaces (APIs). Two examples here are the standards-based directory services provided by LDAP version 3 and database access via Structured Query Language (SQL).
- *Brokering features*—These internal services manage the flow of identity data between datastores. These services detect changes in information and update repositories, aggregate data in central locations, and track object histories. An ordered propagation of changes to multiple repositories is especially important to maintain data consistency.
- *Integrity checks*—These internal services monitor any brokered exchanges of identity data for consistency, ownership, and referential integrity. These integrity checks determine proper execution of business rules applied during the brokering process and confirm or reject changes to the data.

Deployment of Identity Management

Based on the list of requirements in the previous section and the current heterogeneity in application and system software, the management of directory services will most likely be distributed across many different service providers and operating system platforms, even, perhaps, within the same enterprise. To support the previous list of service features, any one service provider is forced to use some combination of technologies, including:

- *Multidirectory access technologies*—These applications utilize published interface specifications to interact directly with data in the datastore that is relevant to some management operation. The technologies help simplify application development by providing a minimum number of API data access paradigms.
- *Synchronization connectors*—These software agents act as readers/distributors that are programmed to recognize changes in the state of data in a repository and then propagate those changes to other data sites.
- *Meta-directory technologies*—These technologies can maximize performance by collecting identity data from various repositories and offering a single access/distribution point and security model.

➤ *Directory consolidation technologies*—These technologies, under intense development, require minimal maintenance. For example, a consolidated directory does not need synchronization, multiple data access paradigms, or synchronization connectors. An example of this trend is Exchange 2000, which uses AD instead of its own data repository.

Microsoft has recognized the importance of identity management, having acquired field-tested technology and having experimented with Metabases in IIS 4, as mentioned in Chapter 2. Windows 2000 provides a mature set of identity management solutions based on AD-related interfaces and services:

➤ *Active Directory Services Interfaces (ADSI)*—Offering multidirectory access through a Component Object Model (COM), ADSI provides an API to access and manage Security Accounts Manager in NT 4, Active Directory Services (ADS) in Windows 2000, Novell's Novell Directory Services (NDS), and any LDAP-based directory.

➤ *Active Directory Connector (ADC)*—This connector specifically synchronizes AD with Exchange Server 5.x, Lotus Notes, Novell GroupWise, and LDAP-based directory systems. These connector technologies (as well as Microsoft Directory Synchronization Services—MSDSS—described in the next bulleted item) are based on an LDAP-based control, DirSync, which enables you to efficiently synchronize AD with heterogeneous directory systems. Figure 7.1 shows how the ADC and MSDSS interoperate with these other applications.

➤ *MSDSS*—Like ADC, MSDSS is a component of Services for NetWare version 5 (SFNW5), which provides a method to synchronize identity data changes between AD and Novell NDS.

➤ *Meta-directory technologies*—With its newly acquired Zoomit product, renamed Microsoft Meta-directory Services (MMS), Microsoft has implemented a hub and spoke architecture for building comprehensive identity management solutions. Some application in the center of Figure 7.2 interfaces with the

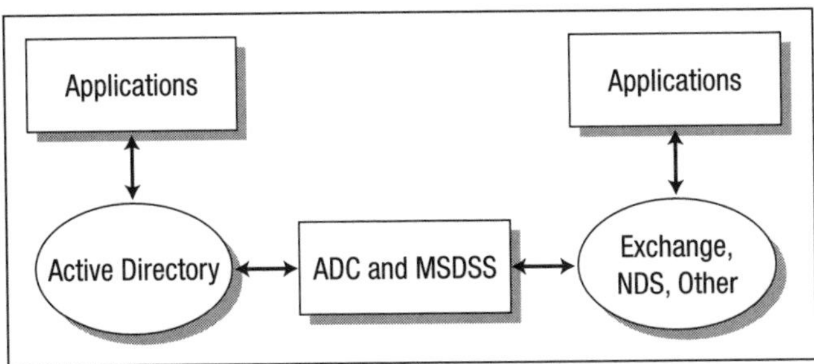

Figure 7.1 The layout of ADCs.

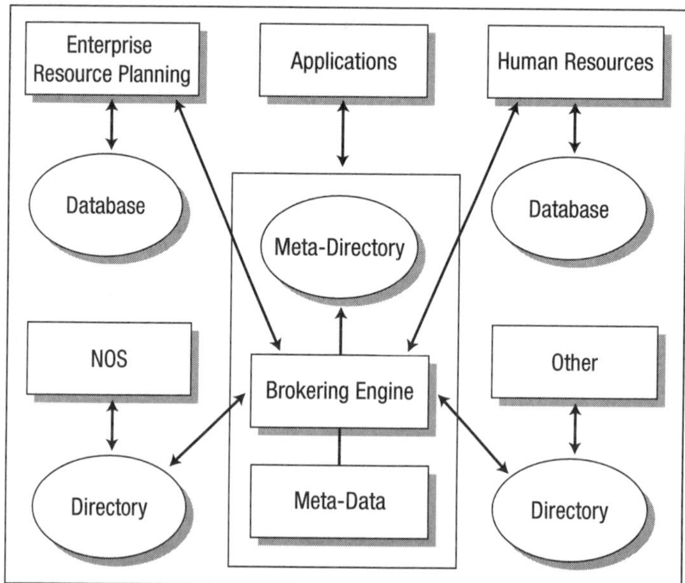

Figure 7.2 Meta-directory hub and spoke architecture.

"hub" meta-directory that represents the aggregate collection of identity data captured from a Human Resources database, some Enterprise Resource Planning (ERP) program, and the network operating system (NOS). Similarly, upon receiving new-hire information from Human Resources, the brokering engine, which follows business rules defined in policy statements, coordinates the creation of mail accounts in the NOS and access rights in the ERP application. All this information is reflected in the aggregate meta-directory repository.

- *Directory consolidation opportunities*—The design of, for example, Exchange 2000, has changed; its own internal datastore has been replaced by the AD enterprise datastores.

Security Objectives

Whether you are protecting information in transit during remote access sessions, during persistent branch network connections, or within the confines of an internal network, network security always complements the actual delivery or accessibility of services. In fact, accessibility is one of the primary IT security controls listed in Chapter 2. It is important to remember, though, that you should measure the deployment costs of any security countermeasure in terms relative to corporate security objectives and an organization's TCO. Corporate security objectives, not the consultant, explicitly determine what the organization "needs" and "wants" in its security plan.

Read every case study carefully. Measure exactly what is said in the documented responses of the participants in each case. Design your responses based on what is written, not what you, as a consultant, consider a "good" design.

As I said in Chapter 2, IT security controls include authentication, authorization, confidentiality, and integrity protection. I include protection against replay attacks under authentication and integrity protection. Similarly, confidentiality in the form of encryption services extends across both distributed and network security subsystems.

TCO and maximized interoperability are important measures of an identity management system's inherent worth. I suggest that the deployment of identity management services requires security subsystems of a similar scope. The strength of these security subsystems directly affects the value of the identity management system. Microsoft emphasizes ease of implementation as a major dimension that measures an identity management system's inherent value. Figure 7.3 shows a diagram of the relationship between ease of implementation and perceived business value. Each service has a different cost versus business benefit ratio because their methods of deployment vary.

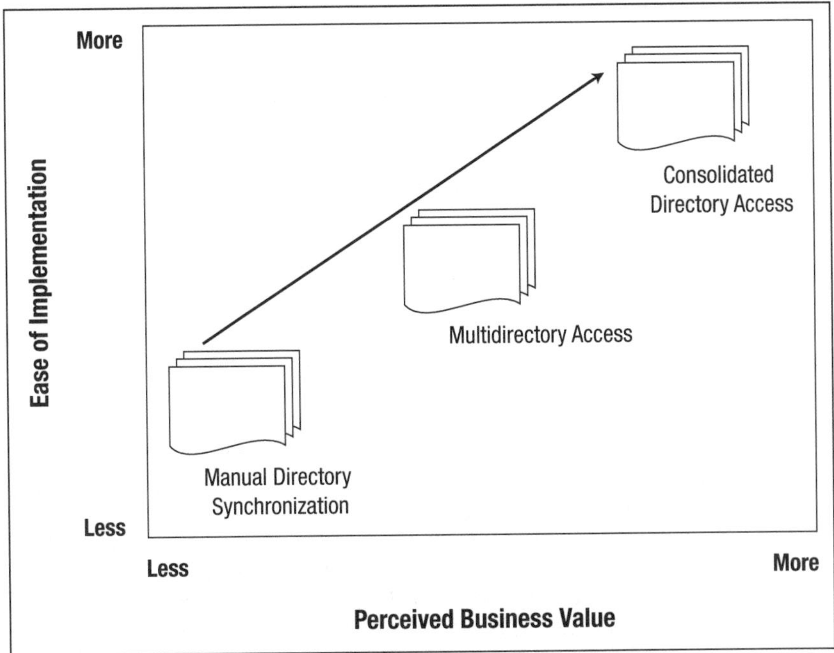

Figure 7.3 Return on investment: identity management and security.

Given the complexity of managing identity data across an enterprise, your deployment plan may involve several technologies applied at the same or different structural layers in terms of an OSI or Microsoft reference model. This affects not only deployment costs but also other TCO variables like maintenance and training. Thus, you can similarly apply the TCO valuation method when you deploy security technologies. As suggested above in the "Requirements for Identity Management" section earlier in this chapter, although theoretically possible and desirable, there is no foreseeable time in the future when all datastores, directory requirements, and support features will be consolidated under one unified service. Similarly, in a security plan, no single system or technology will ever provide all the security controls necessary to protect an enterprise from an intruder assault. Always try to maintain a balance between costs, technologies, and needs.

Practice Questions

Case Study

4Sale, an online bartering company in ThatTherePlace, North Dakota, has merged with Got-a-Deal, and both companies occupy office space in the same office building. They are now running their accounting operation, their bid system, and a knowledge base of their online goods in the same building.

4Sale supports a large Internet audience and many small business brokers around the world. Bids are confidential and must be authenticated. Internet security is important not just for transactions but business reputation. Many of its users, though, are not experienced with the use of secured online services. The Network Manager is considering the addition of a person to support a newly designed Web site and to provide Internet-related help desk support. She is also concerned about securing the IIS server and support for the Proxy Server and certificate services.

Current LAN/Network Structure

4Sale runs native mode Windows 2000 Server in a single domain model with an Exchange 2000 member server, and an IIS 5 and Proxy Server 2 (packet filtering/caching) server. All 100 client machines are running Windows 2000 Professional; Office 2000 is utilized as an applications package. Each system is connected to a 10Mbps hub through 10Mbps local area network (LAN) cards running Category 5 Unshielded Twisted Pair (UTP) cabling in a star topology.

Got-a-Deal is running all 22 client machines in a single child domain under the 4Sale root domain. The client systems are running Windows Professional, with Office 2000 being utilized as an applications package. Each system is connected to a 10Mbps hub through 10Mbps LAN cards running Category 5 UTP cabling in a star topology. These hubs are on the same backbone as 4Sale but have a different subnet.

Proposed LAN/Network Structure

No changes are planned at this time, although management is considering a merger with several business partners running non-Windows environments.

Current WAN Connectivity

4Sale has a T1 connection to an ISP in OverThere, North Dakota. Got-a-Deal has 56Kbps dial-up networking connectivity through the same ISP. The ISP provides simple hosting services and online analysis of traffic.

Directory Design Commentary

No changes are planned at this time.

Current Internet Positioning

4Sale is registered as **4sale.com**. Got-a-Deal has been selling its goods through local companies and through the **4sale.com** Web site.

Company Goal with Windows 2000

Short-term goals are to build enough in-house expertise in handling Web-related issues to bring all online services in-house in six months.

Question 1

The Network Manager at 4Sale asks you to list the security technologies in typical OSI order for the owners of 4Sale. She assumes that the cost of deploying security at higher OSI layers is greater due to installation, support, maintenance, and training. The three OSI reference layers are:

Application

Transport

Network

Place the following positions under the appropriate OSI layer:

IPSec

S-HTTP

SSL

S/MIME

The correct answer is:

Application

S/MIME

Transport

S-HTTP

SSL

Network

IPSec

Question 2

The Network Manager at 4Sale says, "I often receive a help desk call where the user sees a message in her browser saying the certificate issuer is untrusted. What is happening?" Describe the flow in an SSL (Secure Sockets Layer) exchange by placing the following steps in the proper order.

A certificate is issued to the Web server.

You encounter a security alert message that notifies you that you are about to view pages over a secured connection.

You install a certificate on the browser.

Your browser can now read the server's digital certificate, and the encryption of information will provide secured data.

A certificate is installed on the Web server.

SSL is enabled on a virtual server or directory on that Web server.

You access the SSL-enabled virtual server using a secured Uniform Resource Locator.

The correct answer is:

A certificate is issued to the Web server.

A certificate is installed on the Web server.

SSL is enabled on a virtual server or directory on that Web server.

You access the SSL-enabled virtual server using a secured Uniform Resource Locator.

You encounter a security alert message that notifies you that you are about to view pages over a secured connection.

You install a certificate on the browser.

Your browser can now read the server's digital certificate, and the encryption of information will provide secured data.

Question 3

The Network Manager at 4Sale asks, "What can I do to secure the IIS server?" Choose the security methods that will secure IIS. [Check all correct answers]

- ❑ a. Disable unnecessary services.
- ❑ b. Install a dual-homed server.
- ❑ c. Disable directory browsing.
- ❑ d. Disable logging and auditing.
- ❑ e. Disable Server services.

Answers a, b, c, and e are correct. Disabling unnecessary services, installing a second network interface card (a dual-homed server), disabling directory browsing, and disabling Server services are all legitimate security strategies. Another legitimate and highly recommended strategy is to enable (not disable) both logging and auditing on the Web server. Therefore, answer d is incorrect.

Question 4

The Network Manager at 4Sale asks, "Which is the best authentication procedure if 4Sale supports a heterogeneous user population but needs a secured exchange of data?"

- ❍ a. Anonymous access
- ❍ b. Basic authentication
- ❍ c. Digest authentication
- ❍ d. Integrated Windows authentication
- ❍ e. None of the above

Answer e is correct. 4Sale needs to encrypt messages sent over a public network. It also needs to accommodate a heterogeneous population of users. Anonymous access and basic authentication do not support a secure exchange of information. Therefore, answers a and b are incorrect. Digest authentication and integrated Windows authentication are valid only for Windows domain users. Therefore, answers c and d are incorrect. The best answer would have been basic authentication with Secure Sockets Layer, but this is not an option.

Question 5

The Network Manager at 4Sale asks, "What would we be responsible for if we installed our own Certificate Authority?" Answer her question by listing the certificate services.

❑ a. Administration

❑ b. Logging

❑ c. Revocation

❑ d. Consolidation

❑ e. All of the above

Answers a, b, and c are correct. There are three services: administration (creating certificates), logging (tracking requests for certificates), and revocation (maintaining lists of revoked certificates). Consolidation is not one of the services. Therefore, answers d and e are incorrect.

Question 6

The Network Manager at 4Sale asks, "What identity issues would a directory service provider need to handle?" [Check all correct answers]

❑ a. Global address books

❑ b. Hire & fire scenarios

❑ c. E-commerce applications

❑ d. SSL scenarios

❑ e. Applications like Exchange Server

Answers a, b, c, and e are correct. A directory services provider would typically use standards-based directory services that provide global address book services (especially for email servers like Exchange Server), hire & fire scenarios that deal with the propagation of information, and e-commerce applications. Secure Sockets Layer has nothing to do with directory services. Therefore, answer d is incorrect.

Question 7

The CEO at 4Sale asks, "Which service or interface would 4Sale consider if we merged with a company that ran Novell version 5 and Novell Directory Services?" [Choose the best answer]

❍ a. ADSI

❍ b. ADC

❍ c. MSDSS

❍ d. Directory consolidation opportunities

❍ e. MMS

Answer c is correct. Only MSDSS (Microsoft Directory Synchronization Services), a service component of Services for NetWare version 5, provides a method to synchronize identity data changes between Active Directory and Novell Directory Services. ADSI (Active Directory Services Interfaces) offers multidirectory access through a Component Object Model and provides an application programming interface to programmatically access and manage other directory services, including Novell's NDS and any Lightweight Directory Access Protocol-based directory. ADSI is partially correct, but it is not the best answer. Therefore, answer a is incorrect. ADC (Active Directory Connector) specifically synchronizes Active Directory with Exchange Server 5.x, Lotus Notes, Novell GroupWise, and LDAP-based directory systems. Therefore, answer b is incorrect. Directory consolidation opportunities (such as in Exchange 2000) replace their own datastores or repositories with AD. Therefore, answer d is incorrect. Meta-directory technologies like MMS (Microsoft Meta-directory Services) are for building comprehensive identity management solutions. Therefore, answer e is incorrect.

Need to Know More?

Nichols, Randall K. et. al. *Defending Your Digital Assets against Hackers, Crackers, Spies, and Thieves, First Edition*. McGraw-Hill Professional Publishing, New York, NY, 2000. ISBN 0-07-212285-4. Both Chapter 9 (Digital Signatures and Certificate Authorities) and Chapter 10 (Permissions Management: Identification, Authentication and Authorization) discuss topics from a legislative and business viewpoint without sacrificing technical details. The sections on Web security in Chapter 10 are especially relevant from a nontechnical, managerial viewpoint and are an excellent introductory source of issues for constructing a network policy.

Santry, Patrick and Mitch Tulloch. *Administering IIS 5.0*. Computing McGraw-Hill, New York, NY, 2000. ISBN 0-07-212328-1. Chapter 4 (Administering Security) and Chapter 11 (Administering SSL with Certificate Services) offer well-documented, procedural instructions regarding the installation of IIS security services, as well as discussions concerning the strategy behind various option settings.

Stallings, William. *Network Security Essentials: Applications and Standards*. Prentice Hall, Upper Saddle River, NJ, 1999. ISBN 0-13-016093-8. Chapter 7 deals exclusively with Web security and offers a detailed, technical view of the SSL and TLS protocol architectures. Chapter 5 deals specifically with electronic mail security and covers both S/MIME and PGP.

Search the TechNet CD (or its online version through **www.microsoft.com**) and the *Windows 2000 Server Resource Kit* CD using the keywords "security", "meta-directory", "ICS", and "MSDSS". This is Microsoft's definitive online resource for technical papers and bulletins.

www.armadillo.huntsville.al.us/ This site, maintained by members of the Fortezza program office in the Department of Defense, hosts a comprehensive list of technical papers, protocol specifications, product links, cryptographic interface libraries, and other materials related to Fortezza security technologies.

www.ietf.cnri.reston.va.us/rfc/rfc2246.txt?number=2246 This site contains RFC 2246, the TLS Protocol, which is the actual specification for the TLS protocol. TLS provides end-to-end communication privacy over a public network, and it also prevents tampering and message forgery.

www.microsoft.com/windows2000/library/howitworks/iis/iis5techoverview.asp This Windows 2000 Technical Paper, titled *Internet Information Services 5.0 Technical Overview* and originally posted in September 1999, provides information about reliability and performance, security, and the application environment.

www.rsasecurity.com/standards/smime/resources.html This is the RSA Security-hosted Web page of S/MIME resources and related information, including working drafts of S/MIME version 2 and S/MIME version 3 specifications as well as special topics such as certificate handling.

Constructing a Security Policy

Terms you'll need to understand:

- ✓ Network security plan
- ✓ Disaster recovery plan
- ✓ Principals
- ✓ Single Sign-On (SSO)
- ✓ Two-factor authentication
- ✓ Smart card technologies
- ✓ Secure Channel (SChannel) security protocols
- ✓ Microsoft Directory Synchronization Services (MSDSS)
- ✓ Meta-directory
- ✓ Lightweight Directory Access Protocol (LDAP) version 3
- ✓ Active Directory Connectors (ADCs)
- ✓ Remote access technologies
- ✓ Network deployment plan
- ✓ Security Support Provider Interface (SSPI)
- ✓ Security Support Provider (SSP)

Techniques you'll need to master:

- ✓ Developing a network security plan
- ✓ Developing a physical security plan
- ✓ Developing strategies for secure network connections
- ✓ Developing rationales for security policies
- ✓ Applying a performance-oriented, milestone-based methodology for deploying security systems
- ✓ Preparing project deliverables and building an action plan

This chapter shows you how to develop a *network security plan*, which is the integration of security techniques and technologies combined under some formal management policy that grows out of the corporate business objectives. This plan is the balance among acceptable levels of protection, acceptable perceived risk, and acceptable expense. The corporate business objectives explicitly define or help you assess what your client perceives to be network security risks. The first step in this assessment is to determine the scope of the enterprise.

As I explain later in this chapter in the context of identity management, the Windows 2000 enterprise goes far beyond what the legacy NT 4 domain model would typically support. The basic dichotomy of distributed and network security services was especially useful in the NT 4 domain model to determine the initial scope of a security plan. *Distributed security* refers to security features applied within the boundaries of the enterprise; *network security* refers to connectivity beyond enterprise boundaries, specifically through the Internet. With the integration of remote access and Virtual Private Networks (VPNs), however, a Windows 2000 enterprise typically includes various forms of network connectivity outside the boundaries of the enterprise. VPNs are discussed in detail in Chapter 6. You will see that the needs of various components of your user population can radically change the scope of your enterprise as well as the security requirements.

Remember that all security planning is a balance between ease of use and a total system lockdown. In a perfect world, granting the Everyone group full control would be wonderful; conversely, powering down a server or using a pair of wire clippers on a connecting network cable will secure it from an outside attack in the most absolute of ways. Although these extremes are all impractical in a corporate environment, they illustrate the balance which must be struck to deliver reliable computer services. I will distinguish a variety of control and responsibility areas for reasons of design, analysis, and deployment; remember each area contributes specific costs and benefits to the total cost of ownership (TCO).

Steps in Planning Network Security

The network security plan is a fundamental component of any corporate deployment of information technology (IT) services. It is either a part of or complementary to the corporate disaster recovery plan. In developing the network security plan, you should follow these specific steps:

1. Determine short-term corporate objectives and long-term goals.
2. Identify user groups and their specific needs.
3. Determine the scope, sizing, and placement requirements of IT resources.

4. Assess network security risks.
5. Create and publish security policies and procedures.
6. Prepare the support staff for maintenance and help desk services.
7. Conduct pilot studies to test strategies.
8. Formalize a methodology to deploy security technologies.

It is noteworthy that although security technologies tend to come in complicated, highly sophisticated packages, the services must be properly deployed, configured, and managed. The best of services will fail unless they are combined with good business practices and a compliant corporate culture. In fact, your enterprise may require more than one security plan based on functional, operational, or regional considerations. Corporate security objectives, which are discussed in Chapter 2, would indicate the need for such divisions in scope. Distributed security involves coordinating many technologies; thus, a Windows 2000 security policy should also cover these specific topics:

- *Network logon and authentication procedures*—The administration of users and logon authentication practices have now been extended to cover remote access and smart card technologies. The impact of these methods in terms of new protocols, specialized servers, and identity management is covered in Chapter 9.
- *Public key infrastructure (PKI) policies*—The deployment of certificate authorities needs to be planned in advance, especially for use outside the boundaries of the enterprise (such as in e-commerce applications and extranet-based business alliances).
- *Administrative policies*—Administration, authorization, and auditing remain the primary responsibilities of IT personnel. Systematic monitoring and strategically deployed audit logs are cost-effective and typically transparent methods of securing network exchanges.
- *Group Policy and security group descriptions*—It is especially important in the deployment of Windows 2000 to understand the rationale behind the built-in policy structure (for example, Group Policy, default domain policy, and so on) and the mapping of specific policies to user groups in your enterprise. Microsoft has provided policies and security templates that encompass a broad range of business needs and scenarios; using them properly will profoundly impact your TCO.
- *Information security strategies*—The driving forces of e-commerce and Internet connectivity have fostered the need for specific strategies that deal with securing exchanges involving online services such as email and Web-based communications.

Identifying the User Population

Although all business resources and operations are expected to serve the organization's mission statement and corporate objectives, the network infrastructure provides for the functional needs of an organization's members. In general, you can divide employees into three groups: executives, staff, and users, as shown in Figure 8.1.

A relatively new category, business partner, is especially common in organizations that have formed business alliances with different but complementary business concerns that are geographically separated from the primary company. In these situations, network connectivity through an extranet provides the common platform for daily operations. Another category, everyone, includes all principals that access network resources and is critical when you are performing security audits. Although this default built-in group is usually removed from an object's access control list (ACL), the everyone category provides the broadest definition of named objects in a directory namespace. It offers truly comprehensive monitoring of system utilization and intruder activity. Thus, in addition to the classic built-in local groups—administrator, guest, account operator, and so on—I usually categorize members of an organization into the following groups:

- *Everyone*—The universe of principals in the Active Directory (AD) namespace is too comprehensive to individually identify, so this group provides a reliable catchall label.

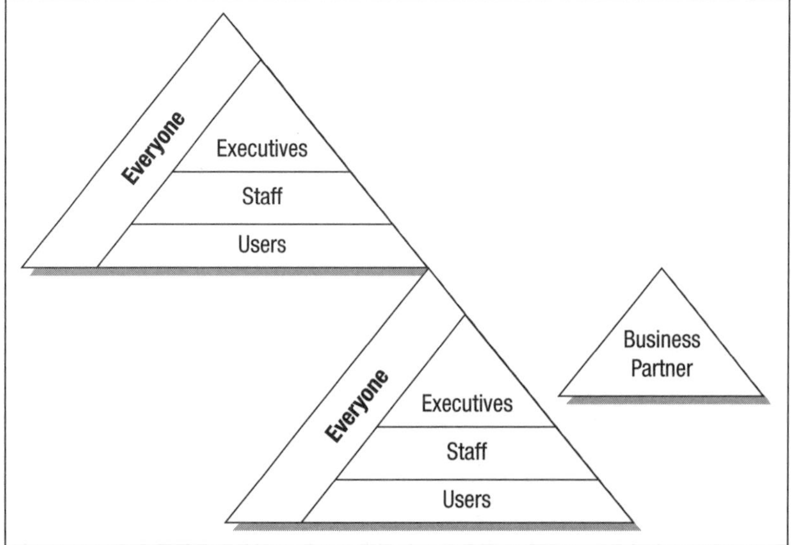

Figure 8.1 Groups in a typical user population.

- *Executives*—This group includes principals with all comprehensive rights, permissions, and/or privileges.
- *Staff*—This group not only works with most (if not all) system resources but is also expected to comply with standard procedures and policies.
- *Users*—This group includes the staff members who access resources and perform their daily functions through software applications.
- *Business partners*—This group includes principals who have some special relationship with the organization. They are expected to comply with all standard policies and procedures, as well as utilize resources exactly like the other groups.

Determining the Scope, Sizing, and Placement of IT Resources

Determining the scope, sizing, and placement of IT resources is a function of business objectives and budget. Often, the functional needs of the different groups in the user population (outlined in the "Identifying the User Population" section earlier in this chapter) also influence these determinations. From a security perspective, security scope, in functional terms, determines where control boundaries lie. I define these boundaries in functional terms wherever possible to both reflect the corporate business objectives and map how people perform their work in an organization.

From a practical, financial, or physical view, number (sizing) and placement of hardware rarely follow textbook descriptions. Although it is possible or necessary to run multiple services on one server machine, doing so is typically not recommended. Workload characteristics of services vary not just in functional terms but also over time with respect to network utilization. Concurrent demands by different services for similar resources on the same hardware platform can cause a server to panic and crash. These concurrently running services may also expose security weaknesses that would never appear if they were run separately. Such security weaknesses could expose all services on that server to unexpected security risks. For purposes of this book, sizing and placement issues are generally operational. With regard to Microsoft certification examination questions, I have and will follow the Windows 2000 Competency guidelines and stress rationales supporting design issues; sizing, placement and related topics on optimization and performance tuning are best left for more comprehensive texts.

Scoping Physical Assets

The scope of any physical security plan, as described in Chapter 2, typically relates to secured server room(s) or wire closet(s). The scope is documented in a physical security plan that describes:

- An inventory of physical assets, including both data and telephone components, routers, printers, tape backup units, and uninterrupted power supplies (all listed with manufacturer, model number, and serial number)
- A diagram of the physical area, including architectural plans that show cabling, power, High Voltage/Air Conditioning (HVAC), and so on
- A definition of the security perimeter that separates the secured facilities from the rest of the world and who has rights of access

The plan would typically document perceived security risks, countermeasures, and, if appropriate, costs and benefits. It might also document policies and procedures regarding personnel allowed access to the facility, emergency personnel call lists, and specific vendors responsible for maintenance of, for example, telephone equipment, air conditioning units, and building maintenance. Backup media sets should be stored in a locked storage area inside this locked facility. Wiring diagrams and emergency contact lists (with account numbers where appropriate) should be prominently displayed. Never overlook the possibility of simple theft of physical equipment or the security risk of a member of the janitorial staff splashing soapy water on a patch panel. The simplest countermeasure is a locked door with a restricted number of keys and a strict company policy regarding accessibility. Any employee handbook should explicitly state that noncompliance of policies—especially relating to physical assets—is grounds for immediate dismissal and possible legal recourse.

Scoping Logical Assets

The security scope that encompasses logical assets is at the heart of identity management and security models, which are covered in Chapter 7. *Identity management*, the services that administer the security credentials of named objects or principals, will become increasingly important as enterprises grow and users roam within them. Windows 2000 uses a security model that determines authentication and authorization of principals based on legitimate credentials administered by AD directory services. The access control mechanism implements authorization and is triggered when the resource is requested; an object-specific ACL that defines various categories of permissions is referenced when the consumer requests access or services. Some strategies applicable in securing these network assets are:

- Authenticating all consumers, clients, and services
- Applying appropriate authorization controls
- Establishing uniform security policies across the domain
- Applying appropriate trust relationships among domains
- Enabling data protection for sensitive data

Determining Scope within the Legacy Domain Model

The domain model in Windows 2000 is a collection of principals or named objects that are stored in a directory repository called the *directory database*. These named objects or principals can be users, machines, or service accounts that log on to remote machines and act as part of the operating system. The domain identifies a security authority that defines internal security policies for this collection and explicit security relationships with other domains.

Determining Scope Regarding Windows 2000 Authentication Services

Windows 2000 authentication services now enable Single Sign-On (SSO) to all network resources using a single password or two-factor authentication using a smart card. Two-factor authentication requires both a physical object and some password to be present when authentication is requested. Smart cards carry integrated circuitry that stores a digital certificate and the holder's private key. The password or personal identification number (PIN) is entered at the keyboard at the same time the data is read from the card.

Both the standards-based Kerberos protocol and the PKI suite have been enhanced to support smart card technologies, which are discussed in greater detail in Chapter 12. Authentication in Windows 2000 is implemented either by the Microsoft Kerberos protocol or NT LAN Manager (NTLM) authentication protocol. Accounts are managed using AD Users And Computers snap-in to Microsoft Management Console (MMC). User accounts can be functionally organized into Organizational Units (OUs) within the AD namespace. Creation of a named account defines that object as a principal and entitles it to access through the enterprise. When domain authentication services are integrated with the enterprise directory namespace, the user account is also a global address book directory entry, thus distributing credentials throughout a domain forest. I further discuss this topic in Chapter 7.

Determining Scope Relating to Trust Management and the Internet

Native Windows 2000 supports SSO for consumers within the domain forest. SSO is transparently supported by several network protocols in providing requested services to some authenticated consumer no matter where they log on to the enterprise. These protocols are the NTLM, Kerberos, and Secure Channel (SChannel) security protocols. NTLM is a legacy authentication protocol used primarily in mixed mode installations where the NT 4 domain model is still operational. Kerberos, the default security protocol in native Windows 2000, makes no assumptions regarding authentication; the identity of both the consumer and service is verified. Trust relationships in the domain forest extend the scope of

Kerberos authentication. Kerberos trusts are bidirectional or transitive by default, so authentication in one domain can be referred or passed-through to service providers in some other domain. With regard to network connectivity, the SSO feature is similarly supported through the SChannel security protocols, such as Secure Sockets Layer (SSL) version 3 and Transport Layer Security (TLS) version 1.

Clients and services are also authenticated when they connect to a domain or when they request services. Computer policies are exchanged during the logon process once authentication is validated. Clients and services in an N-tier architecture need to be "trusted for delegation" where, in the security context of the consumer, one service requests, on behalf of the consumer, additional services from some other client or service. Similarly, you can set the mutual authentication flag so that upon receiving a Kerberos Application Request (KRB_AP_REQ), the service provider authenticates itself to the consumer in the form of a Kerberos Application Reply (KRB_AP_REP).

Assessing Network Security Risks

The concept of a workgroup emphasizes collaboration and communication. With the privilege to share resources comes the ability to intentionally or unintentionally misuse someone else's property. In an enterprise based on collaboration and communication, identity management and security control in the form of authentication, authorization, and auditing (AAA) are critical functions. Although one approach to security controls is to minimize network security risks through isolation ("the best network security control is a pair of wire cutters"), I don't believe this is a realistic way of conducting business operations. Contemporary social and business activities use information technologies; IT is based on network connectivity. Even the most limited access to the Internet exposes an internal network to some form of risk. In my opinion, risks of this nature are a cost of doing business and a fact of contemporary life.

Attack Modalities

The three attack modalities—interference, interception, and impersonation—were discussed in Chapter 2. Acting as a framework, these categories encompass a comprehensive range of possible security assault methods. Chapters 3 through 7 have described various security technologies applied at different structural layers of the Open Systems Interconnection (OSI) model. In the analysis of a security environment, you should systematically work through each network layer to expose possible security risks using samples from each of the three categories. Distributed security systems, working primarily within the boundaries of the enterprise, form a functional core or center security perimeter. To systematically assess network security risks, work outward from that core. Instead of dichotomizing distributed and network security systems, you can think of the various security systems outside the enterprise as a series of concentric rings, each dealing with broader namespaces and more comprehensive identity management. This ring model helps organize the analysis of a case study or a real-life business scenario.

The next section discusses the ring model more in depth. It will help you place several different services in some meaningful perspective. I conceptualize Routing and Remote Access Service (RRAS), Remote Authentication Dial-In User Service (RADIUS), Microsoft's Internet Authentication Service (IAS), and Microsoft Directory Synchronization Services (MSDSS) all on a single dimension that describes greater consolidation of directory services. I believe this concept will help you understand the relationship among these services and how secured boundaries will evolve with increasing interoperability of these meta-directory structures. See Chapter 7 for a discussion of Microsoft's hub-and-spoke meta-directory architecture, where directory services are consolidated under an umbrella directory system of separate directory services.

It is unlikely that you will encounter a case study that deals directly with the services mentioned in Chapter 7's "Identity Management" section. Microsoft's technical papers on this subject and meta-directories are hard to understand but significant in describing future trends.

Ring Model

At the heart of the enterprise is the AD: in the simplest case, a single domain and single namespace. AD makes credential data stores accessible to all objects requiring authentication and authorization services within this inner ring. The trend in consolidation of directory services fosters this directory-centric view. This is similar to the hub in what Microsoft calls its hub-and-spoke architecture, discussed in Chapter 7's "Identity Management" section. If current trends continue, boundaries between heterogeneous network operating systems will gradually dissolve. The business need for functional interoperability will force identity management and directory services to converge. Different namespaces will be consolidated into some universal namescape much like domains link together to form forests. Surrounding the center ring in Figure 8.2 are two additional rings, representing the Internet and extranet, respectively. Lightweight Directory Access Protocol (LDAP)-based meta-directories will assume a position similar to the LDAP version 3 icon, in Figure 8.2, outside any single network operating system but central to all enterprises that have some functional association. Figure 8.2 shows other protocols and services that support the expansion to larger and larger enterprises; this movement is directed outward from the center ring with its core directory services.

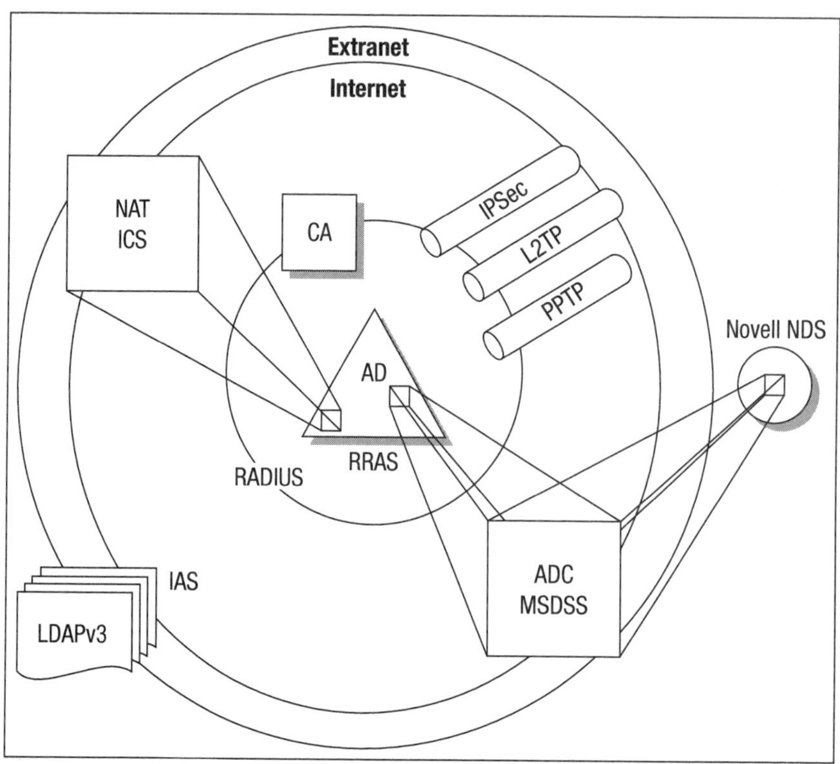

Figure 8.2 Protocols and services in a ring model.

As the enterprise increases in scale, the ability to request and receive services will push its limits beyond its physical boundaries into the Internet. Beyond the capacity to support remote access is the bridging of separate enterprises and the linking of extranets. This shift is toward larger, distributed systems with their greater scalability (meta-directories) and a greater security scope for the credentials they hold. AD and directory services like it, such as Novell Directory Services (NDS), will be at the center of these concentric, logical rings. For example, remote access connectivity on an increasingly large scale is supported by RRAS; on a larger wide area network (WAN), by RADIUS; and finally, between WANs, by IAS. Independent LDAP-based directories either support several IAS servers or eliminate them entirely through consolidation. Similarly, Active Directory Connectors (ADCs), and specifically MSDSS, link the heterogeneous directory services supported by AD and NDS. In the figure, both the Network address translation (NAT) from RRAS and Internet Connection Sharing (ICS) from Dial-Up Connections tool are positioned on the outside physical perimeter of the inner ring, the core enterprise, as features supporting Small Office/Home Office (SOHO) connectivity to the Internet represented by the second ring. The three protocol pipes—Point-To-Point Tunneling Protocal (PPTP), Layer 2 Tunneling Protocol (L2TP), and IP Security (IPSec)—represent VPNs connecting both public networks and extranets. The Certificate Authority (CA) is needed to support the L2TP connections. Some of these services are only meaningful in special heterogeneous or mixed-platform situations. The efforts especially of both Novell through NDS and Microsoft through MSDSS in developing a consolidated directory are very real and significant trends that need to be recognized in today's strategic network planning.

From a case-study perspective, notice the progression of policy management moving outward from the center of the ring, as shown in Figure 8.3. The three different levels are described here:

- *The center ring*—Policy management within the physical boundaries of the enterprise
- *The middle ring*—Policy management outside the enterprise to support remote access services in unsecured, public spaces
- *The outer ring*—Policy management extending session pipes directly out to some extranet

Microsoft is moving toward a consolidation of separate directory services into meta-directory namescapes, as discussed in Chapter 7, which are shared between enterprises. This trend is shown in Figure 8.4. The figure shows that manual directory synchronization requires the most maintenance and is perceived to

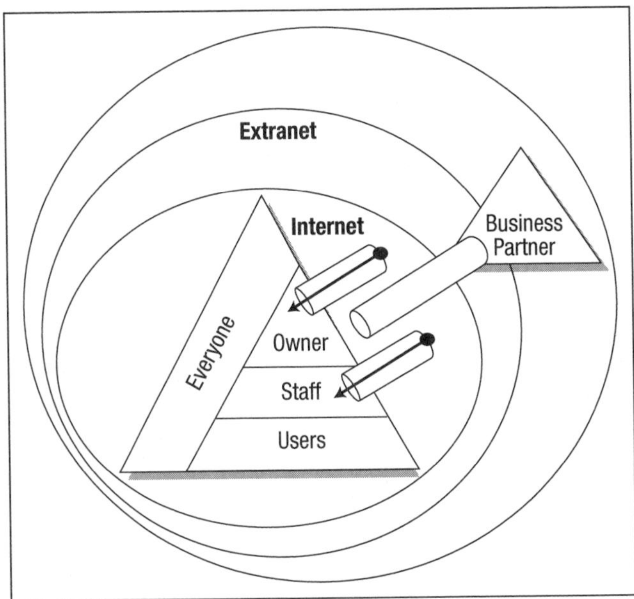

Figure 8.3 A progression of policy management.

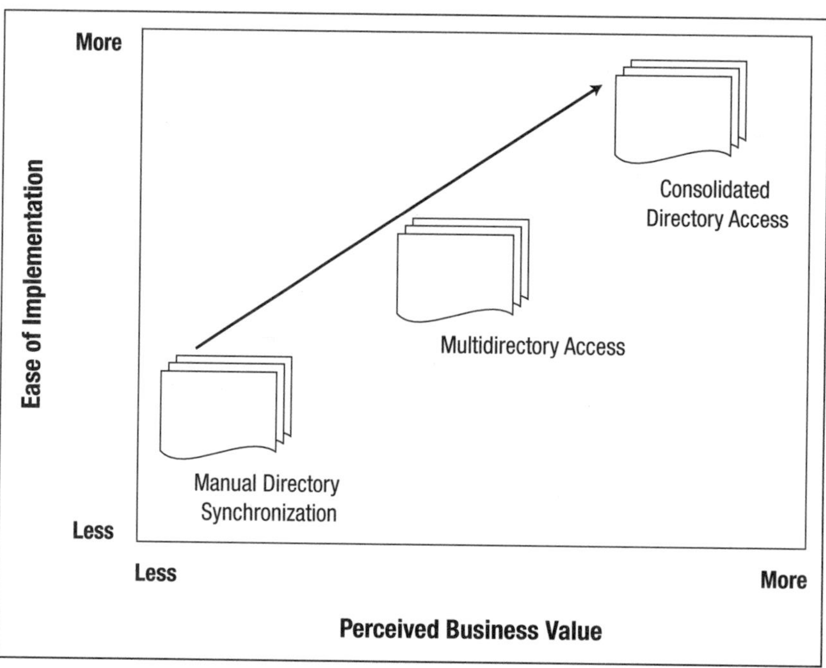

Figure 8.4 Return on investment: identity management and security.

have the least business value, whereas consolidated directory access is superior to both manual directory synchronization and multidirectory access in both ease of implementation and perceived business value. It also suggests that at some point umbrella or meta-directory services will integrate directory services across enterprises in some LDAP-based, "universal" cloud services specializing in identity management.

Creating Secure Boundaries: Physical Scoping

A security perimeter between a more-secured area and a less-secured area depends in general on the way servers running specific services are placed in the network topology. A realistic approach to network security is to isolate specialized and particularly vulnerable servers and services in specially created security zones within your network infrastructure. The classic example of such an area is called a demilitarized zone (DMZ), which uses firewall techniques (discussed in Chapter 6) and technologies that force inbound and outbound traffic to servers and their running services within the zone through restrictive choke points. This approach is said to harden the boundaries around this logical zone to many forms of attack. A DMZ must be secured from physical access and configured to be outside the logical scope of the user population. Similarly, services within the DMZ are both physically and logically scoped in the most restrictive way; only required services, resources, and rights are made available.

Creating Secure Boundaries: Protocol Scoping

Secured boundaries now extend beyond the physical borders of an enterprise; Windows 2000 has integrated services that easily extend secured forms of communication over both private and public networks. These services, now integrated within the operating system, provide transparent security services at the OSI Data Link, Network, and Transport layers, as well as through services at the Application layer. For example, security protocols like L2TP and PPTP operate at the Data Link layer to encrypt messages exchanged through branch network connections as well as remote access sessions. The SChannel security protocols, such as SSL version 3 and TLS, protect Hypertext Transfer Protocol (HTTP) sessions. Finally, the IPSec protocol suite provides client-to-client (end-to-end) security across internal connections.

Creating Secure Boundaries: Application Scoping

Other techniques mentioned in Chapter 6 (besides the DMZ) involve gateways that run as application services. An example is Microsoft Proxy Server 2, which performs both a caching function to improve performance and packet filtering. When this service is installed in a network environment, all client applications must direct their requests for services, such as File Transfer Protocol (FTP) or HTTP, through the Proxy Server. This arrangement restricts the message flow and permits centralized logging, as well as effective monitoring and control of system resources.

Creating Secure Boundaries: Policy Scoping

Distinctions between distributed and network security are blurring because several technologies are now fully integrated into the operating system. Remote access is becoming a necessary business requirement for staff in most enterprises. The management of remote access services is primarily through policy. Windows 2000 policy-based management has been simplified and is now centrally administered primarily because of LDAP version 3 and RADIUS. RRAS provides the remote access services. Microsoft, through the use of the published application programming interface (API) and well-known protocols like LDAP and RADIUS, has extended AD services to include remote access user authentication and to guarantee future interoperability with multivendor directory services. These feature trends are discussed in the "Identity Management" section in Chapter 7.

The call-accounting features of full-featured RADIUS services are incorporated in IAS. Through these features, Windows 2000 can manage large-scale, heterogeneous, remote access environments. Microsoft has integrated IAS with RRAS and AD to build a centrally administered, remote access service that offers policy-based management and detailed call accounting services. The integration of IAS and AD with RADIUS-enforced policy management can control many exchange variables, such as:

- Internet Protocol (IP) address
- Originating client IP address
- Network Access Server (NAS) manufacturer
- Type of service requested
- Type of protocol used
- Transport Control Protocol (TCP)/User Datagram Protocol (UDP) port
- User ID telephone number
- Originating phone number
- User group
- Time of day

Integration of the AD directory service provides centrally managed control of both direct-dial and VPN services. Although previous remote access solutions failed to address both client and management issues, this kind of comprehensive policy management and RADIUS-based accounting services in the form of enhanced directory services reduce TCO while improving staff productivity and the overall security and management efficiency. It changes the way enterprises provide services to their staff. If companies can manage remote access services in this manner, there are few reasons not to offer it as a standard business tool. Windows 2000 now offers these kinds of integrated management tools and policy-based services to its users without the company having to incur additional costs in support, maintenance, or training.

Preparing a Support Team

Security technologies require not just expertise but careful and diligent monitoring. Sophisticated security systems—like, for example, firewall technologies installed as a standalone security system—give an organization a false sense of comfort. These systems are usually deployed in concert with other technologies that carefully fortify them. Two key activities associated with the successful installation of any security system are monitoring and auditing. Your support team must not only have sufficient training to deploy these systems, but also experience using instrumentation that measures system usage and daily activity. They should play an active role in all pilot studies where systems are scrutinized and, often, rebuilt and fine-tuned.

When abnormal or unexpected activity is observed, your support team should first formalize and then systematically follow a set of procedures to isolate the problem, determine its nature, and follow through with some corrective action. These standardized procedures are documented in a disaster recovery plan, a security network plan, or a deployment plan. Help desk support thus plays an integral part in testing the system so that, following deployment, the support team can aggressively and confidently support the system users.

Monitoring and Auditing

The best security technology will fail if it is improperly deployed or configured. Pilot testing is necessary to confirm that systems work as planned. Nevertheless, even the most thorough planning cannot anticipate every conceivable plan of attack within any particular attack modality. In fact, environments will change over time, especially in response to the changing needs of a business or a large user population. Companies need to maintain baselines of network activity. Although ongoing system checks are necessary to maintain system integrity, regularly planned (though randomly scheduled) security audits, especially when you are dealing with network security, are important and can minimize risks. Companies should also systematically apply one or two assault methods from each attack modality to locate security weaknesses and prevent a real attack before it happens.

You should use tools that capture details about network flow so that you can observe system utilization, any changes in baseline behavior, or shifts in workloads. Microsoft Proxy Server 2 automatically produces production reports. Logging data to a text file tracks system usage and errors by supported online service. You can easily import these text files to analysis tools. Alternatively, data can be stored as Open Database Connectivity (ODBC)/Structured Query Language (SQL) database files to facilitate automated analysis and fault management through programmed triggers. Windows 2000 automatically logs events and audits specific activities. IAS also has activity reporting functions. It is important, though, to review the accumulated data, not just collect it.

Another increasingly important approach in network management is Simple Network Management Protocol (SNMP). Based on a simple architecture of management agent (information collector), network management protocol (SNMP), management station (some host server), and an extensive management information knowledge base, a network and its servers can be remotely monitored and maintained. The advantages of this important protocol are a single operator interface and minimal separate equipment outside of the agent and the host. SNMPv3, as specified in RFC 2570 through 2575, defines a framework for incorporating network security and access controls into this architecturally simple system.

Help Desk Support

The support function or user help desk is critical to an organization's health as well as to the implementation of its security policy. You should view the help desk as an in-house service business where performance is measured in terms of quality of service. Employee satisfaction and goodwill are important because both foster compliance with security policies and procedures, as well as shape a corporate culture.

Developing a Security Deployment Plan

At this stage of the process, you begin implementing security plans on a small or pilot scale to test assumptions in the real corporate environment in the hands of nontechnical, perhaps hostile users. Some deployment plans are suggested later in this section. Finally, after the support team has had time to monitor, audit, and analyze the efficacy of the security technologies, the final rollout of the formal security systems is performed. At that point in time, the support staff and help desk are fully empowered and confident in resolving any user issues.

Creating and Publishing a Security Policy

There are social and legal implications in publishing a security policy. It is the management's responsibility to formally communicate its goals, objectives, and restrictions to all employees. It is also necessary to distribute this policy in a way that fosters a sense of compliance among employees. Adding some legal text in a dialog box during the logon process plays an important part in providing an employer with the legal grounds to dismiss an employee for misconduct without fear of legal repercussions.

Developing Strategies for Secure Network Connections

Having prepared an overall strategy and identified the specific needs of various segments of your user population, you must then plan or strategize the deployment of services. Wherever possible, you would have replaced specific user needs with built-in groups and security templates. One of the key benefits of writing a deployment plan is to uncover duplication or overlapping in security services at different layers. Several security systems are mutually dependent, like the dependence of L2TP on IPSec for VPN client-gateway security. IPSec seeks machine certification to authorize the client-server connection. Without certification services provided in that domain, this planned exchange will fail. You must set Group Policy features for auto-enrollment so that clients have the necessary credentials for the IPSec exchange to occur. Group Policy in AD can centralize administration on a domain basis. This topic is discussed in greater detail in Chapter 10.

Thus, the deployment plans also indicate strengths and weaknesses in scoping, especially in the complex area of policy management.

Deploying Network Strategies for the Everyone Group

Depending on the structure of the corporate business objectives, use the Everyone group *conceptually* as the lowest common denominator for assigning network services. Although I do not use the group when assigning access to resources, I use it for security reasons to configure auditing of various objects early in a project. Likewise, I design access for Everyone, so I have to protect myself from Everyone. Deployment of, for example, Proxy Server 2 provides an easily installed and maintained choke for network connectivity as well as a central point for packet filtering and maintaining service logs when Everyone tries to attack my installation. Although it requires slightly more maintenance, deploying an Internet Information Server (IIS) also provides security control over network connectivity and various online services such as FTP and HTTP. Thus, in planning my deployment for the Everyone group, I have actually established three security scopes:

- The Proxy Server at the Application layer implicitly gave me control over TCP/UDP protocols and ports through its packet filtering capabilities.
- IIS gave me similar functionality, except I could control the online services that run at the application level.
- Tracking system auditing (e.g., unsuccessful logon activity) represents policy scoping.

Deploying Network Strategies for Staff Members

The primary security concerns regarding staff members are authentication and confidentiality. This group has some degree of privileges, so you must secure the initial logon. This user group would be assigned to a class of services that would typically include Internet access. Given the low administrative overhead involved in remote access services, it is increasingly common for this to also be included in a class of services for this particular group. Within this broad class of services, both IIS and RRAS allow policy definitions at the user level. Whether implemented as local policies or as part of Group Policy, remote access policies can enforce both authentication and encryption. When you are deploying specifically RRAS security, the following issues are relevant:

- Which groups or users will have access
- What kind of authentication will be used
- What kind of data encryption will be used

Deploying Remote Access Policy Using VPN

Another approach to remote access services is to provide the features of a private network except over unsecured namespace such as the Internet. Windows 2000 provides VPNs as part of the standard operating system and at reduced costs compared to other solutions on the market. Although VPN deployment is more complicated than deployment of unsecured public connections, the full features of a private network across a public network such as the Internet offer significant benefits. A VPN can be deployed between any two sites, even when both are within an internal network, using a variety of connections to enhance security. Windows 2000 includes VPN software as part of RRAS.

When deploying a VPN, consider the following issues:

- Integration of the VPN in your remote access policy
- Choice of either PPTP or L2TP security protocols; if L2TP is used, decide whether to implement IPSec; if you use IPSec, choose what certificate to use
- Placement of the VPN server
- Centralized management tools like Connection Manager, discussed later in this chapter

Remote access policies specifically deal with users of RRAS. Policies can be based on user group, phone number, hours of usage, and other kinds of information. Profiles can be applied to connections that specify session length; maximum idle time; dialup media; allowed addresses; and security methods such as authentication, encryption, or VPN. You can set these policies for RRAS or IAS. It's important that you carefully plan the creation and application of policies to various groups because it is possible to overlap and unintentionally contradict or disallow one specification with another. For a discussion of the VPN protocol choices, see Chapter 6.

Placing Servers

Placement of, for example, a VPN server, especially in relation to a firewall, is very important and is an example of planning, sizing, and placement of server services before deploying security systems. Both VPN technology and firewall technology offer complementary benefits and thus may be deployed at the same time. Their placement in relation to each other is very important. Although both services could be installed on the same physical machine it is best to distribute services across different servers whenever possible to provide fault tolerance, hardware capacity, and so on. At the very least, given the importance of running both services concurrently, the unavailability or loss of this server jeopardizes the network security of an entire enterprise. Figure 8.5 shows a sample VPN/firewall placement.

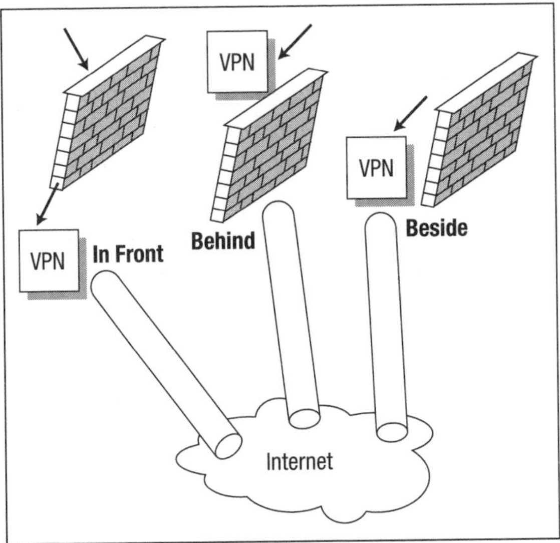

Figure 8.5 An example of VPN/firewall placement.

Figure 8.5 shows three scenarios (I assume that each service is running on a separate server). Each scenario has advantages and disadvantages, as described in Table 8.1.

There is not one single correct relationship between these two security technologies. The final decision is a function of corporate objectives, budget, user population, and in this case, the expertise of the support team responsible for deploying and maintaining the security plan.

An Example of Centralized Administration: Connection Manager

Deploying client software for VPN is labor intensive, especially because the user population is by definition located outside the enterprise's boundaries. Windows

Table 8.1 The advantages and disadvantages of various VPN/firewall configurations.

Configuration	Advantages	Disadvantages
VPN in front of firewall	Firewall is secure	Provides only external services
VPN behind firewall	Firewall provides all services to VPN users	You must configure additional TCP/UDP ports to accommodate which security protocols are chosen; these open ports weaken the wall
VPN beside firewall	Fault tolerance, physical layout of services	Double the costs of support, maintenance, auditing; double the security risks of penetration

2000 provides for relatively simple setup through Connection Manager, which runs on both legacy NT 4 and Windows 9x clients. The Connection Manager Administration Kit (CMAK), like other administration tools such as the Internet Explorer Administration Kit and Outlook Deployment Kit, provides an administrator with a tool that cost-effectively creates customized connections for most if not all end users. From a service business perspective, your support team can distribute an installation kit that efficiently "empowers" nontechnical remote users to configure direct dial-up and VPN remote access connections with little or no dependence on technical support. Like the other administration kits, CMAK permits on-demand updating of remote clients from some centralized source. Here again is an example of Microsoft's integrated administrative features that provide enhanced end-user functionality at little or no increase in TCO.

Deploying Network Strategies for Users and Applications

A security approach, common in relational database management systems such as SQL Server, defines access not in terms of users or groups but in terms of applications. This application role provides a security context within which a user can perform a predetermined task in a controlled environment or security sandbox. The application is secured with either its own dedicated directory database of authorized users or, based on recent trends in directory consolidation (as discussed in Chapter 7), in some centralized global directory. Examples of these applications are time management, company benefits registration, and Web-based e-commerce storefronts. The security technologies that support this kind of application development are rapidly increasing, with the trends toward thinner remote clients and fatter distributed hosts. Relevant security technologies here depend on:

- Specifications of the application
- The sophistication in design with respect to backend integration and security
- Application performance issues
- Complexity of administration required to support the application

Depending upon how the application is integrated with the network through the Security Support Provider Interface (SSPI), application-oriented security technologies include:

- Kerberos, discussed in Chapter 4
- SSL3/TLS1, discussed in Chapters 2 and 7
- Digital certificates, discussed in Chapter 2

These distributed applications interface with SSPI, which in turn negotiates with installed Security Support Providers (SSPs) to establish a mutually supported secured session pipes through which all subsequent information exchanges will occur. Refer to Chapter 4 for a discussion of SSPI and installable SSPs. Figure 8.6 shows how an application interfaces the various communication and security layers. In brief, some distributed application uses a Distributed Component Object Model (DCOM) interface, an Internet API (WinInet), or the Windows Sockets 2 interface (Winsock) to communicate with some host server. These connections, or others using Remote Procedure Calls (RPCs) or Transmission Control Protocol/Internet Protocol (TCP/IP) directly (the Winsock interface) all interface with the SSPI. This common platform gives Windows 2000 a major architectural advantage because it allows any third-party application to negotiate with any one of several installed security libraries (NTLM, Kerberos, or SChannel security protocols) on some host server.

Deploying Network Strategies for Business Partners

With the expansion of communication and the forces of e-commerce, business alliances not only offer complementary services but directly share data and other enterprise resources. This access from outside the boundaries of the enterprise exposes an internal network to considerable risks. The network and security technologies that support such cross-enterprise access are collectively called an *extranet*. Access technologies include VPN and RRAS. One important characteristic that

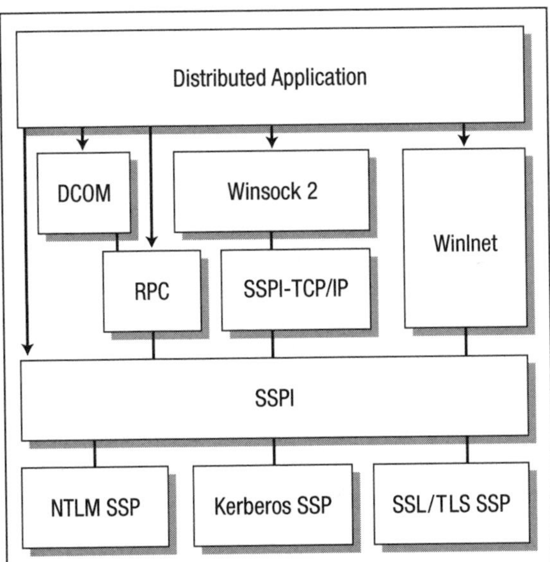

Figure 8.6 Relationships among network application security technologies.

distinguishes the extranet scenario from other remote access situations is that the extranet has location and link specificity. Thus, IP addressing between the two enterprises is predefined.

These predetermined links have both advantages and disadvantages. As with the deployment of all the other population groups, it is critical for daily operation, security, and support that you carefully consider how business units will communicate with each other, their functional relationships, the workflows between units, and the deployment of services. You should carefully monitor traffic patterns across extranet connections because the workloads characteristic among partners are typically several orders of magnitude greater than workloads transferred among staff members. You must carefully consider WAN connection speeds with regard to capacity. Finally, security controls here focus on scalability, availability, accessibility, and timeliness because pipes among partners can be expected to carry mission-critical data. The priorities of these security controls would be detailed in the corporate business objectives.

A Security Policy Case Study

ExamCram Ltd. Reformulates Its Plans

ExamCram Ltd., having merged with MyCompany Inc., located in the same building, has created a new company called ExamCram Company. There is a growing contingent of dissatisfied MyCompany Inc. personnel. At the moment, management is reassessing its financial situation and corporate strategy. There have been some leaks to the press regarding ExamCram Company's plans to increase capitalization through an initial public offering (IPO). This has placed top-level management in an awkward situation. They have hired outside management consultants to evaluate internal policies and procedures, as well as auditors to review the financial data.

MyPartner Inc. still works exclusively for the Sales division of MyCompany Inc. over an extranet.

Company Goal

One immediate objective is to protect the confidentiality of information. Another is to formalize corporate policies and procedures. Outside auditors and consultants agree that ExamCram Company has grown a profitable business from a small, startup company but that it must now develop more sophisticated business policies and procedures before it can take any further strategic steps. A newly formulated Board of Directors wants to plan the growth of the new enterprise carefully.

Exhibit

The original organizational chart for both ExamCram Ltd. and MyCompany Inc. is shown in Exhibit 1.

Current LAN/Network Structure

All 100-client machines are running native mode Windows 2000 in the root domain of a tree. Each workstation is connected to a 10Mbps hub through 10Mbps local area network (LAN) cards, although Category 5 Unshielded Twisted Pair (UTP) cabling connects each system and hub in a star topology. The network protocol is TCP/IP.

MyCompany Inc., composed of 20 users, is in a child domain, **mycompany.examcram.com**, under **examcram.com**. The tree is well connected.

Proposed LAN/Network Structure

The VPN server IP address on the Internet is 201.101.1.1. The HTTP, FTP, and PPTP packet filters are properly configured on the Internet interface.

ExamCram Ltd.				MyCompany Inc.
VP Fin	VP Sales	VP Ops	CEO	President
Accnt Mngr	Sales Mngr	Tech Mngr	Project Mngr1	Vice President/Sales Mngr
			Project Mngr2	Accnt Mngr SysAdmin
		DBA/Developer	Project Mngr3	
		Webmaster	Project Mngr4	
		Programmer	Project Mngr5	
Bookkeep Clerk1 Clerk2 Clerk3	Sales1 Sales2 Sales3 Sales4	Tech1 Tech2 Tech3		Bookkeep Sales1 Tech1 Clerk1 Sales2 Tech2 Clerk2 Sales3 Tech3 Sales4

Exhibit 1 Original organizational chart.

Current WAN Connectivity

Both companies use Internet access to communicate. ExamCram Company wants MyCompany Inc. to continue to work directly with its business partner, MyPartner Inc.

Proposed WAN Connectivity

No plans are proposed at this time.

Design Commentary

The CEO at ExamCram Company says, "We need a methodology to grow our enterprise that is results oriented and milestone based. In my five-year plan, I want to deliver services as quickly and efficiently as possible. I want to shorten the review process of every project so that ExamCram Company adapts quickly to changing business, financial, and technical events in the world of e-commerce."

The IT Director at ExamCram Company says, "I want to create a security blueprint that will address our business, application, and technical needs. I want the IT department to serve as an internal service organization that supports our staff."

Current Internet Positioning

ExamCram Ltd. is registered as **examcram.com**. Its IP address is 201.101.1.1. MyCompany Inc. is registered as **mycompany.com** at IP address 198.2.4.6. ExamCram Company will continue to use the **examcram.com** domain as ExamCram Ltd. has done in the past.

Future Internet Plans

No changes in the current structure are proposed at this time.

Commentary

Figure 8.7 shows the same organizational chart as Exhibit 1, except that it is deployed as a number of organizational global groups that would typically extend across a flat NT 4 legacy domain structure. Figure 8.8 shows the revised categorization of users, as described in the "Identifying the User Population" section earlier in this chapter. However, to support the enterprise, the company would still need two one-way trusts in Windows 2000 mixed mode.

The organization shown in Figures 8.7 and 8.8 can be improved. You can see the transition from the flat NT 4 domain structure (Figure 8.7) and multiple domains with nontransitive trusts (Figure 8.8) to a hierarchical, single domain model (Figure 8.9) using AD without trusts or, worst case, transitive trusts between regional divisions (namely, **east.examcram.com** and **west. examcram.com**).

ExamCram Company is looking for a vision statement. It has little or no idea how to take a first step. The company doesn't know what corporate business objectives

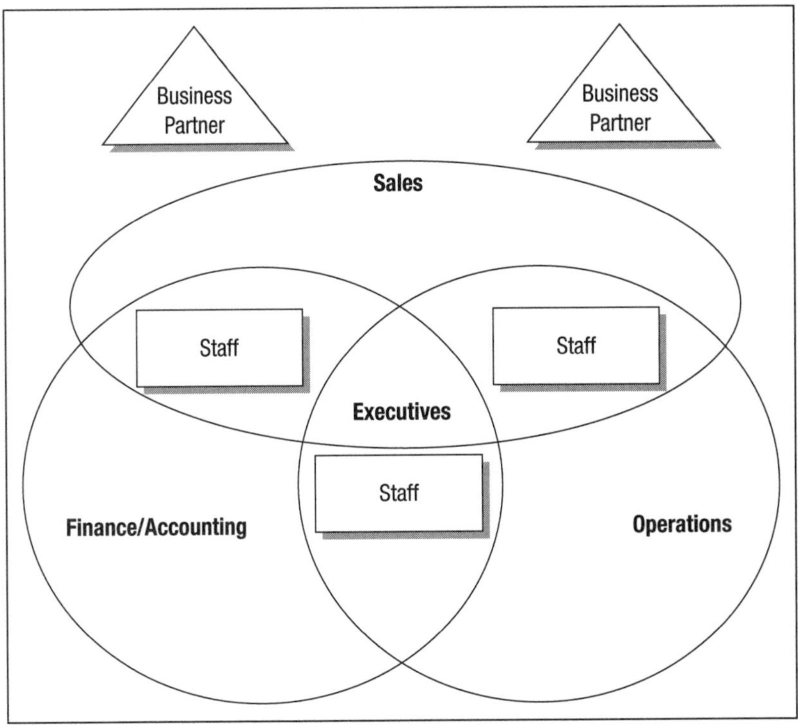

Figure 8.7 Organizational chart: original flat domain structure.

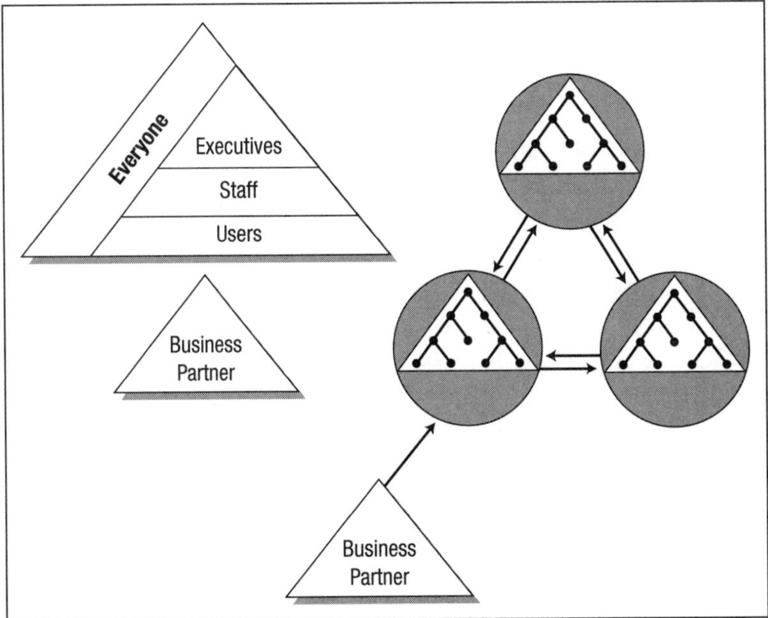

Figure 8.8 Groups in a user population.

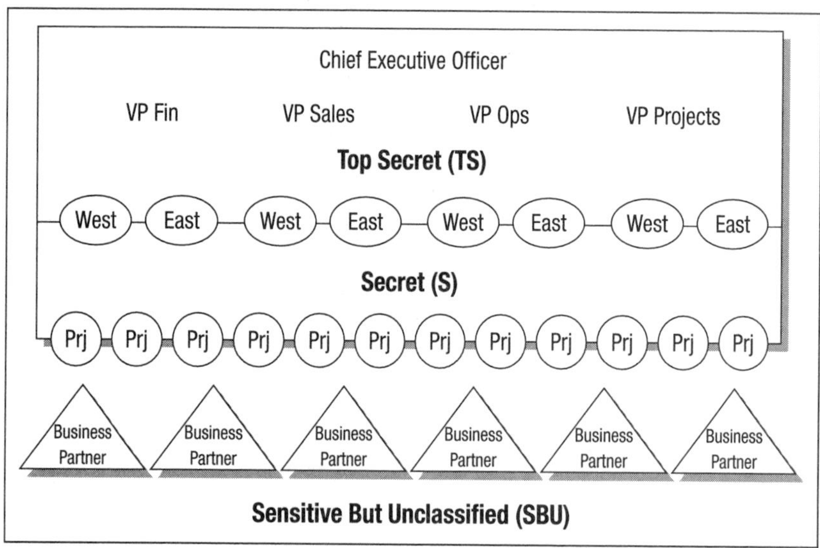

Figure 8.9 Proposed organization after phase 1.

are. However, it does need to evolve into a single corporate structure with unified policies and procedures. The policies and procedures take time to write and will require many revisions and modifications before a final form is achieved.

Note: Always begin with a simple action plan. Approach this task as an iterative process that establishes a specific schedule, a scope of actions to be completed in that timeframe, and a list of required resources. Determine what your deliverables are (scope) and when they are due (schedule), and then determine what you need to complete your action plan (resources).

My action plan is set out in the following sections.

Short-Term Objective 1: Deploy a Technology that Will Correct the Security Leak

The time frame for this objective is as soon as possible. Management believes that future security leaks can be prevented through the deployment of security systems that will limit access to information. The immediate objective is therefore to provide and maintain confidentiality. My initial solution is to establish policies regarding both resource accessibility and user authorization without the need for capital investment. Additional solutions deploying security technologies will typically follow the establishment of policies and procedures based on whether top management wants to allocate financial resources.

I begin by defining four categories of confidentiality. These categories, although arbitrary, would typically be decided by top management and would be based upon perceived damage to the corporation following, for example, full public disclosure. The typical categories are:

- *Top secret (TS)*—The highest level of required confidentiality; unauthorized disclosure of this category of information would result in the gravest of consequences to an organization.
- *Secret (S)*—Disclosure of this type of material would correspond to serious but not irreparable damage.
- *Sensitive but unclassified (SBU)*—This type of material is confidential; disclosure might prove embarrassing.
- *Unclassified (U)*—This type of material would have little or no meaning to outsiders.

Categories should be based on the same criterion or dimension to simplify compliance. For example, in the bulleted list, the constant criterion I use is the amount of damage to the corporation would suffer through disclosure. Next, I simplify job categories by assigning different roles to the user population groups identified in the "Identifying the User Population" section earlier in this chapter: executives, staff, user, and everyone. I then rebuild the organizational chart based on this new classification scheme, as shown in Figure 8.10.

I determine groups by applying the principle of least privilege, where access is permitted only to information that is necessary to accomplish any one job. I focus first on confidentiality by classifying documents in very simple ways. I will suggest to the Board of Directors a second phase of security deployment where I would deploy security technologies that reduce accessibility to all information at any one time, thus reducing the capability of an intruder to cause damage.

Notice how levels of confidentiality decrease from Exec to Staff to User. Nevertheless, these three categories correlate fairly well with job function in that data-entry material is sensitive but not classified. Operational reports typically prepared and reviewed by staff are ranked as S. Financial reporting that represents the consolidation of material is for executive decision support and therefore TS.

Short-Term Objective 2: Deliver a First-Draft Action Plan that Describes a Scalable Enterprise Architecture

The time frame for this objective is two weeks. Once I have placed the users and resources into some manageable framework, I will present my proposed organizational plan; information space has been divided into three specific security levels: TS, S, and SBU resources, as shown previously in Figure 8.9. Instead of adopting the flat domain structure of NT 4, I use a hierarchical arrangement, which offers greater degrees of scalability, especially in the context of regional expansion. This is

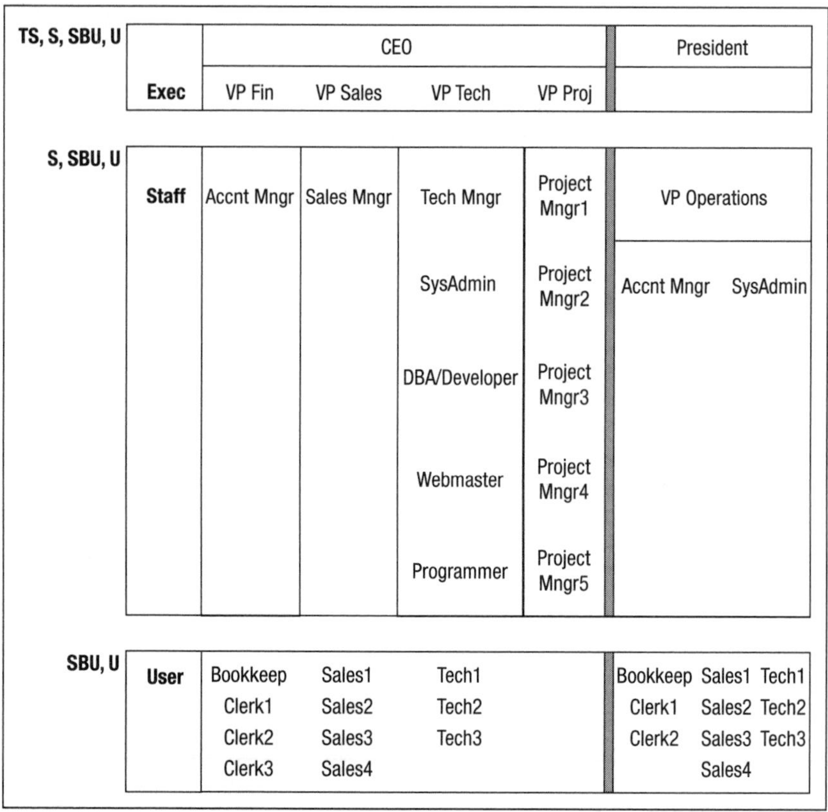

Figure 8.10 Proposed organizational chart of ExamCram Company.

a first draft of the organization that is intended to simplify the flow of information. I will present the Board of Directors with an organizational view that provides a framework within which to develop a more comprehensive policy. The issue of confidentiality needs to be addressed as quickly as possible. By reclassifying users and introducing a conceivably uniform criterion, management can rapidly implement a plan without spending any money.

I will urge the Board of Directors to define policies by creating a security blueprint. I will need to create group policies that begin with account policies, then grow local policies and restricted groups within domains. Figure 8.9 uses a hierarchical domain model with secured, functional boundaries. For example, each project can be isolated from the others. Similarly, as divisions grow, each will join the tree as a child domain under the corporate root domain.

Note: An enterprise is the combination of business, application, information, and technical architectures composed primarily of services. I define a service as a group of related workflows, functions, or outputs that collectively are a named object; the service object has an account in the directory database. Services are implemented through a consistent and documented set of outputs and interfaces composed of these business, application, information, or technical architectures. The value of any service is ultimately determined by the consumer of that service, hence our consumer-service provider relationship. Security controls are based on standards of due care and due diligence, practices that are readily available at a reasonable cost or are in regular use and are applied to reduce risk to that service.

Short-Term Objective 3: What Will My Deliverable Look Like?

It is not appropriate for me to create for ExamCram Company a vision statement that encompasses its business and technical objectives. I can, however, propose a vision statement that includes a framework for a network security plan and recommend some key themes that will help me to eventually create it. I would conceptualize the enterprise as three interdependent areas that provide:

- Business services (services inventory, workflow controls, and business rules)
- User services (services inventory based on the user population's needs)
- Data services (corporate assets)

Note: Create a statement that considers each of the three themes in the context of industry growth trends, frequency of changes, trends in development of competitive businesses, current and future ExamCram Company business needs, and changes in geographic scope associated with sizing issues.

I will create an inventory of business services based on ExamCram Company's business mission and statement. For example, there is a full-charge accounting system that includes Accounts Receivable, Accounts Payable, General Ledger, Payroll, and some kind of purchase order system to take book orders. In addition, a project management system handles book deals..

I create based on the identified user population an inventory of services that includes:

- Line-of-business (LOB) applications
- Internal/external messaging
- Information management (file/print/Web services)
- Data storage and archiving
- Network support
- Service-level guarantees (such as authentication based on a functional WAN link)

I also create a preliminary inventory of internal IT functions, including:

- System administration
- Configuration management
- Problem management
- Contingency planning
- Help desk

I create a physical equipment inventory and a topology that shows WAN and Domain Name System (DNS) architecture. I then create the appropriate domain architecture; create trees; and create a forest based on the inventory of services, the distribution of my user population, and the actual deployment of equipment. I complete site planning by designing a global catalog and DC placement. I conclude by proposing Organizational Units and group policies that mirror the functional organization of the enterprise where appropriate. These latter structures are discussed in Chapters 9 and 10.

From these inventories and needs list, I begin outlining a deployment plan to determine what components are critical and required during the first phase of deployment. I start with as simple a design as possible (such as Figure 8.9). Where possible, I start with a single tree at a single site; I define site, domain, or OUs in terms of hierarchical, functional workflows (geopolitical, business, and technical). In Figure 8.9, top-level management oversees regional divisions, which in turn manage local projects.

Practice Questions

Case Study

4Sale, an online bartering company in ThatTherePlace, North Dakota, has merged with Got-a-Deal, and both companies occupy office space in the same office building. The companies are now running their accounting operation, their bid system, and a knowledge base of their online goods in the same building.

Current LAN/Network Structure

4Sale is presently running Windows 2000 server in native mode. One member server supports Exchange server, and another is running IIS 5 and Proxy Server 2. All 100 client machines are configured in a single domain model. The client systems are running Windows Professional; Office 97 is utilized as an applications package. Each system is connected to a 10Mbps hub through 10Mbps LAN cards running Category 5 UTP cabling in a star topology.

Got-a-Deal has merged with 4Sale and is running all 22 client machines in a single child domain under the 4Sale root domain. The client systems are running Windows Professional, with Office 97 being utilized as an applications package. Each system is connected to a 10Mbps hub through 10Mbps LAN cards running Category 5 UTP cabling in a star topology. These hubs are on the same backbone as 4Sale but have a different subnet.

Proposed LAN/Network Structure

4Sale is developing its online barter/trading business through business alliances. It is investigating the use of secured private networks for branch offices. It has formed several partnerships with brokers throughout the country. These brokers will connect to the system and place bids for clients.

Current WAN Connectivity

4 Sale has a T1 connection to an Internet Service Provider (ISP) in OverThere, North Dakota. Got-a-Deal has 56Kbps dial-up networking connectivity through the same ISP.

Proposed WAN Connectivity

No changes are planned at this time.

Directory Design Commentary

No changes are planned at this time.

Current Internet Positioning

4Sale is registered as **4sale.com**. Got-a-Deal has been selling its goods through local companies and through the **4sale.com** Web site.

Future Internet Plans

No changes in the current structure are proposed at this time.

Company Goal with Windows 2000

Develop the standards and procedures that the IT department will implement.

Exhibit

See Exhibit 2.

4Sale			Got-a-Deal		
	CEO			President	
VP Fin	VP Sales	VP Ops		Vice President/Sales Mngr	
		Webmaster/ SysAdmin			
		DBA/Developer			
Bookkeep	Sales1	Tech1	Bookkeep	Sales1	Tech1
Clerk1	Sales2	Tech2		Sales2	Tech2
	Sales3	Tech3		Sales3	Tech3
	Sales4			Sales4	

Exhibit 2 Original organizational chart of 4Sale and Got-a-Deal.

Question 1

Considering the case study provided, what issue(s) must you consider when you create the 4Sale network security plan?

- ❍ a. Due care and due diligence
- ❍ b. Information security strategies
- ❍ c. Security group descriptions
- ❍ d. None of the above
- ❍ e. All of the above

Answer b is correct. The network plan is a fundamental part of security deployment. Information security strategies are the specific design and strategic choices that need to be made to secure online exchanges such as email and Web-based communications. This is the best answer to the question. Due care and due diligence describes how procedures are to be carried out and is considered part of the IT security control compliance. It should not be part of the actual security plan itself. Therefore, answer a is incorrect. Similarly, security group descriptions are built into the security policy. These default choices and security templates are critical in deployment but are more administrative in function. Therefore, answer c is incorrect. Only answer b is correct, so answers d and e are incorrect.

Question 2

> You have compiled an organizational chart for both 4Sale and Got-A-Deal. You want to categorize the user population into three groups:
>
> Executive
>
> Staff
>
> User
>
> Place the following positions under the appropriate group:
>
> 4Sale VP Finance
>
> Got-a-Deal bookkeeper
>
> 4Sale DBA/developer
>
> Got-a-Deal Tech1

The correct answer is:

- Executive
- Staff
  - 4Sale VP of Finance
  - Got-a-Deal bookkeeper
  - 4Sale DBA/developer
- User
  - Got-a-Deal Tech1

Got-a-Deal is a small company. Often, titles are misleading; never make assumptions about what people do or what responsibilities and security access levels they ought to have. When you assign network access and responsibilities, it is a good practice to have at least one person (preferably, two people) at each functional level to ensure proper workflows. The Got-a-Deal President is in the Executive group. The VP functions more like an office manager in this company than Vice President; this person is in the staff group. The Got-a-Deal bookkeeper, sales staff, and technical staff all report to the VP/Sales Manager. Depending on the "corporate culture," you might recommend that the Vice President could assume the President's role in her absence; there is no backup at the Executive level. Don't be surprised if the President says she doesn't want the Vice President to have an Administrator security role. Remember, the security plan reflects exactly what top-level management wants and needs.

Question 3

Based on the user population in Question 2 and depicted in Exhibit 2, what kind of internal business services does 4Sale offer? [Check all correct answers]

- ❑ a. Line of business (LOB) applications
- ❑ b. Messaging
- ❑ c. Data storage
- ❑ d. Network support

Answers a, b, c, and d are correct. Often, a company (for example, Microsoft) will use its own LOB applications in internal operations, so answer a is correct. 4Sale supports a broad range of business services to its user population in addition to its bidding system. Messaging for communication (answer b), data storage (answer c), and file and print sharing are key to any network environment. In addition, the IT department offers softer services like system and configuration management, contingency planning, and help desk support (answer d). It is important that these business-related functions be included in the inventory of services for a security plan to be complete.

Question 4

VP of Operations for 4Sale says, "What are relevant security issues we need to address when we formulate network strategies for our e-commerce quote and barter applications?" [Check all correct answers]

- ❑ a. Application specifications
- ❑ b. Design sophistication
- ❑ c. Application performance issues
- ❑ d. Administrative complexity
- ❑ e. A consolidated directory

Answers a, b, c, d, and e are correct. When you are dealing with, for example, database management systems, the application specification (answer a) and the design sophistication (answer b) are very important especially in terms of its performance issues (answer c) and level of required administrative support (answer d) during and after installation. There is also a trend among some applications, such as Exchange, to substitute a dedicated directory database of users for a consolidated system database (answer e).

Question 5

VP of Operations for 4Sale says, "What issues should we consider if 4Sale offers its business partners a VPN?" [Check all correct answers]

- ❑ a. Integrating the VPN into a remote access policy
- ❑ b. Choice of PPTP or L2TP
- ❑ c. IIS functionality
- ❑ d. Administrative complexity
- ❑ e. Using Connection Manager

Answers a, b, d and e are correct. Integrating Virtual Private Networks into a remote access policy, choice of Point-To-Point Tunneling Protocol or Layer 2 Tunneling Protocol, administrative complexity, and using Connection Manager are critical themes that you need to explore when deploying a VPN. Aside from these considerations, security protocol is a major consideration because L2TP also depends on IP Security. Administrative complexity is another issue. Connection Manager, however, greatly helps in the installation of remote users. Internet Information Server is not an issue when you are considering VPNs. Therefore, answer c is incorrect.

Need to Know More?

Garfinkel, Simson and Gene Spafford. *Practical UNIX and Internet Security, Second Edition*. O'Reilly & Associates, Sebastopol, CA, 1996. ISBN 1-56592-148-8. Chapter 2, Policies and Guidelines, discusses at great length many components of risk assessment, cost-benefits analysis, and general security issues. This introductory chapter is both descriptive and procedural in its approach and is relevant to any IT installation.

Nichols, Randall K. et al. *Defending Your Digital Assets against Hackers, Crackers, Spies, and Thieves, First Edition*. McGraw-Hill Professional Publishing, New York, NY, 2000. ISBN 0-07-212285-4. Although the entire book is written from a global perspective, discussions in Chapters 3 and 4 are particularly informative about the way the U.S. government and the military handle security issues. Many of the concepts can be applied just as well to a corporate environment.

Search the TechNet CD (or its online version through **www.microsoft.com**) and the *Windows 2000 Server Resource Kit* CD using the keywords "security", "meta-directory", "ICS", and "MSDSS". This is Microsoft's definitive online resource for technical papers and bulletins.

www.microsoft.com/technet/win2000/dguide/ This link offers the *Windows 2000 Server Deployment and Planning Guide* (from the *Windows 2000 Resource Kit*). This Web site provides the text to the entire *Deployment and Planning Guide.*

www.microsoft.com/windows2000/library/howitworks/activedirectory/identity.asp This link takes you to the *Active Directory Interoperability and Metadirectory Overview* technical paper, which gives an overview of how identity information among resources is shared yet remains consistent throughout the enterprise. The concept of identity management is presented as a customer situation that has specific requirements (connectivity, brokering, and integrity management) and specific solutions. The adopted Microsoft solution of a hub and spoke meta-directory architecture is discussed.

www.microsoft.com/windows2000/library/resources/reskit/dpg/default.asp This link takes you to the *Deployment and Planning Guide.* Chapter 7 presents a comprehensive discussion of network connectivity issues, external connectivity from within an organization, and transport and network protocol issues. Chapter 11 provides a detailed guide that outlines sections of a network security plan, administrative policies for a Windows 2000 enterprise, Group Policy issues, and security audit threat detection policies. Chapter 17 describes the network security issues in a security plan, including a discussion of application-oriented network security technologies.

Identity Management Issues

Terms you'll need to understand:

- ✓ Directory services
- ✓ X.500 directory services
- ✓ X.509 recommendations
- ✓ Namespace
- ✓ Simple Authentication and Security Layer (SASL)
- ✓ Microsoft Meta-directory Services (MMS)
- ✓ Microsoft Messaging Application Programming Interface (MAPI)
- ✓ Active Directory Services Interfaces (ADSI)
- ✓ Relative distinguished name (RDN)
- ✓ Distinguished name (DN)
- ✓ Access control list (ACL)
- ✓ Global Catalog (GC)
- ✓ Organizational Unit (OU)
- ✓ Domain controller (DC)
- ✓ Flexible (Floating) Single-Master Operations (FSMO)
- ✓ Encrypting File System (EFS)

Techniques you'll need to master:

- ✓ Identifying the key directory service components
- ✓ Describing the basic components of Windows 2000 architecture
- ✓ Describing the five FSMO roles
- ✓ Describing deployment methods for users
- ✓ Describing deployment methods that control access to resources
- ✓ Understanding how EFS protects data stored on disks

A security threat to a resource depends upon accessibility, a consumer's skills, and consumer motivation. If the built-in Everyone group has access to a file and some authenticated, disgruntled employee with minimal computer skills but malicious intent wants to seek some form of retribution on another company employee or the company itself, that person may attempt to delete a file. If the malicious employee has access and the file provides that person Full Control, he or she will successfully cause damage. If, alternatively, this employee has access to the file but has Read Only object permissions, the malicious attempt will fail. If an administrator has set an account policy to audit such activity, this particular employee's failed attempt is logged for future review, investigation, and possible reprimand.

If you control accessibility, you eliminate most security threats. When someone has access to a resource, however, managing permissions to that object is key to preventing a security incident, no matter what the consumer's skills or motivation. The greater that consumer's skills and motivation to breach security, the more important managing permissions becomes. In fact, permission management is actually a dichotomy: accessibility to resources and management of actions that you can apply to that resource. This chapter begins with a brief discussion of directory services and naming conventions, which provides a foundation for analyzing how systems organize and access directory objects. These objects are primarily users and resources.

This chapter also covers other topics, including a discussion of specific directory services, the X.500 directory standard, and X.509-based directory systems (a subset of X.500) that use public key authentication systems. I then describe Lightweight Directory Access Protocol (LDAP) as an introduction to Active Directory (AD). Having introduced the historical basis for directory services, I briefly discuss each fundamental Windows 2000 logical structure and AD component. I then discuss user and resource topics, as well as how to implement accessibility and permission management in Windows 2000. I conclude this chapter with a discussion of an important Windows 2000 protection technology specifically designed to protect resources themselves—Encrypting File System (EFS).

Basic Directory Services

As you saw in the "A Microsoft Historical Perspective" section in Chapter 2, there is a trend with Windows 2000 toward greater differentiation and specialization of services than earlier versions of the Windows family of operating systems. Windows 2000 provides a greater number of standards-based interfaces than legacy NT. These interfaces provide software hooks for installable extensions to the core system services. As the complexity of information technology expands not only in terms of this specialization but also in terms of distributed objects in and beyond the boundaries of a corporate enterprise, a counterbalancing trend to improve accessibility to these ever-expanding and diversifying services and resources arises. This counterbalancing trend is in a unified directory service that not only catalogs the services and resource objects but also provides access methods to them.

Driving this counterbalancing trend is the need to integrate heterogeneous systems, simplify administration through consolidation and automation, and lower the total cost of ownership (TCO) through easier maintenance, support, and user training. As discussed in Chapter 7, it's a major architectural trend to develop umbrella directory systems that integrate existing directory services across heterogeneous systems called *meta-directories*. A critical maintenance function in identity management systems is synchronizing data across these heterogeneous datastores. It is important that at any given time, changing the credentials of a named object or principal in one datastore is synchronized with copies of credentials or references referring to that principal across all other directory services.

The X.500 Standard

The original idea of directory services is based on a Comité Consultatif International Téléphonique et Télégraphique (CCITT)/International Organization for Standardization (ISO) standard, X.500, which defines a global directory service solution for distributing and retrieving information. Key characteristics of the original specifications as cited in Request for Comments (RFC) 1330 were:

- Decentralized management
- Powerful searching capabilities
- A single global namespace
- A structured framework for storing information

The original X.500 standard is described in terms of four service-related models:

- *Information model*—Defines information
- *Functional model*—Defines how the information is stored and accessed
- *Organizational model*—Defines the policy between entities and the information they hold
- *Security model*—Defines two types of security for directory data: simple authentication (using passwords) and strong authentication (using cryptographic keys)

X.509 is the International Telecommunications Union (ITU) Telecommunication Standardization Sector (ITU-T) recommendation based on X.500 papers on directory services. It defines a framework for delivering the security model and authentication services. This framework, initially recommended in 1988 and subsequently revised several times, recommends specific message formats like the Public Key Cryptography Standards (PKCS) #7, #10, and #12 referred to in Chapter 3, as well as various authentication protocols. The X.509 specification, based on the idea of using public key cryptography and digital signatures, evolved into these PKCS formats. The directory serves as a repository for public key digital certificates and is discussed in both Chapters 3 and 7.

LDAP v3

The original X.500 specification offered users a unified view or namespace of named objects or principals defined in the universe of the organization. To define objects in an unambiguous way, the concept of a hierarchical, inverted tree structure was used. Due to implementation issues with the original X.500 specification that involved its complexity and protocol support, the IT community has actually adopted a simplified version of another protocol, LDAP (RFC 1777), as the favored platform for directory services. Its data model is based on the original X.500 concepts. In it, named objects have attributes, which, in turn, have a data type and a value. The named objects, just like those originally proposed in the X.500 specification, are stored in a hierarchical tree.

LDAP includes operations to select, add, update, and delete data. Authentication in LDAP version 2 uses unencrypted cleartext or Kerberos version 4 password authentication as cited in RFC 1777. LDAP version 3 uses Simple Authentication and Security Layer (SASL), an extensible security model defined in RFC 2222 that negotiates connection protocols like LDAP with different security providers like Kerberos. LDAP version 3 also supports the Secure Sockets Layer (SSL) protocol. Finally, LDAP version 3 has referral capabilities that allow it to appear as a single directory service to the end user; however, it actually interconnects with independent LDAP servers on a global scale. A major disadvantage of LDAP is its inability to synchronize data across servers.

AD Directory Services

At the core of Windows 2000 is the identity management services called Active Directory directory services, modeled on the X.500 specification. Microsoft's initiative in developing identity management solutions like Microsoft Meta-directory Services (MMS), discussed in Chapter 7, is based on the theme of a unified, global namespace. AD is Microsoft's first step toward this goal. Part of this initiative is already realized in the BackOffice mail product, Exchange 2000. The product uses AD, as opposed to its own separate datastore, to store information about objects. AD thus provides some of the original X.500 features:

- A unified catalog of principals

- A common repository in which to store an object's data
- A single point of administration, brokering features, and rules management

In Chapter 4, I discussed how the Key Distribution Center (KDC) was integrated with AD; KDC offers an authentication mechanism, and AD offers an authorization mechanism through security descriptors in the form of an access token and a centralized repository of security credentials. Thus, Microsoft delivers Single Sign-On (SSO) and authentication services by leveraging the existence of this enterprise-wide datastore with the storage of security credentials. With the addition of Microsoft Certificate Server, public key certificates at the heart of the X.509 recommendation are also incorporated into Windows 2000 through its public key infrastructure enhancements, as discussed in Chapter 3. Thus, Windows 2000 has realized much of the security model of the original X.500 standard.

AD supports the following application programming interface (API) sets:

- *LDAP C API (RFC 1823)*—LDAP's de facto C programming standard
- *Microsoft Messaging Application Programming Interface (MAPI)*—The Windows Open Services Architecture (WOSA) Messaging API
- *Active Directory Services Interfaces (ADSI)*—Microsoft's own directory services API, which is the Component Object Model (COM) interface for X.500-based directory services

I will discuss only the third of these—ADSI—here, because the other two have little if any direct connection with Windows 2000 security. ADSI supports popular applications and directory services such as Exchange, Lotus Notes, and Novell Directory Services (NDS). ADSI, which programmatically allows you to manipulate and query data in any of these three examples, is a part of the Open Directory Services Interface (ODSI), which, in turn, is part of WOSA. ADSI provides a single programming interface regardless of which directory services a developer needs. More significantly, ADSI also provides native support for LDAP. Much like AD added both authorization and auditing to Kerberos, integrating LDAP with AD provides much strength and corrects the one LDAP protocol weakness: synchronization.

Objects and Attributes

An *object* is identified in the directory database as some entity that has a name and a set of attributes or properties. *Attributes* could be purely descriptive or a set of security credentials. A *named object* is also called a *principal.* I refer specifically to a user of services as a *consumer*. Similarly, I refer to a service provider and the client machine that the consumer uses as an object (or principal) in the directory database.

Names/Name Resolution

The purpose of directory services is to represent every object or principal in the directory by a name and a directory database account record. Names must therefore be unique. Objects can have many types of names. AD creates a contextual or relative distinguished name (RDN) and an alias or canonical name for each object created in the directory database. The context of the RDN can be explicitly defined by tracing a reverse path up the hierarchy through each parent container within which that object is found to the most exterior container or root domain. This method guarantees the uniqueness of an object's name based upon its location within concentric containers—that is, an object in a domain tree, in a hierarchical path that describes its logical location in same directory namespace.

Because a forest can consist of multiple domain trees, names do not necessarily have to share the same contiguous namespace in the same domain tree. A *distinguished name (DN)* identifies or distinguishes a specific object by using a name that maps the complete path from the root container or root domain down to its exact location in the domain tree. An analogy is an absolute reference of, for example, a text file named mytext.doc, on a physical or logical hard drive. The DN for mytext.doc located in the **examcram.com** domain is:

```
/O=Internet/DC=Com/DC=Examcram/CN=Text/CN=Mytext.doc
```

An alternative naming scheme is an RDN, which includes only the attribute of the object itself—for example, **CN=mytext.doc**. This is also the default common name for security principals (the SAM account name or security principal name). An analogy is the relative addressing of mytext.doc in your present working directory. When you reference the text file mytext.doc, the context of the present working directory and its parent, grandparent, and root directories are all assumed unless otherwise specified.

Like a Web browser, Windows 2000 supports several other naming conventions. Use the format that is easiest to remember and most efficient to enter in the Logon dialog box. Some examples of naming conventions supported by Windows 2000 are:

- *RFC 822 names*—In AD, this is probably the "friendliest" name, the user principal name (UPN), based on RFC 822 and the familiar email syntax—namely, **pschein@examcram.com**. The UPN suffix is the DNS name of the root domain in the domain tree.
- *X.500 names*—LDAP uses the X.500 naming convention called *attributed naming*. This is the DN name used in the previous example in this section, specifically:

```
/O=Internet/DC=Com/DC=Examcram/CN=Text/CN=Mytext.doc
```

- *LDAP Uniform Resource Locators (URLs)*—You can enter in the Locator box a URL (such as **ldap://mycomputer.examcram.com**), accessible from any LDAP-enabled client or browser.
- *Universal Naming Convention (UNC) Names*—You can enter the legacy NT 4 style names to describe resources in Windows 2000-based networks.

Understanding how principals are named is of critical importance. AD domain names are the full name of the domain according to Domain Name System (DNS) records. User accounts have a logon name, a legacy NT4 (SAM) account name, and a user principal name (UPN) suffix which appears to the right of the "@" character according to specifications in RFC 822.This suffix is the DNS name of the root domain in the domain tree. Each AD computer account has a relative distinguished name, a legacy NT 4 (SAM) account name, a primary DNS suffix, a DNS host name, and a service principal name. The service principal name, based on the DNS host name of the computer, is used during mutual authentication of client machine and service provider.

Terms and Components

Most contemporary directory services are based on X.500, so some terms and components are common if not universal across the services. The future trend among network operating systems is to consolidate these services under some integrated meta-directory infrastructure, so it is likely that the commonality and interoperability among components will increase.

Namespaces

Named objects need to be organized to facilitate their location when corroboration of specific data or retrieval of information is necessary. Just as the directory structure organizes resources in the file system, a hierarchy of named objects can be arranged in a branching tree structure with common branches or paths. The endpoint of a path is called a *leaf node*. Nonleaf nodes are containers. A *container*, much like a folder, contains other named objects. In a directory structure, the endpoint of a path is typically some object like a file or document. The leaf node is a noncontainer; it does not contain other objects. In Windows 2000, a contiguous *subtree* describes a circumscribed group of containers all connected by one or more paths or branches.

Hierarchically speaking, a tree has within it a contiguous group of containers that hold objects with specific attributes. This contiguous group forms a *namespace* or *definable context*. I can trace out a specific object by resolving its context in relation to the series of contiguous containers in which it is found. I begin at some root container and literally walk down the contiguous path of connected subcontainers until I reach my destination endpoint or leaf node. In other network operating system cultures, this is called *walking the tree.* In functional terms, a namespace defines the scope of the directory database; it also defines the collection of objects, their context in the namespace, and their replicated attributes. AD contains one or more naming contexts or partitions; this is the *circumscribed contiguous subtree* of the directory structure. It is also the *unit of replication.*

In database terms, a *data dictionary* is a listing of objects you can create and store in the directory database. Each object can be assigned different attributes. In directory service terms, this data dictionary is part of a *schema.* The schema, like the data dictionary of a table, defines the class or list of possible attributes, as well as the syntax of the data types. It is typically extensible, meaning that it allows you to add new attributes and new data types. It is different from a data dictionary in that it can also describe relationships between objects and rules used to determine how objects handle information. Thus, a schema defines files and folders as leaf objects and containers, respectively. An example of some file, mytext.doc, in some folder, myfolder, is an example of an instance of the *file class*; it has specific characteristics such as a name, creation date, and size. It is defined in the context of its container folder. According to Microsoft, AD is implemented as a set of *object class instances.* A user-naming context is defined as the *contiguous subtrees* off the root container that hold the actual objects in the directory tree. Applications read the schema or data dictionary to learn what objects and properties are available in that particular namespace.

Domains

The *domain* in Windows 2000, like in NT 4, is the core administrative unit in AD. It represents a logical collection of objects and is the boundary for both replication and security. Each domain thus stores information only about the objects located within it. Security policies, administrative rights, and access control lists (ACLs) do not extend beyond the domain boundary. Similarly, a domain administrator's jurisdiction is only within that domain. Just as in the legacy NT 4 model, a domain is a logical structure that can span more than one physical drive.

Trees

In the same way that a *contiguous subtree* describes a group of containers connected by at least one path or branch, a *domain tree* is made up of at least two domains that form a contiguous namespace. Domains in a tree share common schema, a *data dictionary*, and replication (or *configuration*) data collectively stored as assorted system information called *metadata.* The connection between domains is described as a *trust relationship.* I can describe the domain tree as a hierarchical naming structure with the initial domain that forms the root of all subsequently attached subordinate or child domains. This full path to the object can be referred to as a distinguished name (DN, defined earlier in this chapter). The DN is unambiguous and unique. In a domain tree, the domain immediately above another is considered its *parent*. The domain name of the *child* domain added to the beginning of the parent domain name forms the RDN of that child domain. Thus, when the east domain becomes a child of another domain, **examcram.com**, its RDN becomes **east.examcram**.

In Windows 2000 and AD, a domain is still a collection computers defined for administrative purposes, sharing the same directory database. For DNS, a domain is any tree or subtree found within the DNS namespace of the enterprise forest. Although DNS domain names may correspond to AD domain names, they aren't necessarily describing the same thing in an enterprise or an examination case study.

Forests

Just as a forest in the real world is a collection of separate trees, Windows 2000 can support a forest of noncontiguous domain trees. In other words, each tree has its own root, so the namespace is not contiguous. Two domain trees with different root names are joined as a forest and display disjointed naming schemes. Each tree, however, trusts other trees and shares a common schema and configuration. Forests can be referred to as *noncontiguous* or *disjointed* namespaces. In directory terms, a *forest* is a cross-referenced set of objects (domains) with trust relationships known to all member trees in the namespace. Access to objects within member trees in a forest is through a Global Catalog (GC) that describes that forest namespace. GC is covered in more detail in the "GC" section later in this chapter.

From a design viewpoint, a domain tree offers the advantage of a contiguous namespace when you are searching for an object. In a forest, a search involves either the local domain tree or the larger GC. When you are providing services, it is always more efficient to establish domain trees rather than forests.

Organizational Units (OUs)

In addition to the domain concept, Windows 2000 provides a second way to partition a logical namespace. *OUs* are containers that can group objects—such as user accounts, groups, clients, printers, and other OUs—into logical administrative units. OUs provide granularity in permission management, such as granting some person the administrative rights for a collection of objects in one OU or in a group of OUs.

GC

AD defines a unified namespace that can consist of partitioned naming contexts such as **east.examcram.com**. A DN provides enough information to allow you to locate that specific object in its partition. In a disjointed namespace or when the DN of some object is not known, the GC provides the location information for objects in the domain tree or the entire forest even when only partial information is known about the object. AD is the repository for all objects in the namespace; GC, a partial index and search engine, stores a replica of each object and a subset of each object's attributes. The subset of object attributes is extensible. The population and synchronization of data is automatic. When a consumer queries the GC for a service provider or resource based on some known attribute, the GC returns the location based on the consumer's access rights. If the consumer doesn't have access rights to that resource, the query for its location fails.

Domain Controllers (DCs)

Although all the terms and components described so far in this section are logical and not bound by physical constraints of equipment, connectivity, or geography, the concepts of site (discussed in the next section) and DCs anchor us in the real world. In native mode Windows 2000, you no longer differentiate primary DCs (PDCs) from secondary or backup DCs (BDCs). All DCs are peers; each contains a writable copy of the domain directory database. Thus, any changes in the directory database of one DC are replicated to all other DCs in the domain.

DC management is further simplified when you are running Windows 2000 Server; the peer controller architecture permits you to promote any standalone or member server to a DC role and vice versa. The AD Installation Wizard (DCPROMO) is an administrative tool that promotes or demotes servers. The act of promoting a standalone or member server to a DC role where one has previously never existed creates a domain. DCs that alternatively join an existing domain receive a copy or replica of the directory database; they are called *replica DCs*. Referential integrity is maintained across databases through directory replication.

DCs provide many services, so it is best to have several in a domain to balance the service load.

DCs fulfill five Flexible (Floating) Single-Master Operations (FSMO) roles:

- *Schema Master (Schema Operations Master)*—Only one per forest; it administers schema updates and changes.

- *Domain Naming Master (Domain Naming Operations Master)*—Only one per forest; it administers addition or removal of domains in a forest or cross-references to external directory services.
- *Relative ID Master (RID Operations Master)*—Only one per domain; it allocates relative ID (RID) sequences, which are the unique portion of the two components that make up a security identifier (SID); the other component is a common domain security ID.
- *PDC Emulator (PDC Advertiser)*—Only one per domain even in native mode; the emulator acts as a PDC for down-level BDCs or clients in mixed mode. In native mode, the emulator assumes a preferential master role over other DCs; it receives replications first and is forwarded logon requests from other DCs before access is denied to the enterprise.
- *Infrastructure Master*—Only one per domain; it administers additions and changes in user/group mappings.

Sites

A *site* is a collection of AD servers that are well connected and use Transmission Control Protocol/Internet Protocol (TCP/IP). Whereas trees are logical groupings based on administration or geography, sites are based on the physical network. Site considerations thus deal specifically with physical topology and bandwidth. In the simplest case, the machines at a site typically have the same TCP/IP subnet address and thus are defined by some common physical boundary such as a local area network (LAN) or LAN segment. Sites are analogous to the site concept used in Exchange server architecture.

Note: Microsoft uses the term "well connected" to suggest sufficient bandwidth for transferring system information such as replication data.

Smaller groupings of computers optimize the discovery of the nearest local AD server (DC) at sites, especially when each LAN segment or subnet has at least one DC. Similarly, it may be expedient in a large enterprise to also include at least one GC at each site to facilitate forest-wide searches despite increased demands on bandwidth due to replication exchanges. You need to carefully define sites according to network topology (physical segments and logical subnets) so that you optimize AD access, DC replication, and GC query performance.

Replication

As mentioned in the "Domain Controllers (DCs)" section earlier in this chapter, all replicas of a particular partition of the AD namespace (the DC directory database) are editable. Information is exchanged among DCs automatically through multimaster replication. If the clocks on DCs are synchronized, some directory services can use timestamps to manage database changes. Alternatively, AD uses a 64-bit Update Sequence Number (USN) maintained on each DC to record the property change in the local directory database and to propagate it to the directory databases on other peer DCs.

Access Control

Although Microsoft suggests reverting to a single domain model in Windows 2000, the AD can consist of more than one domain. Domains organize functional areas, partition the directory database, and create security boundaries. These boundaries affect policies and settings such as administrative rights, security policy, and ACLs. Distributed security and permission management rely on many of the terms and components defined earlier in this chapter. Using these constructs, you should deploy several strategies to secure network resources:

- Limit authenticated access to system resources.
- Manage access controls to available resources.
- Manage security administration through deployment of secure applications using role-based access controls and uniform security policies.
- Establish trust relationships among domains.
- Use protection techniques when storing sensitive or physically exposed data.

Now, I'll discuss each of these in more detail. (Note that protection techniques are covered in the "Resources" section later in this chapter).

Limiting Authenticated Access

The first step in securing resources is limiting access to them. Windows 2000 authenticates users based on user accounts in the AD. Identity management is implemented through the AD Users And Computers snap-in of the Microsoft Management Console (MMC). You can now organize user accounts not only by domain but also by OU, which better reflects the functional needs of your corporation, division, or user population. Creation of an account record is not only integrated with directory services but is added to such items as the global address book as well as other network services. Windows 2000 supports SSO, so the account record is propagated across the forest. In native mode, bidirectional, transitive trust relationships support pass-through or referral authentication to resources and services in other domains in the forest. Any one of the Kerberos, NT LAN Manager (NTLM), or SSL/Transport Layer Security (TLS) security protocols handles the logon process. Windows also supports strong authentication using public key technologies such as smart cards, discussed in greater detail in Chapter 12.

The concept of principals and account records stored in directory service datastores applies to client machines and services as well as consumers. Windows 2000 servers and clients receive policy information from the AD during their startup procedures. Computer policies are applied to the local machine following its authentication but prior to user authentication. In addition to machine authentication during startup and user authentication during logon, Kerberos security provides support for mutual authentication, preventing intruders or rogue users from impersonating a service provider or imposing themselves in the middle of two parties exchanging data (man-in-the-middle attack). You can set policies to permit or deny clients or services to be *trusted for delegation*, where some intermediary creates new network connections on behalf of and in the security context of a consumer. This delegation of authority, discussed in the "Delegation of Authentication" section in Chapter 4, is critical in many applications that use multitier architecture and distributed services.

Deployment

You can harden (strengthen) authentication by using strict account policies that enforce long, complex passwords (which are resistant to dictionary or brute force attacks, discussed in Chapter 2) with reasonable length, lifetime, and constraints on reusability settings. These passive impersonation attacks apply all possible combinations of passwords from a list or dictionary to the authentication mechanism until either the exact combination is found or the list is exhausted. The longer and more complex the character structure of the password, the harder it is to match the exact character combination. However, it is important to balance the need for strong authentication policies (and, for example, strong, long passwords) with concerns for user attitude and compliance (the corporate culture referred to in Chapter 2). A user often will have problems remembering or using too long or complex a password. It is better to have 100 percent compliance with moderate security account policies than compliance of less than 100 percent with especially rigorous security standards. Smart cards and other two-factor authentication methods ("I have something" in addition to "I know something") provide stronger authentication than passwords but also increase TCO. Limit the number of clients and accounts that are trusted for, because their ability to assume an authorized security context of some other party makes them a prime target for an active impersonation attack.

You need to carefully monitor remote access policies, discussed in Chapter 6. Point-To-Point Protocol (PPP) authentication methods offer limited security because they use only username and password. Customized extensions provided by third parties extend the authentication capabilities of Extensible Authentication Protocol (EAP) and provide support for strong two-factor authentication methods. An example of enhancing EAP and providing this two-factor support is EAP-TLS authentication using digital certificates and smart cards. These enhancements harden the dial-up access by basing the authentication process on not just "what you know" but "what you have." Alternatively, using predetermined callback provides another inexpensive countermeasure to impersonation attacks because the system disconnects the caller and calls back a modem-based client located at some prearranged telephone connection. It's always preferable to use Virtual Private Networks (VPNs) as opposed to unsecured remote access despite the increases in overhead that the need for, for example, certificate services creates.

Managing Access Control Lists

After you limit access to resources, the second line of defense is managing accessibility. Access to any resource in the NT File System (NTFS) is based on a collection of permissions or access control entries (ACEs) that specify a user or group and some range of actions they can perform on the specific object. The collection of these ACEs is compiled into a system or discretionary ACL. This topic is discussed in greater detail in the "Managing Security Administration" section later in this chapter.

To simplify administration of ACLs, it is best to use group memberships, not users, when assigning access permissions. Especially when you are creating resources, never assume that default resource permissions are appropriate. Windows 2000 and legacy NT 4 assign the Everyone group Full Control to network shares by default. Make certain you remove this group and replace it with Users or a more appropriate group. Similarly, file system permissions are by default granted to Users. Any authenticated user is part of this built-in group. Always review permissions and minimize access by using Read Only wherever possible.

Individuals and groups are defined in the AD Users And Computers snap-in. Granularity of ACLs has been enhanced in Windows 2000. You must define a group before you can assign it permissions in an ACL. Assign permissions to groups as opposed to users to simplify administration and minimize the need for changes. Although users may change groups often, you should not routinely alter the group assignments at the resource level to minimize errors or misconfigurations. Groups and Group Policies are discussed in greater detail in Chapter 10.

Deployment

Apply the rule of least privilege, where what is not expressly permitted is prohibited. Use the Everyone group for auditing, not for assigning resource permissions.

Managing Security Administration

Three methods for managing the administration of access reflect various approaches to management and security policy. They are:

- Discretionary ACLs (DACLs, sometimes referred to as DACs)

- Mandatory ACLs (MACLs, sometimes referred to as MACs)
- Role-based access controls (RBACs)

The three access schemes typically coexist within a work environment, depending on the kinds of data and job functions people are assigned to perform. There is usually an order of precedence when all three controls are operating; mandatory access control overrides role-based control, which in turn overrides discretionary access. These different forms of access control, as a form of permission management, provide a methodology that helps you manage resources in an environment where all resources are accessible.

DACLs

DACLs require that the owners of the object assume responsibility for the use or misuse of any object they create. The administrator always has the authority to take ownership away from someone. However, of the three approaches, this is the least conservative, exposes resources to the greatest risks, and requires the most monitoring. Aside from internal risks associated with unintentional or malicious acts on the part of authenticated users, DACLs expose resources to manipulation by outside intruders specifically searching for such a target. Intruders can, for example, manipulate read/write access to exploit and further penetrate the operating system. Normally, it's appropriate to use DACLs when you are managing resources in internal workgroup environments where cooperation, collaboration, and sharing are common work themes.

MACLs

MACLs are controlled primarily by the administrator and are typically used in an environment were the principle of least privilege is applied. The administrator assigns only those permissions necessary to complete specific job functions. This form of managing access is appropriate where resources are ranked or categorized—e.g., top secret (TS), secret (S), sensitive but unclassified (SBU), and unclassified (U). The administrator strictly enforces this kind of policy through policy management. Access to all data at any one time is discouraged, and unlikely given the classification scheme. People and processes within a MACL environment are typically in a more secured work environment than a DACL environment because and permissions are administratively controlled.

RBACs

In an RBAC environment, information is categorized in functional terms or by process. Applications can define roles. You—as opposed to the person who accesses the data—could create a specific security context for the application; this technique is used in relational database management systems to simplify permission management. The function of the application determines the scope of permissions; whoever has permission to use the application accesses whatever data is necessary for the application to perform its designed role or function.

Establishing Trust Relationships

Given the scalability of AD, Microsoft recommends migrating even extremely large corporations into a single domain model and eliminating the need for trust relationships. Domains nevertheless remain useful when you are scoping administrative areas and designing enterprises. When migrating to Windows 2000, however, make certain you don't apply old design habits using flat domain models from legacy NT 4 installations. Windows 2000 requires you to re-engineer old design strategies to fully realize the benefits of its hierarchical modeling capability. If you do need to scope administrative or security policies, Kerberos protocol in native mode Windows 2000 has significantly simplified the administration of joining domains. Two-way transitive trusts that are automatically implemented when you add to or create domain trees have replaced legacy nontransitive, one-way trusts. Trust relationships in forests are now implicitly transitive trust relationships; they require little, if any, maintenance. External trusts to either legacy NT 4 domains or across forests, however, still require careful planning because of possible security risks.

Transitive trusts flow up through the domain tree and across the forest, so accounts in any one domain can authenticate in another domain on the other side of the forest. Even though transitive trusts are automatically created between a child and parent domain in Windows 2000, you can still explicitly create one-way nontransitive trusts among, for example, different branches of the same tree or different trees in the same forest. One-way trusts are typically used in one of the following scenarios:

- Between Windows 2000 domains in different forests
- Between Windows 2000 domains and legacy NT 4 domains
- Between Windows 2000 domains and MIT Kerberos 5 realms

Cross-linking domains with transitive relationships shortens trust paths and can facilitate authentication, especially in large, complex forests. Nontransitive trusts, however, are explicitly bound to the two domains; conversely, the nontransitive trust relationship does not flow to neighboring domains.

Deployment

Trust relationships in mixed mode domains continue to function as nontransitive, one-way trusts. Be careful, however, in native mode; trusts are transitive. Any domain administrators can take ownership and modify the Configuration container of any other domain in the forest. Changes are replicated to all other DCs.

The domain administrator of a domain that joins a forest is now immediately trusted and must be considered an equal to other domain administrators. Using explicit one-way (or external) trusts, especially when you are adding new domains, is a good beginning strategy until you have resolved all administrative policies and security issues. An alternative approach is to collapse the domain into an OU, redefine the former domain administrator's administrative scope to that OU, and remove the domain. The administrator continues to have the same scope of responsibilities and authority over resources and users without having administrator-level access to the enterprise.

Resources

In the discussion of attack modalities in the "Scoping Physical Assets" section of Chapter 8, I used the actual theft of equipment as an example of active interception. A CD-ROM burner connected to network drives presents a greater threat to an organization than an intruder roaming your network at will. The CD-ROM can copy organized folders of information; the rogue user or outside hacker typically uncovers data and parts of documents. Another security risk is the road warrior's laptop, which contains perhaps less (but nevertheless well-organized) information, as well as stored passwords; preset, remote access configurations; public and private keys; and internal signatures, such as volume numbers on hard drives. Although many third-party technologies can adequately protect this property, before Windows 2000, no standardized set of tools that specifically addressed these issues was integrated into a Microsoft operating system.

EFS

Encrypting File System (EFS) is a part of Windows 2000 NT File System (NTFS). This enhanced file system is actually different from the NTFS in legacy NT 4 in several ways:

- Storage volumes are monitored and can be limited by disk quotas.
- Changes are tracked through a change journal.
- Data can be protected through an encryption mechanism.

NTFS uses public key technology as the core file encryption technology for securely storing files and folders. EFS is part of the file system, so when the owner of the file or folder works with the object, the owner is actually encrypting or decrypting it in a totally transparent manner. No one except the owner of the files, and an administrator with an EFS Data Recovery certificate, can read the file or folder. Thus, you can configure EFS to encrypt all material saved to specific folders on a local or network drive using NTFS. In the case of a network drive, the data is not encrypted until it is written to the disk. This encryption process would secure material even if someone used a low-level sector editor to read the hard drive directly.

Each file is encrypted with a unique symmetric key. EFS then encrypts the secret, symmetric key using the owner's public key from the EFS certificate. The owner is thus the only person who can decrypt the key used to encrypt the file. There is also a provision for the original encryption key to be encrypted using the public key in an EFS Data Recovery certificate. EFS uses a Data Recovery policy that enables an authorized Data Recovery agent to decrypt the files. In addition, you can use the private key from the EFS Data Recovery certificate to recover the data. It is a good practice for a corporation to establish a recovery agent. Someone can decrypt the file only by first logging on to the network as that original user. The file cannot be read, so it cannot be modified. Thus, EFS supports both confidentiality and integrity.

EFS implementations require that:

- Public key infrastructure (PKI) be installed.
- At least one administrator has an EFS Data Recovery certificate.
- The author of the file has an EFS certificate.

You can encrypt files and folders only on the version of NTFS that is installed with Windows 2000; it does not work with any other file system. To store EFS files on shared drives, EFS "impersonates" the EFS user when making the shared network connection. The servers must be trusted for delegation. You can deploy Certificate Services to issue certificates to EFS recovery agents and EFS users. Cipher.exe is a command-line utility that adds greater functionality to the encryption/decryption process by allowing changes in configuration to be performed from the command line interface.

Practice Questions

Case Study

4Sale, an online bartering company in ThatTherePlace, North Dakota, primarily focuses on selling inexpensive, odd-lot items.

Current LAN/Network Structure

4Sale is presently running Windows 2000 Server in native mode; one member server supports Exchange (Simple Mail Transfer Protocol—SMTP) server, and another is running Internet Information Server (IIS) 4 (Hypertext Transfer Protocol [HTTP] server) and Proxy Server (packet filtering/caching). All 100 client machines are configured in a single domain model. The client systems are running Windows Professional, with Office 97 being utilized as an applications package. Each system is connected to a 10Mbps hub through 10Mbps LAN cards running Category 5 Unshielded Twisted Pair (UTP) cabling in a star topology.

Proposed LAN/Network Structure

4Sale is developing its online barter/trading business through business alliances. It wants secure communications among specific departments. Outside salespeople are using public networks to access the server and office files.

Current WAN Connectivity

No changes in the current structure are proposed at this time.

Proposed WAN Connectivity

No changes in the current structure are proposed at this time.

Directory Design Commentary

No changes in the current structure are proposed at this time.

Current Internet Positioning

No changes in the current structure are proposed at this time.

Future Internet Plans

No changes in the current structure are proposed at this time.

Company Goal with Windows 2000

The Network Manager at 4Sale says, "We are concerned about confidentiality of files, especially among our sales force. A laptop has been stolen, and no one is certain whether valuable customer lists fell into a competitor's hands."

Question 1

The CEO of 4Sale asks, "What is the best interface for future integration with heterogeneous directory services?" [Choose the best answer]

- ❍ a. LDAP C API
- ❍ b. SSPI
- ❍ c. MAPI
- ❍ d. ADSI
- ❍ e. None of the above

Answer d is correct. ADSI (Active Directory Services Interfaces) interfaces natively with Lightweight Directory Access Protocol and with a variety of other directory service products like Lotus Notes, Novell GroupWise, and Exchange Server. LDAP C application programming interface is a de facto C programming standard that allows you to programmatically manipulate directory services structure, but it requires detailed knowledge of each system. Therefore, answer a is incorrect. SSPI (Security Support Provider Interface) does not support directory services; it supports security libraries. Therefore, answer b is incorrect. MAPI (Microsoft Messaging Application Programming Interface) is a Windows API that interfaces with older mail systems and is used primarily for backward compatibility. Therefore, answer c is incorrect.

Question 2

The Network Manager at 4Sale asks, "Are we locked into one naming convention with Windows 2000?" Which of the following are naming conventions you can use with Windows 2000? [Check all correct answers]

- ❑ a. X.509 names
- ❑ b. RFC 822 names
- ❑ c. LDAP names
- ❑ d. email names
- ❑ e. Usernames

Answers b, c, d, and e are correct. RFC 822 and email names are the same answer. LDAP names are actual Uniform Resource Locators that use Lightweight Directory Access Protocol. Finally, usernames are the traditional way to log on to a server. X.509 is a recommendation, referring to X.500 directory services, that specifically regards the use of public keys and digital certificates. It does not deal with names. Therefore, answer a is incorrect.

Question 3

The Network Manager at 4Sale says, "I want to use only one-way trusts. I want to control what administrators can do." Which scenarios support one-way trusts? [Check all correct answers]

- ❑ a. Windows 2000 domains in the same forest
- ❑ b. Windows 2000 domains in a different forest
- ❑ c. Windows NT domains
- ❑ d. MIT Kerberos realms
- ❑ e. All of the above

Answer e is correct. Answer a, a trick answer, is correct because you can still explicitly establish a one-way trust in a Windows 2000 domain. Answers b, c, and d are correct because the only kind of trust you can establish across forests, within NT domains, or within Kerberos realms is a one-way, nontransitive trust.

Question 4

The Network Manager at 4Sale asks, "What are the domain controller FSMO roles?" [Check all correct answers]

- ❑ a. Schema Master
- ❑ b. Domain Naming Master
- ❑ c. RID Master
- ❑ d. PDC Advertiser
- ❑ e. Site Master

Answers a, b, c, and d are correct. The Schema Master administers schema updates and changes. The Domain Naming Master administers the addition or removal of domains in a forest or cross-references to external directory services. The Relative ID Master allocates relative ID (RID) sequences, the unique portion of the two components that make up a security ID. Primary Domain Controller Advertiser acts as a PDC for down-level backup domain controllers or clients in mixed mode. There is no Site Master role. Therefore, answer e is incorrect.

Question 5

The Network Manager at 4Sale says, "The Kerberos protocol is just as strong as a smart card authentication method." Is the Network Manager correct?

❍ a. Yes

❍ b. No

Answer b, no, is correct. The Network Manager is incorrect. Smart cards and other two-factor security techniques provide stronger authentication than the Kerberos protocol because their method requires both "I have something" and "I know something." Kerberos requires just "I know something" (a password).

Question 6

The Network Manager at 4Sale says, "I get confused about which logical component goes where among the Windows 2000 structures." Create an ordered list of only the appropriate logical components/subcomponents.

Objects and attributes

Forest

Namespace

Site

Container

Domain controller

Tree

The correct answer is:

Objects and attributes

Container

Tree

Forest

The question asked for logical structures, so domain controller and site are inappropriate. Namespace is not appropriate because it describes the directory database. Only the four objects listed are correct. Forest and Tree are containers.

Question 7

The Network Manager at 4Sale says, "I prefer to assign permissions to individuals because I then have better control over which of our employees can access any one specific resource as compared to using a specific group classification." Is the Network Manager using a good strategy?

❍ a. Yes

❍ b. No

Answer b, no, is correct. The Network Manager is using a bad strategy. A recommended administrative technique is to assign permissions only to groups. It is more likely that users will change groups than that groups will change their specific resource needs. By assigning permissions to groups, the administrator decreases the possibility of making a mistake.

Question 8

The Network Manager at 4Sale asks, "I want to make certain every salesperson has a secured laptop. What do we have to do?" Which of the following are requirements for deploying EFS on the laptops? [Check all correct answers]

❑ a. PKI must be installed on the laptop.

❑ b. Windows NT must be installed on the laptop.

❑ c. An EFS certificate must be installed on the laptop.

❑ d. All of the above.

Answers a and c are correct. Both public key infrastructure and an EFS (Encrypting File System) certificate must be installed on the laptop. Windows NT does not support EFS, nor is NT File System installed with it. EFS requires you to install Windows 2000 and NTFS. NT is the wrong operating system, so answer b is incorrect, as is answer d.

Need to Know More?

Nichols, Randall K. et al. *Defending Your Digital Assets against Hackers, Crackers, Spies, and Thieves, First Edition*. McGraw-Hill Professional Publishing, New York, NY, 2000. ISBN 0-07-212285-4. Chapter 8 discusses many concepts that relate to access controls.

Shinder, Thomas W. and D. Lynn White. *Configuring Windows 2000 Server Security*. Syngress Media, Inc., Rockland, MD, 2000. ISBN 1-928994-02-4. Chapter 4 covers relationships between directory and security services. Chapter 6 discusses Encrypting File System architecture and user operations.

Stallings, William. *Network Security Essentials*. Prentice Hall, Upper Saddle River, NJ, 1999. ISBN 0-13-016093-8. Subsection 4.2 of Chapter 4 discusses in technical detail the X.509 authentication method, managing certificates and keys, and policies.

Search the TechNet CD (or its online version through **www.microsoft.com**) and the *Windows 2000 Server Resource Kit* CD using the keywords "OU", "EFS", "ACL", and "FSMO".

http://csrc.nist.gov/rbac/ This site offers award-winning RBAC research from the National Institute of Standards and Technology (NIST) and includes technical papers that discuss role-based access control methods.

www.faqs.org/rfcs/ The Internet FAQ Consortium provides a variety of archives, including Internet RFCs, Usenet FAQs, and other FAQs. This page of the site is the RFC search page, which provides searches for material using reference numbers and keywords. This particular page also provides links to Internet-related standards organizations such as IETF, IAB, W3C, and so on.

www.faqs.org/rfcs/rfc1330.html This site offers recommendations for the Phase I Deployment of Open Systems Interconnection (OSI) directory services (X.500) and OSI message handling services (X.400) within the ESnet community.

www.microsoft.com/technet/win2000/win2ksrv/technote/nt5efs.asp At this site, you'll find *Encrypting File System for Windows 2000*, a Windows 2000 Server White Paper that provides an overview of EFS, which is included with Windows 2000.

Group Policy

Terms you'll need to understand:

- ✓ Universal group
- ✓ Security groups
- ✓ Distribution list
- ✓ Distribution groups
- ✓ Organizational Unit (OU)
- ✓ IntelliMirror technology
- ✓ Group Policy Object (GPO)
- ✓ Administrative Template
- ✓ Site
- ✓ System Policy Editor (poledit.exe)
- ✓ Group Policy loopback support

Techniques you'll need to master:

- ✓ Discussing the differences between legacy NT 4 and Windows 2000 policies
- ✓ Utilizing new features in the Windows 2000 concept of groups
- ✓ Understanding the Group Policy Microsoft Management Console (MMC) extensions
- ✓ Outlining Group Policy processing orders
- ✓ Describing Group Policy loopback support modes
- ✓ Using tools and utilities for administration of Group Policy

This chapter begins with a comparison of how NT 4 and Windows 2000 implement group management, system policies, and settings. I explore some of the new features in Windows 2000, including the introduction of Organizational Units (OUs) and the ability to nest containers. I then describe how the desktop environment is secured and user management enhanced while reducing total cost of ownership (TCO) using change and configuration management technologies collectively known as IntelliMirror (also discussed in Chapters 11 and 12). Following this broad view of policy-based management of the user's workspace, I focus specifically on Windows 2000 Group Policies. I briefly discuss their architecture and administrative function. In discussing security groups, I describe the default processing order of Group Policy Objects (GPOs) in relation to Group Policy implementation. In my discussion of the Group Policy Microsoft Management Console (MMC) snap-in, I describe the extensions that enhance and extend the software tool.

In an easily maintained yet secure enterprise, order of policy inheritance is a critical design concept. Each account inherits all GPOs for the entire OU path in which they exist. I discuss how you can modify this inheritance flow through the filtering characteristics of security groups. I also discuss the loopback support technique of controlling the exposure to specific policies. Finally, I briefly discuss specific tools and utilities that assist you in building and maintaining Group Policies. This brief selection of tools complements Chapter 11's more detailed discussion of utilities that are potentially useful when you are working with the daily issues of configuring and maintaining Windows 2000.

The Concept of Group

In Chapter 2 and throughout this book, I have used the basic scenario of consumer and service provider to describe the majority of information exchanges that occur in a computerized environment. In fact, the very access to a file on your local machine is an example of this exchange; you request a file object from a file-keeping service (originally called a *file server*). The "file service provider" authenticates who you are and whether you have the authority to request the file. If you have permission to see the file object, you are given access to it.

Based on the discussion of access control in Chapter 9, you should recognize that authentication is performed during the logon process and that you manage permissions through access control entries (ACEs) associated with the target object. Centralized identity management assumes the administrative overhead and complexity of authenticating and authorizing principals in a networking environment. Permission management, on the other hand, is relegated to the object itself; each resource has its own access control list (ACL) that specifies who can do what to the target resource.

Windows 2000, like the legacy NT system, has always been able to deal directly with the rights and permissions of single users. The peer networking traditions of Windows 3.11, however, have fostered a collective management of users, especially as the size of the user population has expanded. Users are administered as collective groups. As workgroups grew into domains, groups of local users evolved into global user groups. These global groups are then assigned to local groups, who, in turn, have permission to access local resources. This system of group assignment not only becomes another layer of centralized identity management but also actually impacts on TCO by simplifying administration and maintenance of principals in an enterprise.

The NT 4 master domain model best illustrates the functional significance of global versus local grouping. According to this model, global groups are organizational and administrative in function and span one or more trusting resource-laden domains; local groups populate these resource domains and possess the permission to use their local resources. For members of a global group to access a local resource, they must first be assigned local group membership.

Enhancements

To handle enterprise scalability, Windows 2000, in native mode, has added several new group features to the directory database schema. *Group nesting*, in particular, adds a hierarchical dimensionality to the group concept by allowing one group to contain one or more groups within its scope of authority. Other features include the following groups new to Windows 2000:

- *Universal group*—This collection of named accounts, organized into a security or distribution group, can be used anywhere in the domain tree or forest. In other words, universal groups are to the forest what global groups are to the domain. If you use the Windows 2000 group-nesting enhancement, these groups can contain, or nest, other groups, including other universal groups, global groups, and individual users. Universal groups are defined at the forest level, so these groups and their members have Global Catalog (GC) entries (see Chapter 9 for a discussion of the role the GC plays in the enterprise). Universal groups are visible at the forest level, so they can appear in an ACL anywhere in the enterprise namespace.

- *Global groups*—Native mode global groups have the same features as their legacy NT 4 counterparts except that they can now nest other global groups from within their own domain. They are visible from the forest level, so they also appear in the GC; their members, however, do not. In addition, they can appear in an ACL anywhere in the namespace.

- *Domain local groups*—These groups act exactly as they did in the legacy NT 4 model except that they can now contain users, global groups, and universal groups from any domain in the forest. Similarly, because of the change in status of domain controllers (DCs) in native mode (see the discussion of domains in the "Terms and Components" section in Chapter 9), domain local groups are visible. Therefore, you can assign them permissions on both member servers and DCs. Local groups are not visible at the forest level, so they do not appear in the GC.

Universal and global groups, unlike domain local groups, are visible at the forest level and can appear in an ACL anywhere in the enterprise namespace. Local groups act exactly as they did in legacy NT 4 except that they can contain universal groups in addition to global groups and users from any domain in the forest.

In addition, every group in an Active Directory (AD) namespace is a member of one of these groups:

- *Security groups*—You can assign these groups as ACEs to some resource. In addition, you can optionally include them in an email distribution list.
- *Distribution groups*—You cannot assign these groups as ACEs to some resource, but you can use the membership of these groups for email distribution.

Note that distribution groups are actually an extension of the Microsoft Exchange Server distribution lists that have universal scope in an organization. The universal group is also similar to the distribution list in the Exchange Server schema. Another AD object, called contacts, has no network access; however, you can locate contacts through directory services and add them to distribution lists. The addition of distribution groups in the AD directory schema is a direct result of Microsoft's efforts to consolidate directory services, discussed in Chapter 7.

Policies and Settings

You need to understand how profiles, settings, and Group Policy differ to understand how Windows 2000 has evolved from legacy NT 4 and gained greater centralized control over named accounts and a user's work environment. In addition to a Single Sign-On providing access to network resources anywhere in the enterprise, a user should be reliably provided with her own desktop and work environment from any networked machine. A user profile has historically provided this collection of environmental settings either defined for or changed by a user. Customized working environments were saved as a user profile, a home directory, and sometimes login scripts on the legacy NT 4 platform. A local user profile is available only on a specific machine. When these customized settings "follow" the user to different machines, they are called a roaming profile. When a roaming profile is made read-only by an administrator and automatically imposed on the user during the user's logon sequence, the settings are stored as a mandatory user profile. Different aspects of these environmental settings are stored in different places such as the local Registry, Desktop, Profiles directory, Home directory, and so on. A Group Policy, like a mandatory user profile, is specified administratively. It is stored in a central location and always applied during the user logon.

Group policy not only provides rules-based management of network resources and how the OS generally behaves in relation to both users and computers in the enterprise, but is also the primary tool in Windows 2000 for the change and configuration management technologies collectively called IntelliMirror. Policy-based management is applied to named accounts (users and computers) on the basis of membership in AD domains or organizational units through Administrative Templates, security settings, Software Installation, scripts, and folder redirection. Like the ADM files used in the legacy System Policy Editor, the Administrative Templates are a superset of the older files. They are Unicode-based text files with ADM extensions that hierarchically define options displayed in the administrative interface of the Group Policy Editor. They are stored in the Group Policy Template (GPT) folder in the system volume folder of DCs. Although legacy ADM files can extend the Group Policy interface, the new Administrative Templates are not backward compatible with System Policy Editor. Windows 2000 GPO settings also include the legacy option for Registry-based policy settings.

In fact, the Group Policy model of rules-based management is an extension of the older NT 4 legacy System Policy model. In brief, the legacy System Policy Editor (poledit.exe) created a policy file that configured the work environment and enforced system configuration settings that were stored in (and therefore limited by the scope of the Registry of) that particular machine. These policies characteristically were:

- Applied to named accounts in a single domain
- Controlled by security group membership
- Accessible by the user through regedit.exe and therefore not secure
- Persistent in user profiles
- Extensible through the use of ADM files

On the other hand, the Group Policy model is a rule-based management system complementing the enterprise-scale identity management system provided by AD. It not only simplifies administering user profiling, OS, and application installation, but also provides the legacy-style Registry-based desktop system lockdowns of the early NT system. In brief, Windows Group Policy characteristically:

- Is associated with site, domain, OUs, and OUs nested within OUs

- Affects all users and computers in the site, domain, OUs, and OUs nested within OUs
- Is controlled by security group membership
- Cannot be changed by users and therefore is secure
- Is removed and rewritten whenever policy changes
- Offers enhanced granularity to control desktop and computing workspace
- Is extensible through either ADM files or MMC snap-ins

The scope of this rules-based management system, although broader than the legacy Windows NT System Policy model primarily because of its close association with AD still reflects the fundamental dichotomy of computer configurations (historically system.dat in Windows operating systems) and user configurations (historically user.dat). Each family of configurations is composed of general subareas covering software settings, windows settings, and Administrative Templates. This scope is shown in Figure 10.1, where the sublisting of just security settings is shown.

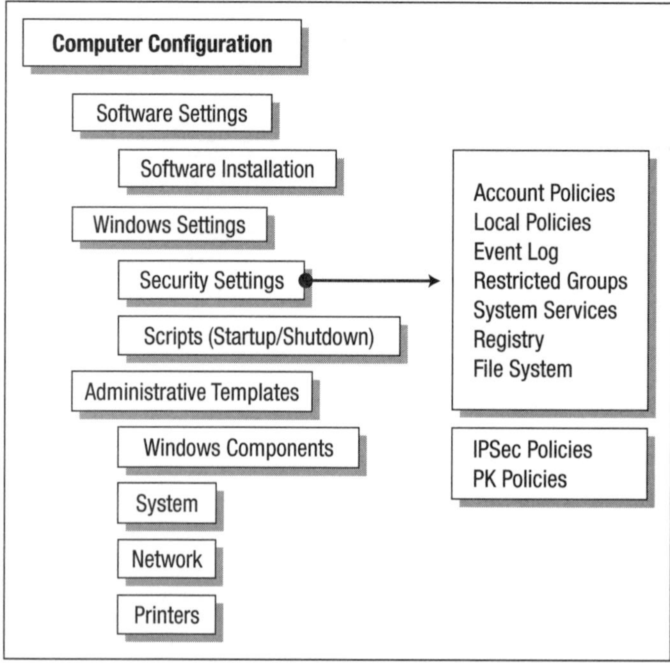

Figure 10.1 Default domain policy: security settings.

Securing the Desktop Environment

A user's working environment is second only to Single Sign-On in importance. Through new management technology, Microsoft provides easy access to your workspace from anywhere in the enterprise. Group Policy simplifies administrative overhead in controlling these environmental settings, and then it relies on Windows 2000 to deliver the policy-managed settings and enforce compliance to corporate security objectives wherever the workspace is used. This theme underlies Windows 2000 change and configuration management services and technologies. One of the IT (information technology) security controls described in Chapter 2 is accessibility to resources and services. Microsoft has developed several desktop management technologies like IntelliMirror, Terminal Services Architecture, and Remote (Operating System) Installation Services (RIS) that provide accessibility to that desktop from anywhere in the enterprise, as well as secure its access from outside interference, intervention, or impersonation without increasing TCO. Both Terminal Services and RIS are discussed in Chapter 12. Windows 2000 change and configuration management services support these security controls and compliance through technologies such as IntelliMirror.

In brief, this Windows 2000 native management technology provides access to a user's computing environment through application management, data protection, and roaming user support based on centralized policy definitions. IntelliMirror centrally manages data resources so that you can replace, restore, or recover users' personal workspace settings, applications, and data anywhere in the Windows 2000 enterprise, whether or not users have permanent network connectivity. An administrator can use the data management, software management, and settings management separately or in combination, depending on the needs of any given situation or working conditions. In concert with AD directory services and Group Policy, IntelliMirror management technology provides policy-based management of users' workspaces in the enterprise. Upon logon authentication, users' desktops are automatically configured according to centrally defined policies based on AD datastores that define their identity, group membership, business role, and location in the enterprise namespace. The ability to roam within an enterprise yet maintain a consistent workspace compliant with the security context within which the user works not only adds to productivity but simplifies the enforcement of security policies and auditing of activities among especially large user populations.

Securing Access and Permissions

Group Policy collectively describes the policy settings that control both user and computer configurations in the Windows 2000 enterprise. The two major themes at the enterprise level are identity management and permission management.

To easily centralize administration of scalable ranges of named accounts, management of users and resources must be applied in both a standardized and systematic way. Especially when applied across a site or organizational unit, policies simplify administration across wide ranges of the user population. You create a GPO and then configure the settings for it. The GPO is a virtual datastore for these settings. By storing settings in separate GPOs, you can describe different configurations for different workspaces. Thus, you define only once the workspaces for a specific group of users or computers; the operating system then automatically delivers the defined workspaces according to the assigned GPO upon network logon. GPO components are stored in the following:

- *Group Policy containers (GPCs)*—This is an AD object that contains GPO attributes and subcontainers for user and computer Group Policy information.
- *Group Policy templates (GPTs)*—This is a folder hierarchy in the system volume (Sysvol folder) on the DC. The GPT contains all Group Policy information on the Group Policy MMC snap-in extensions: policy templates, security, Software Installation, scripts, and folder redirection. For more information on security settings, see the "Group Policy MMC Extensions" section later in this chapter.

Policy Scoping: Secured Boundaries

GPOs create policy-managed scopes of control, as discussed in Chapter 8. Group Policy settings are stored in GPOs that are linked to hierarchically arranged objects in the AD structure: within the site, the domain, the OU, or OUs within an OU. This hierarchical structure organizes the inheritance of these configurations and thereby simplifies administrative tasks. By default, the scope of a Group Policy is defined by the specific container to which it is assigned and possibly modified by a named account's (user or computer) security group membership. Although security group membership can filter Group Policies, you can't associate a Group Policy directly to a security group.

You can remember the order or downward flow of Group Policy inheritance through the AD structure as SDOU (site, domain, Organizational Unit, OU within OU). Microsoft uses this mnemonic device to refer collectively to the AD directory containers. Group Policies and IntelliMirror technologies don't support mixed mode Windows 2000 environments, legacy NT 4, or Windows platforms because both are tightly integrated with AD directory services.

You can scope or define a workspace for your employees as broadly (the site) or as narrowly (members of a single workgroup) as you need when you are administering your network, intranet, or enterprise. The effective settings work like file permissions; the most restrictive apply. They are a function of the scope of the AD object to which the GPOs are linked; this level determines the order in which the GPOs are applied. GPOs are typically stored in a specific domain (nonlocal GPOs), also called the *storage domain*. This domain has nothing to do with the domain to which the GPO is linked, but it does impact cross-domain GPO assignments, discussed shortly.

One way you can access these GPOs is to open the Properties page of a given SDOU, select the Group Policy tab, right-click on the GPO in the GPO list, select Properties, and then click on the Security tab. There are two types of Group Policy objects: local and nonlocal. Local GPOs exist on standalone computers and consist of only the GPT portion of a GPO. Only one local GPO is associated with a Windows 2000-based machine, so the typical objects discussed are nonlocal GPOs.

Local Computer (Group) Policy on a Windows 2000 Professional computer or standalone Windows 2000 Server affects all users who log on locally. In an AD domain, domain group policies, managed by AD, override Local Group Policies.

Types of Policy Management

Centralized or decentralized policy management in conjunction with AD directory services impacts on TCO in the areas of support and maintenance. Although an OU is the smallest scope to which you can apply a Group Policy, different sites, domains, or OUs may use a single GPO, even if it is stored across domains, and thus suffer from slow wide area network (WAN) links and slow performance. Figure 10.2 shows how these cross-domain assignments can cross physical spaces.

Design considerations concerning centralized versus distributed scopes of control impact both performance and maintenance. To simplify administration and enforce corporate security objectives, Group Policy is inherited from upstream GPOs through flows from upper-level directory containers like a site and a domain, to lower-level containers like OUs; everything trickles down. This design optimizes logon times because there are fewer GPOs to process. It also simplifies administering any policy changes because all policies are written at the same level, where they are consolidated as key policy themes; they then trickle downward through the hierarchy. The disadvantage is primarily in the inflexibility of the flow of permissions downstream.

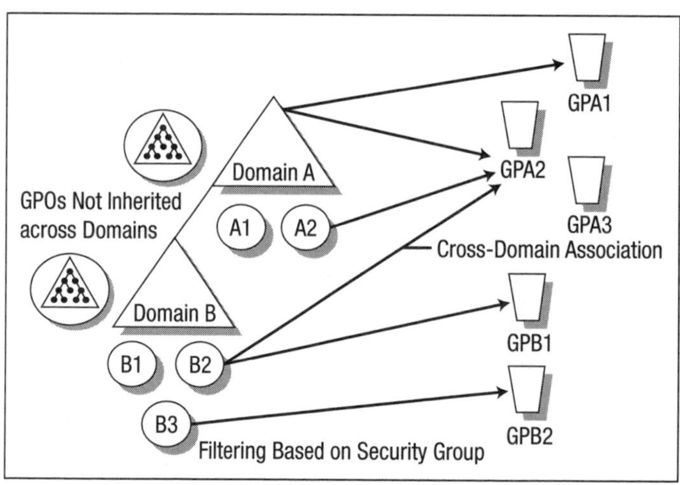

Figure 10.2 How GPOs create secure boundaries through policy management.

Alternatively, a more effective strategy can be to use multiple, decentralized Group Policies in conjunction with OUs that reflect the functional division of labor or authority. The ability to nest OUs within other OUs in a domain adds a dimensionality that was missing in the flat organizational model of legacy NT. Similarly, you can delegate GPO management to different administrative levels. In fact, you can block the setting of policies at various levels, or you can enforce it by object through the use of the No Override option. These features, if you apply them indiscriminately, defeat the effectiveness of a centralized policy management. Finally, once you define policy settings for groups, the operating system automatically and reliably enforces policy settings.

Group Policy Administration

Group Policy handles a wide range of deployment scenarios that scale well in an enterprise environment. The Group Policy MMC snap-in is a familiar tool that integrates with, for example, the AD Users And Computers and AD Site And Services Manager snap-ins, to teach you how to use administrative tools.

In NT 4, System Policy Editor (*poledit.exe*) provided a graphical user interface (GUI) that configured both user and local computer settings stored in the Registry. NT system policies were a list of rules that specified what users saw on their desktops and what they could do at the computer. Thus, you could restrict options in Control Panels, customize desktops, and control network logon and access. Microsoft recommended that the administrator use policy file mode as opposed to Registry mode (directly editing the Registry) to simplify the administration of a uniform domain policy. This mode of operation created or modified the default *ntconfig.pol* file, located in the NETLOGON share on the primary domain controller (PDC). The template ADM files provided policies that appeared in System Policy Editor.

Windows 2000 uses the Group Policy MMC snap-in tool. It not only extends the functionality of System Policy Editor but also provides, in conjunction with AD, enhanced capabilities that go beyond Registry-based policies to include security options, software deployment, scripting, and folder redirection. You set these security settings for a selected SDOU directory container. A Windows 2000 DC must be installed, and you must have Read/Write permission to not only access the system volume on the DC (Sysvol folder), but also permission to change the selected AD object. Group Policy affects all computers and users in a selected AD container by default. However, membership in a security group can filter the effect of a specific policy by overriding the policy and interrupting its inheritance by downstream objects, discussed in the "Security Group Effects" section later in this chapter.

Group Policy MMC Extensions

The Group Policy snap-in includes extensions that can extend either or both the User Configuration and Computer Configuration nodes in Windows Settings or Software Settings. By using the Group Policy MMC snap-in and its extensions, you can specify policy settings using the following extensions:

- *Administrative Templates*—This extension, applicable for both users and computers, includes Registry-based policies that affect the Windows 2000 operating system and applications. You manage them through the Administrative Templates node of the Group Policy MMC snap-in. There are over 450 available settings; you can add more using the ADM files.

- *Security settings*—This extension defines security configuration for computers within a GPO and for network settings, local machine, and domain. It includes, for example, account policies (password policy, lockout policy, Kerberos policy, and so on), local policies (security settings for audit policy, user rights, security options, and so on), and public key policies. Refer back to Figure 10.1 for a listing of the features as they appear under Computer Configuration|Windows Settings in the Default Domain Policy MMC snap-in.

- *Software Installation and maintenance options*—This extension, for users and computers, is for centrally managing software installation as well as removing, repairing, and publishing software (to users) or updates. Utilize this setting on application software that complies with the Microsoft Installer (MSI) technology. Target computers need to have Windows 2000 running as well as the client-side extension for software installation. To install Windows 2000 remotely, use RIS, discussed shortly.

- *Script options*—Scripts use Windows Scripting Host (WSH), discussed in Chapter 11. In Windows 2000, five script types are supported: legacy logon scripts, Group Policy logon/logoff scripts, and Group Policy startup/shutdown scripts.
- *Folder redirection options*—These options redirect users' special folders from their default user profile locations to the alternative network locations where they can be centrally managed. These special folders include My Documents, Application Data, Desktop, and Start Menu.
- *RIS*—Use RIS to manage the Remote Operating System Installation feature as displayed to client computers. Group Policy requires a genuine Windows 2000 client for this operation.

Note: Account policies are set only at the domain level. They are ignored if set at the organizational level.

Security Group Effects

Group Policy leverages the AD hierarchical structure by filtering the scope of GPOs in relation to the associated AD directory containers, SDOU. You create security groups and then assign Apply Group Policy and Read permissions to specific groups within the directory container. Security Groups alter the policy scope of a GPO by filtering Group Policy effects using security group membership and discretionary ACLs (DACLs) (discussed in Chapter 9). You can add named accounts to a group by using the Security tab on the Properties page of the GPO. Filtering affects all settings in the GPO except in the case of folder redirection and Software Installation. These nodes have additional GPO ACLs that can refine scope based on security group membership.

Another refinement in Windows 2000 is the ability to delegate control of these GPOs. Any security group member with both Read and Write permissions can delegate GPO control to other users for administrative reasons. Members of the Enterprise Administrators or Domain Administrators group determine which administrator group can modify GPOs through the Security tab on the GPO Properties page. These network administrators can delegate control of some policy to a specific administrator, who can be defined and provided with Read/Write access to select GPOs. Having Full Control of a GPO does not enable an administrator to link it to some site or other AD object unless the Delegation of Control Wizard grants this ability.

Group Policy Processing

Group Policy is inherited from parent to child containers. Assignment of GPO settings to an upstream container applies to all containers downstream, including the users and computer objects in those containers. Explicitly specifying GPO settings for a child container, however, overrides the parent container's GPO settings. If a parent OU has nonconfigured policy settings, the child OU cannot inherit them. Disabled policies settings are inherited as disabled. If a parent OU has configured settings and a child OU does not, the child inherits the parent's configuration. Policies are inherited as long as they are compatible, so a child inherits the compatible settings of a parent and then overlays its own settings on top. Conversely, when settings are incompatible, the settings aren't inherited, and the child's settings are applied.

When you are considering the ordered sequence with which GPOs are applied to both users and computers, you must consider the local GPO first. The local GPO is the only source of Group Policy for a standalone machine or members in a workgroup, so it is always processed. You cannot block this object.

Although Group Policy settings are processed in the following order, Group Policy settings can alter sequential aspects and behavior:

1. Upon computer startup, Group Policy settings under Computer Configuration from all GPOs associated with the named accounts are processed.
2. Startup scripts are run in sequence.
3. GPOs that affect the computer account are processed before the logon screen is displayed.
4. When the user logs on, all GPOs associated with the user account and associated Group Policy settings under User Configuration are processed simultaneously.
5. Group Policy-applied logon scripts run.
6. The Windows 2000 user interface is loaded.
7. Administrator-defined scripts are run.

Local Group Policy Object Processing

Both the No Override and Block Policy Inheritance options affect the presence or absence of GPOs in the order of GPO processing but do not change the ordering sequence.

Local Group Policy settings are processed in Windows 2000 native mode in the following order:

1. *Local Group Policy Object*—This is the one GPO stored on the local machine.
2. *Site*—GPOs linked to the site are processed synchronously.
3. *Domain*—Multiple domain-linked GPOs are processed synchronously and in a specified order.

4. *OUs*—GPOs linked to the highest upstream OU are processed first, then the rest of the GPOs are processed in order downstream.

At each OU level in the AD hierarchy, you can link one, many, or no GPOs. If several are linked to an OU, they are processed synchronously, and in the order specified. This order means that the local GPO is processed first, and the GPO linked to the OU in which the user and computer are located is processed last, overwriting upstream settings.

Default Order Exceptions

Two options change the inherited flow of Group Policy settings down the AD hierarchy from site to local machine. GPOs that are linked downstream at lower levels of the AD closer to either the specific user or computer cannot override the downward flow of policies when the No Override option is set on a specific upstream GPO link. If you set No Override to a GPO that is linked to a domain, the settings apply to all OUs under that domain. GPOs linked to OUs cannot override that domain-linked GPO. In addition, GPOs linked at the same level are prevented from changing the inheritance flow. If several links are set with No Override at the same AD level, the links higher in the list have priority over the lower ones.

You can alternatively block inheritance of GPO settings from upstream AD objects by checking Block Policy Inheritance on the Group Policy tab of the Properties sheet of the domain or OU. If you set this option at a child object level, the child does not inherit policy settings from its parent-level GPO, on the level above it. This ability to block policies does not exist at the site level. To see what a GPO object is linked to, open the GPO console, right-click on the Root node, click on Properties, and then click on the Links tab. Then, select Domain in the drop-down menu and click on Find Now.

Permissions for GPOs are analogous to file and folder permissions; the most restrictive permissions apply. Be careful when assigning Deny permissions.

Important facts to remember regarding No Override and Block Policy Inheritance are:

- You can set No Override only on a link.
- You can set Block Policy Inheritance on a domain or OU. It applies to all GPOs linked at that AD level or higher. You can also override settings.
- If a No Override option conflicts with a Block Policy Inheritance option, the No Override option takes precedence.

Changes due to inheritance flows regularly occur throughout the network. By default, Group Policy settings are refreshed on client computers every 90 minutes, with a randomized offset difference (plus or minus) of 30 minutes; DCs refresh every 5 minutes. You can change this refresh default value by modifying the Administrative Templates. However, you can apply Software Installation and folder redirection settings during computer startup or user logon. Finally, the user cannot schedule or control the application of GPO settings to a client computer.

Group Policy Loopback Support

GPO settings affect users and computers based on where they are located in the AD hierarchy. Sometimes, however, you must apply policy settings based on the location of the computer object alone. Group Policy loopback provides a way to apply GPOs specifically to one computer that a specific user might use. This feature is supported only in native mode Windows 2000 with both user and computer accounts stored in AD. Thus, in some cases, where processing order is not appropriate, you can specify two additional ways to process the list of GPOs for any user or computer in a specific OU. These two modes are:

- *Merge mode*—In this mode, when the user logs on, the typical list of GPOs is compiled in the typical order. However, a second list of GPOs is then requested, this time with respect to the location of the computer in the AD. This second list is appended to the first, causing the computer's GPOs to be processed after the user's GPO; thus, the computer's GPOs exercise greater control over the user's GPOs because the computer's settings have a higher precedence than the user's settings.
- *Replace mode*—The user's GPO list is ignored; the GPO list of the computer is applied.

I will use the scenario in Figure 10.3 to explain the power of Group Policy loopback support. In this scenario, you have been granted full Administrative rights over the **examcram.com** site. You want your user population to have Group Policy settings defined according to where they work. If an accountant whose office is in the Accounting section is working in the Art department, what policy settings will she receive? You want Group Policies there to be based on computer location to optimize the running of all graphics software. On the other hand, the accountant's ability to work on any workstation and access financial reports is a potential security risk. When she logs on at her graphics workstation, you want the order of Group Policy processing to be GPO3, GPO1, GPO4, GPO5, applied upon computer startup. In Figure 10.3, within the (triangular) Domain A1, there are (circular) organizational units that inherit Group Policy from upstream SDOU container objects. How can you secure the flow of inheritance? Normally, the accountant's Group Policy processing order is GPO3, GPO1, GPO4, and, in

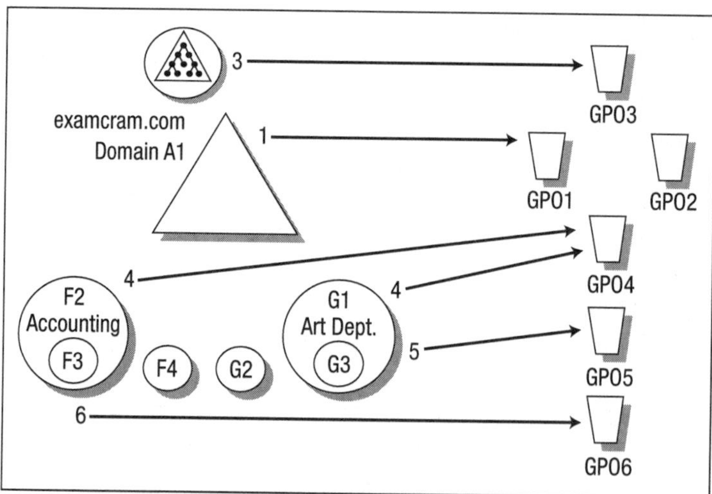

Figure 10.3 How Group Policy loopback support affects policy flow.

the Organizational Unit F3, GPO6, when she logs on to the network. Notice the numbers to the right of each geometric shape indicating these policies.

However, the workstation in question is in the Art department where it's appropriate to manage workspaces based on computer profiles. But what if the accountant attempts to work in the Art department? You can use either Merge or Replace mode to secure the Group Policy processing order. Here's what happens with each mode:

- *Merge mode*—When the accountant logs on, her user's list of GPOs is compiled, but then the computer's list of objects is appended at the bottom of her user list. Therefore, the processing order in Merge mode becomes GPO3, GPO1, GP04, GPO6, GPO3, GPO1, GPO4, and GPO5. The computer GPOs are appended to the user GPO settings, so the computer's GPO list has a higher precedence than the user settings. The workstations will run only graphics applications.
- *Replace mode*—The accountant's list of GPOs is not gathered at all. Instead, only the list of GPOs based on the computer object (GPO3, GPO1, GPO4, GPO5) is applied. This is the only list of settings, so the graphics machines in the Art department remain configured exclusively for graphics.

Permission Management Tools

The tools I discuss in this section are especially designed to work with Group Policy. I include not only what they do but also where you can find them. As mentioned in Chapter 11, support tools are part of the installation CD-ROM and therefore must be considered part of the system. The relevant Group Policy command-line interface (CLI) tools are:

- *floplock.exe*—This tool, FloppyLock, can lock a microdiskette disk drive so that it is accessible by only Administrators and Power Users. It can be used to prevent the installation of unauthorized software or the copying of confidential information to a diskette. The only way to unlock the diskette drive is to stop the FloppyLock service.
- *gpolmig.exe*—This support tool, Group Policy Migration, assists in the migration of NT 4 System Policy settings to Group Policy settings.
- *gpresult.exe and gpotool.exe*—These tools, Group Policy Results and Group Policy Verification, are included in the Windows 2000 Resource Kit. Gpresult.exe is a GPO troubleshooting utility that displays system information about GPOs applied to the local computer and user. Gpotool.exe performs command-line operations like creating and deleting GPOs in the directory, checking GPO/Sysvol replication status, and displaying information about a specific Group Policy object.
- *ldifde.exe*—This utility, LDIF Directory Exchange, is included with the core server application and is used to import and export AD data. It is located in Windows 2000 Server in %systemdir%\System32. It is not automatically installed in Windows 2000 Professional.
- *nltest.exe*—This utility is included with the support tools and is used to test trust relationships between clients and domain controllers as well as to verify relationships between domain controllers. In Windows 2000, nltest.exe accesses information directly from directory services; in legacy NT 4, it queried the browser service for named lists of machines. For more information, see Chapter 11.
- *runapp.exe*—This utility, RunApplication, can launch an application or restart one if it is closed. Be careful running this CLI utility from the command prompt.

You need to gain plenty of hands-on experience with these tools. When using any security utility, but especially those listed in this chapter, carefully test the results following execution of the tool. Centralized policy management simplifies administration but also amplifies even a simple change across an Active Directory container and can unintentionally cause widespread disruption in service.

Practice Questions

Case Study

4Sale, an online bartering company in ThatTherePlace, North Dakota, focuses primarily on selling inexpensive, odd-lot items.

The Network Manager says to you, "I need to deploy very standardized workspaces for the majority of our employees. I really don't have time to develop desktops myself. I want the users to have a standard set of desktop applications. Security needs to extend outside our intranet. We are a Web-based, e-commerce company. I want to make certain that security systems are integrated into as many network layers as possible."

Current LAN/Network Structure

4Sale is presently running Windows 2000 Server in native mode; one member server supports Exchange 5.5, whereas another is running Internet Information Server (IIS) 5 and Proxy Server 2. All 100 client machines are configured in a single-domain model. The client systems are all running Windows 2000 Professional, with Office 2000 being utilized as an applications package. Each system is connected to a 10Mbps hub through 10Mbps local area network (LAN) cards running Category 5 Unshielded Twisted Pair (UTP) cabling in a star topology.

Proposed LAN/Network Structure

No changes are planned at this time.

Current WAN Connectivity

No changes are planned at this time.

Proposed WAN Connectivity

No changes are planned at this time.

Directory Design Commentary

No changes are planned at this time.

Current Internet Positioning

No changes are planned at this time.

Future Internet Plans

No changes are planned at this time.

Company Goal with Windows 2000

4Sale wants to establish a policy-management infrastructure that will allow flexibility in the future but that will keep administrative costs to a minimum.

Question 1

Considering the Network Manager's comments in the case study, which Group Policy extensions are most appropriate? [Check all correct answers]

- ❑ a. Security settings
- ❑ b. Software specifications
- ❑ c. User templates
- ❑ d. Administrative Templates

Answers a and d are correct. Of the listed choices, they are the only answers that are extensions. Although the Network Manager mentions software installation, software specifications is not an extension; software installation and maintenance as well as Remote (Operating System) Installation Services are. Therefore, answer b is incorrect. Answer c is incorrect because user templates are not an extension; Administrative Templates are.

Question 2

The Network Manager at 4Sale says, "I want to delegate responsibility for marketing and sales policies to the supervisors in each department. How can I do this?" [Choose the best answer]

- ❍ a. Only members of the Enterprise Administrators group can modify GPOs; they cannot delegate that responsibility.
- ❍ b. Only members of the Enterprise Administrators and Domain Administrators groups can have Full Control over GPOs; they cannot delegate that responsibility.
- ❍ c. Only members of the Domain Administrators group can have Full Control over GPOs; they cannot delegate that responsibility.
- ❍ d. None of the above.

Answer d is correct. Answer a is incorrect because members of the Enterprise Administrators and Domain Administrators groups cannot only modify Group Policy Objects, but they can also link them to some Active Directory object. They can also delegate the responsibility of modifying a GPO to any administrator or an administrator group, provided all parties have Read/Write access to the specific GPO. Answers b and c are incorrect because you can grant to any administrator Full Control with the Delegation of Control Wizard.

Question 3

The Network Manager at 4Sale says, "I want a child GPO in our Project OU to inherit policy setting from the parent Marketing OU, but the two policies are exact opposites. The project needs Web services running with basic authentication so that Marketing can use integrated authentication to log in. What do I have to do to the parent OU to solve this problem?" [Choose the best answer]

- ❍ a. Modify the Marketing GPO.
- ❍ b. Modify the Project GPO.
- ❍ c. Do nothing.
- ❍ d. None of the above.

Answer c is correct. The parent OU is incompatible with the child OU, so the parent will not overwrite the child. Answer a is incorrect because modifying the Marketing Group Policy Object is not necessary. Answer b is incorrect because the child's GPO settings will not be affected by inheritance from the parent and will apply as always to objects in its own container.

Question 4

The Network Manager at 4Sale asks, "What is the Group Policy processing order?" Place the following in their proper order. Start with the computer startup.

Upon computer startup, Group Policy settings under Computer Configuration from all GPOs associated with the specific computer account are processed.

Group Policy-applied logon scripts run.

Startup scripts are run in sequence.

Administrator-defined scripts are run.

GPOs that affect the computer account are processed before the logon screen is displayed.

When the user logs on, all GPOs associated with the specific user's account and any associated Group Policy settings under User Configuration are processed simultaneously.

The Windows 2000 user interface is loaded.

The correct order is:

Upon computer startup, Group Policy settings under Computer Configuration from all GPOs associated with this specific computer account are processed.

Startup scripts are run in sequence.

GPOs that affect the computer account are processed before the logon screen is displayed.

When the user logs on, all GPOs associated with the specific user's account and any associated Group Policy settings under User Configuration are processed simultaneously.

Group Policy-applied logon scripts run.

The Windows 2000 user interface is loaded.

Administrator-defined scripts are run.

Question 5

The Network Manager at 4Sale says, "If the processing order is inappropriate, I can use Merge mode loopback support to apply only the GPO computer settings." Is this statement true or false?

❍ a. True

❍ b. False

Answer b, false, is correct. The Network Manager is incorrect. Merge mode loopback support appends the computer Group Policy Object settings to the user GPO settings. Replace mode actually replaces the GPO listing because the user GPO list is ignored.

Question 6

The Network Manager at 4Sale says, "Explicit GPO settings of a child container will override a parent containers' settings." Is this statement true or false?

❍ a. True

❍ b. False

Answer a, true, is correct. The Network Manager is correct. Explicit Group Policy specifications override the Group Policy Objects in a parent's container.

Need to Know More?

McLean, Ian. *Windows 2000 Security Little Black Book.* The Coriolis Group, Scottsdale, AZ, 2000. ISBN 1-57610-387-0. In Chapter 3, the author discusses Group Policy capabilities and benefits. He also describes immediate solutions for linking GPOs to objects, configuring a Group Policy Management snap-in, accessing GPOs, creating GPOs, and managing policies.

Nielsen, Morten Strunge. *Windows 2000 Professional Advanced Configuration and Implementation.* The Coriolis Group, Scottsdale, AZ, 2000. ISBN 1-57610-528-8. Chapter 19 not only details the available polices in the Administrative Templates but discusses best practices when you are working in a server environment.

Nielsen, Morten Strunge. *Windows 2000 Server Architecture and Planning.* The Coriolis Group, Scottsdale, AZ, 1999. ISBN 1-57610-436-2. Chapter 9 discusses the planning of user and group management, introduces the group concept, discusses built-in accounts and groups, and covers Group Policies in detail (including scopes of management and best practices).

Simanski, Robert E. *Windows 2000 Reducing TCO Little Black Book.* The Coriolis Group, Scottsdale, AZ, 2000. ISBN 1-57610-315-3. The focus of this book is to show you how to use the new Windows 2000 features to lower the TCO of your network. It is primarily intended for experienced administrators who are migrating from legacy NT or non-Windows platforms. Chapter 5 is dedicated to managing groups and OUs. In addition to a brief discussion of group types, scopes, and built-ins, the chapter has an extensive section on immediate solutions that covers most administrative tasks that involve creating and managing GPOs.

Search the TechNet CD (or its online version through **www.microsoft.com**) and the *Windows 2000 Server Resource Kit* CD using the keywords "Group Policy", "Group Policy Object", "Group Policy template", "OU", and "loopback". This is Microsoft's definitive online resource for technical papers and bulletins.

www.microsoft.com/windows2000/library/howitworks/management/grouppolicy.asp This is the location of *Using Group Policy Scenarios*, originally posted in February 2000. This Windows 2000 White Paper describes six scenarios using Group Policy in detail: Kiosk, TaskStation, AppStation, Public Computing Environment, low TCO desktop, and laptop.

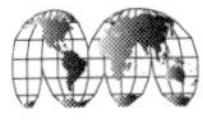

www.microsoft.com/windows2000/library/howitworks/management/grouppolicyintro.asp This is the location for *Introduction to Windows 2000 Group Policy*, originally posted in May 1999. This Windows 2000 White Paper provides an overview of Group Policy and explains the major concepts such as change and configuration management, IntelliMirror, Group Policy and TCO, capabilities and benefits of GPOs, Group Policy and AD, and Group Policy and security groups.

www.microsoft.com/windows2000/library/resources/reskit/samplechapters/dsec/dsec_pol_blsa.asp This is the location for Microsoft's *Windows 2000 Resource Kit* Group Policy chapter. Among the many chapter sections listed here is "Group Policy Processing". Other Group Policy topics you'll find here include an overview, management, storage, object links, loopback, and best practices.

Security and Configuration Tools

Terms you'll need to understand:

- ✓ IntelliMirror
- ✓ Windows Scripting Host (WSH)
- ✓ Terminal Services Architecture (TSA)
- ✓ Remote (Operating System) Installation Services (RIS)
- ✓ Windows Management Instrumentation (WMI)
- ✓ Web-Based Enterprise Management (WBEM)
- ✓ Common Information Model (CIM)
- ✓ Distributed Management Task Force (DMTF)
- ✓ Microsoft Management Console (MMC)
- ✓ Local Computer Policy
- ✓ Security Configuration (SC) Tool Set
- ✓ Security Configuration And Analysis (SCA) snap-in
- ✓ Independent software vendor (ISV)
- ✓ Command-line interface (CLI)
- ✓ Security policy
- ✓ Security templates
- ✓ Microsoft Resource Kit

Techniques you'll need to master:

- ✓ Describing the WBEM initiative
- ✓ Understanding the impact of centralized management on total cost of ownership (TCO)
- ✓ Identifying the security areas of the SCA controls
- ✓ Describing the basic components of the SC Tool Set

This chapter begins with a brief explanation of the many initiatives and technologies that have not only shaped Windows 2000, but which also clearly indicate future trends in how users and resources will be installed and managed. I stress these trends to help put deployment, administration, and maintenance strategies in perspective because the emphasis, especially in security, is changing. As I discussed in Chapter 10, I now rarely have the luxury of dealing with local machines. Instead, the methodology of placing all users in global groups and assigning global groups to local groups now applies to the tools I use in designing, supporting, and troubleshooting security systems. I describe the Microsoft Management Console (MMC) as the framework for tools that are critical in setting baselines, building configuration databases, and conducting security audits. For example, the Security Configuration (SC) Tool Set, and especially the Security Configuration And Analysis (SCA) snap-in, complement but do not replace other legacy NT 4 tools like User Manager For Domains, Server Manager, and Access Control List (ACL) Editor. The SC Tool Set is primarily a wizard that interprets and applies a range of configuration files to standardize security settings.

According to Microsoft, policy management is a scalable approach to system administration, using, for example Group Policy; it is appropriate for a 10-user local area network (LAN) as well as a 10,000-user enterprise. In the legacy domain model, Microsoft urged administrators to assign resource permissions exclusively to groups, never to individual users; now, Microsoft builds on that suggestion by recommending you apply security templates to every workstation, server, and domain controller (DC) to standardize organization, simplify deployment, and lower total cost of ownership (TCO). Having organized users and resources into groups, the application of one central policy simplifies administration and ensures the use of a uniform set of security standards. Nevertheless, there is still a need for command-line interface (CLI) and standalone tools (for example, when automating administrative tasks through the use of batch scripting).

Following a discussion of secedit.exe, one of these CLI utilities, I review a variety of tools: the Microsoft IP Security (IPSec) monitoring tool, Certificate Services CLI tools, security management tools culled from the root directory\Support\Tools directory of the Microsoft Windows 2000 operating system CD-ROM, and tools from the *Windows 2000 Server Resource Kit* CD. The tools in the root directory\Support\Tools directory, which will help you configure the Windows 2000 operating system, are an official part of the operating system. These tools run only on Windows 2000 and it is strongly recommended that both Microsoft support personnel and experienced users should use them. Though Microsoft does not support the tools in the Resource Kits, if information is published in a Resource Kit or online, I assume it will be included somewhere on an exam sometime in the future. Aside from that, the more knowledge technicians accumulate, especially of tools, the more efficiently they will perform their job.

Centralized Administration Tools

This chapter covers a broad range of tools and instrumentation that center on integrated security management and control. The fundamental themes of these various tools are:

- *Desktop management*—Features such as Group Policy and IntelliMirror, discussed later in this chapter, facilitate the management of data, software, and local system and user configuration within an organization and a Windows 2000 enterprise.
- *Centralized administration and control*—With expanding boundaries and 24/7 scheduling, administration must often be automated and performed remotely. Windows Scripting Host (WSH) and Terminal Services Architecture (TSA) support these automated changes and provide remote management from a central location. Terminal Services are discussed in greater detail in Chapter 12.
- *Rapid and inexpensive deployment*—Windows 2000 Professional is easier to deploy than legacy platforms. Aside from using Remote (Operating System) Installation Services (RIS) and creating installation images, you will find that it's fast, efficient, and inexpensive to deploy properly secured local systems. RIS is discussed in greater detail in Chapter 12.

Various security tools, services, and features provide this centralized management and efficient deployment. Security is fundamental in both design and deployment, so it is important that you be at least familiar with these centralized services and features because they provide the foundation for both current and future tools. They include:

- Windows Management Instrumentation (WMI)
- Windows Scripting Host (WSH)
- Terminal Services Architecture (TSA)
- Active Directory (AD)
- Microsoft Management Console (MMC)
- Remote (Operating System) Installation Services (RIS)

WMI

One of the key information technology (IT) initiatives today is Web-Based Enterprise Management (WBEM), which proposes to extend centralized administrative control over software, hardware, networks, and, most significantly, users and security policies. This initiative is based on the Common Information Model (CIM) schema standardized by the Distributed Management Task Force

(DMTF). WMI is WBEM-compliant and provides the basis for many tools that deal with the configuration and operational aspects of Windows 2000. WBEM provides a standardized infrastructure that combines both hardware and software management systems into a unified, common architecture that facilitates easy access from many different networked technologies and platforms. WMI tools are part of this very powerful evolving architecture and will play a future role in remote monitoring and maintenance.

The CIM model catalogs objects that are found in a management environment in an object data dictionary called an *Object Repository*. The CIM Object Manager administers both the collection and manipulation of the objects in this Object Repository. It also collects information from WMI providers, acting as intermediary agents between components that provide operating system services (service providers) and applications that access those components (consumers). These WMI providers collect information by monitoring the session pipes.

You can collect data using the WMI interface for hardware resources installed on the system. WMI can trace data available in AD for core directory service Lightweight Directory Access Protocol (LDAP), Key Distribution Center (KDC), Security Accounts Manager (SAM), Local Security Authority (LSA), and Net Logon service. Trace logging continuously captures events such as network logons, authentication, LDAP operations, and SAM operations.

WSH

WSH is a language-independent, low-memory, scripting platform (host) for 32-bit operating systems. It is a robust and scalable automation engine that supports noninteractive logon, administrative, and maintenance scripting functions. WSH can run from either the desktop as a graphical user interface (GUI)-based host (wscript.exe) or from a command shell-based interface (cscript.exe) as a script file or directly from the command prompt. Microsoft provides Visual Basic Script (VBScript) and JavaScript engines with WSH.

TSA

TSA is now a component of the Windows 2000 operating system rather than a separately purchased legacy NT 4 package. It provides the Windows GUI with remote devices over LANs and wide area networks (WANs), as well as the Internet. Only the data from monitor, keyboard, and mouse is exchanged between the client and host server. Although simultaneous access by multiple remote clients (application server mode) has been the traditional form of deployment, a new feature in Windows 2000 is *remote administration mode*. This operational mode provides remote access to BackOffice server products and DCs. Terminal Services supports up to two remote administration sessions without licenses. Microsoft is apparently encouraging the use of what is intended to be a single-user remote access solution because, at this time, no Terminal Server Client Access License (CAL) is required to use remote administration mode.

RIS

One of the major components of TCO is the initial deployment of new operating systems in the enterprise. RIS for Windows 2000 provides services that install a local copy of the Windows 2000 OS from some central site to remote locations throughout an enterprise. A remote machine would secure an IP address from a Dynamic Host Configuration Protocol (DHCP) server. Using a Client Installation Wizard (CIW) called the Remote Installation Services Setup Wizard, the local machine then receives an RIS image of the operating system and customized file directory structure from a specially designated boot server. This technology will be discussed in greater detail in Chapter 12.

AD

Through centralization of information about named accounts such as users, services and resources, the management of an enterprise is simplified. The arrangement of objects in a hierarchical structure provides AD directory services with a framework to authorize and audit changes and configure users and policies at the physical site level, the domain level, and the organizational unit level within the enterprise. This organizational structure supports enterprise scalability without increasing TCO or compromising the ability to efficiently manage named objects. One way to monitor AD-related activity is to use the NTDS (NT Directory Services) performance object in System Monitor. The NTDS object contains performance counters that provide statistics about AD performance. Counters such as Kerberos Authentications/sec monitor the client authentication rate on a DC, and NT LAN Manager (NTLM) Authentications/sec monitors the DC Service rate of NTLM authentications.

MMC

The MMC is a multiple document interface for an extensible array of administration and management tools. Offering no management functions of its own, the interface hosts a variety of software application components that literally snap into the interface; hence, they are called snap-ins. MMC does not replace any one tool but will over time become an integral part of all other system components. Windows 2000 snap-ins are typically available from the Administrative Tools menu or by typing "mmc" at the Run command line. The collection of tools within the MMC framework is referred to as the *console*.

Performance

Performance, located in the Administrative Tools menu, is an MMC console that displays the performance of many system objects according to selected counters. You can log, print, or view activity according to those counters. It has two tools, both of which can centrally monitor both local and remote computers, periodically collect baseline performance, and summarize data:

- *System Monitor*—This collects and displays realtime data about performance objects like Processor, Memory, Logical Disks, Network Interface, and other system activity in graph, histogram, or report format.
- *Performance Logs And Alerts*—This provides configured logs to record performance data and create alerts that are triggered by user-defined thresholds and sent to the event log for all recorded baseline exceptions. The Performance And Alert snap-in can also record data continuously in the form of trace logs.

NT 4 Performance Monitor has been replaced by the Performance MMC with System Monitor and Performance Logs And Alerts. The Computer Management MMC has consolidated Event Viewer, System Information, Performance Logs And Alerts, Shared Folders, Device Manager, Local Users And Groups, Storage-Related Tools, and Services And Applications.

Event Viewer

Either the standalone Event Viewer or the snap-in displays log files and error messages sent by applications and system services running in local or remote computers. Event Viewer monitors a variety of events, including application or system errors, and the start and stop of services. These events are recorded in event logs. Just as in NT 4, when you activate auditing, events are logged in the Security Log. Here are some examples of auditing events:

- To activate auditing as a local computer policy, select Local Computer Policy|Computer Configuration|Windows Settings|Security Settings|Local Policies|Audit Policy.
- To enable auditing of files and folders, enable Audit Object Access, then select the file or folder and set the access event (successful or failed) in the Auditing Entry dialog box under Properties|Security|Advanced|Auditing. Each entry logs a timestamped successful or failed event as defined in the auditing policy of, for example, object access, logon events, account management, and so on.

Desktop Management with IntelliMirror

Just as WMI provides a key substrate for Windows 2000 tools, the three desktop management components mentioned in the previous section provide the foundation for managing a user's environment. These components are:

- *AD directory services*—Supplies enterprise-wide location and policy information.

- *WSH*—Provides a robust and scalable automation engine.
- *MMC*—Provides a standardized presentation framework for administrative utilities.

These major components will continue to support application deployment and maintenance as much as the need to reduce TCO will drive that deployment and maintenance to greater efficiencies in time and resources. In reality, TCO is greatly affected by issues of deployment and maintenance, and these components all decrease that cost. Another group of technologies, collectively called IntelliMirror, is specifically focused on TCO and desktop management. It offers the following core features:

- *Software/application installation and management*—You can install, maintain, repair, and remove software and applications remotely with little user intervention.
- *Data protection and management*—By using techniques like folder redirection and synchronization, originally provided by the Windows Briefcase utility, you can save user data on network drives with copies cached on the local machine.
- *Roaming user support*—When you centrally manage a user's profile containing his or her desktop preferences, that user's data, applications, and environmental settings follow that user to any client computer connected to the network.

All management is centrally controlled through Group Policies. One significant breach in security will more greatly impact corporate success, goodwill, and reputation in a situation where there is centralized control, than many small deployment and maintenance problems will affect TCO. Network security policy in an enterprise is already as fundamental to the network as its transport protocol. Microsoft and other operating systems like Novell continue to develop initiatives that reduce TCO through consolidating directories, centralizing control, and managing users and resources via policies, and canned scripts, templates, and powerful wizards hide the growing complexity of security infrastructures.

Don't underestimate the ramifications that one poor configuration choice can have on an entire enterprise. Understand not just what the instrumentation can do but also, more importantly, what it doesn't do. Carefully test any policy settings before implementing them on a production platform. Take special care in confirming that all software applications run according to their specifications and intended use. The more tools you know how to use in a variety of situations, the more efficient and versatile your troubleshooting skills will be.

The Security Configuration (SC) Tool Set

Although NT 4 provided adequate tools for maintaining and supporting users and resources, it couldn't analyze security. With security subsystems becoming more complex, companies needed an integrated tools set that could audit security policies of all named objects—namely, users, services, and resources. The SC Tool Set provides a central configuration tool and framework for that analytical functionality. Using MMC provides a multiple document interface for customizable combinations of security-related tools. In addition, the MMC snap-in facilitates task delegation and lower TCO by providing a common, transferable interface with "least privilege features." In other words, an MMC snap-in can be configured with "only the tools needed to get the job done" for some set of specific administrative functions.

The SC Tool Set provides:

- Configuration of one or more NT- or Windows 2000-based computers
- A standardized security audit on one or more computers
- A single, uniform, and integrated point of administration

Security Areas

In providing standardized security functions, the SC Tool Set—specifically in the form of the SCA snap-in—configures and analyzes security configurations or templates, saved as text-based INF files and defined as security attributes, for the following security areas:

- *Account policies*—Settings include access policy, password policies, account lockout policy, and, at the domain level, Kerberos policy.
- *Local policies*—Settings include audit policy, user rights assignments, and a variety of options, such as control of storage devices like micro-diskettes and CD-ROMs.
- *Event log*—Settings include enabling log sizes, access, retention time, and retention methods.
- *Restricted groups*—Settings include group membership for user-defined and built-in groups such as Administrators, Server Operators, Backup Operators, Power Users, and so on. The SC Tool Set also tracks and controls reverse membership of each restricted group in the Members Of column—namely, other groups to which this restricted group can belong. You can use this field to manage which other groups can be joined or limit a group of users exclusively to one group.

- *System services*—Settings include security and startup policy on services ranging from Net Logon, Alerter, and Messenger to uninterruptible power supply (UPS), fax, Domain Name System (DNS) server, and Internet Authentication Service (IAS).
- *Registry*—Settings include the management of system Registry keys by placing a security descriptor on the key object.
- *File System*—Settings include the ability to configure NT File System (NTFS) attributes on all local volumes, including assigning permissions, auditing, and ownership at both the file and folder levels.

This architecture, like so many other aspects of Windows 2000, supports new security configuration areas as the system changes over time. You can import a security template into a GPO. Thus, you can either use the predefined configurations or build customized configurations using the Security Configuration Editor. System services similarly accommodate a security configuration attachment that can analyze and configure any third-party–independent software vendor (ISV) service. Thus, you can configure different NT systems to run different services without complicated options. In addition, the functionality of the SC Tool Set is available as a command-line utility, secedit.exe, for script-based configuration and analysis. The secedit.exe tool is discussed later in this chapter.

Security Settings

The phrase *security settings* describes a specific configuration. When it relates to security, it includes account and local policies (passwords and so on), access control (to services, resources, and so on), logging and auditing (event logs), restricted group memberships, IPSec, and public key policies. The security templates described in the "Security Templates" section later in this chapter are the physical collection of security settings having a common dimension (default, compatible, high security, and so on) stored in one file for simplified administration and maintenance. These templates define roles that can be applied to resources in a standardized way. Two additional settings require more customization and are therefore not included in a security template. These two settings are located in the Windows Settings node in the Computer Configuration portion of the Group Policy node. The two additional security policy nodes are:

- *Public Key Policies*—These policies include subpolicies that public key infrastructure (PKI) uses: X.509 root certificates, certificate trust lists, and encrypted data recovery agents used in Encrypting File System (EFS).
- *IP Security Policies on AD*—These policies point to the IPSec Policy object in the AD, which defines both encryption and signature requirements for IPSec secured information exchanges (discussed in Chapter 5).

Tool Set Components

The SC Tool Set consists of the following components:

- *Security Configuration Service*—This parser engine reads security configuration files and analyzes policy settings on the target machine.
- *Setup Security*—This component creates an initial security configuration database, called the Local Computer Policy, using predefined configurations.
- *Security Templates*—This standalone snap-in manages text-based INF files that define some user-customized security configuration. Templates are covered in more detail in the "Security Templates" section later in this chapter.
- *Security Configuration And Analysis Manager*—This standalone snap-in supports the importing of one or more security configuration databases that, when combined with the original Local Computer Policy, become composite configurations.
- *secedit.exe*—This full-featured CLI tool is used primarily for security configuration and auditing using script applications.
- *Security settings extensions to the Group Policy Editor*—This snap-in tool extends the Group Policy Editor by allowing you to define security configuration as part of a Group Policy Object (GPO), discussed in greater detail in Chapter 10.

The SC Tool Set supports:

- Defining a new, or modifying an existing, security database as a baseline configuration.
- Analyzing current computer security settings, listed by area, against this baseline configuration. A green checkmark indicates consistency between machine and database settings. A red X indicates a discrepancy between the two configurations. A generic icon indicates that the security attribute was not part of the template.
- Configuring the current computer to conform entirely to this baseline or to make individual changes using the Group Policy snap-in. You can define modifications in security policy as part of the GPO at the local machine, domain, or Organizational Unit (OU) in the AD. Thus, GPOs at various levels are imported into the local computer policy database. The composite database configuration, applied to the client computer to ensure compliance, is referred to as its *security policy*.

Familiarize yourself with the steps involved in using the MMC and in adding and removing standalone snap-ins, such as Security Configuration And Analysis, Group Policy, Security Templates, and so on. The MMC is the fundamental Windows 2000 framework for hosting administrative tools.

Security Templates

When you want to deploy a workstation or server, you install the operating system and use a predefined template to modify the new computer's Local and Group Policies. You can apply settings from a selection of predefined templates or customize one for a specific portion of your user population. You can also export a collection of customized settings to a template file for future use. These templates are not actual settings. Changes made to a predefined or customized template do not alter a machine's policies until that template is actually applied. The templates are text-based INF files that you can use as a baseline to analyze the security configuration of a specific machine or as a collection of settings to configure an existing workstation, server, or DC.

The Security Templates (Configuration Editor) provide editing capabilities for security template files, which describe security attributes in each of the security areas defined in the "Security Areas" section earlier in this chapter. You can import or export these template files to a security database on any specific machine. You can also apply them to domain controller GPOs, which replicate them to local computer policy databases on startup.

Predefined security templates that modify newly installed machines are as follows:

- *basicdc.inf*—Basic DC for Windows 2000 Server
- *basicsv.inf*—Default server for Windows 2000 Server
- *basicwk.inf*—Default workstation for Windows 2000 Professional
- *compatws.inf*—Compatible workstation or server
- *hisecdc.inf*—Highly secure DC
- *hisecws.inf*—Highly secure workstation or server
- *securedc.inf*—Secure DC
- *securews.inf*—Secure workstation or server

The templates form classes that satisfy five common security needs:

- *Basic (basic*.inf)*—These templates reapply default settings to all security areas except user and group rights.

- *Compatible (compat*.inf)*—This is not considered a secure environment. These templates implement an ideal Users configuration but a less secure Power Users configuration than a default installation setting. Windows 2000 authenticated users in Windows 2000 Professional (but not Server) are members of the Power Users group by default, so you may need to evaluate their security levels. These templates lower security levels on specific files, folders, and Registry keys that software applications commonly access so that they run successfully under a User security context.
- *Secure (secure*.inf)*—These templates implement security settings for all areas except files, folders, and Registry keys because these objects are configured securely by default or by permissions.
- *Highly secure (hisec*.inf)*—These templates are for IPSec-enabled network traffic and protocols used between Windows 2000 machines, not down-level NT or Windows clients, which are less secure than Windows 2000 machines. All network communication must be digitally signed and encrypted. Communications between a Windows 2000 secure computer and a down-level client cannot be performed.
- *Other INF files*—Special case templates implement specialized configurations. DC security.inf implements ideal file system and Registry permissions settings, especially for local users on Windows 2000 DCs. Microsoft recommends that server-based applications should not be run on DCs, whether under this template or generally. Another file group, ocf*.inf, provides optional component file security for Windows 2000 servers and workstations.

Templates are built on the assumptions that you will apply them to Windows 2000 computers with default configurations, and that these systems will be installed on NTFS volumes. When computers are upgraded from legacy NT, security is not modified. Templates incrementally modify default settings; they do not install default settings and then perform their predefined modifications. Finally, you should not install security templates on production platforms without carefully testing the applications after you apply the templates.

The secedit.exe Tool

When you frequently analyze or configure many machines, you should take advantage of a tool that uses the CLI, which is preferable over the GUI of the SCA tool in terms of both speed and convenience. Command-line operations allow you to configure and analyze security configurations in conjunction with tools like Microsoft System Management Server or the Windows 2000 Task Scheduler. The secedit.exe tool is the CLI version of the SC Tool Set, with which you can view CLI operations. Commands are detailed in the code snippets later in this section only with a usage menu unless details are especially noteworthy; the online help for secedit.exe provides both full command syntax and topical information.

This CLI tool provides five operations:

- *Analyze*—This operation corresponds to the same tasks available using the SCA snap-in.
- *Configure*—This operation corresponds to the same tasks available using the SCA snap-in.
- *Export*—This operation corresponds to the same tasks available using the SCA snap-in.
- *RefreshPolicy*—This operation is not included in the SCA snap-in. This operation automatically triggers a Group Policy propagation event when the machine reboots, every 60 to 90 minutes thereafter, and when local security policy is modified. You can enforce refreshes even if no changes have occurred.
- *Validate*—This operation forces verification of a template's syntax created using the Security Templates MMC snap-in.

To analyze system security, enter the following at the system prompt of the CLI:

```
SECEDIT /analyze [/DB filename ] [/CFG filename ]
  [/log logpath] [/verbose] [/quiet]
```

To configure system security by applying a stored template, enter the following at the system prompt of the CLI:

```
SECEDIT /configure [/DB filename ] [/CFG filename ] [/overwrite]
  [/areas area1 area2...] [/log logpath] [/verbose] [/quiet]
```

where /**areas** specifies the following security areas to be processed separated by a space:

- **filestore**—Security on local file storage
- **group_mgmt**—Restricted group settings only on groups specified in the template
- **regkeys**—Security on local Registry keys
- **securitypolicy**—Local policy and domain policy for the system
- **services**—Security for all defined services
- **user_rights**—User logon rights and granting of privileges

To refresh system security by reapplying the settings to the GPO, enter the following at the system prompt of the CLI:

```
SECEDIT /refreshpolicy {machine_policy | user_policy}[/enforce]
```

To export a stored template from a security database to a security template file, enter the following at the system prompt of the CLI:

```
SECEDIT /export [/mergedpolicy] [/DB filename ] [/CFG filename ]
  [/areas area1 area 2...] [/log logPath] [/verbose] [/quiet]
```

To validate the syntax of a security template that you want to import, enter the following at the system prompt of the CLI:

```
SECEDIT /validate filename
```

Other System and Security Tools

Although the trend in some aspects of Windows 2000 is toward centralization, the operating system promotes remote management through many system-related tools. Many of these are CLI utilities that use a textual user interface (TUI) to minimize bandwidth consumption during operation. The number and power of these tools in Windows 2000 is greater than those of earlier legacy versions. In fact, many utilities, such as netsh (NetShell), are described as both a command-line and scripting utility. This growing class of tools creates separate and distinct programming environments from the command line that support multiple Windows 2000 components on local and remote machines. This trend is clearly associated with the evolution of network architecture that supports distributed servers and services. One way to manage change and configuration in a cost-effective way is to build an infrastructure that can remotely manage objects with minimal impact on bandwidth—namely, in the form of a CLI utility. Many of the CLI utilities in this section have the same or greater functionality than their GUI counterparts, primarily because a CLI utility can be used in an automated script executed, for example, by WSH.

Note: Windows 2000, unlike legacy NT 4 with its fundamental ***net*** *command, increasingly resembles Unix and the standards-based Simple Network Management Protocol (SNMP) with regard to remote monitoring and control.*

Assume unless otherwise indicated that the utilities are run on the local computer as well as remotely (if there is a network connection to the remote computer). To execute any one utility, follow these steps:

1. Click on Start|Run.
2. Type "utility + parameter list".

Following installation of the Windows 2000 Support Tools, a complete, glossary-style listing of support tool syntax and examples is available by typing "w2rksupp.chm" in the Run command dialog box.

IPSec Monitoring Tool

This tool, ipsecmon.exe, though called from the CLI, launches a GUI utility that displays successful, secured communications managed by active security associations on local and remote computers. The refresh rate, updated by default every 15 seconds, is the only option you can configure.

The monitoring tool also:

- Determines authentication or security association failures that indicate incompatible security policy settings.
- Provides statistics, such as number and type of active security associations, total number of master and session keys, and total number of Encapsulated Security Payload (ESP) or combined ESP and Authentication Header (AH) bytes sent or received.

Certificate Services CLI Tools

Windows 2000 includes three CLI tools to assist you in administering Certificate Services. Although they extend the GUI functionality already provided, they are intended for developers and Certificate Authority (CA) administrators. The tools are:

- *CERTREQ*—Used to request certificates from a CA. Here's an example of its usage:

  ```
  CERTREQ -retrieve [-rpc] [-binary] [-config ConfigString]
  [RequestId [Certfile [CertChainFile]]]
  ```

- *CERTSRV*—Runs as a standalone application, typically for diagnostic purposes. Here's an example of its usage:

  ```
  CERTSRV -z
  ```

- *CERTUTIL*—Some of the many features supported by certutil.exe are:
  - Displays Certificate Services configuration information or a file that contains a request, a Public Key Cryptography Standards (PKCS) #7 certificate, or a certification revocation list (CRL).

- Gets the CA configuration string, retrieves the CA signing certificate, revokes certificates, and publishes or retrieves a CRL.
- Determines if a certificate is valid or if the encoding length is incompatible with old enrollment controls, verifies one or all levels of a certification path, and resubmits or denies pending requests.
- Sets attributes or an integer or string value extension for a pending request.
- Verifies a public/private key set, shuts down the server, and displays the database schema.
- Backs up and restores the CA keys and database, displays certificates in a certificate store, and imports issued certificates that are missing from the database.

Use the following help parameter to display a full listing of features:

```
CERTUTIL [options] -?
```

Support Security Management Tools

You use many of the tools described in this section to troubleshoot change and configuration management issues. These tools were included in previous Windows Resource Kits but are now part of the Windows 2000 Support Tools, located on the Windows 2000 operating system CD-ROM in the root directory\ Support\Tools directory. You must install the Support Tools separately from the Windows 2000 operating system.

- *acldiag.exe*—This tool diagnoses and troubleshoots AD objects that have problems with permissions by reading security attributes from ACLs and writing information in either readable or tab-delimited format. This tool displays only the permissions of objects the user has the right to view. You cannot use it on GPOs because they are virtual objects that have no distinguished name.
- *ADSI Edit*—This tool is an MMC snap-in that is a low-level editor for AD. It adds, deletes, and moves objects within the directory services using AD Services Interfaces (ADSI). You can view, change, and delete the attributes of each object. It allows you to create a query and scope it to any level in the tree for searching AD.
- *dsacls.exe*—This tool provides directory services management of ACLs. Like the Security page on various AD snap-in tools, it can query and manipulate security attributes on AD objects.
- *kill.exe*—This tool ends one or more tasks or processes. You can kill processes by entering the process ID number (PID) or by any part of the process name

or the name of the window in which it is running (usually the title of the application's main window). You can use either the Resource Kit tool PuList or TList to find the PID.

- *ksetup.exe*—This tool configures Windows 2000 clients, either Server or Professional, to use an MIT non-Windows–based Kerberos realm. The Windows 2000 client then uses an MIT-based Kerberos realm instead of a Windows 2000 domain, providing a Single Sign-On (SSO) to the MIT KDC and a local Windows 2000 client account.
- *ktpass.exe*—This tool generates Kerberos keytab files as well as sets password and account name mappings for Unix services that will use the Windows 2000 Kerberos KDC. It is part of a group of tools in the Server Resource Kit, including KSetup and Trustdom, which are used to configure Windows 2000 for MIT Kerberos interoperability. With this tool, you can configure a non-Windows 2000 Kerberos service as a security principal in the Windows 2000 AD. It configures the server principal name for the host or service in AD and generates an MIT-style Kerberos keytab file that contains the service's shared secret key. The tool allows Unix-based services that support Kerberos authentication to use the interoperability features that the Windows 2000 Kerberos KDC service provides.
- *ldp.exe*—This is a GUI tool that allows you to perform LDAP operations—including connect, bind, search, modify, add, and delete—against any LDAP-compatible directory, such as AD. You can use this tool to view AD objects along with security descriptors and replication metadata, and to search for *tombstones*, which are deleted but not disposed of AD objects.
- *movetree.exe*—This tool allows you to move AD objects, such as OUs and users with all of the linked GPOs in the old domain intact, between domains in a single forest. The GPO link is moved and continues to work. Clients, however, receive their Group Policy settings from the GPOs located in the old domain.
- *msicuu.exe*—This tool allows you to safely remove Windows Installer settings from a computer. Use this tool to remove Registry entries before reinstalling software applications.
- *netdiag.exe*—This tool performs tests that isolate networking and connectivity problems and determine the state of your network client and whether it is functional. This tool does not require you to specify parameters or switches.
- *netdom.exe*—This tool manages computer accounts for both workstations and servers through add, remove, and query options that allow specification of the OU for the computer account. It also moves an existing computer account for

a member workstation from one domain to another, as well as lists the member workstations or servers in a domain. It manages trust relationships between domains, views all trust relationships, and enumerates direct trust relationships and all (direct and indirect) trust relationships.

- *nltest.exe*—This tool checks trust relationships, as well as the connectivity and traffic flow between a network client and a DC. It also checks the secured interprocess communication (IPC) channel between servers to verify that both Windows 2000- and Windows NT 4-based clients connect to DCs. It can also discover domains and sites, list DCs and available Global Catalog (GC) servers, identify which DCs can log on a specific user and provide specific user information to browsers, force shutdowns, and check the status of trust relationships.
- *ntdsutil.exe*—This tool maintains the AD database, manages and controls single master operations, and removes metadata left behind by DCs that were removed from the network without being properly uninstalled. Only experienced administrators should use this tool. By default, it is installed in the Winnt\System32 folder.
- *PPTP PING*—This tool verifies that Point-To-Point Tunneling Protocol (PPTP) is being routed from a PPTP client to a PPTP server. The pptpclnt.exe and pptpsrv.exe tools work in unison to verify that the required protocol and port for PPTP is being routed from a PPTP client to a PPTP server or vice versa. For a PPTP client to access a remote PPTP server, all routers in between the two hosts *must* allow traffic to pass through Transmission Control Protocol (TCP) port 1723 (PPTP) and must support protocol type 47. Protocol type 47 is the Generic Routing Encapsulation (GRE) protocol. PPTP PING runs on Windows 2000, NT, and 98, but not on 95.
- *reg.exe*—This CLI tool manipulates Registry entries on local or remote computers. It enables you to add, change, delete, search, save, restore, and perform other operations on Registry entries from the CLI or a batch file.
- *remote.exe*—This tool runs command-line programs on remote computers using named-pipes connections. To use it, you start the server end by running **remote /s** from the CLI on the computer where you want to run the selected program. Connect to the server end from another computer by running **remote /c** from the CLI. This tool neither provides security authorization nor permits anyone with a remote client (**remote /c**) to connect to your remote server (**remote /s**). An alternative to the unsecured communications of remote.exe is rcmd.exe (Remote Command Service), a Resource Kit tool, which authenticates all users with standard Windows 2000 user authentication procedures.

- *sdcheck.exe*—This tool displays the security descriptor for any object listed in the ACLs stored in the AD. ACLs define the permissions that users have to manipulate objects. To determine the effective access controls on an object, this tool also displays the object hierarchy and any ACLs that the object has inherited from its parent. It can help determine whether ACLs are being inherited correctly and if ACL changes are being replicated from one DC to another.
- *search.vbs*—This VBScript tool, which requires WSH, performs a search against an LDAP server. You can use it to get information from the AD.
- *SIDWalker*—These tools—showaccs.exe, sidwalk.exe, and the sidwalk.msc MMC snap-in—manage server resources moved between domains and access control policies.
- *snmputilg.exe*—This GUI tool complements the older command prompt SNMP browser tool (snmputil.exe). You can use either tool to obtain information from SNMP-manageable systems on the network.
- *tlist.exe*—This tool displays a list of tasks, or processes, that are currently running on the local computer. It also shows the PID, process name, and (if the process has a window) the title of that window for each process. If you locate the running processes, you can selectively stop any executing process by using the task-killing utility, kill.exe.
- *wsremote.exe*—This tool can start a server application and connect to it from the client using sockets or named pipes. Compare this tool with Remote Command Line (remote.exe), which allows only named-pipes connections.

Because support tools are included as part of the operating system, you should understand how and when they are used. Support tools may be mentioned as parts of provided solutions for administration of various aspects of case studies.

Tools from the *Windows 2000 Server Resource Kit* CD

The *Windows 2000 Server Resource Kit* contains more than 300 separate utilities that range in function from AD and security management to job automation. Unlike Windows 2000 support tools that are included on the operating system CD-ROM, Microsoft does not recommend or support the use of these utilities.

Note:** Legacy tools are no longer included in the Resource Kits; however, they are available at the Microsoft FTP site:* ***ftp://ftp.microsoft.com/bussys/winnt/winnt-public/reskit/.

Based on past trends, many of these tools will most likely become either support or integrated system tools in future versions of Windows operating system products.

Familiarity with their specific functions and interaction with other system components may prove useful in a technician's daily work. Never use these tools on a production platform until you are thoroughly familiar with how they operate.

The following are a selection of these Microsoft "as-is" tools that provide support for change and configuration of security-related objects and services:

- *addiag.exe*—This tool provides information on the state of software either installed or available for installation on a computer managed by IntelliMirror Software Installation And Maintenance. It provides information about software applications such as current user (including logon credentials and SID) and the platform (processor and locale) that could affect the managed software. It also tells you Windows Installer information, installed or advertised information about software derived from the Registry, advertised information about available software stored in AD directory services, and whether Terminal Server is running on the computer.
- *adduser.exe*—This tool creates, writes, and deletes user accounts from a comma-delimited file. Before creating user accounts, execute **addusers /d**, which writes the headings, user accounts, local groups, and global groups to a file and gives a picture of the data structure and headings of the comma-delimited file.
- *auditpol.exe*—This tool modifies the audit policy of the local computer or of any remote computer.
- *gpotool.exe*—This tool checks the state of GPOs on DCs, checks GPO consistency by reading mandatory and optional directory services properties (version, friendly name, extension Globally Unique Identifiers—GUIDs—and SYSVOL data—gpt.ini), compares directory services and SYSVOL version numbers, and performs other consistency checks. It displays information about a particular GPO, including properties that you can't access through the Group Policy snap-in, such as functionality version and extension GUIDs especially in verbose mode. It browses GPOs by searching policies based on friendly name or GUID. It provides cross-domain support for checking policies in different domains. If all policies are valid, a Policies OK message is displayed; if there are validation errors, information about corrupted policies is printed.
- *gpresult.exe*—This tool provides general information about operating system, user information, and computer information. It also provides information about Group Policy (such as the last time policy was applied and the DC that applied policy) for the user and computer and the complete list of applied GPOs and their details (including a summary of the extensions that each GPO contains, applied Registry settings and their details, redirected folders and their details, software management information that details assigned and published applications, disk quota information, IPSec settings, and scripts).

Practice Questions

Case Study

4Sale, an online bartering company in ThatTherePlace, North Dakota, primarily focuses on selling inexpensive, odd-lot items. The Network Manager is preparing to deploy new workstations in the Marketing department and is concerned about setting security policy and configuration.

Current LAN/Network Structure

4Sale is presently running Windows 2000 Server in native mode; one member server supports Exchange (Simple Mail Transfer Protocol—SMTP) server, and another is running Internet Information Server (IIS) (Hypertext Transfer Protocol [HTTP]) and Proxy Server (packet filtering/caching). All 100 client machines are configured in a single domain model. The client systems are running Windows Professional, with Office 2000 being utilized as an applications package. Each system is connected to a 10Mbps hub through 10Mbps LAN cards running Category 5 Unshielded Twisted Pair (UTP) cabling in a star topology.

Got-a-Deal is running all 22 client machines in a single child domain under the 4Sale root domain. The client systems are running Windows Professional, with Office 2000 being utilized as an applications package. Each system is connected to a 10Mbps hub through 10Mbps LAN cards running Category 5 UTP cabling in a star topology. These hubs are on the same backbone as 4Sale but have a different subnet.

Proposed LAN/Network Structure

No changes in the current structure are proposed at this time.

Current WAN Connectivity

No changes in the current structure are proposed at this time.

Proposed WAN Connectivity

No changes in the current structure are proposed at this time.

Directory Design Commentary

No changes in the current structure are proposed at this time.

Current Internet Positioning

No changes in the current structure are proposed at this time.

Future Internet Plans

No changes in the current structure are proposed at this time.

Company Goal with Windows 2000

The 4Sale CEO says, "Make certain our enterprise can operate in a uniform and secure way without increasing TCO given a projected 15 percent growth in sales. I don't want to increase the Technical Services budget line."

The 4Sale Network Manager says, "I need ways to remotely control all machines in the enterprise. I need to have control over what our users can see and do. I want to do this in as transparent a way as possible to nurture our corporate culture of self-reliance. I need tools that will help me troubleshoot system services without concern for slow-link connections or increasing network traffic. I need ways to automate maintenance functions."

Question 1

The CEO of 4Sale asks you, "What sorts of technology help centralize my management services?" [Check all correct answers]

- ❑ a. WMI
- ❑ b. WSH
- ❑ c. TSA
- ❑ d. AD
- ❑ e. None of the above

Answers a, b, c, and d are correct. WMI (Windows Management Instrumentation), WSH (Windows Scripting Host), TSA (Terminal Services Architecture), and AD (Active Directory) all contribute to centralizing installation and support services.

Question 2

The Network Manager at 4Sale asks, "How do I measure user authentication activity?" Which of the following performance objects measures Kerberos Authentications/sec activity?

- ❍ a. NTDS
- ❍ b. NTFS
- ❍ c. Processor
- ❍ d. Process
- ❍ e. None of the above

Answer a is correct. The NTDS (NT Directory Services) is one of the listed performance objects in the System Monitor in the Performance MMC; it measures Kerberos Authentications/sec. NTFS (NT File System) is not a performance object; it is the Windows 2000 file system. Therefore, answer b is incorrect. Although most system activities affect Processor, it does not directly measure Kerberos activity. Therefore, answer c is incorrect. Process provides counters of the application components the processor can measure. Therefore, answer d is incorrect.

Question 3

The Network Manager at 4Sale asks, "Which security areas can I standardize whenever we plan a big rollout of computers?" Which of the following are valid security areas? [Check all correct answers]

- ❑ a. Restricted groups
- ❑ b. System services
- ❑ c. Registry
- ❑ d. DNS server

Answers a, b, c, and d are correct. The restricted groups, system services, Registry, and Domain Name System server (a component of system services) security areas are all correct. Account policies, local policies, event log, and file and folder sharing are missing from the complete list.

Question 4

The Network Manager at 4Sale says, "I don't want to build security profiles myself. What are the default security templates I have to choose from?" [Check all correct answers]

- ❑ a. Basic (basic*.ini)
- ❑ b. Compatible (compat*.ini)
- ❑ c. Highly secure (hisec*.ini)
- ❑ d. Secure (secure*.ini)
- ❑ e. None of the above

Answer e is correct. Although all the category names are correct, security templates are text-based files with the .inf extension (not the .ini extension as in answers a, b, c, and d).

Question 5

The Network Manager at 4Sale says, "I prefer to work with GUI tools. I can use my mouse when I run secedit.exe." Is the Network Manager correct?

- ❍ a. Yes
- ❍ b. No

Answer b, no, is correct. The Network Manager is incorrect. The secedit.exe tool is a command-line utility. It does not work with a mouse.

Question 6

The Network Manager at 4Sale says, "According to my documentation, ntdsutil.exe shows me the security descriptor of any object stored in the AD." Is the Network Manager correct?

- ❍ a. Yes
- ❍ b. No

Answer b, no, is correct. As indicated by its name, ntdsutil.exe is a tool that performs database management on the Active Directory. The utility the Network Manager is probably referring to is sdcheck.exe, which displays the security descriptor information stored in the Active Directory.

Question 7

The Network Manager at 4Sale asks, "What kinds of functions can I perform with secedit.exe?" [Check all correct answers]

- ❑ a. Analyze
- ❑ b. Configure
- ❑ c. Export
- ❑ d. Validate

Answers a, b, c, and d are correct. The secedit.exe tool performs all the operations listed—analyzing, configuring, exporting, and validating—that the graphical user interface tool, SCA (Security Configuration And Analysis) MMC (Microsoft Management Console) snap-in, does. It also provides additional features such as template syntax verification (validate) and on-demand Group Policy propagation (RefreshPolicy).

Need to Know More?

Ivens, Kathy and Kenton Gardinier. *The Complete Reference: Windows 2000*. Osborne McGraw-Hill, Berkeley, CA, 2000. ISBN 0-07-211920-9. Chapter 25 discusses a wide range of configuration tools, including Group Policy management, IntelliMirror, the SCA snap-in, WSH, and WMI. The section on the SCA snap-in gives a concise overview of this MMC snap-in.

McLean, Ian. *Windows 2000 Security Little Black Book*. The Coriolis Group, Scottsdale, AZ, 2000. ISBN 1-57610-387-0. The author discusses SCA tools in Chapter 12. This chapter covers all key areas in a clear, concise manner and provides immediate solutions for analyzing and configuring Windows 2000 clients. It also discusses the use of secedit.exe.

Nielsen, Morten Strunge. *Windows 2000 Professional Advanced Configuration and Implementation*. The Coriolis Group, Scottsdale, AZ, 2000. ISBN 1-57610-528-8. Chapter 15 deals with security design and implementation, in terms of both planning and deployment. Although this book deals with Windows 2000 Professional, it covers other Windows 2000 topics clearly and comprehensively. The author takes great pains to explain the rationale behind many of the new features in the Windows 2000 operating system. The book deals with design and planning as well as configuration and deployment; there is an important chapter that discusses Microsoft's project management methodology, Microsoft Solution Framework (MSF).

Shinder, Thomas. W. and D. Lynn White. *Configuring Windows 2000 Server Security*. Syngress Media, Inc., Rockland, MD, 2000. ISBN 1-928994-02-4. Chapter 5 provides a thorough treatment of the SC Tool Set, including how to create a security tool MMC. This chapter discusses the security areas, how to configure policies, Group Policy integration, and the use of secedit.exe.

Search the TechNet CD (or its online version through **www.microsoft.com**) and the *Windows 2000 Server Resource Kit* CD using the keywords "Active Directory", "GPO", "ACL", and "secedit".

www.microsoft.com/windows2000/library/howitworks/security/sctoolset.asp This site provides the *Security Configuration Tool Set* white paper, posted in April 1999. It describes the SC Tool Set, a set of MMC snap-ins that reduces costs associated with security configuration and analysis of Windows NT and Windows 2000 operating system-based networks.

www.microsoft.com/windows2000/library/technologies/management/default.asp This Web site offers a wide selection of Windows 2000 Server technical papers that cover how to configure and secure Windows 2000-based systems; administer desktop configuration and changes; manage data storage and retrieval; and implement value-added management solutions using technologies such as the AD, IntelliMirror, Group Policy, WMI, MMC, and WSH.

Other Technical Issues

Terms you'll need to understand:

- ✓ Distributed interNet Applications Architecture (DNA)
- ✓ Enterprise identity management
- ✓ Active Directory Services Interfaces (ADSI)
- ✓ Lightweight Directory Access Protocol (LDAP)
- ✓ Microsoft Messaging Application Programming Interface (MAPI)
- ✓ Microsoft Directory Synchronization Services (MSDSS)
- ✓ Remote (Operating System) Installation Services (RIS)
- ✓ Simple Network Management Protocol (SNMP)
- ✓ Server Message Block (SMB) signing
- ✓ Novell Directory Services (NDS)
- ✓ Services for NetWare version 5 (SFN5)
- ✓ Services for Unix 2 (SFU2)

Techniques you'll need to master:

- ✓ Describing the components that support enterprise identity management
- ✓ Identifying Microsoft's strategic positions in the development of smart card technology
- ✓ Comparing Kerberos and Secure Sockets Layer
- ✓ Discussing securing access using SMB signing and the role SMB plays in interoperability
- ✓ Incorporating both Terminal Services and RIS in the secure deployment of network resources
- ✓ Describing how to secure the use of SNMP while monitoring system services
- ✓ Distinguishing parts of the COM+ security model

In this chapter, I discuss enterprise identity management, trends toward network operating system (NOS) consolidation versus coexistence, and securing access to enterprise resources as it relates to the design of Windows 2000, Active Directory (AD), corporate business objectives, and authentication and authorization security controls. I discuss how to standardize user access in a heterogeneous environment. I explore the security aspects of three themes: enterprise consolidation, enterprise enhancement, and enterprise extensibility.

In securing access for users, I discuss two-factor authentication specifically using smart cards as an example of enhancements to the security infrastructure of an enterprise. I then explore other methods of secured access to distributed and network services using Terminal Services and Remote (Operating System) Installation Services (RIS). I discuss how Simple Network Management Protocol (SNMP) can securely monitor subsystems like Dynamic Host Configuration Protocol (DHCP) when providing operating system features like RIS. I also discuss Server Message Block (SMB) signing as an alternative to Kerberos and SChannel security protocols in providing secure exchanges of information at the Open Systems Interconnection (OSI) Application layer. This topic leads to issues of migration and interoperability relating to Novell NetWare and other competitive NOSs.

In my discussion of enterprise consolidation versus coexistence, I examine issues of migration versus interoperability relating to Novell NetWare, Unix, and Macintosh operating systems. I conclude this chapter with a discussion of enterprise extensibility. I discuss the security aspects of COM+ (Component Object Model +), multitier architecture, and Web applications as extensions to the enterprise.

Centralized Identity Management

This book started with corporate business objectives; it also ends with them. Information technology (IT) has evolved into a pantheon of digital technologies that primarily deal with the relationship between consumer and service provider. According to Microsoft, an organization's ability to adapt or evolve depends upon its internal digital processes, or *digital nervous system*. Distributed interNet Applications Architecture (DNA) is a term coined by Microsoft describing multi-tiered, service-providing software technologies that are location-independent, distributed across the enterprise and the Internet. The digital nervous system, another Microsoft term, is the hypothetical collection of these interdependent services. The digital nervous system of an organization, much like its biological analogy, provides a decision support function in recognizing and reacting to changes in the business environment, competitive challenges, and consumer needs in a systematic and timely fashion. DNA extends that concept beyond physical boundaries of site and local area network (LAN) segments through the use of distributed, asynchronous, self-contained, service-providing software components.

We should assume that from an IT perspective, the consumer is as much the corporate employee as the person who buys merchandise in a store. Fundamental to Microsoft's DNA paradigm is enterprise identity management. As we have learned in this book, where there is a principal, there is some form of access/permission management; where there is access/permission management, there must be security systems.

According to Microsoft, enterprise identity management is composed of the following three functional areas:

- *Identity administration*—The data definition function that supports the data of individual entities
- *Community management*—The connectivity function that provides relationships among these entities
- *Identity integration*—The management of repositories and the business rules that govern their operation and interaction

Identity Administration

The central theme in this area is representing the consumer in relation to business processes. Three functions that provide this service are:

- *Existence*—The function that establishes identity
- *Context*—The function that maintains an entity's dynamic inventory
- *Provisioning*—The function that provides materials that the entity needs to operate in its environment

Existence

This function identifies and automates operations that create the individual entity. Active Directory directory services provide open interfaces in the form of application programming interfaces (APIs), such as Active Directory Services Interfaces (ADSI), Lightweight Directory Access Protocol (LDAP), and Microsoft Messaging Application Programming Interface (MAPI), that can programmatically create, copy, or duplicate entity records across applications and platforms. Synchronization and configurable business logic support the systematic propagation of this information.

Context

Context tracks the working environment of a digital identity based on combinations of data, including physical, functional, and organizational location, in association with level, responsibility, role, and time. Tracking the context of an entity is a dynamic function that changes throughout a work period based on the dynamics of the job function and the role. AD provides context support in the form of hierarchical modeling of organizations, security groups, and Group Policy. Migration from one Organizational Unit (OU) to another can dramatically change individuals' contexts in the organization, their privileges and permissions to use resources, and the rules that govern their activity.

Provisioning

Provisioning calls for dynamically providing materials needed to complete a defined job function or role based on a collection of business roles. Job-related provisions include, but are not limited to, application software, different categories of storage (online, inline, and offline), network resources, different modes of access (local, interactive, and remote), and different quotas that pertain to both storage and network bandwidth. AD supports these functions with hierarchical storage and quotas as well as policy-based management. IntelliMirror management technologies, discussed in Chapter 11, provide this sort of provisioning service with its location-independent application distribution and configuration management. In addition to provisioning resources, AD can supply the rules-based engine to force configuration when an inconsistency from some baseline database template is detected.

Community Management

Digital community management tracks, administers, and (when programmed) creates relationships among entities that the enterprise manages. The following three provide this fostered synergy:

- *Authentication*—The function that provides the proof of identity
- *Authorization*—The function that grants the rights and privileges to resources
- *Rendezvous*—The function that connects the objects targeted for synergy

Authentication and Authorization

Authentication and authorization are exactly where I started with security controls in Chapter 2. Entities are granted access to resources based on security credentials. Authentication here extends beyond username and password to smart cards (discussed in greater detail in the "Enhancement: Smart Cards" section later in this chapter), biometrics, and other two-factor forms of authentication ("what I have" and "what I know"). It is clear that to build and manage a community, you must have technologies that will reliably authenticate its members and invited guests. Windows 2000 has an array of security features, including Kerberos authentication, public key infrastructure (PKI), and X.509 certification working through Secure Sockets Layer (SSL), attribute-level permission management spanning security groups within domain partitions, and highly granular access control lists (ACLs).

Rendezvous

Rendezvous connects the consumers with resources for both collaboration and the exchange of services. Once you have verified authentication and authorization, you need to locate resources and make them available as efficiently as possible. AD supports Internet-based protocols and naming conventions that integrate easily into directory services. Naming conventions as well as the control over exposing specific attributes to facilitate cross-referencing and search functions are critical. Active Directory Connectors (ADCs), discussed in Chapter 7, and DirSync technologies (discussed later in this chapter with regard to directory synchronization) allow you to securely populate and update publicly accessible namespaces.

Identity Integration

Identity integration is the management function that recognizes ownership roles of different systems and establishes the business rules regarding how the datastores are maintained. This topic was discussed in the "Requirements for Identity Management" section in Chapter 7. In the context of that chapter, which describes the trend toward consolidation of directory services, I observe that to make identity data accessible, you need to transparently bridge identity management across disparate directory services. Windows 2000 aims to provide a unified, consistent, and reliable view of identities and their associate relationships across heterogeneous systems within the enterprise namespace. The next step, however, is to consolidate views across enterprise namespaces and thus form one unified namescape. The functions that provide that unified view in Windows 2000 are:

- *Connection*—The function that supports cross-system communication within the namespace
- *Brokerage*—The function that supports the translation and exchange of datastores
- *Ownership*—The function that tracks the primary source for each piece of data in the namespace

Although I discuss the details regarding these functions in Chapter 7, I will briefly describe them again. Here, however, I will discuss this topic in the context of a single enterprise or *one homogeneous namespace*, as opposed to the context in Chapter 7, where I discuss different directory systems or *heterogeneous namespaces*.

Connection

Connection refers to linking within *one enterprise* all heterogeneous systems in a unified namescape. These systems refer to several things, such as internalized directory datastores in Exchange 5.5 and SQL (Structured Query Language) Server 7. They also refer to widely distributed datastores and identity repositories across functionally distinct areas of the enterprise, such as Human Resources and a line-of-business (LOB) project management system. AD provides several APIs (discussed in the "AD Directory Services" section in Chapter 9), such as LDAP C API, MAPI, and its own ADSI, to provide support for other enterprise applications. It is noteworthy that AD provides native support for LDAP, shrewdly incorporating the widely accepted, standards-based protocol into its source code.

Brokerage

Brokerage manages the interchange of identity-related data that is based on business rules coming from business processes but fundamentally from corporate business objectives. Data exchanges refer not only to translations in the entries recorded in disparate and widely distributed datastores within the enterprise, but also in the updating process so that consistency and reliability are always maintained. It is noteworthy that a single move, add, or change in any one normalized piece of data can trigger a disproportionate number of associated changes in foreign tables due to referential constraints found in any typical business application. This complexity increases exponentially when you link datastores across intranets and extranets, the latter most likely subscribing to different identity classes and schema. To help clarify this concept, you can make the analogy of mapping fields in data dictionaries when you are importing database tables from proprietary relational database management systems. AD, especially through Microsoft Directory Synchronization Services (MSDSS) and its Zoomit technology, facilitates these rules-based translations and cross-datastore connections.

Ownership

Ownership refers both to the problem of propagating information across many systems in an enterprise and the necessity of relying on one authority as a definitive source for referential integrity of that piece of data. The hub and spoke architecture that Zoomit technology provides directly addresses the issue of ownership of, for example, Human Resources employee records, and the problems of rapid, reliable propagation of data associated with "hire & fire" scenarios, mentioned in Chapter 7. With this technology, Microsoft's Meta-directory Services (MMS) leverages Windows 2000 AD and provides solutions to this and other common business situations not only within, but more importantly beyond, the enterprise.

Standardizing Access for Users

A shift in business strategy is apparent in Windows 2000 with an effort to provide greater support for coexistence with other competing NOSs like Novell NetWare 5, Apple Macintosh, and Unix. Heretofore, the clear bias was not interoperability among competing NOSs, but support primarily for migration of users and resources from those competitive NOSs to the Microsoft NOS family.

You should be very familiar with interoperability and migration issues in terms of the following NOSs: Novell NetWare, Unix, and to a lesser extent, Macintosh.

As mentioned previously, AD is clearly marketed as a potential meta-directory or hub around which other non-Microsoft operating systems can interoperate, interfacing through ADSI to access Windows 2000 core directory services. One major theme that is emphasized in documentation is accessibility to network resources and services characterized by a simple logon process: a Single Sign-On (SSO). With this background theme in mind, Microsoft uses two concepts in its integration strategy:

- *Strong migration tools*—These tools are typically well designed to encourage the move to Microsoft.
- *AD integration as a meta-directory service*—The direction of data sharing remains limited and biased; it is from Microsoft to the other operating systems.

Single Sign-On (SSO)

A key theme in the consolidation of heterogeneous networked environments, and especially in Microsoft and Novell technical and design literature, is the SSO feature, which enables an authenticated consumer to log on and transparently access all authorized resources and services anywhere inside or outside the boundaries of the enterprise. Both Windows 2000 and NetWare NOSs measure their directory services by this feature. Microsoft's evolving strategy with the SSO theme is to have AD provide authentication services no matter from which operating system platform a consumer accesses network resources. This initiative positions Microsoft as the central administrator/manager of security credentials and password account policies. Microsoft has designed Windows 2000 in a truly flexible, scalable manner to encourage the Microsoft meta-directory concept. Not only are the natively implemented security systems like Kerberos, PKI, and SSL/Transport Layer Security (TLS) standards-based, but the operating system security architecture is actually two APIs: Security Support Provider Interface (SSPI) and Cryptographic Application Programming Interface (CAPI). TLS, one of the SChannel security protocols, is the result of the Internet Engineering Task Force (IETF) standardizing SSL version 3, as cited in Request for Comments (RFC) 2246, which the Microsoft implementation supports. References to SSL are thus sometimes written SSL/TLS.

Note: CAPI is covered in Chapter 3 and in the "Enhancement: Smart Cards" section later in this chapter. SSPI is discussed in Chapter 4, and SSL/TLS is covered in Chapter 7.

Kerberos Protocol

As discussed in Chapter 4, the Microsoft Kerberos, with its tight integration to AD, fully complies with the IETF Kerberos 5 specification. Thus, Windows 2000 native mode domains provide SSO to users and, through trust relationships, support cross-realm referrals (discussed in Chapter 4). Alternatively, an administrator of Windows 2000 enterprise can create AD-named accounts and map non-Windows Kerberized consumers to them, thus managing non-Windows accounts just as if they were native AD consumers. It is significant that non-Windows Kerberized consumers require that you initially create and map accounts to gain the same seamless advantages as native AD consumers who seek services in cross-realm environments. In brief, Windows 2000 manages the Kerberos protocol by running both the Kerberos host protocol and AD on a domain controller (DC), more traditionally referred to as a Key Distribution Center (KDC). The Kerberos client is transparently run on every workstation.

SSL

Although the Kerberos protocol is the default authentication method, it is based on an internal logon procedure and replaces NT LAN Manager (NTLM) in native Windows 2000. Growing use of public networks and the Web-Based Enterprise Management (WBEM) initiative (discussed in Chapter 11), however, calls for alternative forms of access using strong authentication methods.

The old dichotomy of distributed versus network security is particularly applicable here; users log on to the enterprise interactively through workstations compared to remote access from outside physical boundaries of the enterprise. Distributed services are actually server components distributed across the enterprise in a codependent manner (see the "Extensibility: COM+" section later in this chapter). Distributed services require distributed security services. Alternatively, it is common to describe network services and network security services as services provided or requested from sources outside the enterprise namespace. The network security protocols supporting these services cannot provide identity and permission management the same way as distributed services do. The namespace is less defined (supporting, for example, anonymous authentication) and more extensible (for example, requiring the mapping of Kerberized principals from non-Windows environments to NT accounts). The trend showing security systems at different levels of the OSI model "negotiating" the appropriate protocol and level of security between two named principals (a consumer and a service provider) exchanging information is an example of this trend toward interoperability among NOSs.

Microsoft relies on SChannel security protocols like SSL to provide SSO to this growing segment of the user population. Windows 2000 provides a native implementation of a standards-based security protocol suite, PKI, which uses X.509 version 3 public key digital certificates to support its strong authentication methods. SSO is maintained through SSL by managing PKI integrated with AD and either enterprise or standalone certificate services.

A digital certificate is a signed (encrypted) data packet that contains a public key and security credentials of the public key's owner. A Certificate Authority (CA) issues a secured, signed certificate consisting of a public key and the key holder's security credentials bound together . The encryption of this bundle with the CA's private key provides corroborative proof that the public key and associated security credentials are authentic. The Web client uses a copy of the CA's public key to decrypt this signed digital certificate and recover the public key of the targeted key holder. From then on, if the Web client's public key can successfully decrypt a message allegedly sent from the key holder, the receiver can assume with great certainty that the message was encrypted using the secret key complementing the public key authorized by the CA. Similarly, only the holder of the public key can read a message encrypted with the key holder's secret key. Thus, both parties are authenticated.

Securing Access for Users

SSO requests information from the consumer one time. This provided information is matched by an authentication, authorization, and auditing (AAA) server against a list of known accounts stored in some protected database. The information may be provided in the context of a controlled, distributed services environment (like a business enterprise) or in a networked services environment (like that found on the Internet or in some dial-up remote access situation). In either case, the AAA server needs to either corroborate the identity of the consumer requesting services or provide services in a controlled environment.

As discussed in Chapter 9, access to resources can either be defined on the basis of per-user and per-group membership, as in the use of discretionary ACLs (DACLs), or in the security context of the provided service, as in role-based access control (RBAC). This section describes technologies that encompass both extremes in securing access for users to enterprise resources—from a two-factor authentication method that corroborates a consumer's identity with information "I have" in addition to information "I know," to the controlled environment of Terminal Services where the only services accessed are centrally distributed, controlled, and monitored. RIS builds that secure, customized user environment on demand. Finally, the last technology described in this section, SMB signing, returns us to the exchange of security credentials at the OSI Application layer (which is transparent to the consumer). Here, service provider exchanges credentials with service provider or consumer to ensure that the session pipe connecting consumer with service provider is authentic, authorized, and managed in a controlled manner.

Enhancement: Smart Cards

Microsoft has approached the use of two-factor authentication ("what I have" and "what I know") by incorporating smart card logon technology into Windows 2000 as an alternative for domain authentication through username and password keyboard entry. This technology is based on both Personal Computer/Smart Card (PC/SC) Workgroup-compliant smart card infrastructure and Rivest-Shamir-Adleman (RSA)-capable smart card devices that support CAPI cryptographic service providers (CSPs). This workgroup promulgates specifications that can be found in the International Organization for Standardization (ISO) original smart card standards, ISO 7810 and 7816. The PC/SC Workgroup initiative, promoted by a consortium of hardware and software manufacturers in this very critical niche industry, proposes to standardize a specification that ensures interoperability across the smart card, the smart card reader, and the software running on various computer platforms that manage smart card-related operations and business transactions. This initiative has garnered worldwide support across many industries. CSPs are covered in more detail later in this section.

Microsoft's Smart Card Business Strategy

Microsoft's approach to smart card interoperability has been to:

- Develop a standard model for interface cards and sensing devices like readers.
- Develop device-independent software APIs.
- Promote software development kits with appropriate tools.
- Integrate the technology into the Windows operating system platform.

This business strategy, a direct extension of the PC/SC Workgroup initiative, has fostered interoperability between the manufacturers of cards and card readers and has especially helped simplify the creation of Win32 software APIs.

The OpenCard Framework (OCF) is an object-oriented software framework for smart card access that complements the PC/SC Workgroup initiative on the hardware interfaces. It also integrates standards such as using Public Key Cryptography Standards (PKCS) #11 formats to standardize the exchange of security credentials and provide extension for inclusion of additional devices like hardware tokens to further harden the digital security schemes. Java Card API 2.1, compliant with the ISO 7816 standard, is another example of an object-oriented software specification where the byte code runs on the card itself.

Device-independent APIs insulate code from future hardware changes and reduce software development costs. By coincidence, the development of these APIs also benefits Microsoft; the Windows 2000 architectural structure is designed much like the MMC. Tomorrow's digital security schemes will "snap in" to either SSPI as security support dynamic link libraries (DLLs) or into CAPI as CSPs.

The Windows 2000 implementation of the smart card technology authentication method uses the Microsoft enhancement to PKI, the Public Key Cryptography for Initial Authentication in Kerberos (PKINIT) protocol, which combines the public key authentication method with the Windows 2000 Kerberos protocol. In brief, an attached card reader or sensing device replaces information retrieved during the Secure Attention Sequence (Ctrl+Alt+Del) on a computer-based system with information stored on the card. Depending on the circumstances, you may need to use a personal identification number (PIN) security code to access the stored information. The smart card may also contain a digital certificate and other security credentials.

Smart Card Types

These credit card sized devices, varying greatly in capability, are typically of two types:

- *Stored-value cards*—Stored-value cards are considered smart cards, but they are similar in function to the magnetic stripe cards that you use to access most ATM machines; they just hold data. They do not perform complex operations; they simply hold information that is useful in, for example, key exchanges or digital signatures. Capacity varies as a function of their design. You can protect the information on them; before you can use them and access their information, you may need to know a PIN. You can subdivide these cards into those that require card readers to retrieve the stored information and those that are contactless, requiring only proximity to some sensor device.
- *Integrated circuit cards (ICCs)*—ICCs can perform tasks that actually facilitate, for example, key exchanges and digital signatures. In fact, they obviate the need for private keys to even be installed on a local computer. Windows 2000 uses the ICC card format.

Microsoft APIs

From the application perspective, three interfaces support different ways to access smart card services:

- *CAPI*—This cryptographic API, for the special, installable CSP, exposes the cryptographic features available in the Windows 2000 operating system. For example, a smart card CSP uses exposed symmetric and asymmetric encryption algorithms already installed in the system as the Microsoft Base Provider CSP while performing its own private key operations.

- *SCard COM*—This noncryptographic interface provides a library of generic smart card related services written in a variety of programming languages.
- *Win32 APIs*—These APIs are the base-level programming interfaces in Windows operating systems that expose system features as well as the hardware-related operations necessary to interface with the card reader and other devices. These APIs also form the protective wrapper that insulates smart card software applications from changes in hardware devices.

There must be at least one CSP for Windows-based applications to access card-based services. CSPs are exclusively software that resides either in the operating system (like the Microsoft Base Provider CSP) or in the cryptographic engine on the ICC. A CSP that resides on a smart card is called a Smart Card Cryptographic Provider (SCCP) to distinguish it from other CSPs. Both SCCPs and CSPs expose and access services through CAPI. Alternatively, Smart Card Service Providers (SCSPs) expose noncryptographic, predefined services that relate to smart card operations. For these services to be accessible through CAPI, you must register them with the operating system. A resource manager, another specific management function, coordinates these registered services and tracks the operations they perform. It is a trusted service that runs as a single process in the operating system. It allocates available resources exposed through the APIs and supports the transactions that actually deliver information to other processes in the operating system.

Smart Card Logons Using Kerberos

Interactive logon means authentication of a user to a network using some shared credentials, such as a hashed password. Windows 2000 has extended the traditional NTLM logon authentication method requesting the entry of a username and password at the Secure Attention Sequence dialog box (Ctrl+Alt+Delete) to include public key interactive logons and two-factor forms of authentication. For example, a smart card is a separate, physical device that contains an X.509 version 3 digital certificate replacing the username portion of the username/password combination typically used in conjunction with legacy logon methods with authenticated security credentials. A password called an access code or PIN releases the credentials on the smart card to some mechanical card reader interface. The authentication method includes not just "what I know" but also "what I have" as a way to harden the security process. Consumers' security credentials and their secret keys are never passed to the client machine; they remain on the card itself. Follow these steps to log on interactively:

1. The smart card is detected by the card reader device that is attached to the operating system running on the local machine.

2. The operating system, through GINA, a Graphical Identification and Authentication interface, prompts for a PIN that validates use of that specific smart card so that its stored security credentials can be released to the card reader.

3. Depending on the contents of the smart card, typically an X.509 version 3 digital certificate is passed to the Local Security Authority (LSA) that is running in the local machine's operating system.

4. The LSA forwards the logon request to the Kerberos client that is running in the operating system on the local machine.

5. The Kerberos client makes a Kerberos Authentication Service Request (KRB_AS_REQ) to the KDC (as discussed in Chapter 4) on some DC. This KRB_AS_REQ includes the X.509 version 3 digital certificate and an authenticator hash, digitally signed with the private key stored on the smart card in its preauthentication data fields.

6. The KDC verifies the digital certificate by tracing the certification path from the digitally signed X.509 version 3 certificate back to possible intermediate CAs to the root CA. It builds this path by using services that the operating system supplies through CAPI. If the KDC can link digital certificates in a valid certificate chain back to the root CA, it can verify that the CA can be trusted and hence that the named principal can be authenticated within the domain namespace.

7. Through CAPI, the KDC accesses services that verify the authenticator in the KRB_AS_REQ. The KDC does this by decrypting the hash using the public key enclosed in the X.509 version 3 certificate, which is now considered valid. Only the holder with the private key could encrypt this hash. The cardholder could not have accessed that private key without entering the correct PIN number into GINA when swiping the original card (in other words, "what I have" on the smart card can be used to encrypt the hash and authenticate me because of "what I know"—specifically, the PIN); hence; the cardholder must be authentic.

8. Upon validating user authenticity, the KDC validates an accompanying timestamp that is part of the authenticator to prevent replay attacks (this is described in detail in Chapter 4).

9. When the KDC validates the authenticity of the request, security credentials are retrieved from AD directory services based on information, such as User Principal Name (UPN), that is stored in the now-validated X.509 version 3 certificate. You use these credentials, including security ID (SID) and group IDs (GIDs), to create the ticket-granting ticket (TGT).

10. The KDC encrypts the TGT with a random key, which it then signs with the cardholder's public key. It includes this random key in a data field in its Kerberos Authentication Service Reply (KRB_AS_REP).
11. The KDC signs the KRB_AS_REP with its private key so the client can verify the KDC's authenticity.
12. The Kerberos client on the local machine, using CAPI-exposed services, verifies the authenticity of the KDC's digital signature by building its own valid certificate chain back to a trusted root CA. Upon validating the digital signature, it uses the CA's public key to verify the KRB_AS_REP.
13. The client, having validated the KRB_AS_REP, now extracts the encrypted random key and decrypts it with its secret key. It uses this random key to decrypt the actual TGT.
14. Upon decrypting the TGT, the client can request services from domain resources.

Smart Card Logons Using SSL/TLS

Client authentication is required when you establish a secure session pipe between a consumer and a service provider across a public network like the Internet. In Web-based, network scenarios, you use a secure protocol such as SSL or TLS with a trusted X.509 version 3 digital certificate to authenticate the client (for example, Internet Explorer) to a server that supports SSL/TLS (like, for example, Internet Information Server [IIS] 5). Hypertext Transfer Protocol (HTTP) is stateless, so the secure session in this scenario requires both the exchange of authenticated public keys to validate parties and the generation of some unique session key to ensure integrity and confidentiality between those parties during the virtual session.

Another smart card logon scenario involves the use of secure email where cardholders carry security credentials with them. Using SSL/TLS network security authentication, security information is independent of both machine and transport protocols. Cardholders can access mail through a smart card enabled client anywhere, anytime, to receive their mail because the smart card stores the PIN-protected private key. This machine-, platform-, and transport protocol-independence is part of the Microsoft business strategy of accessing information technology anywhere at any time and is critical to the future development of both e-commerce and secure multitier architectural design in a distributed services (and server) environment.

Windows 2000, through AD directory services, relies on information contained in a validated digital certificate with possible account name mappings to local accounts to determine the appropriate account records and access rights to domain resources. The following steps outline the client logon procedure:

1. The service provider authenticates an X.509 version 3 digital certificate that a trusted root CA has validated.
2. The service provider then attempts to locate user information in its directory services based upon credentials, such as UPN, included with the authenticated digital certificate.
3. If an account is located, a security context (based upon ACL authorizations listed in the directory services) is established for the account, and requested services are provided through the contacted service provider. Sometimes in this scenario, it is best for the application that is providing the services to define the security context (RBAC) rather than using a DACL based on a specific user or group security account. An example of a scenario that is less secure than RBAC is using an anonymous user or guest account with limited access to a File Transfer Protocol (FTP) directory. The trend toward RBAC (discussed Chapter 9) plays a significant part in Web application development and the extensibility of the enterprise.

Two-factor authentication methods, especially using smart cards, apply to both distributed and network services. It is important that you understand the business, technical, and security requirements necessary for successful deployment of this security methodology.

Terminal Services Uses

In Chapter 11, Terminal Service Architecture was mentioned as supporting automated changes and providing remote management of user desktop environments from a central location. IntelliMirror, mentioned in that chapter, lowers total cost of ownership (TCO) through its focus on deployment and maintenance. Terminal Services leverages those featured advantages by providing services even on legacy hardware platforms through robust terminal emulation features. Older, less efficient hardware can now support the running of application software in a session actually run on a more powerful server platform at some remote location. In effect, this session provides a "window" through which services are accessed, but not performed, on the client machine. There is a parallel here with the RBAC discussed in Chapter 9. Where RBAC creates a security context based on the requirements of a software application, Terminal Services provides a controlled server session that can be configured to the specific needs of a user or group.

Prior to Windows 2000, Terminal Services was available but required an additional purchase of software. All versions of Windows 2000 include this service as part of the core operating system. A Terminal Services connection, Remote Desktop Protocol running on TCP (RDP-TCP), is the session pipe (or link) a remote client uses to log on a server and run a session. From Administrative Tools on a server running Terminal Services, you can right-click on the Connections node from within the Terminal Services Configuration console and configure a wide range of connection properties. Using Terminal Services Configuration console, secure default properties can be configured for all sessions running through that link. To secure a server session, you need to set the amount of time active sessions can run, user and group permissions, and levels for protection involving encryption. Security can be set on a per-user basis when the Terminal Services extension to Local Users and Groups is used. You can also configure the Terminal Server settings specifically in the use of temporary folders, default connection security, and licensing for an Internet Connection.

RIS

One of the management features IntelliMirror provides in Windows 2000 is the ability to install the Windows 2000 Professional operating system on any number of remote clients. This technology secures access to enterprise resources by standardizing a user's desktop environment and remotely providing a predetermined, customized configuration from some centralized point of distribution without increasing TCO. However, this powerful feature is demanding in terms of planning, hardware requirements, and procedural steps. RIS depends on several Windows 2000 services, especially AD, but also Windows 2000 Domain Name Service (DNS) and DHCP. RIS will remotely install Windows Professional operating systems configured with customized parameters that are stored in AD. Based on IntelliMirror technology, installation pushes the installation to the client system when triggered by a user logon. An automatic setup feature automates the entire process but can be modified by the AD's default domain account GPO so that additional system options are possible.

Requirements

Because the installation delivers disk images over the network, one limitation to RIS is that the booting installation image can typically be applied only to clients with the same platform hardware and configuration. Exceptions to this rule use a command-line utility called riprep.exe. RIS will currently install only on single partitioned disks, and require that both source and target hardware have the same version of the Windows 2000 hardware abstraction layer (HAL). The clients, in general, need bootable network adapters or a special boot floppy that is scripted to map to the RIS server and launch the installation of the system image. The RIS boot diskette first requests an IP address from some local DHCP server. It then looks for an operating system using preboot execution environment (PXE) remote boot technology, an Intel Specification for remote OS booting that is embedded in the network adapter ROM. This PXE boot ROM needs to be version .99c or higher to support the RIS installation. Furthermore, RIS supports only Windows 2000 Professional; you cannot install Window 2000 Server remotely.

Once the client boots, it accesses an operating system image stored on the RIS Server. According to Microsoft specifications, these RIS servers must be dedicated Windows 2000 Servers with the installation images stored on a volume that is separate from the system volume. Microsoft recommends that because the workload characterization of a RIS server is high, the distribution volume should be a dedicated SCSI (Small Computer System Interface) disk drive. Another design consideration is to dedicate the same physical server to both the RIS and DHCP services.

RIS manages the providing of installation services through the use of one of the following mechanisms:

- *Prestaging*—Entries in the AD can specify a certain RIS server for a particular client or group. RIS servers receiving requests for the installation of images validate requests based on a group security ID (GUID) against these AD entries.
- *Server referring*—If a RIS server receives an authenticated service request for an image but is not the authorized server to deliver the image, it will forward the service request to the appropriate RIS server.

RIS is an unsecured service vulnerable to both passive interception and impersonation attack modalities like eavesdropping and address spoofing, respectively. Furthermore, the PXE support is available for other operating systems; this support has no way of determining which server to respond to. It is crucial that you use both prestaging and carefully planned network segmentation to manage not only the PXE support but also DHCP and RIS responses to client boot-up requests. You must include other forms of network security to ensure uncompromised software installations, and management systems like SNMP to ensure that support systems are operational.

SNMP

SNMP is a management specification defined by RFCs 1155, 1157, and 1213. The service supports both TCP/IP and IPX protocols and is optionally installed as a service after TCP/IP to provide centralized management of computers through a remotely installed agent. Management software, not included with any version of the Microsoft family of operating systems, must be running on a host machine for information to be configured or collected. To take advantage of the simplification in network management, third-party software, including simple CLI utilities like snmputil.exe, is readily available and is, at times, useful. In brief, management software (also called a management console) exchanges information with an SNMP agent (specialized software running on a client machine). Communication is restricted to members within a predetermined community for administrative and security purposes. Each agent and management console has a community list that requires a minimum of one named community. "Public" is a universally accepted community name.

The agents can monitor specific services on a remote machine such as DHCP or Windows Internet Naming Service (WINS). The agent can be configured to respond to or trap specific data events associated with one of these services occurring on that client machine. Trapped events trigger an alarm message that the agent sends back to its management host. An SNMP agent can communicate only when a trap message is triggered and only with a management host in one of its listed communities. If an agent receives a request from a community not on its list, SNMP agents will generate an authentication trap and send it to a specific trap destination.

SNMP provides security through these community names and authentication traps. Permission levels determine an agent's response to a request by a host in an authenticated community. Thus, an agent can accept SNMP packets from any host or only specifically selected hosts. Regarding best practices, Microsoft recommends that the SNMP communities be organized in some functional way that reflects the pattern of distributed services in that particular enterprise. SNMP can be used to monitor the operation of support services necessary to keep user access to enterprise services and resources running in an optimal manner.

SMB Signing

Another method used to secure access across the session pipe involves the Server Message Block (SMB) file and print protocol. SMB, functioning at the OSI Application layer, is relevant when integrating legacy NT 4 Workstations or Windows 2000 Professional with, for example, NetWare Servers (discussed in the next section). SMB servers, called SAMBA servers, provide similar access to Unix users.

In brief, SMB protocol historically accessed several types of server services: the original LAN Manager servers jointly developed by Microsoft and IBM, IBM's second-generation LAN servers, and legacy NT 4 servers. In Windows 2000, SMB provides a security substrate for the secure transmission of files between client and service provider at the Application layer above where SSL/TLS operates. Thus, along with other Application layer security protocols like S-HTTP, which is used in the exchange of Web-based documents (web pages), SMB signing can complement SChannel security protocols and also provide message authentication and mutual authentication of client and server. When configuring SMB signing, both client and server must be properly configured and have appropriate GPO settings. This form of security is available on both Windows 2000 clients and legacy NT 4 clients (where Service Pack 3 or later has been applied to the operating system). Servers can request SMB signing from Windows clients.

OS Migration vs. Coexistence

Interoperability is a major historical theme driving all IT cultures toward some future point of convergence under the umbrella of a unified directory-based namescape. Microsoft would like the hub of that namescape to be AD directory services. Alternatively, Novell provides Novell Directory Services (NDS). Both network operating system cultures compete for the dominant position. Other cultures, like Macintosh, have through a kind of quasi-selective adaptation found a special niche. Unix, from its inception, has been open, scalable, collaborative, and a technological melting pot. The topic of interoperability is really a business issue and a question of dominance in the IT universe.

Microsoft, on the one hand, does not want to coexist with its desktop competitor Novell. Nevertheless, it must offer IT consumers who use the Novell operating system utilities that bridge the two cultures or, preferably, help migrate them to the Microsoft platform. Macintosh has grown into a niche operating system; it is neither friend nor foe to Microsoft. Hence, Microsoft has provided a means to reliably share resources at no great cost to members of either culture. Finally, Unix, historically uncommon among personal computer users, is nevertheless a giant source of resources, users, and investment capital. Migration paths, though robust and reliable, are only now being considered. In general, Microsoft is still not ready to assert itself in the mini and mainframe computer worlds in which non-Microsoft network operating systems rule and therefore seeks a strategy of growing coexistence, especially with the largest culture, the Unix network operating system.

Interoperability/Migration: NetWare

Microsoft has provided interoperability services—including primarily Client Service for NetWare (CSNW) and Gateway Service for NetWare (GSNW)—that directly interface with its family of NOSs. Both add-ons, especially GSNW, have been designed for occasional and convenient access, not true interoperability and coexistence. These add-ons are designed to function primarily as a segue leading from NetWare-based resources to the Microsoft platform.

Briefly, Microsoft and Novell use different protocols to request services from a server; SMB and NetWare Core Protocol (NCP), respectively. These two protocols are incompatible. To bridge server communications between the two NOSs, you need to either install multiple protocol stacks as client interfaces (CSNW) on all clients, or you need to create one central distribution service provider or gateway (GSNW). CSNW and GSNW automatically install NWLink, the NT/Windows 2000 IPX/SPX/NetBIOS compatible transport protocol necessary to communicate with legacy NetWare platforms (NetWare 2.x to 4.x) as well as NDS and older bindery-based directory information. In a NetWare 5 environment, which, in terms of the two NOS families, is comparable to Windows 2000, the default transport protocol is TCP/IP; CSNW, using exclusively IPX/SPX and NetBEUI, is of little value. CSNW provides the redirector services Windows users need to access NetWare-based file and print resources. This redirection involves the translating from Microsoft's SMB file and print protocol to Novell's NetWare Core Protocol (NCP). From the Novell side, you must install two clients: the NetWare client interface, which understands NCP, and the Microsoft Client interface, which understands the SMB protocol.

Services for NetWare version 5 (SFN5), though similarly designed to encourage users to migrate to Windows 2000, provides a new set of interoperability services and utilities for integrating Windows 2000 platforms into existing NetWare 5 environments. SFN5 also offers older interoperability tools for legacy NT 4 platforms. SFN5 reduces network administration in a mixed platform environment with:

- Microsoft Directory Synchronization Services (MSDSS)
- File Migration Utility (FMU)
- File and Print Services for NetWare version 5 (FPNW5)

Although migration includes conversion of principal and group accounts as well as the access management of resources, specific password assignments, software application configuration, Novell's login scripting, management of Macintosh namespace, and inconsistencies in schema definition and extensions between NDS and AD must be manually modified to conform with Windows 2000 specifications. For a general discussion of issues involving the resolution of inconsistencies in data definitions between directory services, refer to the "Brokerage" section earlier in this chapter. The synchronization of configuration and directory information is stored in the AD service. Access to this AD area is restricted to only authorized administrators in a default MSDSS Admins local security group, specifically responsible for setting up, administering, and monitoring the synchronization process.

MSDSS

MSDSS synchronizes AD datastores with both NDS and NetWare version 3 binderies using Windows 2000 Server. According to Microsoft, MSDSS provides a directory interoperability solution by supporting two-way synchronization with NDS and one-way synchronization with NetWare binderies on a near realtime basis. You can manage principal accounts from either directory service. However, there are differences in how you use the administrative tools and how you deploy directory services. For example, account changes administered through NDS force a two-way synchronization of the entire object between directory services. In comparison, a one-way replication (and a reduction in network traffic) occurs when AD is the point of directory administration because only the object's attribute is changed.

Microsoft suggests that you deploy AD in a NetWare environment without replacing existing directories. MSDSS reduces directory management by:

- Providing centralized administration of identity management
- Maintaining data integrity across multiple directory services
- Synchronizing datastores with different data schema
- Providing SSO

FMU

FMU is a migration tool that encourages the migration of resources from NetWare-based servers to Windows 2000. This wizard-based migration-management interface is integrated with MSDSS and preserves file-access control information and security permissions from loss during the migration process.

FPNW5

FPNW5 provides a NetWare interface and SSO to NetWare users by having Windows 2000 servers emulate the Novell file and print services. This particular product greatly impacts TCO because Novell users do not experience any change in their work environment even though the Windows 2000 operating system is providing the actual services. There is no need for training, nor are there issues of noncompliance that result, in part, from user prejudice or frustration.

Interoperability/Migration: Unix

Unlike Novell, which is considered Microsoft's primary competitor in the desktop NOS market, Unix and its dialects has supported mainframe and minicomputer network environments for decades. Microsoft provides many features in legacy NT 4 systems and Windows 2000. Standards-based protocols, as well as new utilities supplied by Interix, foster true interoperability and coexistence specifically between these two operating system cultures. The inclusion of the Portable Operating System Interface (POSIX) in legacy NT 4 and now Interix, a Windows 2000/Unix interoperability product, clearly shows that Microsoft intends for clients of both NOSs to easily and effectively cross-communicate between different file systems without serious performance penalties. Through Interix, Microsoft also provides a cost-effective migration path for Unix-based proprietary software applications.

Services for Unix 2 (SFU2)

SFU2 fosters true interoperability and coexistence between Windows 2000 and Unix, especially through Sun Microsystems' Network File System (NFS) protocol (RFC 1813). The NFS protocol, which is designed to be independent of machine, operating system, and transport protocols, uses remote procedure calls (RPCs). It is also significant that Windows supported POSIX in the legacy NT architecture. POSIX is an Institute of Electrical and Electronic Engineers (IEEE) standard that facilitates the translation or porting of services from one operating system to another. Windows 2000 uses the POSIX.1-compliant subsystem, which supports case sensitivity, multiple file names, and application execution in protected memory space. Unlike the situation with Novell, where available products are primarily for migration, both NFS and POSIX, in combination with SFU2, are the true sources for interoperability between Windows 2000 and Unix.

Network Resources

Enterprise resources on Windows 2000 and Unix can coexist with a variety of client and gateway services, such as:

- *Client for NFS*—Provides Windows-based clients access to NFS server resources
- *Server for NFS*—Provides NFS clients access to Windows NT and 2000 server resources
- *Gateway for NFS*—Provides any Windows-based client access to an NFS resource without SFU2
- *Server for PCNFS*—Provides NFS user authentication for NFS resources on Windows NT- or 2000-based servers that act as specially assigned servers (through Server for PCNFS services, accessed through the Services for Unix Microsoft Management Console—MMC)

In addition, Microsoft now offers Interix 2.2 as a migration path for Unix applications and scripts to Windows NT/2000. This operating environment, developed by Softway Systems, Inc. and formerly called OPENNT, provides more than 300 utilities and tools that function like their Unix counterparts. Interix 2.2 is not an emulation product like the Mortice Kern Systems (MKS) Toolkit, another Unix utility suite that runs on the non-Unix operating systems discussed in the "Programming Shells as User Interfaces" section later in this chapter; performance of Unix-based legacy applications and scripts will not suffer. It is a complete replacement for the standard Microsoft POSIX subsystem, which contains enhancements, including scripting languages, sockets, interprocess communication, and other features. Interix functions like a peer to the Win32 subsystem and provides both APIs and services that you need to run the legacy Unix system applications. In fact, its software development kit supports more than 1,900 Unix APIs to facilitate migration. Interix provides these Unix legacy applications a single enterprise operating environment that is fully integrated with Windows 2000 services, security, and file system access.

Identity Management

Although Sun Microsystems' Network Information System (NIS), formerly known as the Yellow Pages, is not an Internet standard, it is a common distributed database system that allows you to share system information in Unix-based environments. It employs a client/server model of database information much like Domain Name System (DNS). SFU2 includes an NIS Migration Wizard, which migrates an existing NIS namespace to the AD on a Windows 2000 server. A DC that runs Server for NIS services emulates an NIS master server and maintains database "maps" of system information, such as passwords and host names. Other SFU2tools include:

- *Password synchronization*—This is a two-way utility that synchronizes password changes across Windows NT/2000 and Unix directory services. SFU2 includes SSO daemons (SSODs) provided in both a precompiled form and as source code and complementary make files that run on Unix servers to support the password changes. In addition, a Password Authentication Mapper (PAM), which passes changes back to the Windows NT/2000 directory services, must run on the Unix server. Password synchronization does not include providing an SSO between Unix and Windows NT/2000, nor does it provide for application passwords. It does not provide for a common authentication scheme between the two systems, though native mode Windows 2000 does default to the Kerberos protocol. The Windows-to-Unix synchronization is provided by default; Unix-to-Windows synchronization is optional. Password changes use both Transmission Control Protocol/Internet Protocol (TCP/IP) sockets and triple Data Encryption Standard (3DES) for encryption and decryption. Password synchronization does not require special installation or additional overhead because it uses standard network and security technologies.

- *User name mapping*—This tool bridges differences between the two directory datastores. It can create simple one-to-one maps between principals, as well as bidirectional one-to-many mappings, where you can map a single Unix or Windows NT/2000 principal to multiple accounts in the other directory datastore. For example, you can easily map different Windows NT/2000 administrative accounts to the Unix root account.

Programming Shells as User Interfaces

SFU2 provides a subset of the MKS Toolkit, which has been a very important tool for users of DOS, Windows, and NT operating systems for many years. This toolkit offers a selection of the most common Unix utilities that end users and administrator use, along with a robust implementation of the Korn Shell, a popular Unix programming shell (operating environment). These tools leverage Unix users' knowledge by providing them with the same interface and the same command-line syntax to which they have grown accustomed while working entirely on a Windows-based platform.

Network Administration

Administration tools, which simplify and enhance management, include:

- *Telnet server and client*—This client/host combination provides character mode support, which is faster and more robust than the default graphical mode provided in Windows NT. Windows 2000 uses this newer Telnet client. The Telnet server exclusively supports NTLM authentication for client authentication to provide seamless operation without exposing cleartext passwords across the network. However, for authentication to occur, you must support NTLM on both sides of the connection. The Windows 2000 Telnet client supports NTLM. Using this security protocol, however, effectively prevents Kerberized Unix users from accessing Windows NT/2000 servers because they do not have a client that supports this security protocol.
- *MMC snap-in*—SFU2 provides a single MMC for all SFU2 services and tools except Gateway for NFS. SFU is compatible with Windows Management Instrumentation (WMI), so you can script management functions from the CLI.
- *ActivePerl 5.6*—SFU2 includes ActivePerl 5.6, ActiveState's version of Perl (Practical Extraction and Report Language) 5.6, and Perl Script for Windows NT/2000. This implementation of Perl supports Windows Scripting Host (WSH) for the scripted automation of many administrative system functions.

Interoperability/Migration: Apple Macintosh

Similar to Unix, Macintosh and the Apple OS have not historically been perceived by Microsoft as a true competitor for market share among networked users on the desktop personal computer. The Microsoft strategy with regard to Macintosh is one of mutual coexistence. Besides supporting interoperability with legacy NT operating systems, Windows 2000 continues to support interoperability with Macintosh through File Server for Macintosh (MacFile), an AppleTalk network integration service. AppleTalk network integration (formerly called Services for Macintosh) is a software component of Windows 2000 Server that allows users of both platforms to share enterprise resources. File Services for Macintosh, the Windows 2000 server component that provides Macintosh users with Windows 2000 server access, uses extension-type associations to display Intel-based files with correct icons when viewed through Macintosh Finder. When you install File Services for Macintosh, Windows 2000 creates a directory called the Microsoft User Authentication Module (UAM) volume on an available NT File System (NTFS) partition. Under the Computer Management console tree, you can open Shared Folders to view and manage the properties of the Microsoft UAM volume. Although most applications have cross-platform versions for both Macintosh- and Intel-based clients, both versions can modify the same files stored on this volume. When the UAM volume is mounted on their desktops, Macintosh clients can securely log on and access resources exclusively in this space.

Network Resources

A Windows 2000 server with AppleTalk network integration provides resources to both Intel-based and Macintosh users. Intel-based users see shared files in a shared folder, whereas Macintosh users see the folder as a volume. To use these resources, Macintosh users can mount a Macintosh-accessible volume on their desktop. All Macintosh-accessible volumes must be on an NTFS partition or on a Compact Disc File System (CDFS) volume. Windows 2000 allows you to create and share other Macintosh-accessible volumes in addition to the UAM volume. The four permission levels for a shared volume, as listed in the Create Shared Folder Wizard dialog box, are:

- All users have Full Control.
- Administrators have Full Control; other users have Read Only access.
- Administrators have Full Control; other users have No Access.
- Share and folder permissions can be customized to allow Full Control, Change, and Read.

In addition, Print Server for Macintosh (MacPrint) enables Macintosh clients to send and spool documents on Windows 2000 print servers and, similarly, Intel-based clients to send print jobs to any printer on the AppleTalk network. When Print Services for Macintosh is installed, it automatically installs AppleTalk protocol if it is not already present in the protocol stack.

Identity Management

Authentication is an AppleShare extension that provides secure logon sessions to a Windows 2000 server from a Macintosh client. Passwords are encrypted and stored on the Windows 2000 server. Therefore, to ensure correct authentication, Macintosh users must specify the domain when they log on. They optionally log on to the Microsoft UAM version 5 volume, which requires either an AppleShare client 3.8 or greater, or Mac OS 8.5 or greater. AppleTalk network integration provides an level of authentication in addition to Windows 2000 logon authentication within the Microsoft UAM Volume property sheet, with the use of an optional Macintosh-accessible volume password. This case-sensitive password, required when you are accessing the resource as a Macintosh user, is assigned to the volume when you configure it. Intel-based users do not encounter this additional logon restriction.

Access Management

Access control to Macintosh-accessible volumes, the equivalent of a shared folder for an Intel-based user, is the same as it is for Intel-based machines. Macintosh files, however, inherit permissions that are set on their container folders; they do not carry permissions directly.

Extensibility: COM+

If AD develops into a consolidated meta-directory, it rests on top of a NOS, providing the key "primitive" common information management services of configuration, performance, fault management, and auditability. A component-based Windows 2000 NOS using DNA specifications could spawn components throughout some future universal namescape that extends across other NOSs like Novell and UNIX. Each component would call back to the Windows 2000 AD directory services for identity and security information.

Microsoft proposed a software model in 1993 that described this event in terms of a Component Object Model. A server component provides a service to a consumer that is, in fact, distributed throughout the domain namespace as separate, specialized support service components. A transaction server manages all these distributed service components and tells the primary server when all the components are successfully completed; the primary service provider then delivers the service.

The entire Windows 2000 operating system architecture is based upon the interdependent software components of the Component Object Model. Consumers and clients at all levels of the OSI model access services provided by COM objects, which are a combination of both data and methods of manipulating that data. The operational methods that a component object possesses are grouped into standardized interfaces that totally encapsulate the data defined within the object itself. These interfaces are independent of any one programming language and thus provide services on theoretically any operating system platform. Distributed COM, first released in 1996 as an extension of COM, did not change the fundamentals of the model, only the distance between calls for service between a consumer and service provider, referred to as remote procedure calls (RPCs).

Windows 2000 enhances COM by integrating the previously separate Transaction Server services and the transaction services security model into each individual component; hence, the current version of the model is called COM+. The service-providing server components are now more feature-laden than the older COM components regarding support for transactions, client authorization, and management of their own state. In addition, Windows 2000 distributed COM+ objects are faster because they use TCP as their transport protocol, as compared to the slower UDP protocol legacy COM components communicated with. The security relating to client authorization and issues of integrity and confidentiality are not dictated by the COM server component; COM applications use either Kerberos or NTLM protocols. Details of the COM+ model pertain more to programming and are outside the scope of this book. However, the way COM+ and Microsoft Message Queue Services (MSMQ) handle these security issues, especially in a distributed services environment, needs to be understood, at least in general terms.

Distributed Services

From online service hosting to high-volume transaction processing, Windows 2000 provides a platform for component-based application development. These components achieve high degrees of reliability and manageability because they are tightly integrated with the many services that the Windows 2000 operating system provides. The layered structure of the NOS protects investments in application development. An example of this protection is in the business strategy involved in the development of smart cards mentioned in the "Enhancement: Smart Cards" section earlier in this chapter. Windows 2000 provides the following key services that provide the foundation for both distributed and networked services on which business scenarios (and examination case studies) will be built in the future:

- COM and COM+
- IIS 5
- MSMQ message queuing

COM

When a consumer requests services from a "primary" service provider, these services sometimes require other support services. The primary server (service provider), through delegation of authority (discussed in Chapter 4), can request additional support services on behalf of the consumer from remote service providers. These requests form a chain of dependencies that determine whether or not the primary server provides the requested service to the consumer. These mutually dependent support service requests are called *transactions*. The success or failure of a transaction depends upon the successful completion of all support service requests. In the simplest case, the primary server provides the requested services and the transaction between the two parties is completed. In the common e-commerce scenario, the consumer makes a request to a Web server that authenticates the client, establishes the session, and presents the consumer with scripted questions. Answers to the questions are processed according to predefined business rules and executed. Processing the information, no matter how many separate service components are involved, is considered one transaction.

IIS 5

Developers can easily build and run Web-based scripts that combine HTML, scripts, and procedure calls to COM+ objects. IIS 5 goes beyond providing the simple Web services of its predecessors by providing developers with an extensible environment that fosters rapid development of these scripts based on powerful technologies like Active Server Pages (ASP). ASP scripts integrate with other component-based software applications because ASP itself is a COM+ application. The real power of this scripting, however, lies in its manageability; developers control how scripts are processed (process isolation), where scripts are processed (through Windows Load Balancing Services—WLBS), and which scripts are processed as single, smart transactional units.

MSMQ

MSMQ fundamentally provides communication services between distributed COM+ server components. Queued components let server components logically participate in transactions whether they are online, unavailable, or offline; messages are stored in queues until you retrieve them. In other words, server components can send asynchronous messages to other COM+ components and continue processing without waiting for a response. MSMQ, when requested, journalizes these messages and automatically notifies components whether messages were received.

MSMQ digitally signs and encrypts messages that are transferred across the network. You can request authentication on a per message basis by including in a message the message sender's X.509 digital certificate and digital signature. Thus,

MSMQ provides authentication and integrity controls by using CAPI and an appropriate CSP. In fact, MSMQ provides the same security services among COM+ server components that are provided to consumers and client machines. MSMQ reduces dependency on synchronization requirements among COM+ server components, so greater interoperability can occur across different software architectures. Finally, all the MSMQ features are independent of network protocols; COM+ server components can send messages based on the name of another application's request queue regardless of the network on which it runs.

Security and RBAC

COM+ server objects, at the component level, provide the same security services as consumer and service provider information exchanges at the intranet, Internet, and extranet levels—namely, authentication, integrity, confidentiality, and authorization. Although authentication, integrity, and confidentiality are functions primarily of PKI, COM+ authorization depends on access controls and permission management. The COM+ runtime engine uses RBAC to provide security within the application (see the discussion of RBAC in Chapter 9). You can set role-based authorization at various application levels, including the server object level.

Practice Questions

Case Study

4Sale, an online bartering company in ThatTherePlace, North Dakota, focuses primarily on selling inexpensive, odd-lot items.

Current LAN/Network Structure

4Sale is presently running Windows 2000 Server in native mode; one member server supports Exchange 5.5, whereas another is running IIS 5 and Proxy Server 2. All 100 client machines are configured in a single-domain model. The client systems are all running Windows 2000 Professional, with Office 2000 being utilized as an applications package. Each system is connected to a 10Mbps hub through 10Mbps local area network (LAN) cards running Category 5 Unshielded Twisted Pair (UTP) cabling in a star topology.

Proposed LAN/Network Structure

No changes are planned at this time.

Current WAN Connectivity

No changes are planned at this time.

Proposed WAN Connectivity

No changes are planned at this time.

Directory Design Commentary

No changes are planned at this time.

Current Internet Positioning

No changes are planned at this time.

Future Internet Plans

No changes are planned at this time.

Company Goal with Windows 2000

4Sale plans to install smart cards at some workstations. The management is also contemplating a merger with another Internet company that has about 45 people on a Novell 5 network.

Question 1

Considering the case study, what issue might be a major concern when you are installing smart cards? [Check all correct answers]

- ❑ a. Device specification
- ❑ b. Software specification
- ❑ c. User account information
- ❑ d. Operating system

Answers a and b are correct. Although Microsoft supports the major specification initiatives, there is still no specific standard among hardware and software manufacturers regarding smart card hardware and software integration. The PC/SC Workgroup is an initiative that is gaining international support but is not a recognized standard. Smart card installation raises no real issues with user account information or operating system because 4Sale is using Windows 2000, which provides PKINIT support. Therefore, answers c and d are incorrect.

Question 2

The Network Manager at 4Sale asks, "If we were to merge with a company running Novell, what could we use to help keep both directory services talking to each other by having the systems run independently?"

- ❍ a. MSDSS
- ❍ b. MDSS
- ❍ c. FMU
- ❍ d. FPNW5

Answer a is correct. MSDSS (Microsoft Directory Synchronization Services) synchronizes Active Directory datastores with Novell Directory Services. Answer b is incorrect because there is no Microsoft product called MDSS that relates to Novell NetWare. Answer c is incorrect because FMU (File Migration Utility) is a migration tool. Answer d is incorrect because FPNW5 (File and Print Services for NetWare version 5) provides a NetWare interface and Single Sign-On for Novell users who are running on Windows 2000.

Question 3

The Network Manager at 4Sale asks, "How can we port Unix applications to our NT system?" [Choose the best answer]

❍ a. Interix

❍ b. Enterix

❍ c. Imterix

❍ d. None of the above

Answer a is correct. Interix 2.2 is the preferred migration path from Unix to Windows 2000. Answers b and c are incorrect because there are no such companies that offer Unix-to-Windows migration tools.

Question 4

The Network Manager at 4Sale asks, "How does Kerberos authenticate using smart cards?" Place the following in the proper order to indicate how authentication occurs. Start with the card reader detecting the smart card.

The card reader device detects the smart card, and then Graphical Identification and Authentication prompts for a personal identification number.

The Key Distribution Center encrypts the ticket-granting ticket with a random key and signs the Kerberos Authentication Service (AS) Reply with its own private key.

The Kerberos client makes a Kerberos Authentication Service (AS) Request.

The Local Security Authority forwards the logon request to the Kerberos client.

The client can request services from domain resources.

The client extracts the encrypted random key and decrypts the ticket-granting ticket.

The Key Distribution Center verifies the digital certificate and authenticator.

The correct order is:

The card reader device detects the smart card, and then Graphical Identification and Authentication prompts for a personal identification number.

The Local Security Authority forwards the logon request to the Kerberos client.

The Kerberos client makes a Kerberos Authentication Service (AS) Request.

The Key Distribution Center verifies the digital certificate and authenticator.

The Key Distribution Center encrypts the ticket-granting ticket with a random key and signs the Kerberos Authentication Service (AS) Reply with its own private key.

The client extracts the encrypted random key and decrypts the ticket-granting ticket.

The client can request services from domain resources.

Question 5

The Network Manager at 4Sale says, "FMU will keep our Novell people happy." Is the statement true or false?

❍ a. True

❍ b. False

Answer b, false, is correct. The Network Manager is incorrect. FMU (File Migration Utility) is primarily a migration tool. It is doubtful the Novell people are looking forward to a network migration. The tool that would make the Novell people happy is File and Print Services for NetWare version 5, which provides a NetWare interface and Single Sign-On for NetWare users running on Windows 2000.

Question 6

The Network Manager at 4Sale says, "UAM is the only Macintosh-accessible volume we can configure on a Windows 2000 Server." Is the statement true or false?

❍ a. True

❍ b. False

Answer b, false, is correct. The Network Manager is incorrect. The UAM (User Authentication Module) is created when you install File Services for Macintosh. You can, however, install additional shares that Macintosh users can access as volumes.

Need to Know More?

McLean, Ian. *Windows 2000 Security Little Black Book.* The Coriolis Group, Scottsdale, AZ, 2000. ISBN 1-57610-387-0. In Chapter 9, the author discusses smart card installation and how smart cards affect interactive logon and client authentication using SSL/TLS protocols.

Nielsen, Morten Strunge. *Windows 2000 Professional Advanced Configuration and Implementation.* The Coriolis Group, Scottsdale, AZ, 2000. ISBN 1-57610-528-8. Chapter 19 discusses Microsoft's integration and migration strategy, the importance of providing SSO across platforms, and coexistence issues for Windows and the most popular operating systems—Novell, Macintosh, Unix, and Systems Network Architecture (SNA).

Nielsen, Morten Strunge. *Windows 2000 Server Architecture and Planning.* The Coriolis Group, Scottsdale, AZ, 1999. ISBN 1-57610-436-2. In Chapter 19, the author clearly and concisely discusses current support for migration to Windows 2000 from Novell and Unix.

Shinder, Thomas W. and D. Lynn White. *Configuring Windows 2000 Server Security.* Syngress Media, Inc., Rockland, MD, 2000. ISBN 1-928994-02-4. In Chapter 8, the authors describe the history of ISO 7816 and the PC/SC Workgroup initiative. They then discuss various APIs, types of cards, and smart card installation and logon procedures.

Search the TechNet CD (or its online version through **www.microsoft.com**) and the *Windows 2000 Server Resource Kit* CD using the keywords "MMS", "CAPI", "SFN", "MSDSS", and "SFU". This is Microsoft's definitive online resource for technical papers and bulletins.

www.interix.com The Interix Web site provides details about the company and its Unix migration products.

www.iso.ch/search.html This site offers the ISO search engine, which is provided as part of the ISO's Web site, ISO Online. This is an excellent site to use when you are researching ISO standards.

www.microsoft.com/windows2000/guide/server/solutions/EIM.asp Here, you will find *Enterprise Identity Management within the Digital Nervous System*, originally posted in July 1999. This Windows 2000 White Paper provides a framework and discussion about managing identity data, the advantages of AD and the digital nervous system, and the functional architecture that supports business relationships and internal business processes.

www.microsoft.com/windows2000/library/howitworks/activedirectory/adinterface.asp Here, you will find *Active Directory Service Interfaces*, originally posted in April 1999. This Windows 2000 White Paper outlines how Microsoft integrates multiple directory services through ADSI.

www.microsoft.com/windows2000/library/resources/reskit/samplechapters/dsec/dsec_pol_blsa.asp At this site, you can find topics related to the Group Policy chapter of the *Windows 2000 Resource Kit*. This particular section discusses Group Policy processing orders.

www.microsoft.com/windows2000/sfu/sfu2wp.asp This site offers the *General Services for Unix version 2.0 White Paper*, originally posted in March 2000. This Microsoft White Paper discusses interoperability and management using SFU2.

www.pcscworkgroup.com The PC/SC Workgroup Web site provides technical specifications, including PC/SC Version 1 specifications, compatible products, and other information relating to smart card technologies.

Sample Test

Case Study 1

4Sale, an online bartering and auction company in ThatTherePlace North Dakota, focuses primarily on selling inexpensive, odd-lot items. 4Sale provides customized front-end client application software to its online customers. It uses its Web site to distribute this software. The 4Sale client connects directly with the 4Sale Web site and provides an Internet customer with realtime lists of available items, research material about an item and its history, and a screen with which to bid for the item during online auctions. Due to the nature of this online auction business, all internal and Internet email correspondence is digitally signed.

4Sale has merged forces with a smaller company, Got-a-Deal, which rents space in the same office building. Got-A-Deal is an online association of international brokers of all kinds of retail and wholesale merchandise. This brokers association is looking for an e-commerce company that can provide a centralized marketplace for its odd lot goods. There is no formal set of corporate business objectives or a formal security policy.

Current LAN/Network Structure

4Sale is currently running NT Server 4 on three machines:

- A primary domain controller (PDC)
- A backup domain controller (BDC) that serves as the Exchange Server 5.5
- A member server that is running Internet Information Server 4 and Proxy Server 2

All 100 client machines are configured in a single-domain model. The client systems are running Windows NT Workstation 4, with Office 2000 being utilized as an applications package. Each system is connected to a 10Mbps hub through 10Mbps local area network (LAN) cards running Category 5 Unshielded Twisted Pair (UTP) cabling in a star topology.

The corporate side of the merger between 4Sale and Got-A-Deal has gone well, but the network infrastructure is under construction. Got-a-Deal is undergoing changes to upgrade from its Ethernet bus topology, which uses coaxial cabling, to a more modern configuration. Got-a-Deal is using an NT server in a 22-person workgroup configuration as a file and print server. The network is stable but does not provide scalability.

Proposed LAN/Network Structure

4Sale will use native mode Windows 2000 and develop its online barter/trading business. Some of the security features would help leverage development of its e-commerce plans and future corporate goals. In addition, 4Sale would like to improve the network's speed by implementing newer cards and hubs that support 100Mbps.

Got-a-Deal would also like to upgrade to Windows 2000 under a domain arrangement but has concerns regarding performance, deployment costs, maintenance, and training. The company will be hiring an in-house network engineer to be part of a newly formulated information technology (IT) team that administers the resources of both companies. Got-a-Deal needs a faster network infrastructure in place within the next two months. It will depend on 4Sale for most of its network services.

Current WAN Connectivity

4Sale has a T1 connection to its Internet Service Provider (ISP). Got-A-Deal uses dial-up clients and integrated services digital network (ISDN) to connect to its ISP.

Proposed WAN Connectivity

No changes in the current structure are proposed at this time.

Directory Design Commentary

The CEO of 4Sale says, "My first objective is to integrate Got-a-Deal as seamlessly as possible into our daily operational flow. I will instruct the Human Resources Manager to give you a list of security access levels for both 4Sale and Got-a-Deal personnel. At least for this interim period, I want to defer all internal Got-a-Deal issues to my business associate, the Got-a-Deal president. I want you to talk to other people in our organization and compile a strategic corporate plan, organization layout, and IT program. Remember, though, that 4Sale is the parent company."

The President of Got-a-Deal says, "I don't feel very secure about impending changes in how Got-a-Deal will do business. I want to be the only one who sees top-secret material at Got-a-Deal for the next couple of months!"

The Human Resources Manager at 4Sale says, "The cost of training end users and tech people is rising every month. The CEO wants me to maintain a budgetary range for retraining Got-a-Deal personnel. He also wants me to plan for future changes in the company so that with future mergers, we will not have to go through this same process again."

The Network Manager at 4Sale says, "Software upgrades for applications and operating systems, as well as technical support, cost more than the capital investment in equipment. The CEO is very strict about budget ranges and holds me responsible for making the correct strategic decisions in our short-term purchases and long-term capital investment plans. I am also concerned about security issues like secure email and signed documents. The CEO wants the environment to be as secure as possible."

Current Internet Positioning

4Sale uses virtual hosting services and is registered as **4sale.com**. Got-a-Deal has been selling its goods through local companies, pages on other broker Web sites, and through a Web page on the **4sale.com** Web site.

Future Internet Plans

Got-a-Deal will use the **4sale.com** Web site.

Company Goal with Windows 2000

The CEO of 4Sale says, "4Sale has hired you as an outside consultant to manage the network issues involved in the merger of the two companies. I am giving you strict and confidential instructions. I want all control centralized under the 4Sale Network Manager, no matter what people from 4Sale or Got-A-Deal propose to you on an individual basis. I want the transition to run smoothly. To ensure that employee relations remain upbeat and optimistic, you should not publicize our emphasis on centralized control. Over the next year, I plan to grow 4Sale first by building a scalable base, then by extending lines of communication out to organizations with whom we form business alliances, and finally, by acquiring other mature online service companies. We need our IT infrastructure to support these corporate objectives."

The VP of Finance at 4Sale says, "4Sale is expecting 10 percent quarterly growth in its online catalog. It expects larger growth in online business partners acting as field agents. We will need to assimilate companies and their in-house systems as quickly as possible without interrupting any online services. Depending on the financial markets and our capitalization, you need to prepare the IT department for consolidation of several online businesses, each with its own operating system platform, at the same time."

The 4Sale Network Manager says, "Based on our business, our computer systems need to deliver accessibility, accuracy, and confidentiality 24/7. I want to utilize Windows 2000 Active Directory by using its default schema because I don't have much experience with Windows 2000. I also need you to help develop the standards and procedures that our newly formulated IT team will implement."

Question 1.1

Considering the case study provided, what type of domain structure that allows for all relevant concerns would you recommend? [Choose the best answer]

- ❍ a. Two distinct forests with an extended trust connecting them
- ❍ b. An empty root domain with one domain in place and two Organizational Units (OUs), one at 4Sale and one for Got-a-Deal
- ❍ c. One domain with the root **4sale.com**, with a child domain being **gotadeal.4sale.com**
- ❍ d. One domain called **4sale.com** with two OUs, one at 4Sale and one for Got-a-Deal

Question 1.2

Considering the case study provided, place total cost of ownership (TCO) components in descending order of importance. Choose only the appropriate answers and list the most expensive component first.

Cost of system upgrades

System maintenance

Cost of hardware and software

Cost of disposables

Technical support

User training

Question 1.3

Based on the case study provided, 4Sale provides internal messaging, accounting, data storage, and network support to its client base. These are the only business services you need to provide with primary support.

❍ a. True

❍ b. False

Question 1.4

Considering the case study provided and the conclusions you reached in Question 1.3, choose only the appropriate IT security objectives from the list below and order them in descending order of importance.

Confidentiality

Training

Firewall technology

Software authentication

Accessibility

Nonrepudiation

Question 1.5

Considering the case study provided, what primary issue(s) must you consider when you create the 4Sale network security plan? [Choose the best answer]

❍ a. Due care and due diligence

❍ b. Information security strategies

❍ c. Security group descriptions

❍ d. All of the above

❍ e. None of the above

Question 1.6

The Network Manager at 4Sale asks, "Which Performance MMC snap-in object do I use to measure Key Distribution Center (KDC) Authentication Service (AS) request activity?" [Choose the best answer]

- ❍ a. NT Directory Services (NTDS)
- ❍ b. Kerberos
- ❍ c. KDC
- ❍ d. None of the above

Question 1.7

The Network Manager at 4Sale asks, "Which security areas can I standardize as we deploy our systems?" [Check all correct answers]

- ❑ a. Executive, Staff, and User groups
- ❑ b. Application files
- ❑ c. A 4Sale proprietary application extension
- ❑ d. Smart card services
- ❑ e. All of the above

Question 1.8

The Owner-Network Manager at Got-a-Deal asks, "Which authentication method do you suggest for our staff?" [Choose the best answer]

- ❍ a. PC/smart card technology
- ❍ b. NT LAN Manager (NTLM)
- ❍ c. Kerberos protocol
- ❍ d. SChannel (Secure Channel) protocols

Question 1.9

Considering the case study provided, which security technology would have an optimal effect on TCO? [Choose the best answer]

❍ a. Kerberos protocol

❍ b. Microsoft IP Security (IPSec) protocol suite

❍ c. SChannel protocols

❍ d. All of the above

❍ e. None of the above

Question 1.10

The Network Manager at 4Sale asks, "From a technical point of view, which security technology would give me confidentiality, data integrity, and flexible security protocols?" [Check all correct answers]

❑ a. Kerberos

❑ b. Secure Sockets Layer (SSL) 3

❑ c. IPSec

❑ d. Transport Layer Security (TLS) 1

❑ e. All of the above

Question 1.11

The Network Manager at 4Sale asks you in what order you would deploy the following security technologies to deliver as many security services as quickly as possible at the cheapest cost:

Secure Multipurpose Internet Mail Extensions (S/MIME)

IPSec

Secure Hypertext Transfer Protocol (S-HTTP)

Secure Sockets Layer (SSL)

Question 1.12

The Network Manager at 4Sale says, "We run an online barter service and our primary business focus is our proprietary front-end client, so we do not have to concern ourselves with directory service issues." Is this statement true or false?

❍ a. True

❍ b. False

Question 1.13

The Network Manager is a member of the Enterprise Administrators group. She asks, "I want to delegate responsibility for Got-a-Deal administration to the Got-a-Deal Vice President of Operations. How can I do this?" [Choose the best answer]

❍ a. She can modify GPOs, but she cannot delegate that responsibility.

❍ b. She has Full Control over GPOs, but she cannot delegate that responsibility.

❍ c. She has to be added to the Got-a-Deal Domain Administrators group to have Full Control over GPOs, but she cannot delegate that responsibility.

❍ d. None of the above.

Question 1.14

The Network Manager at 4Sale says, "Assuming Got-a-Deal is configured as a child domain under 4Sale, I want our 4Sale Corporate News folder to appear on its desktop in addition to whatever the Got-a-Deal Vice President of Operations wants. What is the easiest way to have this automatically happen?" [Choose the best answer]

❍ a. Create an OU and assign the appropriate settings.

❍ b. Modify the Got-a-Deal domain GPO.

❍ c. Do nothing.

❍ d. None of the above.

Case Study 2

4Sale, an online bartering company in ThatTherePlace North Dakota, focuses primarily on selling inexpensive, odd-lot items. 4Sale has merged operations with an online brokerage company, Got-a-Deal. Got-a-Deal rents space in the same office building.

As part of the expansion plan proposed by the 4Sale CEO, the online company is now learning how to use its infrastructure and focusing on learning how to leverage the many new Windows 2000 features as they relate to the corporate business objectives.

MyPartner is an antique broker and independent contractor located in Somewhere, New York.

The 4Sale proprietary front end is growing in popularity. This front end provides an interface to the 4Sale online bidding system and online auction services. The back-end application is actually composed of an accounting system, a cataloging system, and an online communication package that supports virtual auction rooms in which Internet customers can participate in realtime bidding. The application is composed of COM+ components that allow third-party developers to rapidly configure their own in-house systems to the 4Sale application.

Current LAN/Network Structure

4Sale is currently running native mode Windows 2000 Server on five Pentium III 600MHz machines:

- One member server runs Exchange Server 5.5 with Service Pack (SP) 1
- One member server runs Internet Information Server 5 and Proxy Server 2
- One member server runs Certificate Server

The client systems are running Windows 2000 Professional, with Office 2000 being utilized as an applications package.

Got-A-Deal is currently running native mode Windows 2000 Server on two Pentium III 600MHz machines.

Got-a-Deal is running 22 client machines on Windows 2000 Professional, with Office 2000 being utilized as an applications package.

The 4Sale system is connected to a 10Mbps hub through 10Mbps LAN cards running Category 5 UTP cabling in a star topology. Got-a-Deal is connected to a 10Mbps hub through 10Mbps LAN cards running Category 5 UTP cabling in a star topology. These hubs are on the same backbone as 4Sale but have a different subnet.

My Partner has no direct connection to the 4Sale domain tree at this time.

Proposed LAN/Network Structure

Network Manager at 4Sale says, "We need My Partner to have a secured connection to Got-a-Deal."

Current WAN Connectivity

4Sale has a T1 connection to its ISP. Got-a-Deal uses dial-up clients and ISDN to connect to its ISP.

Proposed WAN Connectivity

No changes in the current structure are proposed at this time.

Directory Design Commentary

4Sale uses native mode Windows 2000 for its online barter/trading business. All 125 client machines are configured in a single-domain model. Got-a-Deal is a child domain under the root **4sale.com**.

Current Internet Positioning

4Sale is registered as **4sale.com**. Got-a-Deal uses the **4sale.com** Web site.

Future Internet Plans

No changes in the current structure are proposed at this time.

Company Goal with Windows 2000

With the possible extension of communication to online companies that have a business alliance with 4Sale, the immediate goal is to secure 4Sale infrastructure and distributed services. An important theme is to centralize management so that any future expansion does not increase TCO.

Question 2.1

The Network Manager at 4Sale asks, "Based on our needs, what is the best security template to deploy to workstations?"

- ❍ a. Basic (basic*.inf)
- ❍ b. Compatible (compat*.inf)
- ❍ c. Secure (secure*.inf)
- ❍ d. Highly secure (hisec*.inf)
- ❍ e. None of the above

Question 2.2

Considering the case study provided, what component(s) that you need to deploy smart cards is/are missing? [Check all correct answers]

- ❑ a. Hardware
- ❑ b. Security Support Provider (SSP)
- ❑ c. Operating system specifications
- ❑ d. User account Information
- ❑ e. All of the above

Question 2.3

The Network Manager at 4Sale says, "I want to automate configuring security policies using secedit.exe." You want to perform the following operations:

Create a verbose log file named sec001215.log.

Use securedb1.sdb as your database file.

Configure the user logon rights only.

You use the following syntax:

```
SECEDIT /configure /db securedbl.sdb /areas user_rights /log
  c:\winnt\security\logs\sec001215.log /verbose
```

The Network Manager at 4Sale says, "This operation will work as intended."

- ❍ a. True
- ❍ b. False

Question 2.4

The Network Manager at 4Sale says, "Got-a-Deal wants to have its own certificate server independent of our root certificate server. I want to be able to validate the certificates from both Certificate Authorities (CAs). How should I install this server?" [Choose the best answer]

- ❍ a. Install an enterprise root CA with a two-way networked trust to the 4Sale root CA.
- ❍ b. Install a standalone root CA with a two-way networked trust to the 4Sale root CA.
- ❍ c. Install a subordinate CA with a two-way networked trust to the 4Sale root CA.
- ❍ d. None of the above.

Question 2.5

The Vice President of Marketing at 4Sale says, "We have received offers from other online services to integrate our front-end client with their software. What protocol would provide 4Sale with the highest levels of security and flexibility?" [Choose the best answer]

❍ a. PPP

❍ b. DPA

❍ c. EAP

❍ d. PCT

Question 2.6

The Network Manager at 4Sale asks, " Which is the best authentication procedure if 4Sale supports a heterogeneous user population but needs a secured exchange of data?"

❍ a. Anonymous access

❍ b. Basic authentication

❍ c. Basic authentication with SSL

❍ d. Integrated Windows authentication

Question 2.7

The Network Manager at 4Sale says, "I want to install a Virtual Private Network (VPN) using L2TP/PPP for a secured connection with MyPartner. The VPN connection won't have any problems passing through our proxy server."

❍ a. True

❍ b. False

Question 2.8

The Network Manager at 4Sale gives you the following list and says, "Here are the actions I performed to harden our IIS server. This list is complete and I covered all the major security areas."

1. Disable unnecessary services.
2. Install a dual-homed server.
3. Disable directory browsing.
4. Disable Server services.

Is the Network Manager's statement true or false?

❍ a. True

❍ b. False

Question 2.9

The Network Manager at 4Sale asks, "Given the heterogeneity of our user population, at which level is it best to apply access controls?"

❍ a. User

❍ b. Group

❍ c. Application

❍ d. NT File System (NTFS) level

❍ e. None of the above

Question 2.10

The Network Manager at 4Sale says, "I have applied RBACs (role-based access controls) to our barter software but am now having problems running the accounting portion of it in-house. What is the first thing I should do?"

❍ a. Modify NTFS permissions.

❍ b. Modify user rights.

❍ c. Modify domain GPOs.

❍ d. Apply a different security template.

❍ e. None of the above.

Case Study 3

4Sale, an online bartering company in ThatTherePlace North Dakota, has been building an infrastructure that will support its corporate plans for expansion. Having focused on securing the distributed services within the boundaries of its enterprise network, the company is now extending its virtual boundaries and building both functional and network bridges across public networks to outside online business concerns that share the same or related business interests.

MyPartner is an antique broker and independent contractor located in Somewhere, New York.

Current LAN/Network Structure

4Sale is currently running native mode Windows 2000 Server on six Pentium III 600MHz machines:

- One member server runs Exchange Server 2000
- One member server runs Internet Information Server 5 and Proxy Server 2
- Two member servers manage certificate services: one root Certificate Server and one subordinate Certificate Server

The client systems are running Windows 2000 Professional, with Office 2000 being utilized as an applications package.

Got-a-Deal is currently running native mode Windows 2000 Server on two Pentium III 600MHz machines.

Got-a-Deal is running 22 client machines on Windows 2000 Professional, with Office 2000 being utilized as an applications package.

All 100 client machines at 4Sale are configured in a single domain model. The client systems are running Windows 2000 Professional, with Office 2000 being utilized as an applications package. Each system is connected to a 10Mbps hub through 10Mbps LAN cards running Category 5 UTP cabling in a star topology.

Got-a-Deal has undergone changes. It is running all 22 client machines in a single child domain under the 4Sale root domain. Got-a-Deal client systems are running Windows 2000 Professional, with Office 2000 being utilized as an applications package. Each system is connected to a 10Mbps hub through 10Mbps LAN cards running Category 5 UTP cabling in a star topology. These hubs are on the same backbone as 4Sale but have a different subnet.

Proposed LAN/Network Structure

Network Manager at 4Sale says, "I need to secure all network communications in the most efficient way. I would prefer to do this at the OSI Network layer as opposed to the OSI Application layer."

Current WAN Connectivity

4Sale has a T1 connection to its ISP for its online business.

Proposed WAN Connectivity

The installation of IP Security protocols and the successful deployment of Virtual Private Networks (VPNs) may lead to use of a RADIUS server.

Directory Design Commentary

4Sale is currently running Windows 2000 Server in native mode. No changes in the current structure are proposed at this time. Got-a-Deal is running all 22 client machines in a single child domain under the 4Sale root domain.

Current Internet Positioning

4Sale uses virtual hosting services and is registered as **4sale.com**. Got-a-Deal has been selling its goods through local companies, pages on other broker Web sites, and through a Web page on the **4sale.com** Web site.

Future Internet Plans

No changes in the current structure are proposed at this time.

Company Goal with Windows 2000

Network Manager at 4Sale says, "With the building of business alliances, I need to prepare for the deployment of more persistent VPN connections to extranets all over the country. As we expand our online auction rooms, I will also need to support brokers who will require secure connections when they contact our network."

Question 3.1

Considering the case study provided, for which choice does the IPSec specification not provide countermeasures?

❍ a. Passive interception like sniffing

❍ b. Passive impersonation like address spoofing

❍ c. Active interference like a virus from someone you know

❍ d. Active interception like man-in-the-middle attacks that reroute a data exchange

❍ e. None of the above

Question 3.2

For future growth projections, including the probability of new branch offices, what would be the best OU design for the **4sale.com** domain?

❍ a. Location then organization

❍ b. Organization then location

❍ c. Department

❍ d. Project

Question 3.3

The Network Manager at 4Sale says, "We need to build a firewall. We have put our Web server behind it. What issues would we face if we put the VPN server in front of the firewall?" [Check all correct answers]

❑ a. User Datagram Protocol (UDP) port number 1701

❑ b. VPN server IP address

❑ c. HTTP packets

❑ d. All of the above

Question 3.4

The Network Manager at 4Sale says, "We need to build a firewall. We have put our Web server behind it. What issues would we face if we put the VPN server behind the firewall?" [Check all correct answers]

❑ a. Transmission Control Protocol/User Datagram Protocol (TCP/UDP) ports for tunnel maintenance

❑ b. VPN server IP address

❑ c. HTTP packets

❑ d. All of the above

Question 3.5

The Network Manager at 4Sale says, "Only MyPartner uses the VPN. My plan is to put the VPN in front of the firewall so that we can use it to restrict MyPartner's access to areas inside our intranet." Who will this plan affect and will it work?

❍ a. This plan will affect only MyPartner and will work as planned.

❍ b. This plan will affect only MyPartner but will not work as planned.

❍ c. This plan will affect others in addition to MyPartner and will work as planned.

❍ d. This plan will affect others in addition to MyPartner but will not work as planned.

Question 3.6

The Network Manager at 4Sale asks, "What protocol would I need if I wanted remote access using smart cards?"

❍ a. EAP-MD5

❍ b. EAP-TLS

❍ c. EAP-RADIUS

❍ d. TLS

❍ e. None of the above

Question 3.7

Considering the case study provided, during the deployment of L2TP over IPSec, the only thing the Network Manager at 4Sale must do is install a computer certificate on the 4Sale VPN server by configuring an auto enrollment Group Policy or manually using the Certificate snap-in.

❍ a. True

❍ b. False

Question 3.8

The Network Manager at 4Sale asks, "If MyPartner wanted to switch to a non-Microsoft VPN client, what special configurations are necessary for a secure connection?" [Check all correct answers]

❑ a. For PPTP, MPPE must be supported.

❑ b. For L2TP, IPSec encryption must be supported.

❑ c. No configuration is needed; the VPN client will not work.

❑ d. No configuration is needed; the VPN client will negotiate all settings.

Question 3.9

The Network Manager at 4Sale asks, "If we implement IPSec and the VPN server is behind the firewall, what packet filters do I have to set?" [Check all correct answers]

❑ a. Inbound/outbound IP port 50

❑ b. Inbound/outbound IP port 51

❑ c. UDP port 500 for key exchange

❑ d. UDP port 1701 for L2TP

Question 3.10

The Network Manager at 4Sale says, "Even though I use ipsecmon.exe to monitor IP traffic, I am sure I can find similar counters in Performance."

❍ a. True

❍ b. False

Question 3.11

The Network Manager has asked you to compile a flowchart showing how a company like My Partner will securely connect to Got-a-Deal in a way that minimizes exposure of the firewall to outside attack. The following objects represent the components of the network:

VPN Client | Web Server | Firewall | Domain Controller | VPN Server

Use items from the following list to connect the objects so that they are correct. The diagram should flow from the VPN client on the left side to the 4Sale domain controller on the right. Some items may be used more than once, and some items may not be used at all.

PPP

TCP/IP

RDP/TCP

VPN

Case Study 4

4Sale, an online bartering company in ThatTherePlace North Dakota, focuses primarily on selling inexpensive, odd-lot items. The CEO at 4Sale has slowly implemented a business plan that began with consolidation of the parent company, 4Sale, gradually expanded operations through the use of remote access and Virtual Private Networks (VPNs), and is now concerned primarily with building cost-effective operations with the consolidation of IT resources and the merging of or interoperation with other business platforms such as Macintosh, Novell, and Unix.

Fred Smith, an artist and Web designer, is an independent contractor at 4Sale.

MyPartner is an antique broker and independent contractor located in Somewhere, New York. MyPartner formed a business alliance with 4Sale over one year ago.

Future Inc. is a 15-year old data warehousing service that has developed several proprietary search engines customized for various industries.

Current LAN/Network Structure

4Sale is currently running native mode Windows 2000 Server on six Pentium III 600MHz machines:

- One member server runs Exchange Server 2000
- One member server runs Internet Information Server 5 and Proxy Server 2
- Two member servers manage certificate services: one root Certificate Server and one subordinate Certificate Server
- One member server runs RRAS and provides VPN services

All 100 client machines are configured in a single domain model. The client systems are running Windows 2000 Professional, with Office 2000 being utilized as an applications package. Each system is connected to a 10Mbps hub through 10Mbps LAN cards running Category 5 UTP cabling in a star topology.

Fred Smith has 1 iBook laptop and two Power Macintosh G4 workstations running MacOS 8.5 using both MacTCP and AppleTalk.

MyPartner has a 25-user Novell 5.1 network running BorderManager VPN Services, BorderManager FireWALL Services, and Oracle 8i for NetWare 5.1 (8.1.5.0.4c).

Future Inc. has 300 users on an AT&T 6386 System V Unix operating system platform running several proprietary packages and Oracle 8i Release 3.

Proposed LAN/Network Structure

The Network Manager at 4Sale says, "We want Fred to store all his work for us on our system. We will be merging with MyPartner in about three months; I will need a deployment plan from you as soon as possible. Future Inc. will be handling all our data storage. It has proprietary search engine applications that we will need to run on our system to access our data."

Current WAN Connectivity

4Sale has a T1 connection to its ISP for its online business. 4Sale supports remote access through VPN connections provided by its RRAS Server.

Proposed WAN Connectivity

No changes in the current structure are proposed at this time.

Directory Design Commentary

We want the administration of directory services between My Partner and 4Sale to be as simple and efficient as possible.

Current Internet Positioning

4Sale has a registered domain, **www.4sale.com,** and uses virtual hosting services to connect to the Internet. Got-a-Deal has been selling its goods through local companies, pages on other broker Web sites and through a Web page on the **4sale.com** Web site.

Fred Smith has his own registered domain, **www.fredsmith.com**, and uses an Apple AirPort base station to interface with his ISP, which provides him with virtual hosting services. The base station provides NAT services for all his AirPort clients.

MyPartner has its own registered domain, **www.mypartner.com**, and uses an ISP to connect to the Internet.

Future Inc. has its own registered Class B domain, **www.futureinc.com**, and runs its own in-house DNS servers.

Future Internet Plans

No changes in the current structure are proposed at this time.

Company Goal with Windows 2000

The CEO of 4Sale says, "My personal goal over the next three months is to seamlessly incorporate Fred, MyPartner, and Future Inc. into our daily 4Sale operations."

Question 4.1

Considering the case study provided and the proposed merger with MyPartner, what type of domain structure would you recommend allowing for all relevant concerns?

❍ a. Two distinct forests (**4sale.com** and **mypartner.com**), with an extended trust connecting them

❍ b. One domain with the root **4sale.com**, with a child domain being **mypartner.4sale.com**

❍ c. One domain called **4sale.com** with two OUs, one for 4Sale and one for MyPartner

❍ d. One domain called **4sale.com** with one OU for MyPartner

Question 4.2

The CEO of 4Sale says, "In terms of migration, rank our three projects in descending order, from the best candidate to the worst candidate."

Fred Smith: Macintosh

MyPartner: Novell

Future Inc.: Unix

Question 4.3

The CEO of 4Sale says, "In terms of interoperability, rank our three projects in descending order, from the best candidate to the worse candidate."

Fred Smith: Macintosh

MyPartner: Novell

Future Inc.: Unix

Question 4.4

The Network Manager at 4Sale asks, "We are not merging for at least six months, so it might be better to run 4Sale and MyPartner as separate entities but allow them to share data. We need to control access to 4Sale resources. What service will handle our security issues?"

❍ a. Microsoft Directory Synchronization Services (MSDSS)

❍ b. File Migration Utility (FMU)

❍ c. File and Print Services for NetWare version 5 (FPNW5)

❍ d. Gateway and Client Services for NetWare

Question 4.5

The Network Manager at 4Sale asks, "When we are ready, how do we migrate the Novell user accounts and permissions from Novell Directory Services (NDS) to Windows 2000?" Which of the following is an alternative naming convention you can use with Windows 2000?

❍ a. MSDSS

❍ b. DSMigrate

❍ c. FMU

❍ d. None of the above

Question 4.6

The Network Manager at 4Sale says, "Using default settings, we can control Fred Smith's access to our printers." Is this statement true or false?

❍ a. True

❍ b. False

Question 4.7

The Network Manager at 4Sale asks, "What is the fastest way to port the source code of Future Inc.'s proprietary search engine?" [Choose the best answer]

❍ a. Interix

❍ b. Portable Operating System Interface for Unix (POSIX)

❍ c. Unicode

❍ d. Services for Unix 2 (SFU2)

Question 4.8

The Owner-Network Manager at Got-a-Deal says, "I want our people to be as proficient as possible in creating batch scripts to automate many of the administrative functions and dealing with security issues on both the Future Inc. and 4Sale platforms. What is our best strategy?" [Check all correct answers]

- ❑ a. Interix
- ❑ b. POSIX
- ❑ c. Korn Shell programming
- ❑ d. All of the above
- ❑ e. None of the above

Question 4.9

The Network Manager has asked you how various acquisition candidates will either merge or fully interoperate over a long term with 4Sale directory services. To answer this question, you must move the labels on the right side of the graphic to their appropriate positions inside the blank connector arrows in the middle of the screen. Some items may be used more than once, and some items may not be used at all.

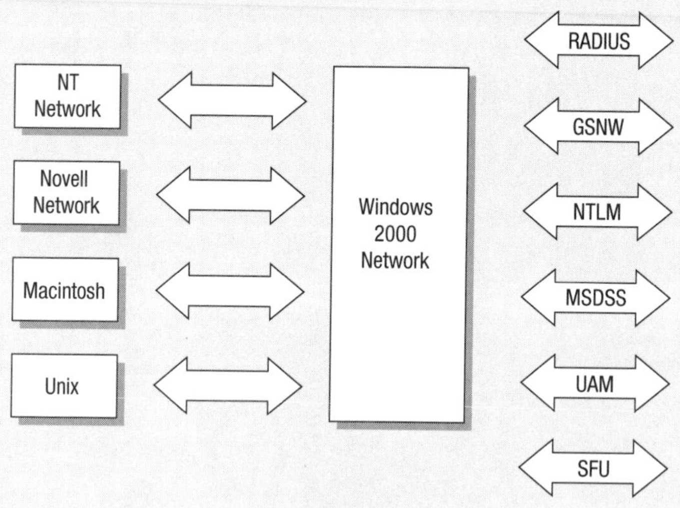

Case Study 5

4Sale, an online bartering company in ThatTherePlace North Dakota, is now a major player in the electronic bidding and online auction business. It has business alliances with major companies in related business such as data warehousing, virtual hosting services, online retail portals, and wholesale dealers. Evidence shows a security breach where a competitor has received copies of interoffice email that details a major business innovation.

Current LAN/Network Structure

4Sale is currently running native mode Windows 2000 Server on 10 Pentium III 600MHz machines:

- Two member servers runs Exchange Server 2000
- One member server runs Internet Information Server 5 and Proxy Server 2
- One member server runs SQL Server 7
- Three member servers manage certificate services: one root Certificate Server and two subordinate Certificate Servers
- Two member servers run RRAS and provide VPN services

4Sale is currently running Windows 2000 Server in native mode. All 150 client machines are configured in a single domain model. The client systems are running Windows 2000 Professional, with Office 2000 being utilized as an applications package. Each system is connected to a 100Mbps hub through 100Mbps LAN cards running Category 5 UTP cabling in a star topology.

Proposed LAN/Network Structure

No changes in the current structure are proposed at this time.

Current WAN Connectivity

4Sale has a T3 connection to its ISP for its online business. 4Sale supports remote access through VPN connections provided by its several RRAS Servers.

Proposed WAN Connectivity

No changes in the current structure are proposed at this time.

Directory Design Commentary

No changes in the current structure are proposed at this time.

Current Internet Positioning

Although 4Sale has several registered domains, **www.4sale.com** is still the published home page. It runs its Web sites from an affiliated virtual hosting service.

Future Internet Plans

No changes in the current structure are proposed at this time.

Company Goal with Windows 2000

The CEO of 4Sale says, "The Board of Directors is pleased with our substantial increase in market share and our growth in earnings. But the fact that our competitor acquired a copy of an internal memo may cost us a major share of the market. I don't want to just respond to this single incident, however; I want our computer systems to provide a foundation that will support the security needs for the currently planned projects that I have promised will be implemented in the next six months. Over the next six months, I want to deploy persistent branch VPN systems, digital document signing, and two-factor authentication security for our applications within the enterprise."

The Network Manager at 4Sale says, "We must implement both encryption and authentication of email transmissions as soon as possible. I am also worried about the data on laptops that leave our building."

Question 5.1

Considering the case study provided, what is the best security technology that allows for all relevant concerns? [Choose the best answer]

❍ a. Kerberos protocol

❍ b. SChannel protocols

❍ c. PKI technologies

❍ d. IPSec protocol suite

Question 5.2

The Network Manager at 4Sale says, "I am concerned about deploying technologies that require the presence of a Certificate Authority infrastructure. Which of the corporate projects and my personal objectives do not require the presence of a CA?" [Choose the best answer]

❍ a. EFS

❍ b. SSL

❍ c. VPN

❍ d. None of the above

Question 5.3

The Network Manager at 4Sale asks, “In addition to supporting our other objectives, what do we need to validate a signed document?” [Check all correct answers]

❑ a. A standalone Certificate Authority

❑ b. A root Certificate Authority

❑ c. Active Directory

❑ d. All of the above

❑ e. None of the above

Question 5.4

The Network Manager at 4Sale asks, “What are the key components of a public key infrastructure?” [Check all correct answers]

❑ a. Certificate Authority architecture

❑ b. Public keys and certificates

❑ c. Active Directory integration

❑ d. SSL/TLS protocols

❑ e. None of the above

Question 5.5

The Network Manager of 4Sale asks, “How can we harden the following types of security around the Certificate Server?”

Physical security

Logical security

Place any appropriate answers under the appropriate heading:

Run the root Certificate Authority offline.

Place the Certificate Server in a locked enclosure.

Place the Certificate Server on a machine equipped for two-factor authentication.

Install the Certificate Server inside a demilitarized zone (DMZ) with a Web server.

Place the Certificate Authority private key on a smart card.

Place the Certificate Authority root certificate on a smart card.

Create the longest private key possible.

Regularly run the Security Configuration And Analysis MMC Snap-in using a batch script.

Question 5.6

The Network Manager at 4Sale asks, "What are the key components when you are securing email?" [Check all correct answers]

- ❑ a. Hash-based signature
- ❑ b. DSS
- ❑ c. Fortezza cards
- ❑ d. MD5
- ❑ e. All of the above

Question 5.7

The Network Manager at 4Sale asks, "How can I monitor the policy module on a Certificate Authority?"

- ❍ a. Use the **certsvr.exe -z** command.
- ❍ b. Right-click on the appropriate CA node and select Properties on the Certificate Authority MMC snap-in.
- ❍ c. Both of the above.
- ❍ d. None of the above.

Answer Key

For asterisked items, please see textual representation of answer on the appropriate page within this chapter.

1.1. c
1.2. *
1.3. b
1.4. *
1.5. b
1.6. a
1.7. e
1.8. a
1.9. b
1.10. c
1.11. *
1.12. b
1.13. d
1.14. c
2.1. d
2.2. a
2.3. a
2.4. b
2.5. c
2.6. c
2.7. a
2.8. b
2.9. c
2.10. d
3.1. c
3.2. a
3.3. b, c
3.4. d
3.5. c
3.6. b
3.7. b
3.8. a, b
3.9. a, b, c
3.10. b
3.11 *
4.1. d
4.2. *
4.3. *
4.4. a
4.5. b
4.6. b
4.7. a
4.8. d
4.9 *
5.1. c
5.2. a
5.3. b, c
5.4. a, b, c
5.5. *
5.6. e
5.7. c

Question 1.1

Answer c is correct. One domain with the root **4sale.com**, with a child domain being **gotadeal.4sale.com**, is one of the solutions that would allow for the relevant concerns. For example, the company already has **4sale.com** registered and plans to continue with this naming convention for both companies when they are merged. Having two separate domains allows for distinct password structures, yet having 4Sale as the root still provides a way of implementing strong control. Another solution might have been an empty root with two distinct domains beneath, but this was not an option. Answer a is incorrect because it offers two distinct forests, and this provides a poor solution of unification and control. Answers b and d are incorrect because they offer an empty root but then provide Organizational Units, which will not handle the issue of control over password security between the two locations.

Question 1.2

The correct answer is:

Technical support

System maintenance

Cost of hardware and software

Cost of system upgrades

User training

The prioritized order of total cost of ownership (TCO) components is culled from the discussions with key participants in network deployment. TCO includes cost of system upgrades, system maintenance, and technical support. Cost of disposables is not included in the list because it is not a component of TCO; disposables are typically considered an expense.

Question 1.3

Answer b, false, is correct. 4Sale provides a front-end client to its online customers to facilitate the exchange of bidding information. It also uses its own line-of-business applications in its internal accounting operations. 4Sale supports a broad range of business services to its user population in addition to its bidding system, but messaging and accounting are critical. 4Sale must provide fault-tolerant online transaction processing and storage. Network support is also a business service because its primary information technology security control is accessibility.

Question 1.4

The correct answer is:

Accessibility

Software authentication

Confidentiality

Nonrepudiation

The most important business corporate objective, though not formally written down, is access to the online services; therefore, accessibility is first. The 4Sale online customers must have confidence in the services. Authenticating the software not only instills that confidence but provides a level of guarantee that both the customer and 4Sale are exchanging data in a predictable way. If the online customer has access and uses the front-end client, the necessary confidentiality will be provided. Finally, from the 4Sale perspective, nonrepudiation is an important business concern because customers bid for product. When bids are placed, they must be considered final and irrefutable. Training and firewall technology are not included in the list because training is not a typical security objective, and firewall technology is not a security objective; it is considered one of many possible solutions.

Question 1.5

Answer b is correct. 4Sale is an online service. Information security strategies are the specific design and strategic choices necessary to secure online exchanges and Web-based communications. Due care and due diligence typically describe those actions that relate to the information technology security control compliance. This IT control is not of primary consideration in this case study. Therefore, answer a is incorrect. Similarly, security group descriptions are built into the security policy. Use of default choices and security templates, as stated in the case study, is critical in deployment and will be automatically carried out assuming proper installation and maintenance. Therefore, answer c is incorrect.

Question 1.6

Answer a is correct. NTDS (NT Directory Services) provides a variety of counters for directory replication, directory services, Lightweight Directory Access Protocol services, Security Accounts Manager (SAM) activity, address book activity, Kerberos activity, and specifically Key Distribution Center activity. Neither Kerberos nor KDC are performance objects. Therefore, answers b and c are incorrect.

Question 1.7

Answer e is correct. You can standardize specific security against some baseline profile in specific areas covered in the security templates supplied with the Security Configuration And Analysis Microsoft Management Console snap-in. The answer options are examples of the following security areas: Executive, Staff, and User groups are restricted groups; application files pertain to the file system; a proprietary application extension is part of machine\software\classes in the Registry; and smart card services are part of system services. Thus, answers a, b, c, and d are all examples of security areas included in security templates.

Question 1.8

Answer a is correct. Smart cards are the best recommendation because 4Sale is running in Windows 2000 native mode, and digitally signed documents are required for exchanges of information. Because 4Sale is running in native mode with the security protocol defaulting to Kerberos and a two-factor authentication method is preferred, NT LAN Manager authentication is not a good answer. Therefore, answer b is incorrect. Although Kerberos is the default authentication protocol, it supports only interactive logons. Therefore, answer c is incorrect. Secure Channel protocols support network logons. Therefore, answer d is incorrect.

Question 1.9

Answer b is correct. Microsoft IP Security adds features like strong encryption, which 4Sale requires, without affecting the total cost of ownership (specifically in terms of software upgrades, training, and hardware). IPSec works at the Open Systems Interconnection Transport layer; 4Sale line-of-business software, system software upgrades, training, and hardware are not directly affected. Kerberos protocol and Secure Channel protocols support public key infrastructure and the use of smart cards. These technologies, however, increase the investment in hardware and software to support the two-factor authentication method. Therefore, answers a and c are incorrect.

Question 1.10

Answer c is correct. The key feature here is flexible security protocols. Only one listed security technology is technically a protocol suite: IPSec. It provides both Authentication Header and Encapsulated Security Payload protocols. Kerberos and Secure Sockets Layer 3/Transport Layer Security 1 provide confidentiality and data integrity but are actual protocol specifications. Therefore, answers a, b, and d are incorrect.

Question 1.11

The correct answer is:

IPSec

Secure Multipurpose Internet Mail Extensions (S/MIME)

Secure Sockets Layer (SSL)

Secure Hypertext Transfer Protocol (S-HTTP)

You should deploy IPSec first because it will have the greatest effect in the shortest period of time at the lowest total cost of ownership. S/MIME is a standard component of most email services, so you should deploy it shortly after IPSec. You can outsource the immediate need for some Certificate Authority to a third party. Both SSL and S-HTTP will most likely require that you modify the 4Sale proprietary front-end software. SSL working at the Open Systems Interconnection Transport layer provides a broader range of support services than the application-specific S-HTTP, so its deployment as a security protocol tends to be more cost-effective when dealing with many HTTP applications. Because S-HTTP works at the OSI Application layer, in comparison to the other four security choices, this choice requires more time to modify specific application software, as well as more money to deploy. You should use S-HTTP on a per-case basis when more broad-based security protocols like SSL/TSL do not provide the necessary support or are not appropriate due to your specific network configuration.

Question 1.12

Answer b, false, is correct. 4Sale uses signed documents and therefore requires public key technologies. It also plans to deploy smart cards, so it will use enterprise certificate services to minimize administrative overhead. Directory services will be a very important part of 4Sale's long-term business strategy to scale its business without incurring additional costs for administration and support.

Question 1.13

Answer d is correct. The Network Manager is a member of the Enterprise Administrators and Domain Administrators group, so she cannot both modify GPOs (Group Policy Objects) and link them to some Active Directory object. Members of either of these administrative groups can also delegate the responsibility of modifying a GPO to any administrator or an administrator group, provided the administrator or group to whom they are delegating this responsibility has Read/Write access to the specific GPO. Answer a is incorrect because the Network Manager specifically wants the Got-a-Deal VP of Operations to have administrative authorization. Remember, the President of Got-a-Deal wants to have exclusive access to top secret information. Under the circumstances, a simpler choice—assigning the VP of Operations membership in the Domain Administrators group—is not an option. Answers b and c are incorrect because the Delegation of Control Wizard can grant Full Control to any administrator.

Question 1.14

Answer c is correct because a child domain will inherit policy settings unless those inherited settings contradict policy about those same settings or are blocked in the child domain. Answer a is incorrect because it is not necessary to create an OU (Organizational Unit) and assign the appropriate settings. Answer b is incorrect because inheritance from the parent domain applies unless incompatibilities exist between the GPO (Group Policy Object) settings across the two domains.

Question 2.1

Answer d is correct. Given the requirement that all correspondence be digitally signed, the only appropriate security configuration template is the hisec*.inf, which is specifically designed for network communications. These machines communicate only with other Windows 2000 workstations. Internet communication is through the proxy server. Answer a is incorrect because basic*.inf is used for reapplying the default security settings of a modified configuration file. Answer b is incorrect because compat*.inf is used for giving the local Users group strict security settings, whereas Power Users receive security levels comparable to legacy NT 4 Users. Compat*.inf templates also lower the security levels on files, folders, and Registry keys commonly used by applications to run. Answer c is incorrect because secure*.inf is used for recommended security settings for all areas except files, folders, and Registry keys. The latter are typically secured by the administrator or by default.

Question 2.2

Answer a is correct. An enterprise mode certificate server is already in place, so the only missing components are the actual card reader hardware and the accompanying software for the appropriate workstations. The Security Support Provider is either Kerberos (Public Key Cryptography for Initial Authentication in Kerberos) or SSL/TLS (Secure Sockets Layer/Transport Layer Security), both of which are provided as part of the operating system. Therefore, answer b is incorrect. There are no issues with operating system or user account information because 4Sale is using native mode Windows 2000. Therefore, answers c and d are incorrect.

Question 2.3

Answer a, true, is correct. This is the correct syntax for using secedit.exe to execute the operations listed.

Question 2.4

Answer b is correct. Got-a-Deal's only choice is to run a standalone Certificate Authority (CA) with a networked trust to the 4Sale root CA. This configuration will permit Got-a-Deal to administer its own certificates for transactions that require Secure Sockets Layer or Secure Multipurpose Internet Mail Extensions and will allow the sharing of certificates between the two CAs. Got-a-Deal is a child domain in the 4Sale enterprise tree. An enterprise root CA already exists, so Got-a-Deal cannot run a second enterprise root certificate server. Therefore, answer a is incorrect. Got-a-Deal wants to have an independent CA, so running a subordinate CA is also not acceptable. Therefore, answer c is incorrect.

Question 2.5

Answer c is correct. EAP (Extensible Authentication Protocol) is an extension to PPP (Point-To-Point Protocol) that works with dial-up, PPP, and Layer 2 Tunneling Protocol clients. EAP provides support for two-factor authentication such as smart cards and public keys. It also plays an important role in Virtual Private Networks. PPP is a communications protocol standard that provides interoperability for remote access protocols and supports a variety of authentication methods so that other authentication protocols run on it. Therefore, answer a is incorrect. DPA (Distributed Password Authentication) is an asymmetric authentication protocol used by online services and part of Microsoft Commercial Internet Systems. Therefore, answer b is incorrect. PCT (Private Communications Technology) is one of the Secure Channel Security Support Providers along Secure Sockets Layer 3 and Transport Layer Security 1. Therefore, answer d is incorrect.

Question 2.6

Answer c is correct. Basic authentication using SSL (Secure Sockets Layer) is supported by most Web browsers and thus supports a heterogeneous population. By using SSL support, which most browsers also support, you make basic authentication more secure. Neither anonymous access nor basic authentication provide for the secure exchange of information. Therefore, answers a and b are incorrect. Integrated Windows authentication is more secure than basic authentication, but it is designed primarily for intranets. Therefore, answer d is incorrect.

Question 2.7

Answer a, true, is correct. L2TP/PPP (Layer 2 Tunneling Protocol/Point-To-Point Protocol) will not have any problems with the Network Address Translation used in Proxy Server because it will not use IPSec for authentication. There are incompatibilities when IPSec components like Internet Key Exchange attempt to exchange session keys and create secured sessions, because internal network IP addresses are translated by NAT and never actually disclosed outside the network. IKE needs the actual destination address to properly encrypt and decrypt packets during a secured exchange of information.

Question 2.8

Answer b, false, is correct. The Network Manager forgot to enable both logging and auditing on the Web server. This one step is the least expensive in terms of overhead and maintenance and is probably the most important action to perform when you are securing an Internet Information Server server.

Question 2.9

Answer c is correct. Role-based (application) access control is the best way to handle 4Sale security. If you assign permissions to the user or group, you have more administrative overhead and more possibilities of a security weakness or conflicts in configuration and permission levels. Therefore, answers a and b are incorrect. Assigning permissions to an applications-based role simplifies administration but also hardens security; the role's security context provides the least privileges for completing that application's specific tasks. Users log on to perform some work function, and then they log out. You should always apply NT File System permissions within an enterprise, but you must carefully test for unpredictable results. Therefore, answer d is incorrect.

Question 2.10

Answer d is correct. The first step should be to apply the compatws.inf template to the appropriate local machines. This security maintains a secure internal environment while possibly allowing all aspects of the software to run successfully. Changing specific NT File System permissions would be a second choice. Therefore, answer a is incorrect. Only part of the software is malfunctioning, so a rights issue pertaining to the application role is unlikely. Therefore, answer b is incorrect. Similarly, Group Policy settings at the domain level are less likely than local permissions to be causing this problem. Therefore, answer c is incorrect.

Question 3.1

Answer c is correct. IP Security does not stop the spread of a virus from a sender you trust primarily because a virus can be incorporated in the message packet. Answers a and b are incorrect because IPSec does provides countermeasures for passive interception and impersonation attack modalities. Answer d is incorrect because IPSec decreases the possibility of active interception attacks (man-in-the-middle) that intercept the data exchanged between the two parties.

Question 3.2

Answer a is correct. The rule is to keep the structure as simple as possible. Even though 4Sale is an e-commerce company, the business infrastructure is still based by location. It's conceivable that an organization subdivided by location schema might help structure 4Sale if it were to specialize in categories of objects. For example, all business functioning and personnel involved in the bartering of automobiles would be assigned to a specific Organizational Unit (OU) separate from other 4Sale operational areas. This OU would then have regions throughout the country. This division of business by organization rather than location, however, would add more complexity at this time without any obvious advantage, so it is not appropriate. Therefore, answer b is incorrect. Answer c is incorrect because separating specific departments would not provide any clear business advantage. Similarly, because 4Sale does not have specific projects requiring a separate organizational structure or special policies, answer d is incorrect. Creating OUs within geographical areas (location) for 4Sale at this time is the simplest and most logical design.

Question 3.3

Answers b and c are correct. Because the VPN (Virtual Private Network) server is in front of the firewall, the firewall must filter traffic to and from the VPN server's designated Internet Protocol address to allow traffic to flow. Therefore, answer b is correct. The Network Manager must also decide whether to force all traffic through the VPN server or allow outbound HTTP packets to pass through the firewall. Therefore, answer c is correct. Answer a is inccorect because the VPN server is in front of the firewall. L2TP encapsulates message packets inside a PPP frame when it creates a tunnel, then puts that package inside a UDP packet assigned to port 1701. If the VPN server were behind the firewall, port 1701 would have to allow UDP packets to pass through it to reach the internally located VPN server. Because the VPN Server is outside the firewall, port 1701 does not have to allow inbound or outbound traffic to pass through the wall. Placing the VPN server in front of the firewall also restricts Internet traffic on the intranet because inbound packets must first pass through the VPN server.

Question 3.4

Answer d is correct. The firewall input and output filters must be able to pass tunnel maintenance traffic, as well as any other server behind it. Answer a is correct because both TCP and UDP packets must be able to pass through ports like 1701 to reach the internally located VPN server. Answer b is correct because the tunneled data must be able to pass to the VPN server where it is then authenticated. Answer c is correct because HTTP (Hypertext Transfer Protocol) packets must cross the wall.

Question 3.5

Answer c is correct. The firewall will restrict access to MyPartner as intended. However, outbound Internet traffic will also have to go through the Virtual Private Network, so the VPN will therefore restrict the use of Internet resources to VPN users. Therefore answers a, b, and d are incorrect.

Question 3.6

Answer b is correct. EAP-TLS (Extensible Authentication Protocol - Transport Layer Security) is used in a certificate-based exchange. You must use this protocol for remote access authentication. EAP-MD5 (Extensible Authentication Protocol - Message Digest 5) is a challenge-handshake protocol that uses EAP messages. This protocol is used in remote access situations when username and password are exchanged. Therefore, answer a is incorrect. EAP-RADIUS (Extensible Authentication Protocol-Remote Authentication Dial-In User Service) passes EAP messages to a RADIUS server for authentication. It does not deal with smart cards. Therefore, answer c is incorrect. TLS (Transport Layer Security) is used in conjunction with EAP packets. Therefore, answer d is incorrect.

Question 3.7

Answer b, false, is correct. The Network Manager must make certain both the Virtual Private Network server and VPN client have computer certificates.

Question 3.8

Answers a and b are correct. For PPTP (Point-To-Point Tunneling Protocol), MPPE (Microsoft Point-To-Point Encryption) must be supported, and for L2TP (Layer 2 Tunneling Protocol), IP Security encryption must be supported. No other configuration is necessary. Therefore answers c and d are incorrect.

Question 3.9

Answers a, b, and c are correct. Ports 50 and 51 support Authentication Header and Encapsulated Security Payload traffic. Port 500 allows Internet Key Exchange traffic. No filters are required for L2TP (Layer 2 Tunneling Protocol) traffic because the tunnel maintenance and tunneled data are encrypted as an ESP payload. Therefore, answer d is incorrect.

Question 3.10

Answer b, false, is correct. There are no relevant performance objects related to IP Security in Performance. The best utility is ipsecmon.exe. Therefore, answer a is incorrect.

Question 3.11

The correct answer is:

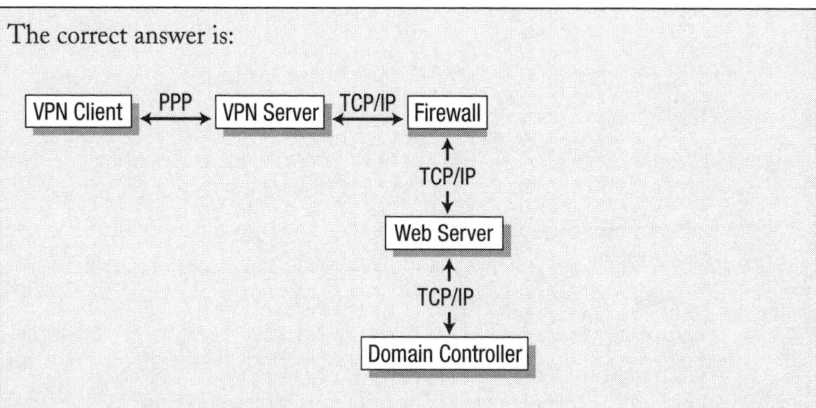

A VPN client connects to a VPN server using a communication protocol like Point-To-Point Protocol (PPP). The VPN server is positioned outside the firewall; only inbound packets with the VPN server's IP address will be permitted through the firewall. 4Sale would typically position its Web server behind the firewall. Between the VPN server, the Web server, and the domain controller, TCP/IP is the protocol of choice.

Question 4.1

Answer d is correct. Creating a separate Organizational Unit within the 4Sale domain is the most cost-effective way to merge the two companies. Answer a is incorrect because MyPartner will be merged with 4Sale, so there is no reason to create a separate namespace by extending a trust across two separate forests. Creating a separate child domain would increase administrative costs as compared to other choices in this question. MyPartner would need a domain administrator. Although the creation of a child domain might be "politically correct," especially in view of how Got-a-Deal is managed in the enterprise, members of a MyPartner Domain Administrators group, because of the transitive trust relationship, would automatically have administrative rights in the 4Sale root domain. Arbitrarily adding a child domain to the domain tree, although administratively easy, can compromise security within the enterprise. A more conservative approach, especially from a security perspective, is to use an organizational unit. Therefore, answer b is incorrect. Answer c is incorrect because the 4Sale CEO has emphasized that 4Sale is the parent company; two OUs under one domain implies more of a sibling relationship between companies. No statement in the case study suggests this kind of relationship.

Question 4.2

The correct answer is:

MyPartner

Fred Smith

Future Inc.

Migration would mean that an entire working environment would change for the user. Employees at MyPartner would see the least amount of change because Novell provides support services; the working interface is typically Windows-based. MyPartner is the best candidate for migration. Fred Smith, on the other hand, uses a Macintosh interface with a different presentation of the workspace, directory services, and access control than a Windows-based interface. Creating a Macintosh-accessible User Authentication Module share would support all of Fred's storage needs and would have little impact on his daily job. Data storage would be under 4Sale's centralized control. Future Inc. is the worst candidate for migration in this case study; not only is it a large company, but its operating system is also well suited to its line-of-business applications and business mission.

Question 4.3

The correct answer is:

Future Inc.

Fred Smith

MyPartner

Windows 2000, like legacy NT, provides several tools that provide a high degree of interoperability. Portable Operating System Interface for Unix remains a native subsystem in the Windows 2000 architecture. Services for Unix 2 provides tools that allow greater levels of interoperability and coexistence than for either Macintosh or Novell. Fred Smith is using the Macintosh operating system, which like Unix, coexisted with legacy NT 4. It can reliably share the same files and, except for slight differences in permission management, coexists well with Windows 2000. Novell is the worst candidate for interoperability because most of the Services for NetWare version 5 are designed for migration.

Question 4.4

Answer a is correct. MSDSS (Microsoft Directory Synchronization Services) synchronizes Active Directory datastores with Novell Directory Services. FMU (File Migration Utility) is a migration tool. Therefore, answer b is incorrect. FPNW5 (File and Print Services for NetWare version 5) provides a NetWare interface and Single Sign-On for Novell users running on Windows 2000. Therefore, answer c is incorrect. Gateway and Client Services for NetWare do not support access to the NWAdmin utility. Administrative control must be handled from the Novell operating system. Therefore, answer d is incorrect.

Question 4.5

Answer b is correct. DSMigrate (Directory Services Migration Tool) migrates user accounts, groups, files, and permissions from MyPartner's Novell Directory Services directory services. MSDSS (Microsoft Directory Synchronization Services) does not migrate accounts. Therefore, answer a is incorrect. FMU (File Migration Utility) migrates only files. Therefore, answer c is incorrect.

Question 4.6

Answer b, false, is correct. Using default settings, you cannot impose user-level access permissions on Macintosh print clients. Macintosh networking provides access control on files but not printers. By default, a Macintosh print client has implicit permission to access a printer because it runs in the security context of a system account.

Question 4.7

Answer a is correct. Interix 2.2 provides a Portable Operating System Interface for Unix-compliant software platform with developer tools and functions that assist in the migration of the source code to the Windows 2000 operating system. POSIX is a set of standards and specifications to facilitate the migration of software. Therefore, answer b is incorrect. Unicode is a character set standard that uses 16 bits; it has nothing to do with Unix. Therefore, answer c is incorrect. Services for Unix 2 is not primarily concerned with the porting of source code. Therefore, answer d is incorrect.

Question 4.8

Answer d is correct. Interix and the Mortice Kern Toolkit working on the POSIX (Portable Operating System Interface for Unix) subsystem on the Windows 2000 platform provide full integration with the Unix-style command line and environment. The Korn Shell is the command-line interpreter used in the Mortice Kern Toolkit.

Question 4.9

The correct answer is:

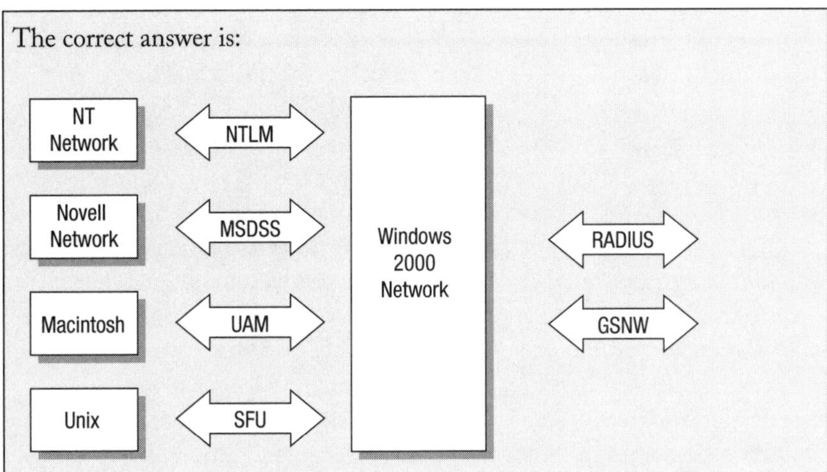

Legacy NT 4 networks will integrate with 4Sale directory services using their default authentication protocol, NTLM, and Novell will use Microsoft Directory Synchronization Services (MSDSS). Although Gateway Service for NetWare (GSNW) provides a method to connect the two operating systems, it does not provide the support for long-term interoperability. The Macintosh OS can use the User Authentication Module (UAM) share to store folders and documents. Unix can use a variety of tools provided by the Services For Unix version 2. The last choice, Remote Authentication Dial-in User Service (RADIUS), is an authentication and auditing system used by many Internet Service Providers; it specifically deals with remote access services.

Question 5.1

Answer c is correct. Public key infrastructure provides the foundation for applications and technologies that require strong authentication. The use of public keys provides support for secure Web transactions (Secure Sockets Layer), secure mail (Secure Multipurpose Internet Mail Extensions), file system encryption (Encrypting File System), IP Security tunneling (Virtual Private Network), smart card logon (Public Key Cryptography for Initial Authentication in Kerberos), and so on. The CEO specifically wants a solution that will also support smart card–based applications, VPN systems, and digital document signing. Kerberos is the default protocol in Windows 2000 for interactive authentication and authorization issues; it does not provide a platform for these other system needs. Therefore, answer a is incorrect. Secure Channel protocols like SSL and Transport Layer Security are the security methods of choice for authentication across a public network and for smart cards, but they do not support VPNs. Therefore, answer b is incorrect. IPSec technologies support encryption and authentication but at the Open Systems Interconnection Network layer; answer d is therefore not the best answer.

Question 5.2

Answer a is correct. EFS (Encrypting File System) on laptops does not require the presence of a Certificate Authority. Secure Sockets Layer and Virtual Private Networks both rely on the authentication of digital certificates issued by some CA to function. Therefore, answers b and c are incorrect.

Question 5.3

Answers b and c are correct. For large enterprise solutions and the 4Sale goals listed in the case study, a hierarchical trust model consisting of a root Certificate Authority (CA) and subordinate CA with Active Directory integration is the best solution because it provides both scalability and administrative flexibility. For security reasons, you can take the root CA offline while keeping the subordinate CA online to handle the authentication process. Through integration with Active Directory, certificates and other security information like certification revocation lists are replicated throughout the domain tree or forest. The standalone CA is an acceptable solution for Secure Sockets Layer and Secure Multipurpose Internet Mail Extensions—that is, issuing certificates to external users—but it is not integrated with the Active Directory. Therefore, answer a is incorrect.

Question 5.4

Answers a, b, and c are correct. The Certificate Authority architecture allows you to administer public keys and digital certificates. Therefore, answers a and b are correct. Active Directory integration is important because it contains the location of Certificate Servers and it supports the publication of digital certificates and certificate revocation lists by automatically replicating this security material as part of the Global Catalog. Therefore, answer c is correct. (Secure Sockets Layer/Transport Layer Security) protocols use public key infrastructure security services but are not critical components. Therefore, answer d is incorrect.

Question 5.5

The correct answer is:

- Physical security
  - Place the Certificate Server in a locked enclosure.
  - Place the Certificate Server on a machine equipped for two-factor authentication.
- Logical security
  - Run the root Certificate Authority offline.
  - Place the Certificate Authority private key on a smart card.
  - Create the longest private key possible.

Several items were not included. You should not install a Certificate Server inside a demilitarized zone with a Web server because you must adjust packet filtering to include all public key infrastructure-related traffic, especially from the internal side of the network. A Web server is also inside the DMZ, so adding a certificate server seriously weakens the DMZ. The root Certificate Server is best installed offline on its own subnet and domain in a separate DMZ. Certificate Authority (CA) root certificate on a smart card is incorrect because the only key that you need to protect is the CA's private key; the public key is distributed throughout the network. Regularly running the Security Configuration And Analysis Microsoft Management Console snap-in using a batch script is incorrect; you cannot run the Security Configuration And Analysis MMC snap-in in a batch mode; the correct tool to accomplish the same function is secedit.exe.

Question 5.6

Answer e is correct. S/MIME (Secure Multipurpose Internet Mail Extensions) uses Secure Hash Algorithm or MD5 (Message Digest 5) for the hash function used to create the digital signature. S/MIME incorporates three public key algorithms, of which DSS (Digital Signature Standard) is preferred. Fortezza cryptocards are smart cards developed by the National Security Agency that securely store public key credentials.

Question 5.7

Answer c is correct. Both methods (using the **certsvr.exe -z** command, or right-clicking on the appropriate CA node and selecting Properties on the Certificate Authority MMC snap-in) will expose policy information such as the identity of the requestor, the state of the request, and so on.

Glossary

access control
The service that manages permissions of an authenticated principal (user or group) to perform an operation or manipulate an object.

access control entry (ACE)
The identifying entry of a principal (user or group) in a list that grants or denies permission to perform an action on an object.

access control list (ACL)
Part of the security descriptor of an object, a list of principals (or trustees) described in individual access control entries (ACEs) that grant or deny permission to perform an operation on an object. The discretionary ACL (DACL) lists the permissions granted or denied to principals listed in separate ACEs. The mandatory ACL (MACL) is a list of permissions centrally controlled by an administrator. The system ACL (SACL) specifies which events the system is to audit per user or group.

Active Directory (AD)
The Windows 2000 directory service that authenticates and authorizes named objects to access network resources based on provided security credentials and other information.

Active Directory Connector (ADC)
The application interface that replicates directory objects between a Microsoft Exchange Server directory (version 5.5 or later) and Active Directory directory services.

Active Directory Services Interfaces (ADSI)
The set of programming interfaces based on the Component Object Model (COM) that enable client applications to access network directory services.

Administrative Template
Special files with the .adm file extension that provide baseline security profiles with access through the Group Policy Microsoft Management Console (MMC) snap-in or the legacy System Policy Editor.

American National Standards Institute (ANSI)
The voluntary organization composed of computer professionals and companies that create standards for the computer industry.

American Standard Code for Information Interchange (ASCII)
A standard (based on an 8-bit character system) for transferring data between systems.

application programming interface (API)
The interface through which you can access program routines, procedures, and functions in an application or operating system component.

architecture
The logical design or schema of a system, such as Windows 2000, or hypothetical construct, such as the Open Systems Interconnection (OSI) Reference Model.

attribute
A single characteristic or property of an object described by a variable within a defined range.

authentication
The process of verifying the identity of a user who is attempting to access computer resources against some trusted credentials. Alternatively, the process of verifying the integrity of a received transmitted message against its content when it is originally sent.

authentication, authorization, and auditing (AAA) server
Taken from the triple A security model, which addresses remote access security, an AAA server performs authentication, authorization, and accounting functions. In this book, I have replaced the more general accounting function with an auditing function to conform to an Open Systems Interconnection (OSI) model of specific functional management areas in a network operating system.

bulk data encryption
A high-speed method of encryption that typically uses a symmetric encryption algorithm. In Encrypting File System (EFS), a unique file encryption key (FEK) is generated for the bulk encryption of data.

Certificate Authority (CA)
A trusted source that issues digital certificates that corroborate the identity of a named principal. This issued certificate contains supporting credentials and a public key of the private key holder authenticated by the CA. With the public key, secured information can be exchanged with the private key holder.

certificate practices statement (CPS)
Defines operational procedures on a Certificate Authority (CA) level based on certificate policies (CPs). These policies include the kinds of policies linked to the CA, method of certificate distribution, how the CA is administered, how revocations are handled, how access to the CA is secured, and so on.

command-line interface (CLI)
A textual user interface, commonly called a command prompt, that enables the communication of instructions to an operating system.

Common Information Model (CIM)
See *Windows Management Instrumentation (WMI)*.

container
An Active Directory (AD) object that is a holder of other objects or other containers.

cross-domain exchange
With regard to Group Policy Objects (GPOs), the linking to Group Policy settings in GPOs stored outside the current domain.

cryptanalysis
Methods and techniques involved in decrypting a message encoded in an unreadable format.

Cryptographic Application Programming Interface (CAPI)
A Microsoft application programming interface (API) that provides programmable support for cryptographic applications through independent modules called cryptographic service providers (CSPs).

data encryption standard (DES)
A symmetric-key encryption method standardized by the American National Standards Institute (ANSI) in 1981 as ANSI X.3.92. This method uses a 56-bit key.

delegation
The transferring of administrative authority or rights from one principal to another.

demilitarized zone (DMZ)
The type of firewall technology that consists of a bastion host sandwiched between two packet-filtering routers that provide the highest level of security among firewall technology configurations. Also called a screened-subnet firewall.

digital certificate
Used for security purposes, an attachment to an electronic message that a Certificate Authority (CA) usually generates. It is used to verify that the message sender is who he or she claims to be; it also provides the receiver with the means to encode a reply to the sender in the form of the sender's public key.

digital envelope
The encryption of a secret key within a message that uses a public key.

digital nervous system
Describes distributed services used to obtain and understand information.

digital signature
An encrypted digital message attached to another message that uniquely identifies the sender.

directory
An Active Directory (AD) container object that stores information about objects on the network.

directory consolidation technology
A technology that substitutes an application's native directory services with the data repositories that the operating system directory services provide.

directory service
Provides services for storing and making accessible object-related information datastores to system services and users.

Directory Services Migration Tool (DSMigrate)
A special tool provided with Windows 2000 that is used to migrate NetWare users and resources to a Windows 2000 enterprise.

disaster recovery plan
Formal documentation outlining policies and procedures that must be followed if an unexpected disaster occurs. This document sometimes includes a network security plan that outlines the information technology (IT) security controls most important to the functioning of the corporation.

discretionary ACL (DACL)
See *access control list (ACL).*

distinguished name
A unique object description that identifies the domain that holds the object as well as the complete path through the container hierarchy by which the object is reached.

distribution group
A group that is not security enabled, is used exclusively for email distribution, and has no effects on logon times or network traffic.

distribution list
A datastore of contact information for easy retrieval by mail programs.

domain
An administrative and security grouping of Windows NT/2000-based computers that can span more than one physical location and have common user accounts. With regard to the Domain Name System (DNS), a domain consists of a group of domains that share a common DNS namespace.

domain controller (DC)
A Windows NT/2000-based server that holds an Active Directory (AD) partition.

domain local group
An Active Directory (AD) object that contains users and global groups from any domain in the forest, universal groups, and other domain local groups in its own domain.

Domain Name Service
A Windows NT/2000 system service that uses static, hierarchically arranged information for name/address resolution to TCP/IP addressing.

Domain Name System (DNS)
An Internet service that uses a hierarchical, distributed database for name/address resolution to Transmission Control Protocol/Internet Protocol (TCP/IP) addressing.

Encrypting File System (EFS)
A file system that supports the encryption and decryption of files.

enterprise identity management
The management of centralized services that provide authentication and authorization of named objects in

a scalable environment that spans multiple namespaces.

File and Print Services for NetWare version 5 (FPNW5)
An add-on service that NetWare clients use to access Windows 2000-based shared files and printer resources.

firewall technology
A combination of hardware and software solutions that prevent unauthorized access from external sources to an internal network. A screened-host firewall (also called a single-homed bastion) consists of a packet-filtering router and a bastion host with a single network interface card (NIC). A dual-homed bastion is more secure than a single-homed one because the server has two separate network interface cards (NICs) and thus creates an internal router that filters the flow of packets across the two connected networks.

Flexible (Floating) Single-Master Operations (FSMO)
According to the single-master model in an Active Directory (AD) forest, the five operations master roles assigned to at least one domain controller (DC) are, for the entire forest, domain naming and schema master; for the domain, infrastructure, primary DC (PDC), and relative ID (RID).

forest
A group of one or more Active Directory (AD) trees that trust each other and share a common schema, configuration, and Global Catalog (GC).

Fortezza Crypto Card technology
A group of peripheral products, most commonly smart cards, that use security technologies developed by the National Security Agency (NSA) to support public key encryption technologies.

Global Catalog (GC)
Located on domain controllers (DCs) called Global Catalog (GC) servers, a partial replica of every Windows 2000 domain in the directory. It also contains the schema and configuration of directory partitions.

global group
One of the Active Directory (AD) container objects that can appear on access control lists (ACLs) anywhere in the forest and may contain users and other global groups from its own domain.

Group Policy
Refers to applying Registry-based and other types of control settings to groups of computers and/or users within Active Directory (AD) containers. The collections of policies are referred to as Group Policy Objects (GPOs).

Group Policy loopback support
An advanced Group Policy setting that reorders the inheritance sequence in which Group Policy settings for a computer are applied to a user logging on to that specific machine.

Group Policy Object (GPO)
A collection of settings given a unique name stored in either a Group Policy container (GPC) (preferred) or a Group Policy template (GPT) used for file-based data. It stores software policy, script, and deployment information. The GPT is located in the system volume folder of the domain controller (DC).

hash function
A mathematical function that produces hash values for security purposes. A hash value (or simply hash) is a number generated from a string of text.

hash message authentication code (HMAC)
The mechanism for message authentication, which uses cryptographic hash functions.

hierarchical namespace
A hierarchically structured namespace that provides a mechanism that allows the namespace to be partitioned or organized into functional subsections.

Hypertext Transfer Protocol (HTTP)
The stateless protocol on which the World Wide Web is based.

independent software vendor (ISV)
A company that produces software.

IntelliMirror technology
A set of native Windows 2000 features providing desktop change and configuration management technology, which combines centralized computing with the flexibility of distributed computing. Users' data, applications, and settings are centrally managed and controlled anywhere in the enterprise environment. Services include user data management, software installation and maintenance, user settings management, and remote installation services.

Internet Authentication Service (IAS)
Software services specifically designed for wide area network (WAN) deployment that provide centralized remote access authentication, authorization, and auditing for both the remote access server and the Virtual Private Network (VPN) server.

Internet Protocol Security (IPSec) protocol suite
A set of protocols that support secure exchange of packets at the IP layer. The suite consists of two security protocols: Authentication Header (AH) and Encapsulated Security Payload (ESP), two encryption modes (transport and tunnel), and Internet Key Exchange (IKE) security associations for exchanging public keys during secured transmissions.

IP addressing scheme
An identifier for a computer or device on a Transmission Control Protocol/ Internet Protocol (TCP/IP) network.

Kerberos Authentication Service (AS) request/reply
Using the Kerberos protocol, the request a client makes to a Key Distribution Center (KDC) for authentication and a ticket-granting ticket (TGT), along with the KDC reply with that TGT.

Kerberos Client/Server (CS) Authentication Service (AS) exchange
Using the Kerberos protocol, the request a client makes to a Key Distribution Center (KDC) for a ticket-granting ticket (TGT).

Kerberos protocol
The default Windows 2000 authentication method, a security protocol that authenticates users but doesn't provide authorization to services or resources.

Kerberos ticket-granting service (TGS) request/reply
Using the Kerberos protocol, the request a client makes to the TGS side of the Key Distribution Center (KDC) for a service-granting ticket, along with the reply.

Key Distribution Center (KDC)
A Kerberos 5 service, run on a domain controller (DC), which issues ticket-granting tickets (TGTs) and service-granting tickets (which Microsoft refers to as service tickets) for obtaining network authentication in a domain.

Knowledge Consistency Checker (KCC)
A built-in service that runs on all domain controllers (DCs) and automatically establishes network connections (or site links) between machines for replicating AD information. These network connections, known as Windows 2000 Active Directory directory services connection objects, are the actual connections through which domain controllers exchange directory services information within (and outside) their own site.

Lightweight Directory Access Protocol (LDAP)
A simplified version of the Directory Access Protocol (DAP), the native Windows 2000 protocol that provides access to a directory service that is currently being implemented in Web browsers and email programs. It is used to gain access to X.500 directories.

local computer policy
The initial security template applied to a computer.

mandatory ACL (MACL)
See *access control list (ACL)*.

message digest
The process by which a one-way hash function transforms a block of text into a single string of digits. When this transformed block of text is encrypted with a private key, it creates a digital signature, which is used for authentication.

Messaging Application Programming Interface (MAPI)
A Microsoft application programming interface (API) that provides programmable support for messaging applications.

meta-directory
Directory datastores centralized in one location, allowing applications to access them using a single access model and security system instead of having to interact with many different datastores and access methods.

Microsoft four-layer network model
Similar to the Open Systems Interconnection (OSI) Reference Model except that there are four distinguishing layers: Application Programming Interface (API), Transport Driver Interface (TDI), Network Device Interface Specification, and Physical.

Microsoft Management Console (MMC)
A customizable frame that provides an interface for administrative tools, installable on demand, in the form of snap-ins.

Microsoft Point-To-Point Encryption (MPPE)
An encryption algorithm, especially useful when the IP Security suite is not appropriate or available, providing confidentiality between a remote access client and the remote access or tunnel server. The algorithm uses either 128-bit or 40-bit key encryption and is compatible with Network Address Translation. However, it is only available when either EAP-TLS or MS-CHAP authentication protocols are used.

Microsoft Resource Kit
Subsidiary documentation accompanied by tools and utilities that elaborate on or enhance features and services that are included in the installation CD-ROM for every operating system and BackOffice application.

mixed mode
The mode that allows domain controllers (DCs) that run on both Windows 2000 and Windows NT to coexist in the domain.

multimaster replication
An Active Directory (AD) feature that provides writable copies of the directory database across multiple servers in a domain.

Multipurpose Internet Mail Extensions (MIME)
An Internet mail system specification specifically for non-ASCII (binary or non-ASCII character sets) message packages so that they can be transmitted across a network. These packages typically carry non-HTML information like graphics, audio, and video files that sometimes require add-in applications to enable the browser to properly display their contents.

name resolution
In a defined namespace, the process of resolving a name into an object or information that the name represents.

namespace
Based on a naming convention, a named account (user, computer, group, or service) in a bounded area in which that given name can be resolved.

native mode
The mode in which all the domain controllers (DCs) in a given domain are running on the Windows 2000 operating system and taking full advantage of Active Directory (AD) features.

Network Address Translation (NAT)
An Internet standard that translates one set of Internet Protocol (IP) addresses for internal traffic in a local

area network (LAN) to a second set of addresses for external traffic.

network security plan
Formal documentation that describes the security policy based upon corporate business objectives.

network security policy
A formal document that defines the services that will be explicitly allowed or denied on a network, how those services will be used, and special conditions and/or exceptions to rules.

Novell Directory Services (NDS)
Proprietary directory services, provided by Novell NetWare, that offer services similar to Microsoft Active Directory (AD).

object
A distinct, named set of attributes that represent some definable entity, such as a user, a printer, or an application.

Open Systems Interconnection (OSI) Reference Model
An International Organization for Standardization (ISO) standard reference tool for worldwide communications that defines a network in seven protocol layers.

Organizational Unit (OU)
An Active Directory (AD) object that is a container object. It is used to create an administrative partition, which can contain users, groups, resources, and other OUs.

parent-child trust relationship
The two-way, transitive trust relationship that is established in a domain and added to an Active Directory (AD) tree, providing pass-through logon authentication.

policy
The set of rules that govern the interaction between a subject and an object.

primary domain controller (PDC)
In legacy NT 4 or an earlier domain, the computer running Windows NT Server that maintained the directory database for a domain and authenticated domain logons. In Windows 2000, a domain controller still manages user access and shares in authentication through multimaster replication of the Active Directory data stores.

principal
A named object, resolvable in the namespace, that has a database record in the directory datastore.

profile
A collection of settings information that is applied to the interaction between a subject and an object.

public key infrastructure (PKI)
An integrated set of services and administrative tools for creating, deploying, and managing public key-based authentication processes, including the cryptographic methods, the use of digital certificates and Certificate Authorities (CAs), and the system for managing the process.

relative distinguished name (RDN)
The part of the name of an object that is an attribute of the object itself.

remote access technology
The ability to log on to or to connect to a network from a distant location.

Remote Authentication Dial-In User Service (RADIUS)
A distributed security system designed for centrally administering remote access across a wide area network (WAN).

replication
In database management, the service that synchronizes distributed databases by copying the entire database or subsets of the database to other servers in the network.

schema
The definition of the data language used to create an entire database, including the objects that can be stored in that database.

schema master
The domain controller (DC) assigned to control all updates to the schema within a forest.

screened-host architecture
See *firewall technology*.

screened-subnet architecture
See *demilitarized zone (DMZ)*.

Secure Channel (SChannel) security protocols
The protocols—including Secure Sockets Layer 3 (SSL3)/Transport Layer Security 1 (TLS1)—that Security Support Provider Interface (SSPI) provider supports.

Secure Hypertext Transfer Protocol (S-HTTP)
An extension to Hypertext Transfer Protocol (HTTP) that supports sending data securely over the World Wide Web. It sends individual messages, as opposed to data packets, securely.

Secure Multipurpose Internet Mail Extensions (S/MIME)
A version of the Multipurpose Internet Mail Extensions (MIME) protocol that supports encryption of messages based on the public-key encryption technology of RSA (named after Rivest, Shamir, and Adelman).

security association (SA)
In an IP Security (IPSec) exchange, a unidirectional connection between two IPSec systems in either of two modes—tunnel or transport—depending on the protocol involved.

security ID (SID)
A number that uniquely identifies a named principal in the namespace.

Security Parameters Index (SPI)
In IP Security (IPSec) exchanges, a 32-bit value used to identify different security associations with the same destination address and security protocol. See *security association (SA)*.

single-master operations
Active Directory (AD) operations that are not permitted to occur at different places in the network at the same time. See *Flexible (Floating) Single-Master Operations (FSMO)*.

Single Sign-On (SSO)
The process by which an NT/ Windows 2000 domain user or guest can log on to the network once and gain access to all network resources and services within the domain or the enterprise.

site
In a network, a physical location that holds Active Directory (AD) servers and that is defined as one or more well-connected Transmission Control Protocol/Internet Protocol (TCP/IP) subnets. See *well connected*.

store
The physical storage for each Active Directory (AD) replica.

system ACL (SACL)
See *access control list (ACL)*.

transitive trust
The two-way trust relationship between Windows 2000 domains in a domain tree or forest, or between trees in a forest, or between forests. A transitive trust is automatically established, through the Kerberos authentication protocol, when a domain joins an existing forest or domain tree in native mode Windows 2000. In mixed-mode environments, where NTLM is the default authentication protocol, two domains form nontransitive trusts.

Transmission Control Protocol/Internet Protocol (TCP/IP) protocol suite
A suite of networking protocols and utilities used on the Internet that provide an exchange of information in the form of packets across interconnected, heterogeneous networks of diverse hardware and operating system architecture.

tree
A set of Windows NT/2000 domains connected through transitive, bidirectional trusts that share a common schema, configuration, and Global Catalog (GC). These domains form a contiguous hierarchical namespace.

tunneling protocol
A protocol that supports a logical connection over which data is exchanged in an encapsulated form. Usually, the data is both encapsulated and encrypted. When this occurs, the tunnel is considered a private, secure link between a consumer and a host.

two-factor authentication
An authentication method that requires two separate sets of security credentials: "what I know" and "what I have."

universal group
The simplest form of group in the enterprise that can appear in access control lists (ACLs) anywhere in the forest and that can contain other universal groups, global groups, and users from anywhere in the forest.

Unix-to-Unix encoding (UUEncoding)
A set of algorithms for converting files into a series of 7-bit American Standard Code for Information Interchange (ASCII) characters that can be transmitted over the Internet; it is especially popular for sending email attachments.

Virtual Private Network (VPN)

A network that is constructed by using public networks to connect private nodes. These systems use encryption and other security mechanisms to ensure that only authorized users can access the network and that the data cannot be intercepted.

Web-Based Enterprise Management (WBEM)

An initiative, using Windows Management Instrumentation (WMI), to establish standards for accessing and sharing management information over an enterprise network.

well connected

Network connectivity that is highly reliable and fast—local area network (LAN) speeds of 10Mbps or greater—to make Windows 2000 and Active Directory (AD) perform in a useful way. The precise meaning of the term is determined by your particular needs.

Windows Management Instrumentation (WMI)

An Web-Based Enterprise Management (WBEM)-compliant initiative that provides integrated support for the Common Information Model (CIM), a data model that describes objects existing in a management environment. It proposes universal access to management information for enterprises by providing a consistent view of the managed environment.

Windows Scripting Host (WSH)

Programming platform or host that enables scripts to be run directly in Windows 2000 through the graphical user interface (GUI) or at the command prompt. It has very low memory requirements and runs in both interactive and noninteractive scripting modes.

X.500

A set of standards that define a distributed directory service developed by the International Organization for Standardization (ISO).

X.509

Used for defining digital certificates, an International Telecommunications Union (ITU) recommendation that has not yet been officially defined or approved.

Index

Bold page numbers indicate sample exam questions.

3DES, 64
64-bit encryption, 64
128-bit encryption, 64

A

AAA, 41, 91–94, **117**
AAA servers, 104
Access, securing
- about, 333–334
- desktop, 339–340
- IntelliMirror, 339–340
- prestaging, 341
- RIS, 340–341
- server referring, 341
- smart cards, 334–339, **355**
- SMB signing, 342–343
- SNMP, 341–342
- terminal services, 339–340
- two-factor authentication, 334

Access, standardizing
- about, 330–331
- Kerberos, 332
- SSL, 332–333
- SSO, 331–333

Access control, **365**
- ACLs, managing, 264
- active interception, 267–268
- authenticated access, limiting, 262-264
- DACLs, 265
- deploying, 263–264
- EAP, 263–264
- EAP-TLS, 263–264
- MACLs, 265
- password length, 263
- PPP, 263
- RBACs, 265–266, 275, **373**
- remote access policies, 263–264
- resources, 267–268, 273
- security administration, managing, 264–266
- strategies, 262
- trust relationships, establishing, 266–267
- trusted for delegation, 263

Access control entities. *See* ACEs.
Access control lists. *See* ACLs.
Access management, Apple Macintosh, 350
Account database, Microsoft Kerberos 5, 101
Account mapping, Microsoft Kerberos 5, 103
Account policies, 306
ACEs, 41
acldiag.exe, 314
ACLs, 41–42, 73, 264
Action plan
- for deployment, 34, **56**
- network security, 234–242

Active Directory. *See* AD.
Active Directory Connectors. *See* ADCs.
Active Directory Installation Wizard. *See* DCPROMO.
Active Directory Services. *See* ADS.
Active Directory Services Interfaces. *See* ADSI.

ActivePerl 5.6, 348
AD, **387.** *See also* Access control; Groups.
    about, 38
    APIs, 255
    attributes, 255, **272**
    computer account names, 257
    contacts, 278
    containers, 257, **272,** 282
    DCs, 260–261, **271**
    directory services, 254–255
    domain names, 257
    domains, 258–259, 262
    forests, 39, 259, **272**
    FSMO roles, 260–261, **271**
    GC, 260
    Group Policy, 278–280
    group types, 277–278
    icons, 39
    identity management, 201–202, **210**
    KDC integration, 255
    namespaces, 257–258
    naming conventions, 256–257
    network security plan, 226
    objects, 255, **272**
    OUs, 259
    replication, 261–262
    SDOU, 282
    server collections, 261
    sites, 261
    trees, 258–259, **272**
AD Installation Wizard.
  See DCPROMO.
Adaptive format, 13–14, 17–18
ADCs, 201
addiag.exe, 318
adduser.exe, 318
Administration, Group Policy, 284–286
Administration tools, 301–304
Administrative templates, 279, 285, **293**
ADS
    about, 38–41
    as directory service provider, 40–41
    KDC and, 94
    LDAP and, 40–41
    tools, 303–305
ADSI, 201, 255, **270**
ADSI Edit snap-in, 314
AH, 126, 131–132, 138, 161
AH packet type, 162
Aliases, directory services, 256
American National Standards Institute
  X3.92. *See* ANSI X3.92.
Analyze operation, 311, **322**
Anonymous access, 186–187
ANSI X3.92, 64
Answering routers, 165, **175**
Anti-replay, 131
API layer, 36–37
APIs
    AD, 255
    smart cards, 335–336
Apple Macintosh migration, 349–350, **357**
AppleTalk interoperability, 349–350
Application layer security technologies,
  194–195, **207**
Application programming interfaces.
  See APIs.
Application-level encryption, 128
Application-level gateway, 167
Applications group, 232–233
Application-specific security, 194–196
AS exchange, 90, 94–96
Asymmetric encryption
    PKI, 66–68
    procedural steps (diagram), 67, **82**
    symmetric vs., 67–68, 72, **82**
ATMs, 70
Attack modalities
    categorizing, 45–48
    e-commerce, 48–49
    firewalls, 168
    IIS server, 191–192
    Internet, 49
    IPSec, 126–127
    layered models and, 49–50
    network security plan, 220–221
    RIS, 341
    types of, 28–30, **56–57**
Attributed naming, 256
Auditing
    data flows, 172
    IIS server, 191
    network security plan, 227
auditpol.exe, 318
Authenticated access, limiting, 262–264
Authentication, **366, 372.**
  See also IPSec; Kerberos.
    client/server Kerberos exchange, 90
    cross-domain, 98–100
    e-commerce, 104–106, **119**
    heterogeneous population with
      secured exchange, 187–189,
      195, **208**
    HTTP, 78, 187–188

identity management, 328
IIS, 186, 191–192
Internet, 105
intranets, 187
IPSec, 138, 162
Microsoft Kerberos 5, 105–106
most secure, 188
network security plan, 219
NTLM vs. Kerberos, 106–107, 109, **116**
PKI, 68–71
subdirectories, 186
through comparison, 69–70
through proof of possession, 70–71
two-factor authentication, 263, **271**, 334
virtual directories, 186
virtual servers, 186
Web content, 186

Authentication, authorization, and auditing. *See* AAA.
Authentication delegation, 93, 100
Authentication Header. *See* AH.
Authentication Service exchange. *See* AS exchange.
Authenticity not assumed, 130, **147**
Authenticode, 77, 196
Authorization. *See also* Kerberos.
Microsoft Kerberos 5, 105–106
MIT Kerberos 5, 105
security controls, 329

Automatic teller machines. *See* ATMs.

B

Backup DCs. *See* BDCs.
Bandwidth Allocation Protocol. *See* BAP.
Banking industry and encryption, 79
BAP, 155
Basic authentication, 186–188, **372**
basic*.inf, 309
Bastion, 126, 166
Bastion hosts, 166
BDCs, 259
Bindings, disabling on IIS server, 190
Blank answers, 17, 19
Block Policy Inheritance, 288–289
Bogies, 49
Bogus nameserver cache loading, 128
Boundaries, secured, 34
Broadcast media, 128
Brokerage function, 330
Brute force attacks, 29
Budgeting your time, 17
Build-list-and-reorder format, 7–8
Bulk data encryption, 64, 68, 71, **82**
Business objectives
in disaster recovery plan, 30
e-commerce and, 43
importance of, 326
from key personnel, 30, 32, **55**
from surveys, 28, 30

Business partners
case studies, 217, 230, **247**
defined, 217
network security plan, 233–234
VPNs and, 217, 230, **247**

Business strategy, smart cards, 334–335

C

CA certificate stores. *See* Certificate stores.
CA hierarchies, 74–75, **84**
Cable TV interception risk level, 128
Calling routers, 165, **175**
Canonical name, 256
CAPI
overview, 78–79
supported services, 78, **83**

Carnegie Mellon CERT Coordination Center Web site, 21
CAs, **386–387**
internally managed, 193
IT security controls provided by, 193
PKI, 73
services, list of, 193–194, **209**
standalone, 75, **371**
Thawte, 193
VeriSign, 193
Web exchanges, verifying parties, 193

Case studies
access control, 269
business partners and VPNs, 217, 230, 247
confidentiality, 269
e-commerce security issues, 220–226, 247
exam format, 4–5, 13
exam strategy, 15–16
Group Policy, 292
IIS server, 205–206
internal business services, 241–242, 244, 246
IPSec, 141–145
Kerberos, 110–113
network issues, 205–206
network security plan, 234–242
Novell migration, 354

organizational charts, 216–217, 236–238, 244, 245–246
security decisions, 114–115
security policy, 234–242
sharing resources with other companies, 110–113
smart cards, 354
tools, 319–320

Case studies, 4Sale
access control, 269
business partners and VPNs, 217, 230, 247
confidentiality, 269
e-commerce security issues, 220–226, 247
Group Policy, 292
IIS server, 205–206
internal business services, 241–242, 244, 246
IPSec, 144–145
network issues, 205–206
Novell migration, 354
organizational charts, 216–217, 236–238, 244, 245–246
remote access, 173–174
security decisions, 114–115
smart cards, 354
tools, 319–320
VPNs, 173–174

Case studies, ExamCram Ltd.
IPSec, 141–143
Kerberos, 110–113
network security plan, 234–242
security policy, 234–242
sharing resources with other companies, 110–113
VPNs, 154–155

CDFS, 349
Center for Education and Research in Information Assurance and Security, 21
Center for Education and Research in Information Assurance and Security page. *See* CERIAS Web page.
Center for Information Technology/ National Institutes of Health. *See* CIT/NIH Web site.
Centralized administration tools, 301, **320**
CERIAS Web page, 21
CERT Coordination Center, 21
Certificate Authorities. *See* CAs.
Certificate Authority snap-in, 194
Certificate extensibility, 73
Certificate management services, 78–79
Certificate Revocation List v2. *See* CRL v2.
Certificate Server services, 194
Certificate Services CLI tools, 313–314
Certificate stores, 78–79
Certificates, 73–74
Certification exams. *See* Exams.
Certified for Microsoft Windows logo, 196
CERTREQ, 313
CERTSRV, 313
CERTUTIL, 313–314
Challenge Handshake Authentication Protocol. *See* CHAP.
CHAP, 156, **178**
Child domains, 259, **368**
Choke points, 126, 165, 172
Chokes, 166
Ciphertext, 63
Circuit-level gateway, 167
Circumscribed contiguous subtree, 258
CIT/NIH Web site, 21
Cleartext, 63
Cleartext challenge, 70–71

CLI tools
Certificate Services, 313–314
Group Policy, 290–291
SC Tool Set, 310–311

Client configuration, Microsoft Kerberos 5, 103
Client flooding, 128
Client management, VPNs, 165
Client policy, IPSec, 139
Client Service for NetWare. *See* CSNW.
Client/server authentication exchange. *See* CS authentication exchange.
CM, 231–232
COM+, 350–353
COM service, 352
Command-line interface tools. *See* CLI tools.
Community management, 328–329
Compact Disc File System. *See* CDFS.
compatible*.inf, 310, **373**
Competency Model, 27–28, 50–51, **57**
Component Object Model+. *See* COM+.
Compulsory tunnels, 159
Computer account names, 257
Computer emergency response team Coordination Center. *See* CERT Coordination Center.
Computer profiles, 278–280, 281–282

Confidentiality, **367**. *See also* IPSec; VPNs.
  categories of, 238–239
  EFS, 268
  IPSec, 162
  messages, and key length, 64
  using symmetric encryption, 63–65
Configuration tools, 306–312. *See also* Tools.
Configure operation, 311, **322**
Connection function, 329–330
Connection Manager. *See* CM.
Consumer, defined, 255
Consumer-provider model, 44–48, 61–62, 103
Consumer-Web server flow, 192, **207**
Contacts, 278
Containers, 257, **272**, 282
Context function, 327–328
Contiguous subtrees, 258
Corporate business objectives. *See* Business objectives.
Corporate culture, 35
Corporate objectives, 61–62
Costs. *See* TCO.
Countermeasures, 61–62
Counters, exam, 3, 17
Crack attacks, 29, 49
Create-a-tree format, 8–10
Credentials cache, 93, 101, **120**
CRL v2, 77
Cross-domain authentication, 98–100
Cryptanalysis, 65–66
Crypto Archive Web site, 21
Cryptographic Application Programming Interface. *See* CAPI.
Cryptographic Resources, Inc. Web site, 21
Cryptographic service providers. *See* CSPs.
Cryptography Archives Web site, 21
CS authentication exchange, 90
CSNW, 343
CSPs, 78–79, 105

D

DACLs, 42, 106, 265
Data dictionary, 258
Data Encryption Standard. *See* DES.
Data Encryption Standard-Cipher Block Chaining. *See* DES-CBC.
Data protection and management tools, 305
Database configuration tools, 308
DCPROMO, 99, 260
DCs, 260–261, **271**
Default deny, 171, 185–186, **383**
Default permit, 171, 185–186
Default protocol, IPSec, 161
Definable context, 257
Delegating Group Policies, 286, **293**, **368**
Delegation of authority, 263
Deliverables, security plan, 234–242
Demilitarized zone. *See* DMZ.
Denial of service. *See* DOS attacks.
Deny permissions, 288
Deployment
  access control, 263–264
  Basic authentication, 187–188, **372**
  enterprise security system, 34, **56**
  Group Policy, 284–286
  identity management, 200–202, 204
  IIS permissions, 189–190
  Integrated Windows authentication, 188
  IPSec, 128–129
  IPSec strategy, 136–140
  network security plan, 228–234
  SSL, 192
  steps, 34, **56**
  tools, 301
DES, 64
DES-CBC, 131, 134
Desktop
  Group Policy, 281
  management tools, 301, 304–305
  securing, 281, 339–340
DH, 134
Diffie-Hellman. *See* DH.
Digest authentication, 186, 188
Digital certificates, 105, 193
Digital envelopes, 71
Digital nervous system, 326
Digital Signature Standard. *See* DSS.
Digital signatures, 28, 49, 71, 73, 196
Directory browsing, disabling on IIS server, 191
Directory consolidation, 232
Directory containers. *See* Containers.
Directory database, defined, 219
Directory service provider, 198–199, **209**
Directory services, **368**, **384**
  about, 252–253
  AD, 254–255
  AD server collections, 261
  aliases, 256
  attributes, 255, **272**
  canonical name, 256

child domains, 259, **368**
circumscribed contiguous subtree, 258
components, 257–262
consumers, 255
containers, 257, **272**
contiguous subtrees, 258
data dictionary, 258
DC, 260–261, **271**
definable context, 257
disjointed namespaces, 259
DN, 259
DNs, 256
DNS domains, 259
Domain Naming Master, 261, **271**
domain trees, 258–259
domains, 258
features, 254–255
file class, 258
forests, 259, **272**
FSMOs, 260–261, **271**
GC, 259–260
heterogeneous, 255, **270**
identity management, 199–200
Infrastructure Master, 261, **271**
instances, 258
LDAP v3, 254
leaf nodes, 257
metadata, 258
meta-directories, 201–202, 223–224, 253
named objects, defined, 255
namespaces, 257–258
naming conventions, 256–257
noncontiguous namespaces, 259
object class instances, 258
objects, 255, **272**
OUs, 259
parent domains, 259
PDC Advertiser, 261, **271**
PDC Emulator, 261
principals, defined, 255
purpose of, 256
RDNs, 256
Relative ID Master, 261, **271**
replica DCs, 260
replication, 260, 261–262
RID Operations Master, 261, **271**
schema, 258
Schema Master, 260, **271**
search engine, 260
sites, 261
subtrees, 257
terms, 257–262
trees, 257–259, **272**
trust relationships, 258
unit of replication, 258
walking the tree, 258
well connected, 261
X.500, 253–254
X.509, 253–254
Disabling directory browsing, 191
Disabling services, protocols, and bindings, 190
Disaster recovery plans, 30, 48, 214
Discretionary ACLs. *See* DACLs.
Disjointed namespaces, 259
Distinguished names. *See* DNs.
Distributed interNet Applications Architecture. *See* DNA.
Distributed Password Authentication. *See* DPA.
Distributed security
defined, 214
risk analysis, 33
Distributed services, COM+, 351–353
Distribution groups, 277–278
DMZ
firewalls, 170–171
network security plan, 224
DNA, 326
DNS, 185–186
DNs, 256, 259
DNS domains, 259
DNS servers, 128
DoD four-layer model, 36–37
Domain controllers. *See* DCs.
Domain local groups, 277–278
Domain model features, 42
Domain Name System. *See* DNS.
Domain names, 257
Domain Naming Master, 261, **271**
Domain trees, 39, 258–259
Domains
AD, 258–259, 262, **364**, **382**
directory services, 258
functions of, 262
single domain model, 41
DOS attacks, 29
Down-level, defined, 93
DPA, 78, 105
Drag-and-connect format, 10–11
dsacls.exe, 314
DSS, 70, 72, **388**
Dual-ported hosts, 169

E

EAP, 105, 155, **178**, 263–264, **372**
EAP-TLS, 263–264
Eavesdropping, 127, 172
E-commerce
  attack modalities, 48–49
  authentication, 104–106, **119**
  business objectives and, 43
  case studies, 220–226, 247
  identification, 197–198
  IPSec and, 129
  permission management, 197–198
  security issues, 220–226, 247
  TCO, 43
EFS, 267–268, 273, 275, **386**
Email, smart cards, 338–339
Encapsulated Security Payload. *See* ESP.
Encapsulation, IPSec, 133
Encrypting File System. *See* EFS.
Encryption and Security Related Resources Crypto-farm Web site, 21
Encryption techniques, 133–134
Encryption technologies, 62–63, **80**
Encryption Web sites, 20–22
End-to-end, defined, 154
End-to-end encryption, 127
End-to-end network security, 157
Enterprise CA, 75
Enterprise security system, 34, **56**
ESP, 126, 131–132, 138, 161
ESP packet type, 162
Ethernet interception risk level, 128
Event log, 306
Event Viewer snap-in, 304
Everyone user population, 216, 229
Exams
  adaptive format, 13–14, 17–18
  blank answers, 17, 19
  budgeting your time, 17
  build-list-and-reorder format, 7–8
  case study format, 4–5, 13, 15–16
  counters, 3, 17
  create-a-tree format, 8–10
  drag-and-connect format, 10–11
  exam-readiness, assessing, 2
  exhibits, 4
  fixed-length format, 13, 16–17, 19
  guessing, 18–19
  marking questions for later, 16
  multiple-choice format, 5–6
  number of questions, 15
  partial credit, 6
  practice questions, 19–20
  process of elimination, 18
  question formats, 5
  questions remaining counter, 17
  revisiting questions, 14, 16
  select-and-place format, 11–12
  short-form format, 14, 16–17, 19
  simulations, format, 13
  simulations, practice questions, 13
  test formats, about, 13–14
  test formats, determining, 15
  testing centers, 3–4
  Web sites of interest, 19–22
Exams, strategies
  adaptive format, 17–18
  case study format, 15–16
  fixed-length format, 16–17, 19
  short-form format, 16–17, 19
Exchange 2000, 254
Exchanges. *See* Subprotocols.
Executing utilities, 312
Executive user population, 217, 239–240
Exhibits (exam), 4
Existence function, 327
Expired certificates, 76
Export operation, 311, **322**
Export restrictions on encryption, 79
Extensibility. *See* COM+.
Extensible Authentication Protocol. *See* EAP.
Extensible Authentication Protocol-Transport Layer/Level Security. *See* EAP-TLS.
Extensible ticket fields, 92–93
Extranets, 129, **146**, 233. *See also* Business partners; VPNs.

F

FDDI, 128
Federal information processing standard 180. *See* FIPS PUB 180.
Fiber Distributed Data Interface. *See* FDDI.
File and Print Services for NetWare version 5. *See* FPNW5.
File class, 258
File Migration Utility. *See* FMU.
File System tool, 307
Filter actions, IPSec, 139
Filter lists, IPSec, 138, **378**
FIPS PUB 180, 134

Firewalls, **376–377, 379.** *See also* VPNs.
- about, 165–166
- attack modalities, 168
- choke points, positioning at, 172
- components, 166–167
- DMZ, 170–171
- network security plan, 224
- packet filter architecture, 168
- packet filter routers, 166
- packet flow, 167–171, **176**
- policies, 171–172
- proxy servers, 166–167
- screened host architecture, 168–170
- screened-subnet architecture, 170–171
- topologies, 167–171
- topologies, most secure, 171

Fixed-length format, 13, 16–17, 19
Flags, Microsoft Kerberos 5, 92
Flexible (Floating) Single-Master Operations. *See* FSMOs.
FMU, 345, **357**
Folder redirection, 286
Forests, 259, **272**
Fortezza, 21, 197, 211, **388**
Forwarded TGTs, 100
FPNW5, 345
FSMOs, 260–261, **271**

G

Gates, 166
Gateway Service for NetWare. *See* GSNW.
GC, 259–260
General Security Services API. *See* GSS-API.
Generic Routing Encapsulation. *See* GRE.
Global Catalog. *See* GC.
Global encryption policies, 79
Global groups, 277
GPOs, 276, 283, 286, **293**, **368**
gpotool.exe, 318
gpresults.exe, 318
GRE, 316
Group Policy
- AD, 278–280
- administration, 284–286
- administrative templates, 279, 285, **293**
- Block Policy Inheritance, 288–289
- CLI tools, 290–291
- computer profiles, 278–280, 281–282
- delegating, 286, **293**, **368**
- Deny permissions, 288
- deployment, 284–286
- desktop, securing, 281
- folder redirection, 286
- GPOs, 276, 283, 286, **293**
- Group Policy MMC extensions, 285–286, **293**
- groups, about, 276–277
- groups, nesting, 277
- groups, types of, 277–278
- identity management, 281–282
- inheritance, 282–283, 288, **368**
- Local Group Policy processing order, 287–288
- loopback support, 289–290, **295**
- Merge mode, 289, **295**
- mixed mode environments, 282
- MMC extensions, 285–286, **293**
- multiple, 284
- nesting OUs, 284
- No Override, 288–289
- permission management, 281–282, 288, 290–291
- policy management, 283–284
- processing order, 286–290, **294**
- Replace mode, 289
- RIS, 286
- roaming profiles, 278
- rules-based management, 278–280
- scope of control, 282–283
- scripts, 286
- security groups, 282–283, 286
- security settings, 285, **293**, **368**
- security settings extensions, 308
- software installation and maintenance, 285
- storage domains, 283
- user profiles, 278–280, 281–282
- Web sites, 297
- Windows 2000 vs. NT 4, 276–280

Group Policy MMC, 42
Group Policy Objects. *See* GPOs.
Groups
- about, 276–277
- Group Policy, 276–277
- nesting, 277–278, 284
- policies, 278–280
- restricted, 306
- security settings, 278–280
- types of, 277–278

GSNW, 343
GSS-API, 41, 103
Guessing on exam, 18–19

H

Hacker Libraries Web site, 21
HAL, 37
Hardening the boundaries, 34
Hardware Abstraction Layer. *See* HAL.
Hardware compatibility list, 21
Hash function, 28, 67, 69–70
Hash message authentication code. *See* HMAC.
Hash message authentication code-Message Digest 5. *See* HMAC-MD5.
Hash signatures, 72
Help Desk support, 228
Heterogeneous directory services, 255, **270**
Heterogeneous environments. *See also* Access, standardizing.
  authentication with secured exchange, 187–189, 195, **208**
  Kerberos, 195
  SSL/TLS, 195
Hierarchy of authorities, 74–75
hisec*.inf, 310, **370**
HMAC, 68, 131, 134, **388**
HMAC-MD5, 134
Homogeneous environments
  Kerberos, 195
  SSL/TLS, 195
HTTP, 187–188
HTTP authentication, 78, 187–188
Hypertext Transfer Protocol. *See* HTTP.

I

ICCs, 335
Icons for AD, 39
Identification, 197–198
Identity administration, 327–328
Identity integration, 329–330
Identity management. *See also* AD.
  about, 198–199, 252, 326–327
  AD and, 201–202, **210**
  Apple, 350
  authentication, 328
  community management, 328–329
  context function, 327–328
  deployment, 200–202, 204
  directory service provider, 198–199, **209**
  directory services and, 199–200
  existence function, 327
  Group Policy, 281–282
  identity administration, 327–328
  interoperability, 203
  LDAP, 199
  NDS, 201, **210**
  provisioning function, 328
  ROI, 203
  security controls, 328
  security objectives, 202–203
  TCO, 203
  Unix, 347–348
IETF Web site, 21
IIS 5
  authentication schemes, 186
  COM+, 352
  DNS, 185–186
  network addressing, 185–186
  security control layers, 185
  security restriction, configuring, 185–186
IIS permissions
  deploying, 189–190
  with NTFS, 189–190
IIS servers
  attack modalities, 191–192
  auditing, 191
  authentication, 191–192
  disabling directory browsing, 191
  disabling services, protocols, and bindings, 190
  logging, 191
  secured end-to-end pipe, 192
  securing, 190–191, **208**, **373**
  SSL3/TLS1, 192
  traffic security, 191–192
IKE, 132, 161–162
Impersonation
  attack techniques, 29–30, 49
  IPSec, 127
  public keys, 72
  thwarting with encryption, 127–128
Import restrictions on encryption, 79
INF files, 306–307, 309–310, **321**
Information exchange steps, 140, **146**
Information technology security controls. *See* Security controls.
InfoSecurity News Web site, 21
Infrastructure Master, 261, **271**
Inheritance, Group Policy, 282–283, 288, **368**
Inside attacks. *See* IPSec.
Instances, 258
Integrated circuit cards. *See* ICCs.
Integrated Windows authentication, 186, 188
Integration strategy, 331

Integrity. *See also* IPSec.
- EFS, 268
- IPSec, 162
- PKI, 68–69

Intelligence Briefing Web site, 21
IntelliMirror, 281–282, 304–305, 339–340
Interception
- active, 68, 267–268
- attack techniques, 29
- broadcast media, 128
- cable TV, 128
- Ethernet, 128
- FDDI, 128
- IPSec, 127
- passive, 127–128
- thwarting with encryption, 127–128

Interference attack techniques, 29
Interix 2.2, 346–347, **383–384**
Internal business services, 241–242, 244, **244**, 246, **246**
International Organization for Standardization search engine. *See* ISO search engine.
Internet
- about, 22
- architectural weaknesses, 127
- attack modalities, 49
- authentication protocols, 105
- deployment examples, 128–129
- IPSec deployment examples, 128–129
- Microsoft licensing violations and, 190
- passive interception, 127–128
- SMB, 190
- SSPs, 104–106

Internet Engineering Task Force Web site. *See* IETF Web site.
Internet Information Server. *See entries beginning with* IIS.
Internet Key Exchange. *See* IKE.
Internet Protocol. *See entries beginning with* IP.
Internet Protocol Exchange. *See* IPX.
Internet Protocol Security. *See* IPSec.
Internet Security Association and Key Management Protocol. *See* ISAKMP.
Internet sites, blocking access to, 172
Interoperability, **121, 384**
- about, 102–103
- access management, Apple, 350
- ActivePerl 5.6, 348
- Apple Macintosh migration, 349–350, **357**
- AppleTalk, 349–350
- FMU, 345, **357**
- FPNW5, 345
- identity management, 203
- identity management, Apple, 350
- identity management, Unix, 347–348
- Interix 2.2, 346–347, **383–384**
- IPSec, 163
- Microsoft Kerberos 5, 94, 102–103
- migrations vs. coexistence, 343, **378**
- MKS Toolkit, 347–348
- MSDSS, 345, **355**
- NetWare migration, 343–345, **357**
- network administration, 348
- OPENNT, 346
- password synchronization, 347
- SFU2, 346, 348
- smart cards, 334–335
- Telnet, 348
- Unix migration, 345–348, **356**
- user name mapping, 348

Intranets authentication, 187
IP 50 packet type, 162, **378**
IP 51 packet type, 162, **378**
IP attack modalities, 126–127
IP and DNS, 128
IP Security. *See* IPSec.
IP Security Policies on AD, 307
IPSec, **367, 373**
- about, 126
- advantages, 130, **145**
- advantages of, 130
- AH, 126, 131–132, 138, 161
- AH packet type, 162
- architecture, 132–133
- attack modalities, 126–127
- authentication, 138, 162
- authenticity not assumed, 130, **147**
- case study, 4Sale, **144–145**
- case study, ExamCram Ltd., 141–143
- components, 131–132, **147**
- confidentiality, 162
- connection types, 138
- cryptographic key management, 136
- data flow, impact on, 139
- default protocol, 161
- defined, 77
- deployment examples, 128–129
- deployment strategy, 136–140
- DES-CBC, 131, 134
- DH, 134
- disadvantages, 140

encapsulation, 133
encryption techniques, 133–134
ESP, 126, 131–132, 138, 161
ESP packet type, 162
extranet connectivity, 129, **146**
filter actions, 139, **378**
filter lists, 138
HMAC, 131, 134
IKE, 132, 161–162
impersonation, 127
information exchange steps, 140, **146**
integrity, 162
interception, 127
Internet deployment examples, 128–129
interoperability, 163
IP attack modalities, 126–127
IPX and, 133
ISAKMP, 132, 134–135, 161
key management, 161
key management protocols, 134–135
legacy support, 163–164
methods, 138
NAT incompatibility, 162
NetBIOS and, 133
Oakley, 132, 135, 161
OSI Network layer, 127, 131–132, **148**
packet encryption, 163
passive interception, 127–128
public networks and, 140
remote access, 129, **146**
rules, 138–139
SA, 132–133
SA bundles, 133
security descriptor, 132–133
security policies, 137–138
security policies, built in, 139
security protocols, 131–132
security services, 132, **149**
software upgrades, 135
TCO, 126, 129, 135–136, **367**
TDI layer, 126
training, 135
transform, defined, 134
transport mode, 162
tunnel mode, 162
tunneling, 133, 138, **148**
VPNs, 161–164
Web sites, 21, 151, 180–181
IPSec monitoring tool, 313, **378**
IPSec Transport, 163–164
IPSec Tunnel, 163–164
IPX, 133
ISAKMP, 132, 134–135, 161
ISO search engine, 22
IT security controls. *See* Security controls.
IT Security Cookbook Web site, 21
IT security objectives. *See* Security objectives.
IUSR_*Servername,* 187

K

KDC, 94, **119**, 255
Kerberos. *See also* Microsoft Kerberos 5; MIT Kerberos 5.
AAA, 41
AAA servers, 104
access, standardizing, 332
authenticity not assumed, 130
consumer/provider schema, 103
design of, fictional account, **58**
in heterogeneous environment, 195
in homogeneous environment, 195
as installable SSP, 107–109
lifetime, 104
logon, smart cards, 336–338, **356**
non-Windows 2000 service, 315
NTLM vs., 106–107, 109, **116**
policy, 101–102, **120**
principals, defined, 103
smart cards, 336–338, **356**
SSL/TLS vs., 195
subprotocols, 90, **117**
trusts, 219–220
TTL, 104
user authentication, 78
Key agreements, 71
Key distribution, 66
Key Distribution Center. *See* KDC.
Key length
message confidentiality and, 64
PKI, 72, 79
Key management
IPSec, 134–136, 161
methods, 63
PKI, 72–76
Key-escrow systems, 79
kill.exe, 314
ksetup.exe, 315
ktpass.exe, 315

L

L2TP, 155, 160–162, **176**, **372**, **378**
L2TP/IPSec, 160–161, 163–164, **174**, **377**

LAN Rover software, 156
Layer 2 protocols, 155–156, 160, **178**
Layer 2 Tunneling Protocol. *See* L2TP.
Layer 2 Tunneling Protocol/Internet Protocol Security. *See* L2TP/IPSec.
Layered models, 36–37. *See also* DoD four-layer model; Microsoft four-layer model; OSI model.
LDAP, 40–41, 199, 254, 255
ldp.exe, 315
Leaf nodes, 257
Least privilege principle, 135, 239
Legacy domain model, 219
Legacy one-way trusts, 107
Legacy support, IPSec, 163–164
Legacy tools, 317
Lifetime, 104
Lightweight Directory Access Protocol. *See* LDAP.
Link-level encryption, 127
List-and-reorder questions, 7–8
Local Area Network Rover software. *See* LAN Rover software.
Local Group Policy processing order, 287–288
Local machine, 36, 42
Local policies, 306
Local Security Authority. *See* LSA.
Logging, IIS server, 191
Logical access, defined, 31
Logon, smart cards
  with Kerberos, 336–338, **356**
  with SSL/TLS, 338–339
Long-term keys, 94
Loopback support, 289–290, **295**
LSA, 37

M

MAC, 70–71
Macintosh migration, 349–350, **357**
MACLs, 265
MACs. *See* MACLs.
Management policies, VPNs, 164–165
Mandatory ACLs. *See* MACLs.
Man-in-the-middle attack, 29
MAPI, 255
Marking questions for later, 16
Massachusetts Institute of Technology Kerberos 5. *See* MIT Kerberos 5.
MD5, 70, 134, **388**
Merge mode, 289, **295**
Message Authentication Code. *See* MAC.
Message confidentiality and key length, 64
Message digest, 68
Message Digest 5. *See* MD5.
Message Queue Services. *See* MSMQ.
Messaging Application Programming Interface. *See* MAPI.
Metabase, 38
Metadata, 258
Meta-directories, 201–202, 223–224, 253
Microsoft Certificate Server, 255
Microsoft Certified Professional Web site, 20
Microsoft Cryptographic Application Programming Interface. *See* CAPI.
Microsoft Directory Synchronization Services. *See* MSDSS.
Microsoft four-layer model
  attack modalities and, 49–50
  compared to others, 36–37
  protocols, 37, 50, **57**
Microsoft Kerberos 5
  account database, 101
  account mapping, 103
  authentication delegation, 93, 100
  authentication services, 105–106
  authorization services, 105–106
  client configuration, 103
  credentials cache, 93, 101
  cross-domain authentication, 98–100
  AS exchange, 94–96
  extensible ticket fields, 92–93
  flags, 92
  forwarded TGTs, 100
  GSS-API, 103
  interoperability, 94, 102–103
  KDC, defined, 94
  Kerberos policy, 101–102
  mutual authentication, 93
  native mode, 102
  Negotiate SSP, 105–106
  non-Microsoft clients, 103
  one-way trust, 103
  PKI, 92
  PKINIT, 92
  proxy tickets, 93
  realms, defined, 99
  service account, 103
  service tickets, 102
  session tickets, 102
  session-granting exchange, 97–98
  smart card support, 92
  system-wide audits, 93
  TGS exchange, 96–97

TGTs, 102
ticket structure, 92
trust management, 93–94
user tickets, 102
Windows 2000 features, 93–94
Microsoft licensing violations, 190
Microsoft Management Console. *See* MMC.
Microsoft Message Queue Services. *See* MSMQ.
Microsoft Messaging Application Programming Interface. *See* MAPI.
Microsoft Meta-directory Services. *See* MMS.
Microsoft recommendations, VPNs, 161–162
Microsoft User Authentication Module. *See* UAM.
Microsoft Web site, 22
Microwaves interception risk level, 128
Migration, **382**, **382–383**
Apple Macintosh, 349–350, **357**
coexistence vs., 343
NetWare, 343–345, **357**
Unix, 345–348, **356**
MIT Kerberos 5
AAA support, 91–94, **117**
assumptions, 89
authorization services, 105
components of, 89–90
goals, 88–89
requirements, 88–89
RFC 1510 enhancements, 90–91
subprotocols, 90
Web site, 21
Mixed mode environments, 282
MKS Toolkit, 347–348
MMC, 42, 303, 305
MMS, 201–202, 223–224, 253
Mnemonic device for AD directory containers, 282
Mobile IP, 133
Monitoring, 227
Moore's Law, 43
Mortice Kern Systems Toolkit. *See* MKS Toolkit.
movetree.exe, 315
MSDSS, 201, **210**, 345, **355**, **378**
msicuu.exe, 315
MSMQ, 352–353
Multiple-choice format, 5–6
Mutual authentication, 93
MY certificate store, 79

N

Named objects, 255
Namespaces, 257–258
Naming conventions, 256–257, **270**, **383**
NAT, 159, 162, **175**
National Institute of Standards and Technology. *See* NIST.
National Institute of Standards Web site, 22
National security, 79
National Security Agency. *See* NSA.
National Security Agency Web site, 22
National Security Institute Web site, 21
Native mode, 102
NDIS layer, 37
NDS identity management, 201, **210**
Negotiate SSP, 105–106
Nesting groups, 277–278, 284
NetBIOS, 133
netdiag.exe, 315
netdom.exe, 315
NetWare migration, 343–345, **357**
Network Address Translation. *See* NAT.
Network addressing, 185–186
Network administration, 348
Network Basic Input/Output System. *See* NetBIOS.
Network Device/Driver Interface Specification. *See* NDIS layer.
Network layer security technologies, 194, **207**
Network operating system. *See* NOS.
Network security, defined, 214
Network security plan
action plan, 234–242
AD integrations, 226
Applications group, 232–233
attack modalities, 220–221
auditing, 227
authentication, 219
business partners, 233–234
case studies, 234–242
CM, 231–232
content, 215
defined, 214
deliverables, security plan, 234–242
deployment, 228–234
disaster recovery plan, 214
DMZ, 224
Everyone user population, 229
ExamCram Ltd. case study, 234–242
firewalls, 224
Help Desk support, 228

Kerberos trusts, 219–220
legacy domain model, 219
Meta-directory, 223–224
monitoring, 227
physical security plan content, 217–218
policy management, 223–224
publishing policy, 228
ring model, 220–224
scope, application, 225
scope, logical assets, 218–219
scope, physical, 217–218, 224
scope, policy, 225–226
scope, protocol, 225
server placement, 230–231
SSO, 219–220
SSPI, 232–233
Staff user population, 229–232
steps for developing, 214–215, **244**
support team, 226–227
trust management, 219–220
user population, identifying, 216–217, 236–238
Users user population, 232–233
VPNs, 230–232, **247**

Network security plan strategies, 215, 228–229, **244**, **365**
New Technology. *See* NT.
NIST, 70
nltest.exe, 316
No Override, 288–289
Nonce, defined, 92
Noncontiguous namespaces, 259
Non-Microsoft clients, 103, **378**
Nonrepudiation, 63, **83**
Nontechnical procedures, documenting, 48
Non-Windows 2000 service, 315
NOS, 326, 331
Novell Directory Services identity management. *See* NDS identity management.
Novell migration, 343–345, **355**, **357**
NSA, 70
NT, 37–38
NT File System. *See* NTFS.
NT LAN Manager. *See* NTLM.
NTBugTraq Web site, 21
ntdsutil.exe, 316, **322**
NTFS
ACLs, 263
EFS vs., 267–268
IIS permissions, 189–190
NTLM
authentication service, limitations of, 41
Kerberos vs., 106–107, 109, **116**
user authentication, 78

O

Oakley, 132, 135, 161
Object class instances, 258
Objectives. *See* Business objectives; Security objectives.
Objects, 255, **272**
OCF, 334
128-bit encryption, 64
One-way trust, 103, 266–267, **271**
Open Systems Interconnection. *See entries beginning with* OSI.
OpenCard Framework. *See* OCF.
OPENNT, 346
Organizational charts, 216–217, 236–238, 244, **244**, 245–246, **245–246**
Organizational data, compiling, 35
Organizational Units. *See* OUs.
OSI layer security technologies, 194–195, **207**
OSI model
attack modalities, 49–50
compared to others, 36–37
mapping protocols to, 49–50
security schema, 44
OSI Network layer, 127, 131–132, **148**
OUs, **376**
AD, 259
defined, 40
directory services, 259
nested, 279–280, 284
Ownership function, 330

P

Packet encryption, 163
Packet filter architecture, 168
Packet filter routers, 166
Packet flow, 167–171, **176**
Packet Internet Groper. *See* Ping.
Packet sniffing, 127
PAP, 156, **178**
Paper trail, need for, 48
Parent domains, 259
Partial credit, 6
Pass-through SSP, 105–106
Password Authentication Protocol. *See* PAP.
Password length, 263

Password synchronization, 347
Payload. *See* Tunnels.
PDCs
  PDC Advertiser, 261, **271**
  PDC Emulator, 261
Performance Log And Alerts, 304
Performance snap-in, 303–304, **366, 378**
Permission management
  e-commerce, 197–198
  Group Policy, 281–282, 288, 290–291
  identification and, 197–198
Permissions, Web server, 189–190
PGP, 22, 197
Physical access, defined, 31
Physical organization, 42–43
Physical security plan, 217–218
PING, 316
Ping, 139
PKCS, 76–77
PKI, **386–387**
  ACLs, 73
  active interception, 68
  asymmetric key encryption, 66–68
  asymmetric vs. symmetric, security, 72
  asymmetric vs. symmetric, speed, 67–68, **82**
  authentication controls, 68–71
  authentication through comparison, 69–70
  authentication through proof of possession, 70–71
  CA, 73
  CAPI overview, 78–79
  certificate extensibility, 73
  certificate management services, 78–79
  certificate stores, 78–79
  certificates, 73–74
  cleartext challenge, 70–71
  consumer-provider model, 61–62
  cryptanalysis, 65–66
  CSPs, 78–79
  digital envelopes, 71
  digital signatures, 73
  DSS, 72
  encryption technologies, 62–63, **80**
  expired certificates, 76
  features of, 76–77
  global encryption policies, 79
  hash functions, one-way, 69–70
  hash signatures, 72
  hierarchy of authorities, 74–75
  HMAC generation, 68
  integrity controls, 68–69
  key length, 72, 79
  key management, 72–76
  MD5, 70
  message digest, 68
  Microsoft Kerberos 5, 92
  national security, 79
  public key certificates, 75–76
  public keys and impersonation, 72
  revoked certificates, 76
  RSA, 72
  secret key agreements, 71
  secret key distribution, 66
  security schema, 61–62
  SHA-1, 70
  symmetric key encryption, 63–66
  Web site, 22
PKINIT, 77, 92
PKIX, 77
Point-To-Point Protocol. *See* PPP.
Point-To-Point Tunneling Protocol. *See* PPTP.
Policies, **371, 388**
  application-specific, 195–196
  built in (IPSec), 139
  case studies, 234–242
  content, 215
  defined, 137
  firewalls, 171–172
  groups, 278–280
  IP Security Policies on AD, 307
  IPSec, 137–138
  Public Key Policies, 307
Policy management
  Group Policy, 283–284
  network security plan, 223–224
Portable Operating System Interface for Unix. *See* POSIX.
POSIX, 346, **384**
PPP
  access control, 263
  VPNs, 160, 162–163, **372**
PPTP
  features, 163
  VPNs, 156, 160, 164, **378**
PPTP PING, 316
Practice questions, 19–20
Prestaging, 341
Pretty Good Privacy. *See* PGP.
Pretty Good Privacy Web site, 22
Primary DCs. *See* PDCs.

Principals
 defined, 40, 103, 255
 naming conventions, 256–257
 security schema and, 44–45
Principle of least privilege, 135, 239
Private communication channels. *See* VPNs.
Private network infrastructures, 156–157
Procedural paradigm, 34–35
Process of elimination, 18
Processing order, Group Policy, 286–290, **294**
Protocols, disabling on IIS server, 190
Provisioning function, 328
Proxy servers, 166–167
Proxy tickets, 93
Public key certificates, 75–76
Public Key Cryptography for Initial Authentication in Kerberos. *See* PKINIT.
Public Key Cryptography Standards. *See* PKCS.
Public key infrastructure. *See* PKI.
Public Key Infrastructure X.509. *See* PKIX.
Public Key Policies, 307
Public key-based protocols, 105
Public keys and impersonation, 72
Public networks, 140
Publishing policy, 228

Q

Question formats, 5
Questions-remaining counter, 17

R

Radio interception risk level, 128
RADIUS, 155, 164–165, **178**
Rainbow Series Library, DoD Web site, 22
RBACs, 265–266, 275, 353, **373**
RDNs, 256
Realms, 99
RefreshPolicy operation, 311
reg.exe, 316
Registry, 37–38
Registry tools, 307
Relative distinguished names. *See* RDNs.
Relative ID Master. *See* RID Master.
Remote access, **377**
 application-specific security, 196
 design flow, 164–165, **177**
 incorporated into network operating system, 157–158
 IPSec, 129, **146**
 policies, 263–264
 policy management, 164–165
 VPNs, 156–157
Remote administration mode, 302–303
Remote Authentication Dial-In User Service. *See* RADIUS.
Remote (Operating System) Installation Services. *See* RIS.
Remote site connectivity, 129, **146**
remote.exe, 316
Replace mode, 289
Replay attacks, 29
Replica DCs, 260
Replication, 260, 261–262
Request for Comments. *See entries beginning with* RFC.
Resources
 access control, 267–268, 273
 Group Policy, 278–280
 rules-based management, 278–280
Restricted groups, 306
Return on investment. *See* ROI.
Revisiting questions, 14, 16
Revoked certificates, 76
RFC 822, 197, 257
RFC 822 names, 256
RFC 1330, 253
RFC 1334, 162
RFC 1510, 90–91, **118**
RFC 1636, 127
RFC 1777, 254
RFC 2003, 133
RFC 2069, 188
RFC 2078, 105
RFC 2222, 254
RFC 2246, 192, 212
RFC 2401, 151
RFC 2402, 151
RFC 2406, 151
RFC 2408, 151
RFC 2411, 131
RFC search page, 275
RFC Web sites, 21
RID Master, 261, **271**
RID Operations Master, 261, **271**
Ring model, 220–224
RIS, 281, 286, 303, 340–341
Risk analysis
 attack modalities, 60
 basic components, 60
 distributed security, 33

Risk management steps, 32–33, 45–48
Roaming profiles, 278
Roaming user support, 305
Rogue attacks, 49, 128
ROI, 203
Role-based access controls. *See* RBACs.
Root CA, 74, 193, **387**
ROOT certificate store, 79
Routers, VPN, 165
Routing and Remote Access Service integration. *See* RRAS integration.
RRAS integration, 157–158
RSA, 72
Rules
  Group Policy, 278–280
  IPSec, 138–139

S

S, 239, 265
SA bundles, 133
SACLs, 42
SAs, 132–133
SBU, 197, 239, 265
SC Tool Set, 306–312
  CLI version, 310–311
SCA snap-in, 306–307, **366**
Scalable organization structure, 41
SCard COM, 336
SChannel protocols, 191–194
SChannel services, 105
SChannel SSPs, 78
Schema. *See* Security schema.
Schema Master, 260, **271**
Scope, Group Policy, 282–283
Scope, network security plan
  application, 225
  logical assets, 218–219
  physical, 217–218, 224
  policy, 225–226
  protocol, 225
Screened host architecture, 168–170
Screened-subnet architecture, 170–171
Scripts, 286
sdcheck.exe, 317
SDOU, 282
Search engines, directory services, 260
Search tools, 22
Searching for Web sites, 22
search.vbs, 317
secedit.exe, 308, 310–312, **322**, **371**
Secret. *See* S.
Secret keys. *See entries beginning with* Key.
Secure authentication, 188
Secure Electronic Transaction LLC Web site, 22
Secure Hash Algorithm. *See* SHA; SHA-1.
Secure Multipurpose Internet Mail Extensions. *See* S/MIME.
Secure Server policy, IPSec, 139
Secure Sockets Layer. *See* SSL.
Secure Sockets Layer/Transport Security Layer. *See* SSL/TLS.
Secured end-to-end pipe, 192
secure*.inf, 310
Securing IIS servers, 190–191, **208**, **373**
Security account management, 41–42
Security administration, managing, 264–266
Security analysis, 60–61
Security areas, list of, 306–307, **321**, **366**
Security Associations. *See* SAs.
Security attack modalities. *See* Attack modalities.
Security attributes, configuring, 306–307
Security component schema, 44–45
Security Configuration And Analysis Manager, 308
Security Configuration And Analysis snap-in. *See* SCA snap-in.
Security Configuration Service, 308
Security Configuration Tool Set. *See* SC Tool Set.
Security control layers, 185
Security controls
  attack modalities, 28–30
  authorization, 329
  brokerage function, 330
  business objectives and, 28
  categorizing, 46–48
  connection function, 329–330
  examples of, 28
  identity integration, 329–330
  identity management, 328
  matching with corporate objectives, 61–62
  matching with countermeasures, 61–62
  ownership function, 330
  VPNs, 164
Security deployment plan, 228–234
Security descriptor, 132–133
Security groups, 278, 282–283, 286
Security Negotiation Mechanism. *See* SNEGO.
Security objectives, 28, **54**, 202–203

Security overview
AAA, 41
AD, 38
ADS, 38–41
attack modalities, 28–30, 45–48
boundaries, secured, 34
business objectives, from key personnel, 30, 32, **55**
business objectives, from surveys, 28, 30
business objectives, in disaster recovery plan, 30
Competency Model, 27–28
consumer/provider schema, 44–48
corporate culture, 35
deployment steps, 34
digital signatures, 28, 49
disaster recovery plans, 30, 48
distributed security, risk analysis, 33
DoD four-layer model, 36–37
domain model features, 42
enterprise security system, deploying, 34
group policies, 42
hash function, 28
historical trends, 35–38
impersonation attack modality, 49
IT security controls, 28–30, 46–48
layered models, 36–37
LDAP, 40–41
logical access, defined, 31
Microsoft four-layer model, 36–37
MMC, 42
nontechnical procedures, documenting, 48
organizational data, compiling, 35
OSI model, 36–37, 44, 49–50
OUs, 40
physical access, defined, 31
physical organization, 42–43
procedural paradigm, 34–35
questions to ask, 26
risk management steps, 32–33, 45–48
security account management, 41–42
security component schema, 44–45
security policy contents, 30–31
security protocols and layered models, 49–50
single domain model, 41
social layer, 35
system administrator capabilities, 42
system security audits, 27, 31–32
system security plan, 27
TCO, 27
troubleshooting paradigm, 43–44
Windows Registry, 37–38
Security plan for Windows 2000
about, 198–199
AD, 201–202, **210**
deployment, 200–202, 204
directory service provider, 198–199, **209**
interoperability, 203
LDAP, 199
NDS, 201, **210**
ROI, 203
security objectives, 202–203
TCO, 203
Security plans, 27–28, **53**, **55**
Security policies. *See* Policies.
Security policy categories, 30–31, **54**
Security policy contents, 30–31
Security Portal for Information Security Professionals Web site, 21
Security protocols
IPSec, 131–132
layered models and, 49–50
Microsoft four-layer model, 37, 50, **57**
VPNs, 155–156, 159–164
Security restriction, configuring, 185–186
Security rules. *See* Rules.
Security schema
about, 44–45
active vs. passive attacks, 47
attack modalities, applying security controls to, 47–48
attack modalities, types of, 45–47
consumer-to-provider model, 44–45
interception attack modality, 46–47
interference attack modality, 46
PKI, 61–62
principals, defined, 44
risk analysis, 47–48
security controls, applying to attack modalities, 47–48
security controls, categorizing, 46–47
security exposures, targets of, 45
Security services, IPSec, 132, **149**
Security settings
extensions (Group Policy Editor), 308
Group Policy, 285, **293**, **368**
groups, 278–280
tools, 307
Security support provider interface. *See* SSPI.

Security support providers. *See* SSPs.
Security templates, 308–312, **321**, **370**, **373**
Security tools. *See* Tools.
Security Web sites, 20–22
Select-and-place format, 11–12
Sensitive But Unclassified. *See* SBU.
Server Gateway Cryptography. *See* SGC.
Server Message Block. *See* SMB.
Server placement, 230–231
Server policy, IPSec, 139
Server referring, 341
Service accounts, 103
Service pack Web site, 21
Service principal names, 257
Service tickets, 102
Services, disabling on IIS server, 190
Services for NetWare version 5. *See* SFN5.
Services for Unix 2. *See* SFU2.
Session pipe. *See* Tunnels.
Session tickets, 102
Session-granting exchange, 97–98
Setup Security tool, 308
SFN5, 344
SFU2, 346, 348
SGC, 78
SHA, 134
SHA-1, 70
Shiva LAN Rover software, 156
Shiva Password Authentication Protocol. *See* SPAP.
Short-form format, 14, 16–17, 19
SIDWalker, 317
Simple Network Management Protocol. *See* SNMP.
Simulations, 13
Single domain model, 41, **382**
Single Sign-On. *See* SSO.
Site, domain, Organizational Unit, OU within OU. *See* SDOU.
Sites, 261
64-bit encryption, 64
Smart cards, **366**, **371**, **377**
- access, securing, 334–339, **355**
- APIs, 335–336
- authentication, 263
- business strategy, 334–335
- email, 338–339
- ICCs, 335
- interoperability, 334–335
- logon with Kerberos, 336–338, **356**
- logon with SSL/TLS, 338–339
- Microsoft Kerberos 5, 92
- SCard COM, 336
- stored-value cards, 335
- two-factor authentication, 334
- types of, 335
- Win32 API, 336

SMB, 190
SMB signing, 342–343
S/MIME, 50, 197, 212, **387**
Snap-ins
- about, 42
- ADSI Edit snap-in, 314
- Certificate Authority snap-in, 194
- Event Viewer snap-in, 304
- Performance snap-in, 303–304, **366**
- SCA snap-in, 306–307, **366**
- where to get, 303

SNEGO, 105
SNMP, 341–342
snmputilg.exe, 317
Social layer, 35
Sockets for Unix compatibility. *See* SOCKS.
SOCKS, 50
Software installation and maintenance
- Group Policy, 285
- tools, 305

SPAP, 156, **178**
Spheres of responsibility, 40
Spoke and hub, 201–202
Spoofing, 29–30, 49
SSL, **372**
- access, standardizing, 332–333
- consumer/Web server flow, 192, **207**
- defined, 77
- deployment, 192

SSL3/TLS1, 192
SSL/TLS, 195, 331–332, 338–339
SSO, 94, 219–220, 255, 331–333
SSPI, 105–106, 108–109, 232–233
SSPs, 104–106, **119**
Staff user population, 217, 229–232, 239
Standalone CA, 75, **371**
Storage domains, 283
Stored-value cards, 335
Strategies
- access control, 262
- network security plan, 215, 228–229, **244**, **365**

Strategies (exam)
- adaptive format, 17–18
- case study format, 15–16
- fixed-length format, 16–17, 19
- short-form format, 16–17, 19

Study guide, Competency Model as, 27–28, 50–51, **57**
Subdirectories, 186
Subordinate CA, 74–75
Subprotocols, 90, **117**
Subtrees, 257
Surveys, 28, 30
Symmetric encryption
- asymmetric encryption vs., 67–68, 72, **82**
- confidentiality, 64–65
- PKI, 63–66
- prerequisites, 64–65
- procedural steps (diagram), 64, **81**

Syntax for tools, 312–313
System ACLs. *See* SACLs.
System administrator capabilities, 42
System Monitor, 304
System Policy Editor, 42
System Policy (NT 4). *See* Group Policy.
System security
- analyzing, 311
- audits, 27, 31–32, **55**, 93
- plan, 27

System services tools, 307

T

TCO, **364**
- application-specific security, 194–196
- defined, 27, **53**
- e-commerce, 43
- identity management, 203
- IPSec, 126, 129, 135–136, **367**
- single domain model, 41

TCP/IP layered model. *See* DoD four-layer model.
TDES, 64
TDI, 36–37, 126
Technical expertise. *See* Competency model.
Telephone, interception risk level, 128
Telnet, 348
Terminal services access, securing, 339–340
Terminal Services Architecture. *See* TSA.
Test. *See* Exams.
Testing centers, 3–4
Testlets. *See* Case studies.
TGS, 96–97
TGS exchange, 90
TGTs, 102
Thawte, 193
3DES, 64
Ticket structure, 92
Ticket-granting service. *See* TGS.
Ticket-granting service exchange. *See* TGS exchange.
Ticket-granting tickets. *See* TGTs.
Time remaining counter, 3
Time to live. *See* TTL.
tlist.exe, 317
TLS, 77, 156, 212
TLS1, 192
Tools. *See also* Group Policy.
- account policies, 306
- acldiag.exe, 314
- AD directory services, 303–305
- addiag.exe, 318
- adduser.exe, 318
- administration tools, 301–304
- ADSI Edit snap-in, 314
- auditpol.exe, 318
- centralized administration, 301, **320**
- Certificate Services CLI tools, 313–314
- CERTREQ, 313
- CERTSRV, 313
- CERTUTIL, 313–314
- CLI, Certificate Services, 313–314
- CLI, Group Policy, 290–291
- CLI, SC Tool Set, 310–311
- configuration tools, 306–312
- data protection and management, 305
- database configuration, 308
- deployment, 301
- desktop management, 301, 304–305
- dsacls.exe, 314
- event log, 306
- Event Viewer snap-in, 304
- executing utilities, 312
- File System, 307
- gpotool.exe, 318
- gpresults.exe, 318
- Group Policy CLI tools, 290–291
- INF files, 306–307, 309–310, **321**
- IntelliMirror, 304–305
- IP Security Policies on AD, 307
- IPSec monitoring tool, 313
- kill.exe, 314
- ksetup.exe, 315
- ktpass.exe, 315
- ldp.exe, 315
- legacy tools, 317
- local policies, 306
- MKS Toolkit, 347–348
- MMC, 303, 305

movetree.exe, 315
msicuu.exe, 315
netdiag.exe, 315
netdom.exe, 315
nltest.exe, 316
ntdsutil.exe, 316, **322**
Performance Log And Alerts, 304
Performance snap-in, 303–304
PPTP PING, 316
Public Key Policies, 307
reg.exe, 316
Registry, 307
remote administration mode, 302–303
remote.exe, 316
restricted groups, 306
RIS, 303
roaming user support, 305
SC Tool Set, 306–312
SC Tool Set, CLI version, 310–311
SCA snap-in, 306–307, **366**
sdcheck.exe, 317
search.vbs, 317
secedit.exe, 308, 310–312, **322**
security areas, list of, 306–307, **321**
security attributes, configuring, 306–307
Security Configuration And Analysis Manager, 308
Security Configuration Service, 308
security settings, 307, **368**
Security settings extensions (Group Policy Editor), 308
security templates, 308–312, **321**, **370**
Setup Security, 308
SIDWalker, 317
snap-ins, where to get, 303
snmputilg.exe, 317
software/application installation, 305
syntax, 312–313
System Monitor, 304
system services, 307
tlist.exe, 317
TSA, 302–303
Windows 2000 Server Resource Kit, 317–318
Windows 2000 Support Tools, 314–317
WMI, 301–302
WSH, 302, 305
wsremote.exe, 317
Top Secret. *See* TS.
Topologies, firewalls, 167–171
Total cost of ownership. *See* TCO.
Traffic security, 191–192
Training and Certification Web site, 22
Transforms, 134
Transmission Control Protocol/Internet Protocol layered model. *See* DoD four-layer model.
Transport Driver/Device Interface layer. *See* TDI.
Transport Layer Security. *See* TLS.
Transport layer security technologies, 194, **207**
Transport mode, 162
Tree format questions, 8–10
Trees, 257–259, **272**
Triple DES. *See* TDES.
Troubleshooting paradigm, 43–44
TRUST certificate store, 79
Trust management
Microsoft Kerberos 5, 93–94
network security plan, 219–220
Trust relationships
CA-based, 75
deploying, 266–267
directory services, 258
establishing, 266–267
transitive, 266–267
Trusted for delegation, 263
Trusted network infrastructures, 156–157
TS, 239, 265
TSA, 281, 302–303
TTL, 104
Tunnel mode, 162
Tunneling, 133, 138, **148**, 158–159
Tunnels, 158
Two-factor authentication, 263, **271**, 334

U

U, 239, 265
UAM, 349, **357**
UNC, 257
Unclassified. *See* U.
Uniform Resource Locators. *See* URLs.
Unit of replication, 258
Universal groups, 277
Universal Naming Convention. *See* UNC.
Unix migration, 345–348, **356**
Up-level, defined, 93
UPNs, 256–257
URLs, 257
User accounts naming conventions, 257
User Authentication Module. *See* UAM.
User name mapping, 348

User population, identifying, 216–217, 236–238
User principal names. *See* UPNs.
User profiles, 278–280, 281–282
User tickets, 102
UserDS certificate store, 79
Users, deploying access control, 263–264
Users user population, 217, 232–233, 239
UUEncoding, 187

V

Validate operation, 311, **322**
VeriSign, 193
Virtual directories, 186
Virtual Private Network Consortium. *See* VPNC.
Virtual Private Networks. *See entries beginning with* VPN.
Virtual servers, 186
Vision statements, 241–242
Voluntary tunnels, 158
VPN answering routers, 165, **175**
VPN calling routers, 165, **175**
VPN client, 158
VPN Consortium Web site, 22
VPN server, 158
VPN tunneling protocols, list of, 159
VPNC, 180
VPNs, **372**, **376–379**. *See also* Firewalls.
  business partners and, 217, 230, **247**
  client management, 165
  defined, 154
  design considerations, 160
  ExamCram Ltd. diagram, 154–155
  IPSec, 161–164
  L2TP, 160–162, **372**
  management policies, 164–165
  Microsoft recommendations, 161–162
  NAT, 159, 162, **175**
  network security plan, 230–232, **247**
  PPP, 160, 162–163, **372**
  PPTP, 156, 160, 164, **378**
  RADIUS, 165
  remote access models, 156–157
  remote access policy management, 164–165
  RRAS integration, 157–158
  security controls required, 164
  security protocols, 155–156, 159–164
  tunneling, 158–159
  Web sites, 180–181

W

Walking the tree, 258
Web content authentication, 186
Web exchanges, verifying parties, 193
Web server. *See* IIS servers.
Web sites
  blocking access to, 172
  finding, 22
  IPSec, 151, 180–181
Web-Based Enterprise Management. *See* WEBM.
WEBM, 301–302
Well connected, 98, 261
Win32 API, smart cards, 336
Windows 2000
  components. *See* AD
  Microsoft Kerberos 5, 93–94
  naming conventions, 256–257, **270**
  NT 4 (Group Policy) vs., 276–280
  remote administration mode, 302–303
  remote installation, 285
Windows 2000 Hardware Compatibility List Web site, 22
Windows 2000 security policy. *See* Network security plan.
Windows 2000 Server Resource Kit, 317–318
Windows 2000 Support Tools, 314–317. *See also* Tools.
Windows for Workgroups, 36
Windows Management Instrumentation. *See* WMI.
Windows Registry, 37–38
Windows Scripting Host. *See* WSH.
WMI, 301–302
World Wide Web, 22. *See also* Internet.
WSH, 302, 305
wsremote.exe, 317

X

X.400 Web site, 275
X.500
  directory services, 253–254
  names, 256
  Web site, 275
X.509
  Authenticode, 196
  directory services, 253–254
  S/MIME, 197